CLYMER®

YAMAHA

YZ100-490 MONOSHOCK · 1976-1984

The world's finest publisher of mechanical how-to manuals

PRIMEDIA
Information Data Products

P.O. Box 12901, Overland Park, Kansas 66282-2901

FIRST EDITION
First Printing December, 1980
Second Printing April, 1981
Third Printing August, 1981
Fourth Printing May, 1982

SECOND EDITION
Revised by Ron Wright to include 1981-1983 models
First Printing April, 1984

THIRD EDITION
Revised by Ron Wright to include 1984 models
First Printing May, 1985
Second Printing April, 1986
Third Printing February, 1987
Fourth Printing April, 1988
Fifth Printing June, 1989
Sixth Printing March, 1990
Seventh Printing June, 1991
Eighth Printing May, 1992
Ninth Printing May, 1993
Tenth Printing May, 1994
Eleventh Printing January, 1996
Twelfth Printing August, 1997
Thirteenth Printing January, 1999
Fourteenth Printing December, 2000
Fifteenth Printing December, 2002
Sixteenth Printing July, 2005

Printed in U.S.A.

CLYMER and colophon are registered trademarks of PRIMEDIA Business Magazines & Media Inc.

ISBN: 0-89287-309-4

COVER: Cover illustration by Tony Barmann.

TOOLS AND EQUIPMENT: K & L Supply Co. at www.klsupply.com.

1

2

3

4

5

6

7

8

9

10

11

12

13

14

CLYMER®

Publisher Shawn Etheridge

EDITORIAL

Managing Editor
James Grooms

Associate Editors
Lee Buell

Technical Writers
Jay Bogart
Jon Engleman
Michael Morlan
George Parise
Mark Rolling
Ed Scott
Ron Wright

Editorial Production Manager
Dylan Goodwin

Senior Production Editor
Greg Araujo

Production Editors
Holly Messinger
Darin Watson

Associate Production Editors
Susan Hartington
Julie Jantzer-Ward
Justin Marciniak

Technical Illustrators
Steve Amos
Errol McCarthy
Mitzi McCarthy
Bob Meyer

MARKETING/SALES AND ADMINISTRATIO

Marketing Director
Rod Cain

Trade Show & Retention Marketing Manager
Elda Starke

Sales Channel & Brand Marketing Coordinator
Melissa Abbott Mudd

New Business Marketing Manager
Gabriele Udell

Art Director
Jennifer Knight
Chris Paxton

Sales Managers
Justin Henton
Dutch Sadler
Matt Tusken

Business Manager
Ron Rogers

Customer Service Manager
Terri Cannon

Customer Service Representatives
Shawna Davis
Courtney Hollars
Susan Kohlmeyer
Jennifer Lassiter
April LeBlond

Warehouse & Inventory Manager
Leah Hicks

PRIMEDIA
Business Magazines & Media

P.O. Box 12901, Overland Park, KS 66282-2901 • 800-262-1954 • 913-967-1719

The following books and guides are published by PRIMEDIA Information Data Products.

More information available at *primediabooks.com*

CONTENTS

QUICK REFERENCE DATA

MOTORCYCLE INFORMATION

MODEL:_____ YEAR:_____

VIN NUMBER:_____

ENGINE SERIAL NUMBER:_____

CARBURETOR SERIAL NUMBER OR I.D. MARK:_____

RECOMMENDED LUBRICANTS AND FUEL

Engine oil	Yamaha Yamalube "R"; Shell Super M; Castrol R30
Transmission oil	SAE 10W/30 "SE" motor oil
Front forks	SAE 10W/20, SAE15, or special fork oil
Air filter	SAE 10W/30 motor oil
Drive chain	Chain lube or 10W/30 motor oil
Control cables	Cable lube or 10W/30 motor oil
Control lever pivots	10W/30 motor oil
Steering head, wheel bearings, swing arm	Medium weight wheel bearing grease (waterproof type)
Brane cam	Lithium base
Fuel	Premium grade – research octane 90 or higher

TRANSMISSION OIL CAPACITY

Model	Drain/refill	Rebuild
YZ490L, K, J	750 cc	800 cc
YZ465H	700 cc	750 cc
YZ465G*	700-800 cc	750-850 cc
YZ400F	750-850 cc	800-900 cc
YZ400E, D, C	1,050-1,150 cc	1,150-1,250 cc
YZ250L, K, J	850 cc	900 cc
YZ250H	750 cc	800 cc
YZ250G*	700-800 cc	750-850 cc
YZ250F, E	750-850 cc	800-900 cc
YZ250D, C	1,050-1,150 cc	1,150-1,250 cc
YZ175C	650 cc	750 cc
YZ125L, K, J	800 cc	850 cc
YZ125H	700 cc	750 cc
YZ125G, F, E, D, C, X	600 cc	700 cc
YZ100K, J	550-650 cc	650-750 cc
YZ100H, G, F, E, D, C	600-700 cc	700-800 cc

*Note—add an aditional 150 ± 50 cc to certain models. Refer to the text for specific engine serial numbers involved.

TIRE INFLATION PRESSURE

Tire Size	Air Pressure
Front	
3.00-21-4PR	14 psi (1.0 kg/cm^2)
Rear	
4.10-18-4PR	18 psi (1.2 kg/cm^2)
4.50-18-4PR	15 psi (1.1 kg/cm^2)
5.10-18-4PR	14 psi (1.0 kg/cm^2)

SPARK PLUG TYPE AND GAP

Model	Type	Gap	
		in.	mm
YZ490L, K, J	Champion N-86	0.020-0.024	0.5-0.6
YZ465G	Champion N-3	0.024-0.028	0.6-0.7
YZ400F	Champion N-3	0.024-0.028	0.6-0.7
YZ400E, D, C	Champion N-3G	0.024-0.028	0.6-0.7
YZ250L, K, J	Champion N-86	0.020-0.024	0.5-0.6
YZ250H, G, F, E, D, C, B	Champion N-2G	0.018-0.022	0.45-0.55
YZ175C	Champion N-59G	0.020-0.024	0.5-0.6
YZ125L	Champion N-84	0.020-0.024	0.5-0.6
YZ125K	Champion N-86	0.020-0.024	0.5-0.6
YZ125J	Champion N-84	0.020-0.024	0.5-0.6
YZ125H, G, F, E, D, C, X	Champion N-59G	0.024-0.028	0.6-0.7
YZ100K, J	Champion N-84	0.020-0.024	0.5-0.6
YZ100H	Champion N-59G	0.020-0.024	0.5-0.6
YZ100G, F, E, D, C, B	Champion N-59G	0.024-0.028	0.6-0.7

DRIVE CHAIN SLACK

Model	inches	millimeters
YZ490L	1.2-1.6	30-40
YZ490K	0.8-1.2	20-30
YZ490J	0.79-1.18	20-30
YZ465H, G	0.4-0.6	10-15
YZ400F, E	0.4-0.6	10-15
YZ400D*	2.6-3.0	65-75
YZ400C*	2.2-2.6	55-65
YZ250L, K	1.2-1.6	30-40
YZ250J	0.79-1.18	20-30
YZ250H, G, F	0.4-0.6	10-15
YZ250E	1.4-1.6	35-40
YZ250D*	2.6-3.0	65-75
YZ250C*	2.2-2.6	55-65
YZ175C	1.5-1.7	40-45
YZ125L, K	1.2-1.6	30-40
YZ125J	1.18-1.38	30-35
YZ125H, G, F	0.4-0.6	10-15
YZ125E*	2.2-2.6	55-60
YZ125D, C, X	2.6-3.0	65-75
YZ100K, J	1.4	35
YZ100H	1.6-1.8	40-45
YZ100G, F, E, D	0.4-0.6	10-15
YZ100C	0.8-1.0	20-25

* Push down on chain tensioner until it is free from the drive chain on these models.

NOTE: If you own a 1981 or later model, first check the Supplement at the back of the book for any new service information.

1

CHAPTER ONE

GENERAL INFORMATION

This detailed, comprehensive manual covers the Yamaha YZ100 to YZ490 seriew monoshock motocross bikes from 1976-1984. The expert text gives complete information on maintenance, tune-up, repair, overhaul and performance improvement. Hundreds of photos and drawings guide you through every step. The book includes all you need to keep your Yamaha running right and performing in top condition.

General information on all models and specific information on 1976-1981 models is contained in Chapters One through Twelve. Specific information on 1981 and later models that differs from earlier years is in the supplement at the end of the book.

A shop manual is a reference. You want to be able to find information fast. As in all Clymer books, this one is designed with you in mind. All chapters are thumb tabbed. Important items are extensively indexed at the rear of the book. All procedures, tables, photos, etc., in this manual assume that the reader may be working on the bike or using this manual for the first time. Finally, all the most frequently used specifications and capacities are summarized on the *Quick Reference Data* pages at the front of the book.

Keep the book handy in your tool box, or tow vehicle. It wil help you to better understand how your YZ runs, lower repair and maintenance costs, and generally improve your satisfaction with your bike.

Refer to **Figure 1A** and **Figure 1B** for location of the major controls.

MANUAL ORGANIZATION

All dimensions and capacities are expressed in English units familer to U.S. mechanics as well as in metric units.

This chapter provides general information and specifications. It also discusses equipment and tools useful both for preventive maintenance and troubleshooting. See **Table 1** at the end of this chapter for model serial numbers.

Chapter Two provides methods and suggestions for quick and accurate diagnosis and repair of problems. Troubleshooting procedures discuss typical symptoms and logical methods to pinpoint the trouble.

Chapter Three explains all periodic lubrication and routine maintenance necessary to keep your Yamaha YZ running well. Chapter Three also includes recommended tune-up procedures, eliminating the need to constantly consult chapters on the various assemblies.

Subsequent chapters describe specific systems such as the engine, clutch,

MAJOR CONTROLS AND COMPONENTS

1. Kickstarter
2. Choke lever or knob
3. Front brake lever
4. Fuel shutoff valve
5. Air filter
6. Rear brake pedal
7. Clutch/transmission oil fill
8. Clutch lever
9. Fuel/oil mixture fill cap
10. Throttle grip
11. Exhaust silencer
12. Gearshift lever
13. Foot peg
14. Side stand
15. Drive chain adjusters

MAJOR CONTROLS AND COMPONENTS

1. Kickstarter
2. Choke lever or knob
3. Front brake lever
4. Fuel shutoff valve
5. Air filter
6. Rear brake pedal
7. Clutch/transmission oil fill
8. Clutch lever
9. Fuel/oil mixture fill cap
10. Throttle grip
11. Exhaust silencer
12. Gearshift lever
13. Foot peg
14. Side stand
15. Drive chain adjusters

transmission, fuel, exhaust, suspension and brakes. Each chapter provides disassembly, repair, and assembly procedures in simple step-by-step form. If a repair is impractical for a home mechanic, it is so indicated. It is usually faster and less expensive to take such repairs to a dealer or competent repair shop. Specifications concerning a particular system are included at the end of the appropriate chapter.

Some of the procedures in this manual specify special tools. In all cases, the tool is illustrated either in actual use or alone. Well equipped mechanics may find they can substitute similar tools already on hand or can fabricate their own. The terms NOTE, CAUTION, and WARNING have a specific meaning in this manual. A NOTE provides additional information to make a step or procedure easier or clearer. Disregarding a NOTE could cause inconvenience, but would not cause damage or personal injury.

A CAUTION emphasizes areas where equipment damage could result. Disregarding a CAUTION could cause permanent mechanical damage; however, personal injury is unlikely.

A WARNING emphasizes areas where personal injury or even death could result from negligence. Mechanical damage may also occur. WARNINGS *are to be taken seriously.* In some cases serious injury or death has resulted from disregarding similar warnings.

Throughout this manual keep in mind 2 conventions. "Front" refers to the front of the bike. The front of any component such as the engine is the end which faces toward the front of the bike. The left and right hand side refer to the position of the parts as viewed by a rider sitting on the seat facing forward. For example, the throttle grip is on the right-hand side. These rules are simple, but even experienced mechanics occasionally become disoriented.

SERVICE HINTS

Most of the service procedures covered are straightforward and can be performed by anyone reasonably handy with tools. It is suggested, however, that you consider your own capabilities carefully before attempting any operation involving major disassembly of the engine.

Some operations, for example, require the use of a press. It would be wiser to have these performed by a shop equipped for such work, rather than to try to do the job yourself with makeshift equipment. Other procedures require precise measurements. Unless you have the skills and equipment required, it would be better to have a qualified repair shop make the measurements for you.

Repairs go much faster and easier if your bike is clean before you begin work. There are special cleaners, like Gunk Cycle Degreaser, for washing the engine and related parts. Just brush or spray on the cleaning solution, let it stand, then rinse it away with a garden hose. Clean all oily or greasy parts with cleaning solvent as you remove them.

> *WARNING*
> *Never use gasoline as a cleaning agent. It presents an extreme fire hazard. Be sure to work in a well-ventilated area when using cleaning solvent. Keep a fire extinguisher, rated for gasoline fires, handy in any case.*

Special tools are required for some repair procedures. These may be purchased at a dealer, rented from a tool rental dealer, or may be fabricated by a mechanic or machinist often at a considerable savings.

Much of the labor charged for repairs made by dealers is for the removal and disassembly of other parts to reach the defective unit. It is frequently possible to perform the preliminary operations yourself and then take the defective unit in to the dealer for repair at considerable savings.

Once you have decided to tackle the job yourself, read the entire section in this manual which pertains to it, making sure you have identified the proper one. Study the illustrations and text until you have a good idea of what is involved in completing the job satisfactorily. If special tools are required, make arrangements to get them before you start. It is frustrating and time-consuming to get partly into a job and then be unable to complete it.

Simple wiring checks can be easily made at home; but knowledge of electronics is almost a necessity for performing tests with complicated electronic testing gear.

During disassembly of parts keep a few general cautions in mind. Force is rarely needed to get things apart. If parts are a tight fit, like a bearing in a case, there is usually a tool designed to separate them. Never use a screwdriver to pry apart parts with machined surfaces such as crankcase halves. You will mar the surfaces and end up with leaks.

Make diagrams (or take a Polaroid picture of it) wherever similar-appearing parts are found. For instance, crankcase bolts are often not the same length. You may think you can remember where everything came from—but mistakes are costly. There is also the possibility you may be sidetracked and not return to work for days or even weeks—in which interval carefully laid out parts may have become disturbed.

Tag all similar internal parts for location and mark all mating parts for position. Record number and thickness of any shims as they are removed. Small parts such as bolts can be identified by placing them in plastic sandwich bags. Seal and label them with masking tape.

Wiring should be tagged with masking tape and marked as each wire is removed. Again do not rely on memory alone.

Protect finished surfaces from physical damage or corrosion. Keep gasoline off painted surfaces.

Frozen or very tight bolts and screws can often be loosened by soaking with penetrating oil, like WD-40 or Liquid Wrench, then sharply striking the bolt head a few times with a hammer and punch (or screwdriver for screws). Avoid heat unless absolutely necessary, since it may melt, warp, or remove the temper from many parts.

No parts, except those assembled with a press fit, require unusual force during assembly. If a part is hard to remove or install, find out why before proceeding.

Cover all openings after removing parts to keep dirt, small tools, etc., from falling in.

When assembling 2 parts, start all fasteners, then tighten evenly.

Wiring connections, and brake shoes should be kept clean and free of grease and oil.

When assembling parts, be sure all shims and washers are replaced exactly as they came out.

Whenever a rotating part butts against a stationary part, look for a shim or washer. Use new gaskets if there is any doubt about the condition of the old ones. A thin coat of oil on gaskets may help them seal effectively.

Heavy grease can be used to hold small parts in place if they tend to fall out during assembly. However, keep grease and oil away from electrical and brake components.

High spots may be sanded off a piston with sandpaper, but fine emery cloth and oil will do a much more professional job.

A carburetor is best cleaned by disassembling it and soaking the parts in a commercial carburetor cleaner. Never soak gaskets and rubber parts in these cleaners. Never use wire to clean out jets and air passages; they are easily damaged. Use compressed air to blow out the carburetor only if the float(s) has been removed first.

A baby bottle makes a good measuring device for adding oil to the transmission and front forks. Get one that is graduated in ounces and cubic centimeters.

Take your time and do the job right. Do not forget that a newly rebuilt engine must be broken in the same as a new one. Keep the rpm within the limits given in your owner's manual when you get back in the dirt.

TORQUE SPECIFICATIONS

Torque specifications throughout this manual are given in foot pounds (ft.-lb.) and Newton meters (N.m). Newton meters are being adopted in place of meter-kilograms (mkg) in accordance with the International Modernized Metric System. Tool manufacturers are beginning to introduce torque wrenches calibrated in Newton meters, and Sears has introduced a Craftsman line calibrated in both values.

Existing torque wrenches, calibrated in meter kilograms, can be used by performing a simple conversion. All you have to do is move the decimal point one place to the right, e.g., 4.7 mkg = 47 N.m. This conversion is sufficient for use in this manual even though the exact mathematical conversion is 3.5 mkg = 34.3 N.m.

SAFETY FIRST

Professional mechanics can work for years and never sustain a serious injury. If you observe a few rules of common sense and safety, you can enjoy many hours servicing your own machine. You could hurt yourself or damage the bike if you ignore these rules.

1. Never use gasoline as a cleaning solvent.
2. Never smoke or use a torch in the vicinity of flammable liquids such as cleaning solvent in open containers.
3. If welding or brazing is required on the machine, remove the fuel tank (and monoshock) to a safe distance, at least 50 feet away.
4. Use the proper sized wrenches to avoid damage to nuts and injury to yourself.
5. When loosening a tight or stuck nut, be guided by what would happen if the wrench should slip. Protect yourself accordingly.
6. Keep your work area clean and uncluttered.
7. Wear safety goggles during all operations involving drilling, grinding, or use of a cold chisel.
8. Never use worn tools.
9. Keep a fire extinguisher handy and be sure it is rated for gasoline and electrical fires.

SPECIAL TIPS

Competition machines are subjected to loads and wear far beyond those encountered in normal dirt riding. One race may take as much out of a machine as several days of trail riding. Because of the extreme demands placed on a racing machine, several points should be kept in mind when performing service and repair. The following items are general suggestions that may improve the overall life of the machine and help avoid costly failures.

1. Use a locking compound such as Loctite Lock N' Seal No. 2114 (blue Loctite) on all bolts and nuts, even though they are secured with lockwashers. This type of Locktite does harden completely and allows easy removal of the bolt or nut. A screw or bolt lost from an engine cover or bearing retainer could easily cause serious and expensive damage before its loss is noticed.

When applying Loctite, use a small amount. If too much is used, it can work its way down the threads and stick parts together not meant to be stuck.

Keep a tube of Loctite in your tool box; when used properly it is cheap insurance.

2. Use a hammer driven impact driver tool to remove and install all screws, particularly engine cover screws. These tools help prevent the rounding off of screw heads as well as ensure a tight installation.

3. When straightening out the "foldover" type lockwasher (used on the clutch nut and drive sprocket), if possible, use a wide blade chisel such as an old and dull wood chisel. Such a tool provides a better purchase on the folded tab, making straightening out easier.

4. When installing the "fold-over" type lockwasher always use a new washer if possible. If a new washer is not available always fold-over a part of the washer that has not been previously folded.

Reusing the same fold may cause the washer to break, resulting in the loss of its locking ability and also a loose piece of metal adrift in the engine.

When folding the washer over, start the fold with a screwdriver and finish it with a pair of pliers. If a punch is used to make the fold, the fold may be too sharp, thereby increasing the chances of the washer breaking under stress.

These washers are relatively inexpensive and it is suggested that you keep several of each size in your tool box for field repairs.

5. When replacing missing or broken fasteners (bolts, nuts, and screws), especially on the engine or frame components, always use Yamaha replacement parts. They are specially hardened for each application. The wrong 25 cent bolt could easily cause many

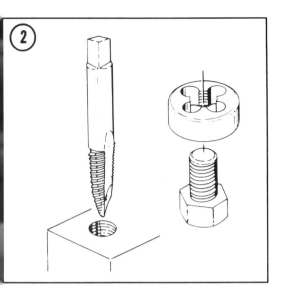

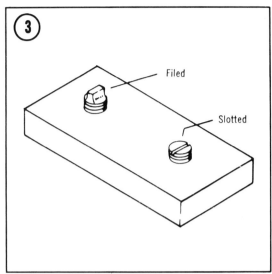

dollars worth of serious damage, not to mention rider injury.

6. When installing gaskets in the engine, always use Yamaha replacement gaskets *without* sealer, unless designated. These gaskets are designed to swell when they come in contact with oil. Gasket sealer will prevent the gaskets from swelling as intended, which can result in oil leaks. These Yamaha gaskets are also cut from material of the precise thickness needed. Installation of a too thick or too thin gasket in a critical area could cause engine damage.

MECHANIC'S TIPS

Removing Frozen Nuts and Screws

When a fastener rusts and cannot be removed, several methods may be used to loosen it. First, apply penetrating oil such as Liquid Wrench or WD-40 (available at any hardware or auto supply store). Apply it liberally. Rap the fastener several times with a small hammer; do not hit it hard enough to cause damage.

For frozen screws, apply penetrating oil as described, then insert a screwdriver in the slot and rap the top of the screwdriver with a hammer. This loosens the rust so the screw can be removed in the normal way. If the screw head is too chewed up to use a screwdriver, grip the head with Vise-Grip pliers and twist the screw out.

Remedying Stripped Threads

Occasionally, threads are stripped though carelessness or impact damage. Often the threads can be cleaned up by running a tap (for internal threads on nuts) or die (for external threads on bolts) through threads. See **Figure 2**.

Removing Broken Screws or Bolts

When the head breaks off a screw or bolt, several methods are available for removing the remaining portion.

If a large portion of the remainder projects out, try gripping it with Vise-Grips. If the projecting portion is too small, try filing it to fit a wrench or cut a slot in it to fit a screwdriver. See **Figure 3**.

If the head breaks off flush, try using a screw extractor. To do this, centerpunch the exact center of the remaining portion of the screw or bolt. Drill a small hole in the screw and tap the extractor into the hole. Back the screw out with a wrench on the extractor. See **Figure 4**.

PARTS REPLACEMENT

Yamaha makes frequent changes during a model year—some minor, some relatively major. When you order parts from the dealer or other parts distributor, always order by engine and frame number. Write the numbers

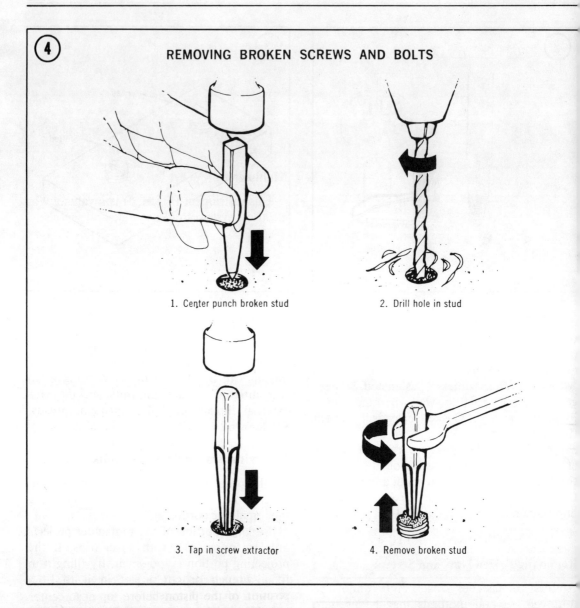

REMOVING BROKEN SCREWS AND BOLTS

1. Center punch broken stud

2. Drill hole in stud

3. Tap in screw extractor

4. Remove broken stud

down and carry them with you. Compare new parts to old before purchasing them. If they are not alike, have the parts manager explain the difference to you.

EXPENDABLE SUPPLIES

Certain expendable supplies are also required. These include grease, oil, gasket cement, wiping rags, and cleaning solvent. Ask your dealer for the special locking compounds, silicone lubricants and lube products which make motorcycle maintenance simplier and easier. Solvent is available at some service stations.

TOOLS

To properly service your motorcycle, you will need an assortment of ordinary tools. As a minimum, these include:

a. Combination wrench
b. Socket wrenches
c. Plastic mallet
d. Small hammer
e. Circlip pliers
f. Phillip's head screwdrivers
g. Slot head screwdrivers
h. Impact driver
i. Pliers
j. Feeler gauges

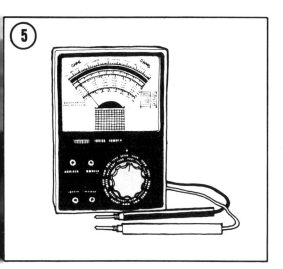

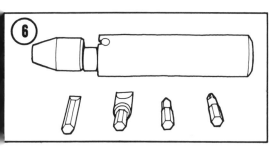

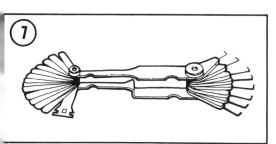

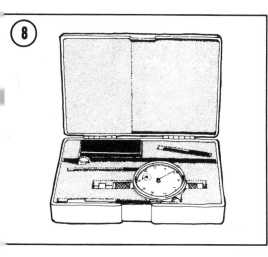

k. Spark plug gauge and gapping tool
l. Spark plug wrench
m. Drift
n. Torque wrench
o. Allen wrenches

Engine tune-up and troubleshooting procedures require a few more tools, described in the following sections.

Multimeter or VOM

This instrument (**Figure 5**) is invaluable for electrical system trouleshooting and service. A few of its functions may be duplicated by locally fabricated substitutes, but for the serious hobbyist, it is a must. Its uses are described in the applicable sections of this book. Multimeters are available at electronic hobbyist stores and mail order outlets.

Impact Driver

This tool might have been designed with the motorcyclist in mind. It makes removal of engine cover screws easy and eliminates damaged screw slots. Good ones run about $15 at large hardware and auto parts stores. See **Figure 6**.

Ignition Gauge

This tool has round wire gauges for measuring spark plug gap. See **Figure 7**.

Timing Gauge

This device is used to precisely locate the position of the piston before top dead center to achieve the most accurate ignition timing. The instrument is screwed into the spark plug hole and indicates inches and/or millimeters.

The tool shown (**Figure 8**) is available from most dealers and mail order houses. Less expensive tools, which use a vernier scale instead of a dial indicator, are also available.

Circlip Pliers

These special pliers are used to remove the circlips on transmission shaft assemblies and some engine bearing retainers. These are available in hardware and auto parts stores. See **Figure 9**.

Other Special Tools

A few other special tools may be required for major service. These are described in the appropriate chapters and are available either from Yamaha dealers or other manufacturers as indicated.

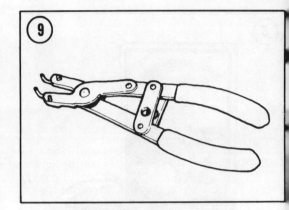

WHAT YEAR IS IT?

It's not easy to tell one year from the other. External changes throughout the years by the factory have been relatively minor. Also, after the bike has been thrashed around on the motocross circuit for a few years and/or any modifications have been done by a previous owner to the suspension or fuel tank you may be left guessing as to what year it is.

The only *positive* way to correctly identify the specific year of the engine and chassis is with the factory serial numbers. Refer to the following section for their specific location. **Table 1** is a comprehensive list of all YZ100 to YZ465 series monoshock motocross motorcycles. This table includes the engine and chassis serial numbers from beginning to the end of production for each year that that particular model was produced.

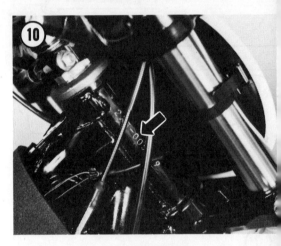

Remember that the engine may have been swapped in the frame and may not be from the same year. So always use the engine serial number for engine parts and the chassis serial number for chassis related components.

SERIAL NUMBERS

You must know the model serial number for registration purposes and when ordering replacement parts.

The frame serial number is stamped on the right-hand side of the steering head (**Figure 10**). The engine number is located on the top rear section of the engine (**Figure 11**). This location varies with the different models, but the basic location is the same.

Table 1   ENGINE AND CHASSIS NUMBERS

Model Number and Year	Engine Serial No. Start to End	Frame Serial No. Start to End
YZ465G 1980	3R5-000101-on	3R5-000101-on
YZ400F 1979	2X5-000101-Not available	2X5-000101-Not available
YZ400E 1978	2K8-000101-007406	2K8-000101-007406
YZ400D 1977	1W4-000101-006720	1W4-000101-006720
YZ400C 1976*	510-100101-102838	510-100101-102838
YZ250G 1980	3R4-000101-on	3R4-000101-on
YZ250F 1979	2X4-000101-Not available	2X4-000101-Not available
YZ250E 1978	2K7-000101-009850	2K7-000101-009850
YZ250D 1977	1W3-000101-006520	1W3-000101-006520
YZ250C 1976	509-100101-103405	509-100101-103405
YZ175C 1976*	1L8-000101-001610	1L8-000101-001610
YZ125G 1980	3R3-000101-on	3R3000101-on
YZ125F 1979	2X3-000101-Not available	2X3-000101-Not available
YZ125E 1978	2K6-000101-015080	2K6-000101-015080
YZ125D 1977	1W1-000101-015610	1W1-000101-015610
YZ125C 1976*	537-000101-01 4044	537-000101-014044
YZ125X 1976**	1G8-000101-007120	1G8-000101-007120
YZ100G 1980	3R2-000101-on	3R2-000101-on
YZ100F 1979	2W5-000101-Not available	2W5-000101-Not available
YZ100E 1978	2K5-000101-006572	2K5-000101-006572
YZ100D 1977	1J4-000101-103550	1J4-000101-103550
YZ100C 1976*	1J4-000101-003470	1J4-000101-003470

*First year of production
**Produced in that model year only

CHAPTER TWO

TROUBLESHOOTING

Diagnosing mechanical problems is relatively simple if you use orderly procedures and keep a few basic principles in mind.

The troubleshooting procedures in this chapter analyze typical symptoms, and show logical methods of isolating causes. These are not the only methods. There may be several ways to solve a problem, but only a systematic, methodical approach can guarantee success.

Never assume anything. Do not overlook the obvious. If you are riding along and the engine suddenly quits, check the easiest, most accessible problems first. Is there gasoline in the tank? Is the fuel shutoff valve in the ON position? Has the spark plug wire fallen off?

If nothing obvious turns up in a cursory check, look a little further. Learning to recognize and describe symptoms will make repairs easier for you or a mechanic at the shop. Describe problems accurately and fully. Saying that "it won't run" isn't the same as saying "it quit climbing a hill and won't start," or that it "sat in my garage for three months and then wouldn't start."

Gather as many symptoms together as possible to aid in diagnosis. Note whether the engine lost power gradually or all at once, what color smoke (if any) came from the exhaust, and so on. Remember that the more complicated a machine is, the easier it is to troubleshoot because symptoms point to specific problems.

After the symptoms are defined, areas which could cause the problems are tested and analyzed. Guessing at the cause of a problem may provide the solution, but it can easily lead to frustration, wasted time, and a series of expensive, unnecessary parts replacements.

You do not need fancy equipment or complicated test gear to determine whether repairs can be attempted at home. A few simple checks could save a large repair bill and time lost while the bike sits in a dealer's service department. On the other hand, be realistic and do not attempt repairs beyond your abilities. Service departments tend to charge heavily for putting together a disassembled engine that may have been abused. Some dealers won't even take on such a job—so use common sense, don't get in over your head.

OPERATING REQUIREMENTS

An engine needs 3 basics to run properly correct gas/air mixture, compression, and a spark at the correct time. If one or more are missing, the engine won't run. The electrical

system is the weakest link of the 3 basics. More problems result from electrical breakdowns than from any other source. Keep that in mind before you begin tampering with carburetor adjustments and the like.

If the bike has been sitting for any length of time and refuses to start, check and clean the spark plug and then look to the gasoline delivery system. This includes the fuel tank, fuel shutoff valve and fuel line to the carburetor. Gasoline deposits may have formed and gummed up the carburetor jets and air passages. Gasoline tends to lose its potency after standing for long periods. Condensation may contaminate it with water. Drain old gas and try starting with a fresh tankful.

TROUBLESHOOTING INSTRUMENTS

Chapter One lists many of the instruments needed and detailed instructions on their use.

EMERGENCY TROUBLESHOOTING

When the YZ is difficult to start or won't start at all, it does not help to wear out your leg kicking the kickstarter or to kick the tires. Check for obvious problems even before getting out your tools. Go down the following list step-by-step. Do each one; you may be embarrased to find your kill switch is stuck in the ON position, but that is better than

wearing out your leg. If it still will not start, refer to the appropriate troubleshooting procedure which follows in this chapter.

1. Is there fuel in the tank? Remove the filler cap and rock the bike. Listen for fuel sloshing around.

WARNING
Do not use an open flame to check in the tank. A serious explosion is certain to result.

2. Is the fuel mixture correct? If there is any doubt, drain the tank and refill with the correct fuel/oil mixture.
3. Is the fuel shutoff valve in the ON position (**Figure 1**).
4. Make sure the kill switch (**Figure 2**) is not stuck in the ON position.
5. Is the spark plug wire on tight (**Figure 3**).
6. Is the choke (**Figure 4**) in the right position? It should be pulled UP for a cold engine and DOWN for a warm engine.

ENGINE STARTING

An engine that refuses to start or is difficult to start can try the patience of anyone. More often than not, the problem is very minor and can be found with a simple and logical troubleshooting approach.

The following items provide a beginning point from which to isolate engine starting problems.

Engine Fails to Start

Perform the following spark test to determine if ignition system is operating properly.

1. Remove the spark plug.

2. Connect the spark plug connector to the spark plug and place the spark plug base to a good ground like the engine head. Position the spark plug so you can see the electrode.

3. Crank the engine over with the kickstarter. A fat blue spark should be evident across the spark plug electrode.

> *WARNING*
> *Do not hold the spark plug, wire, or connector or serious electrical shocks may result.*

4. If the spark is good, check for one or more of the following possible malfunctions:
   a. Obstructed fuel line
   b. Leaking head or cylinder base gasket

5. If spark is not good, check for one or more of the following:
   a. Weak ignition coil
   b. Loose electrical connections
   c. Ignition coil ground wire—it may be loose or broken

Engine Is Difficult to Start

Check for one or more of the following possible malfunctions:

a. Fouled spark plug
b. Improperly adjusted choke
c. Contaminated fuel system
d. Improperly adjusted carburetor
e. Weak ignition coil or CDI unit
f. Incorrect ignition coil
g. Poor compression

Engine Will Not Crank

Check for one or more of the following possible malfunctions:

a. Defective kickstarter
b. Siezed piston
c. Siezed crankshaft bearings
d. Broken connecting rod

ENGINE PERFORMANCE

In the following discussion, it is assumed that the engine runs, but is not operating at peak efficiency. This will serve as a starting point from which to isolate a performance malfunction.

The possible causes for each malfunction are listed in a logical sequence and in order of probability.

Engine Will Not Idle

a. Carburetor incorrectly adjusted
b. Fouled or improperly gapped spark plug
c. Head gasket leaking
d. Fuel mixture incorrect
e. Obstructed fuel line or fuel shutoff valve

Engine Misses at High Speed

a. Fouled or improperly gapped spark plug
b. Improper ignition timing
c. Improper carburetor main jet selection
d. Weak ignition coil or CDI unit
e. Obstructed fuel line or fuel shutoff valve

Engine Overheating

a. Too lean fuel mixture—an incorrect carburetor adjustment or jet selection
b. Improper ignition timing
c. Improper spark plug heat range
d. Intake system or crankcase air leak
e. Damaged or blocked cooling fins

Smoky Exhaust and Engine Runs Roughly

a. Carburetor adjustment incorrect-mixture too rich
b. Incorrect fuel/oil mixture
c. Choke not operating correctly
d. Water or other contaminants in fuel
e. Clogged fuel line
f. Clogged air filter element

Engine Loses Power

a. Carburetor incorrectly adjusted
b. Engine overheating
c. Improper ignition timing
d. Incorrectly gapped spark plug
e. Weak ignition coil or CDI unit
f. Obstructed muffler
g. Dragging brake(s)

Engine Lacks Acceleration

a. Carburetor mixture too lean
b. Clogged fuel line
c. Incorrect fuel/oil mixture
d. Improper ignition timing
e. Dragging brake(s)

ENGINE NOISES

Knocking or pinging during acceleration Caused by using a lower octane fuel than recommended. May also be caused by poor fuel available at some "discount" gasoline stations. Pinging can also be caused by a spark plug of the wrong heat range. Refer to *Correct Spark Plug Heat Range* in Chapter Three.

2. *Slapping or rattling noises at low speed or during acceleration*—May be caused by piston slap, i.e., excessive piston-cylinder wall clearance.

3. *Knocking or rapping while decelerating* —Usually caused by excessive rod bearing clearance.

4. *Persistent knocking and vibration*—Usually caused by excessive main bearing clearance.

5. *Rapid on-off squeal*—Compression leak around cylinder head gasket or spark plug.

EXCESSIVE VIBRATION

This can be difficult to find without disassembling the engine. Usually this is caused by loose engine mounting hardware. High speed vibration may be due to out-of-round or out-of-balance tire(s).

TWO-STROKE PRESSURE TESTING

Many owners of 2-stroke bikes are plagued by hard starting and generally poor running, for which there seems to be no cause. Carburetion and ignition may be good, and compression tests may show that all is well in the engine's upper end.

What a compression test does not show is lack of primary compression. The crankcase in a 2-stroke engine must be alternately under pressure and vacuum. After the piston closes the intake port, further downward movement of the piston causes the entrapped mixture to be pressurized so that it can rush quickly into the cylinder when the scavenging ports are opened. Upward piston movement creates a slight vacuum in the crankcase, enabling fuel/air mixture to be drawn in from the carburetor.

If crankcase seals or cylinder gaskets leak, the crankcase cannot hold pressure or vaccum, and proper engine operation becomes impossible. Any other source of leakage such as a defective cylinder base gasket or porous or cracked crankcase castings will result in the same conditions.

It is possible, however, to test for and isolate engine pressure leaks. The test is simple and does not require elaborate equipment. Briefly, what is done is to seal off all natural engine openings, then apply air pressure. If the engine does not hold air, a leak or leaks is indicated. Then it is only necessary to locate and repair all leaks.

The following procedure describes a typical pressure test.

1. Remove the carburetor.
2. Install the pressure adapter and its gasket in place of the carburetor.
3. Block off the exhaust port, using suitable adapters and fittings.
4. Connect the pressurizing bulb and gauge to the pressure fitting installed where the carburetor was, then continue to squeeze the bulb until the gauge indicates approximately 9 lb.
5. Observe the pressure gauge. If the engine is in good condition, pressure should not drop more than 1 psi in several minutes. Any pressure loss of 1 psi in 1 minute indicates serious sealing problems.

Before condemning the engine, first be sure that there are no leaks in the test equipment itself. Then go over the entire engine carefully. Large leaks can be heard; smaller ones can be found by going over every possible leakage source with a small brush and soap suds solution. The following lists of possible leakage points:

a. Crankshaft seals
b. Spark plug
c. Cylinder head joint
d. Cylinder base joint
e. Carburetor base joint
f. Crankcase joint

FRONT SUSPENSION AND STEERING

Poor handling may be caused by improper front and/or rear tire pressure, a damaged or bent frame or front steering components, worn front fork assemblies, worn wheel bearings, or dragging brakes. Also check front end alignment as described in Chapter Eight.

BRAKE PROBLEMS

Sticking brakes may be caused by worn or weak return springs, improper cable adjustment, or dry pivot and cam bushings. Grabbing brakes may be caused by greasy linings which must be replaced. Brake grab may also be due to an out-of-round drum. Glazed linings will cause loss of stopping power.

CHAPTER THREE

LUBRICATION, MAINTENANCE, AND TUNE-UP

If this is your first experience with a motorcycle, you should become acquainted with products that are available in auto or motorcycle parts and supply stores. Look into the tune-up tools and parts, check out the different lubricants such as 2-stroke motor oil, fork oil, locking compounds, and greases (**Figure 1**). Also check engine degreasers, like Gunk Cycle Degreaser, for cleaning your engine after each event, or prior to working on it.

The more you get involved in your Yamaha the more you will want to work on it. Start out by doing the simple tune-up, lubrication, and maintenance. Tackle more involved jobs as you gain experience.

The Yamaha YZ motocrosser is a relatively simple machine but to gain the utmost in safety, performance, and useful life from it, it is necessary to make periodic inspections and adjustments. It frequently happens that minor problems are found during such inspections that are simple and inexpensive to correct at the time, but which could lead to major problems if not corrected.

This chapter explains lubrication, maintenance, and tune-up procedures required for the YZ. **Table 1** is a suggested maintenance schedule. (**Tables 1-13** are at the end of the chapter.) However, each owner will have to determine his own maintenance requirements based on the type and frequency of use that each machine is subjected to. Full-time racing each weekend naturally requires a much more stringent maintenance schedule than occasional trail or sport riding.

NOTE
Due to the number of models and years covered in this book, be sure to follow the correct procedure and specifications for your specific model and year. Also use the correct quantity and type of fluids as indicated in the tables.

PRE-CHECKS

The following checks should be performed prior to each event or before the first ride of the day in the dirt.

1. Inspect all fuel lines and fittings for wetness.
2. Make sure the fuel tank is full and has the correct fuel/oil mixture; refer to **Table 2**.
3. Make sure the air cleaner is clean and that the cover is securely in place.
4. Check the transmission oil level.
5. Check the operation of the clutch and adjust if necessary.
6. Check that the accelerator and brake levers operate properly with no binding.
7. Inspect the condition of the front and rear suspension; make sure it has a good solid feel with no looseness.
8. Check the condition of the drive chain for wear and correct tension.
9. Check tire pressure. Refer to **Table 3**.
10. Check the exhaust system for damage.
11. Check the tightness of all fasteners, especially engine mounting hardware.

TIRES AND WHEELS

Tire Pressure

Tire pressure should be checked and adjusted to maintain the smoothness of the tire, good traction and handling, and to get the maximum life out of the tire. A simple, accurate gauge (**Figure 2**) can be purchased for a few dollars and should be carried in your tool box. The appropriate tire pressures are shown in **Table 3**.

Tire Inspection

The tires take a lot of punishment due to the variety of terrain they are subject to. Inspect them periodically for excessive wear, cuts, abrasions, etc. If you find a nail or other object in the tire, mark its location with a light crayon prior to removing it. This will help locate the hole for repair. Refer to Chapter Eight for tire changing and repair information.

Wheel Spoke Tension

Tap each spoke with a wrench. The higher the pitch of sound it makes, the tighter the spoke. The lower the sound frequency, the looser the spoke. A "ping" is good, a "klunk" says the spoke is too loose.

If one or more spokes are loose, tighten them as described under *Wheels* in Chapter Eight.

Rim Inspection

Frequently inspect the condition of the wheel rims. If a rim has been damaged it may be enough to knock it out of alignment. Improper wheel alignment can cause severe vibration and result in an unsafe riding condition.

LUBRICANTS

Oil

Oil is graded according to its viscosity, which is an indication of how thick it is. The Society of Automotive Engineers (SAE) system distinguishes oil viscosity by numbers. Thick oils have higher viscosity numbers than thin oils. For example, an SAE 5 oil is a thin oil while an SAE 90 oil is relatively thick.

Grease

A good quality grease (preferably waterproof) should be used for many of the parts on the YZ. Water does not wash grease off parts as easily as it washes off oil. In addition, grease maintains its lubricating qualities better than oil on long and strenuous events. In a pinch, though, the wrong lubricant is better than none at all. Correct the situation as soon as possible.

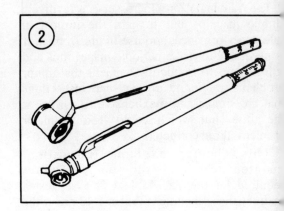

3

CLEANING SOLVENT

A number of solvents can be used to remove old dirt, grease, and oil. Kerosene is readily available and comparatively inexpensive. Another inexpensive solvent similar to kerosene is ordinary diesel fuel. Both of these solvents have a very high temperature flash point and can be used safely in any adequately ventilated area away from open flames.

WARNING
NEVER USE GASOLINE. Gasoline is extremely volatile and contains tremendously destructive potential energy. The slightest spark from metal parts accidently hitting, or a tool slipping, could cause a fatal explosion.

PERIODIC LUBRICATION

Refer to **Figure 3** for lubrication points.

Engine Lubrication

WARNING
Serious fire hazards always exist around gasoline. Do not allow any smoking in areas where fuel is being mixed or while refueling your machine. Always have a fire extinguisher, rated for gasoline and electrical fires, within reach just to play it safe.

The engines in all YZ models are lubricated by oil mixed with gasoline. Refer to **Table 4** for recommended oils and fuel. Mix the oil and gasoline thoroughly in a separate, clean, sealable container larger than the quantity being mixed to allow room for agitation. Always measure the quantities exactly. Fuel capacity for the various models is given in **Table 5**. Use a good grade of premium fuel rated at 90+ octane.

Use a baby bottle (**Figure 4**) with graduations in both fluid ounces (oz.) and cubic centimeters (cc) on the side.

Pour the required amount of oil into the mixing container and add approximately 1/2 the required amount of gasoline. Agitate the mixture thoroughly, then add the remaining fuel and agitate again until all is mixed well.

NOTE
Always mix a fresh amount of fuel the morning of the race or ride; do not mix more than you will use that day. Do not keep any fuel overnight; dispose of any excess properly.

To avoid any contaminants entering into the fuel system, use a funnel with a filter when pouring the fuel into the bikes tank.

Transmission Oil
Checking and Changing

Proper operation and long service for the clutch and transmisions require clean oil. Oil should be changed at the intervals indicated in **Table 1**. Check oil level frequently and add any to maintain the correct level. Refer to **Table 6** for oil capacities for the various models.

CAUTION
On early 1980 models YZ250 and YZ465 the oil quantity was changed by the factory. The models affected by this change are YZ250 serial numbers 3R4-000101 through 3R4-005505 and YZ465 serial numbers 3R5-000101 through 3R5-003260. These models require an additional 150 +/- 50 cc of oil than specified in the owner's manual for proper lubrication. These affected models cannot use the inspection screw to check oil level as oil level is now above this screw hole.

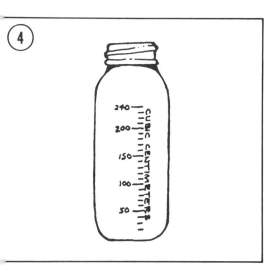

(4)

LUBRICATION POINTS

1. Front brake cam
2. Steering head bearings
3. Control cables
4. Throttle grip
5. Rear brake cam
6. Front wheel bearings
7. Front forks
8. Clutch/transmission oil
9. Side stand pivot
10. Drive chain
11. Rear wheel bearings

NOTE
See preceding note for some affected models that cannot use this inspection method. To play it safe, remove the oil level screw and let the oil drain out into a clean container. When it stops running out reinstall the screw. Measure out the correct amount of additional oil needed (150 +/- 50 cc) from the expelled oil and any additional oil and refill to bring oil up to the correct level.

4. To add oil, remove the oil fill cap (B, **Figure 5**) and add oil until it just begins to run out the screw hole.

5. Install the oil fill cap and oil level screw.

Changing

To drain the oil you will need the following (**Figure 6**):

   a. Drain pan
   b. Funnel
   c. Can opener or pour spout
   d. 1 quart of oil

There are a number of ways to discard the old oil safely. The easiest way is to pour it from the drain pan into a half gallon plastic bleach or milk bottle. Some service stations and oil retailers will accept your used oil for recycling; some may even give you money for it. Check local regulations before discarding the oil in your household trash.

Try to use the same brand of oil; do not mix brand types at the same time as they all vary slightly in their composition.

Checking

1. Start the engine and let it warm up approximately 2-3 minutes. Shut it off.

2. Place the bike in an upright position; place small piece of wood under the kickstand.

3. To check the oil level remove the screw A, **Figure 5**). If oil runs out the level is correct. If not, oil must be added.

1. Start the engine and let it reach operating temperature.

2. Shut it off and place a drip pan under the engine.

3. Remove the drain plug (**Figure 7**). Remove the oil fill cap (B, **Figure 5**); this will speed up the flow of oil.

NOTE
*On some models the drain plug is also the transmission shift drum stopper housing (containing a spring and cam stopper). See **Figure 8**. Make sure these parts are not lost in the drain pan.*

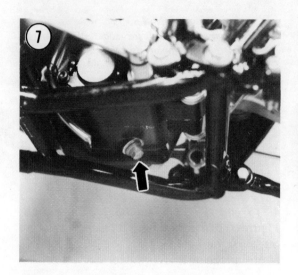

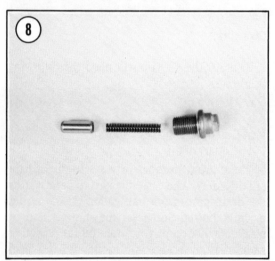

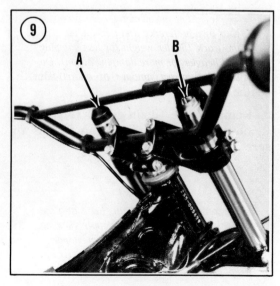

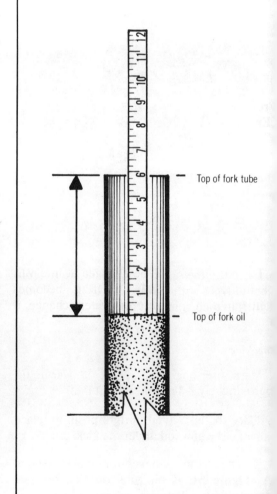

Top of fork tube

Top of fork oil

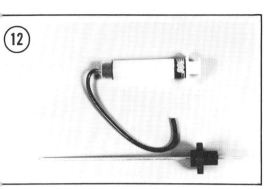

⑫

3

4. Let it drain for at least 15-20 minutes.
5. Inspect the condition of the sealing washer on the drain plug. Replace it if its condition is in doubt.
6. Install the drain plug (reassemble the transmission shift drum stopper on models so equipped). Tighten it securely.
7. Fill the transmission with the correct weight and quantity oil. Refer to **Table 6**.
8. Screw in the oil fill cap and start the engine; let it idle for 2-3 minutes. Check for leaks.
9. Turn the engine off and check for correct oil level; adjust as necessaary.

Front Fork Oil Change
(Except Models YZ400C,
YZ250C, YZ175C, YZ125X)

The following procedure describes how to change the fork oil with the forks installed in the frame. If desired, the forks can be removed and disassembled if the fork oil is really contaminated and you want to flush out the fork assembly. Refer to *Front Forks* in Chapter Eight.

The fork oil should be changed at intervals as described in **Table 1**. If it becomes contaminated with dirt or water, change it immediately.

1. Remove the upper black protective cap (A, **Figure 9**) on the top of the fork tube. Remove the dust cap (B, **Figure 9**).
2. Use a small slot-head screwdriver or similar tool and expel all air pressure in the fork.

NOTE
Release the air pressure gradually. If released too fast, oil will spurt out with the air. Protect your eyes and clothing accordingly.

3. Remove the top fork cap assembly, spacer and fork spring. Remove the fork cap slowly as the fork spring is under pressure and will push itself out when the fork cap is removed.
4. Place a drip pan under the drain screw (**Figure 10**). Allow the oil to drain for at least 5 minutes. *Never reuse the oil.*

CAUTION
Do not allow the fork oil to come in contact with any of the brake components.

5. With both of the bike's wheels on the ground and the front brake applied, push down on the handlebar grips to work the forks up and down. Continue until all oil is expelled.
6. Inspect the condition of the gasket on the drain screw; replace it if necessary. Install the drain screw.
7. Repeat for the other fork.
8. Fill each fork with the specified weight and quantity fork oil. After pouring in the oil, measure the distance from the top of the fork tube to the top of the oil with the forks fully bottomed. Refer to **Table 7** and **Figure 11**. To assure a precise oil level, you may want to invest in S & W Products "Fork Oil Level Adjuster Kit" shown in **Figure 12**. Follow the manufacturer's simple and easy to use instructions and you will end up with the exact same oil level in each fork leg.

NOTE
The weight of the oil can vary according to your own preference and the conditions of the track (lighter weight for less damping and heavier for more damping action). Do add the correct amount of oil as this specification should be followed.

9. Inspect the condition of the O-ring seal on the top cap (**Figure 13**) and replace if necessary.
10. Install the fork spring(s), spring seat and spacer (**Figure 14**). Install the fork top cap while pushing down on the spring. Start the fork cap slowly and don't cross thread it. Tighten it to the torque specifications listed in **Table 8**.

11. After assembling each fork tube, slowly pump the fork several times to expel air from the upper and lower fork chambers and to distribute the oil.

12. Inflate each fork tube to the correct amount of air pressure as indicated in **Table 9**. Refer to *Front Fork Air Pressure* following.

13. Road test the bike and check for leaks.

Front Fork Air Pressure (Excpet Models YZ400C, YZ400C, YZ175C, YZ125X)

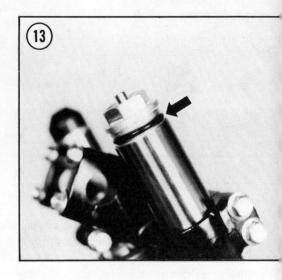

For proper damping action of the front forks the air pressure must be maintained at the correct pressure and both forks must have the same pressure.

1. Place wood blocks or a milk crate under the frame to elevate the front wheel off the ground. There must be no weight on the front wheel.

2. Remove the black rubber cap (A, **Figure 9**).

3. Remove the dust cap.

4. Use a small manual air pump like S & W Mini-Pump. Attach it to the air fitting (**Figure 15**) on top of each fork and inflate to the inflation pressure as shown in **Table 9**.

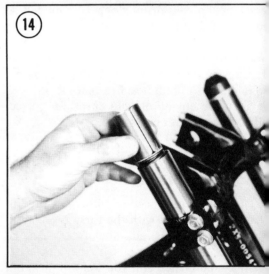

> *CAUTION*
> *Never use a high pressure air supply to pressurize the forks. Never exceed the maximum allowable air pressure of 36 psi (2.5 kg/cm2) as the oil seal will be damaged. The air pressure difference between the 2 forks should be 1.4 psi (0.1 kg/cm2) or less.*

> *CAUTION*
> *Use only compressed air or nitrogen—DO NOT use any other type of compressed gas as an explosion may result. Never heat the front forks with a torch or place them near an open flame or extreme heat.*

5. Install the dust cap and black rubber cap.

Front Fork (Models YZ400C, YZ250C, YZ175C, YZ125X)

This particular fork was used only in 1976 on models YZ400C, YZ250C, YZ175C, and YZ125X. This fork is unique in that

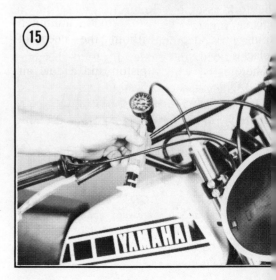

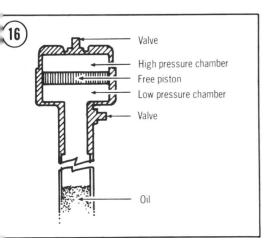

Valve
High pressure chamber
Free piston
Low pressure chamber
Valve

Oil

ompressed air takes the place of the typical rk spring. This was to provide unlimited ning possibilities without the need of placing fork springs.

There is a floating piston and a dual air essure chamber—one low pressure and one gh pressure, mounted on top of each fork igure 16). Each has its own air pressure lve. The low pressure chamber responds to nall road shocks but under severe load or rge road shock, the piston compresses the r in the upper or high pressure chamber for mping.

Changing fork oil and changing air pressure different from all other fork semblies—always refer to this procedure for ur bike.

Changing Fork Oil

1. Remove the rubber cap from the air valve on the low pressure chamber and expel all air pressure.

2. Place a drain pan under the fork and remove the drain screw (**Figure 17**). Allow the oil to drain for at least 5 minutes. *Never reuse the oil.*

> *CAUTION*
> *Do not allow the fork oil to come in contact with any of the brake components.*

3. Remove the safety wire securing each air chamber to the handlebar.

4. Unscrew the air chamber from each fork.

> *WARNING*
> *Make sure all air pressure is expelled from the air chamber prior to removing it. Failure to do so may result in personal injury.*

5. With both of the bike's wheels on the ground, and the front brake applied, pump the forks several times to drain any remaining oil. Continue until all oil is expelled.

6. Install the drain screws.

7. Pour in about 200 cc of 20W fork oil into each fork tube. Distribute the oil by pumping the fork up and down until smooth damping can be felt. Add any additional oil until the level is correct.

8. Measure the oil level from the top of the fork tube with a tape measure (**Figure 11**) with the forks *fully extended.* Refer to **Table 7**.

> *NOTE*
> *This is just the opposite of all other forks used on the YZ. The forks must be FULLY EXTENDED—not fully bottomed.*

9. Check again that the fork oil is exactly the same in both forks. Hold the bike vertical, with the forks fully extended, and remeasure; add or remove to achieve the same level in both fork legs.

10. Inspect the condition of the O-ring seal in the base of the air chamber. Replace if necessary.

11. Install the air chambers onto the forks and tighten to 10-15 ft.-lb. (15-20 N.m).

12. Safety wire the air chamber to the handlebar.

Front Fork Air Pressure

For proper damping action of the front forks the air pressure must be maintained at the correct pressure and both forks must have the same pressure.

The high pressure chamber must be filled first and then the low pressure chamber.

1. Place wood blocks or a milk crate under the frame to elevate the front wheel off the ground. There must be no weight on the front wheel and the forks must be FULLY EXTENDED.

2. Remove the air cap on the high pressure chamber.

3. Use a small manual air pump like S & W Mini-Pump (**Figure 18**). Attach it to the air fitting on the high pressure chamber and inflate to 51-56 psi (3.5-3.9 kg/cm2).

4. Repeat for the low pressure chamber and inflate to 29-32 psi (2.0-2.3 kg/cm2).

> *CAUTION*
> *Never use a high pressure air supply to pressurize the forks. Never exceed the maximum allowable air pressure of 36 psi (2.5 kg/cm2) for the upper chamber or 70 psi (5.0 kg/cm2) for the lower chamber. If this pressure is exceeded the fork oil seal will be damaged. The air pressure difference between the 2 forks should be 1.4 psi (0.1 kg/cm2) or less.*

> *CAUTION*
> *Use only compressed air or nitrogen — DO NOT use any other type of compressed gas as an explosion may result. Never heat the front forks with a torch or place them near an open flame or extreme heat.*

5. Install the air caps on both chambers of both forks.

6. Test ride the bike for a couple of laps and recheck the air pressure in each chamber on both forks. Readjust if necessary.

Drive Chain

Clean and lubricate the drive chain at intervals as described in **Table 1**, or more frequently if desired.

A properly maintained chain will provide maximum service life and reliability.

1. Disconnect the master link (**Figure 19**) and remove the chain from the motorcycle.

2. Immerse the chain in a pan of cleaning solvent and allow it to soak for about a half hour. Move it around and flex it during this period so that the dirt between the pins and rollers may work its way out.

3. Scrub the rollers and side plates with a stiff brush and rinse away loosened dirt. Rinse it a couple of times to make sure all dirt and grit are washed out. Hang up the chain and allow it to thoroughly dry.

4. Lubricate the chain with a good grade of chain lubricant, carefully following the manufacturer's instructions. If a chain lubricant isn't available use 10W/30 motor oil.

5. Reinstall the chain on the motorcycle. Use a new master link clip and install it so that the closed end of the clip is facing the direction of chain travel (**Figure 20**).

> *WARNING*
> *Always check the master link clip after the bike has been rolled backwards such as unloading from a truck or trailer. The master link clip may have snagged on the chain guide or tensioner and become disengaged. Obviously, losing a chain while riding can cause a serious spill not to mention the chain damage which may occur.*

Control Cables

The control cables should be lubricated at intervals as described in **Table 1**. Also they should be inspected at this time for fraying and the cable sheath should be checked for chafing. The cables are relatively inexpensive and should be replaced when found to be faulty.

The control cables can be lubricated either with oil or with any of the popular cable

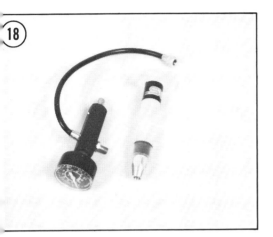

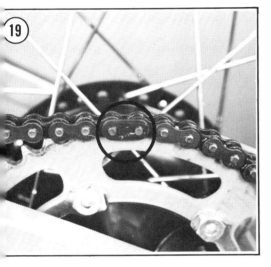

lubricants and cable lubricator. The first method requires more time and the complete lubrication of the entire cable is less certain.

Oil Method

1. Disconnect the cables from the clutch lever and the throttle grip assembly.
2. Make a cone of stiff paper and tape it to the end of the cable sheath (**Figure 21**).
3. Hold the cable upright and pour a small amount of light oil (SAE 10W/30) into the cone. Work the cable in and out of the sheath for several minutes to help the oil work its way down to the end of the cable.

> NOTE
> *To avoid a mess at the end of the cable, place a shop cloth at the end to catch the oil as it runs out the end.*

4. Remove the cone, reconnect the cable and adjust the cable(s) as described in this chapter.

> NOTE
> *While the throttle housing is separated, apply a light coat of grease to the metal surfaces of the grip assembly and to the handlebar.*

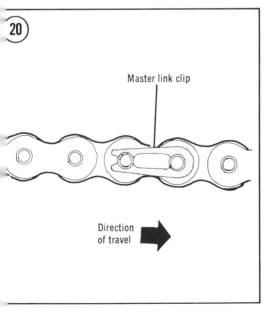

Master link clip

Direction of travel

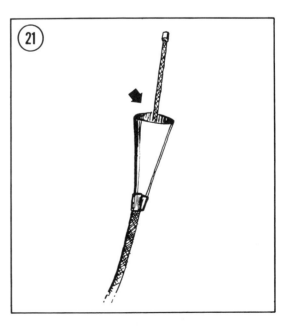

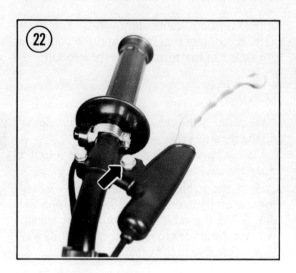

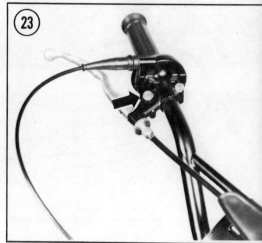

Lubricator Method

1. Disconnect the cables from the clutch lever and the throttle grip assembly.
2. Attach a lubricator following the manufacturer's instructions.
3. Insert the nozzle of the lubricant can in the lubricator, press the button on the can and hold down until the lubricant begins to flow out of the other end of the cable.

> *NOTE*
> *Place a shop cloth at the end of the cable(s) to catch all excess lubricant that will flow out.*

4. Remove the lubricator, reconnect the cable(s) and adjust the cable(s) as described in this chapter.

Miscellaneous Lubrication Points

Lubricate the clutch lever (**Figure 22**), front brake lever (**Figure 23**), rear brake pedal pivot point (**Figure 24**), and the side stand pivot point (**Figure 25**).

PERIODIC MAINTENANCE

Front Fork Air Pressure

Refer to *Front Fork Air Pressure* and *Periodic Lubrication* in this chapter.

Monoshock Adjustment

Refer to *Monoshock Adjustments* in Chapter Nine for complete details.

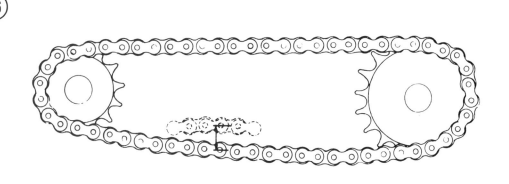

3

Drive Chain Adjustment

The drive chain should be checked and adjusted prior to each race or weekend ride.
1. Place the bike on the sidestand.

> *NOTE*
> *This adjustment must be made with the bike vertical with both wheels on the ground, and **without a rider sitting on it**.*

2. The free movement of the chain, pushed up midway between the sprockets, should be as indicated in **Table 10**. Refer to **Figure 26**.
3. To adjust, remove the cotter pin (on models so equipped) and loosen the rear axle nut (A, **Figure 27**).
4. Loosen the axle adjuster locknut (B, **Figure 27**) and turn the adjuster bolts (C, **Figure 27**) in or out as required, in equal amounts. Be sure that the marks on both adjusters align wth the same marks on each side of the swing arm (**Figure 28**).

> *NOTE*
> *Rotate the rear wheel to move the chain to another position and recheck the adjustment; chains rarely wear or stretch evenly and, as a result, the free play will not remain constant over the entire chain. If the chain cannot be adjusted within these limits, it is excessively worn and stretched and should be replaced.*

5. Sight along the top of the drive chain from the rear sprocket to see that it is correctly aligned. It should leave the top of the rear

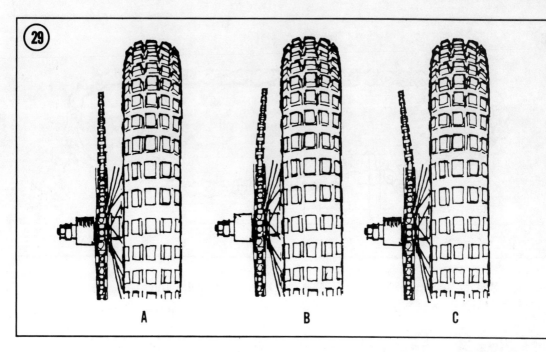

A   B   C

sprocket in a straight line (A, **Figure 29**). If it is cocked to one side or the other (B and C, **Figure 29**) the wheel is incorrectly aligned and must be corrected. Refer to Step 4.

6. Tighten the rear axle nut to 58-61 ft.-lb. (80-85 N.m) and intall a new cotter pin (on models so equipped).

> *NOTE*
> *Always install a new cotter pin; never reuse an old one.*

7. After the drive chain has been adjusted, the rear brake pedal free play has to be adjusted as described in this chapter.

Drive Chain Inspection

> *NOTE*
> *Prior to removing the drive chain from the bike, pull back on the chain with your fingers at the driven sprocket. If the chain can be pulled away from the sprocket by 1/2 the length of the sprocket teeth (**Figure 30**) it has stretched and must be further inspected as described in the following.*

1. Remove the drive chain and clean it as described under *Drive Chain Lubrication* in this chapter.

2. After cleaning the chain, examine i carefully for wear or damage. If any signs ar visible, replace the chain.

3. Lay the chain alongside a ruler (**Figure 31** and compress the links together. Then stretc them apart. If more than 1/4 in. (6.3 mm) c movement is possible, replace the chain; it i too worn to be used again.

> *NOTE*
> *Refer to **Table 11** for replacement chain type and number.*

> *CAUTION*
> *Always check both sprockets (**Figure 32**) every time the chain is removed. If any wear is visible on the teeth, replace the sprocket(s). Never install a new chain over worn sprockets or a worn chain over new sprockets.*

4. Check the inner faces of the inner plate (**Figure 33**). They should be lightly polishe on both sides. If they show considerable wea on both sides, the sprockets are not aligned Adjust alignment as described under Steps and 5 of *Drive Chain Adjustment* in this chapter

5. Lubricate the drive chain with a good grad of chain lubricant carefully following th

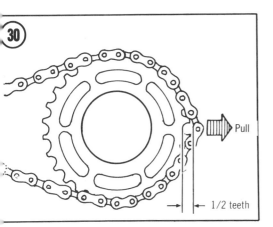

Pull

1/2 teeth

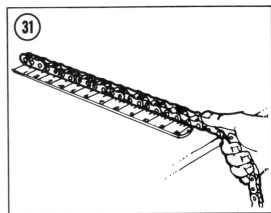

3

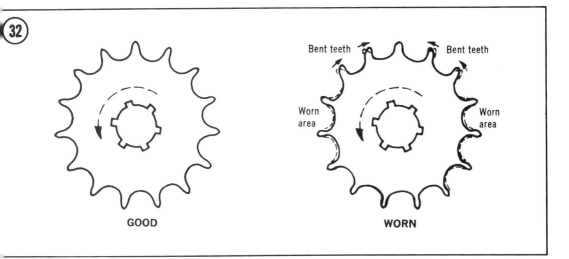

GOOD

Bent teeth   Bent teeth

Worn   Worn
area   area

WORN

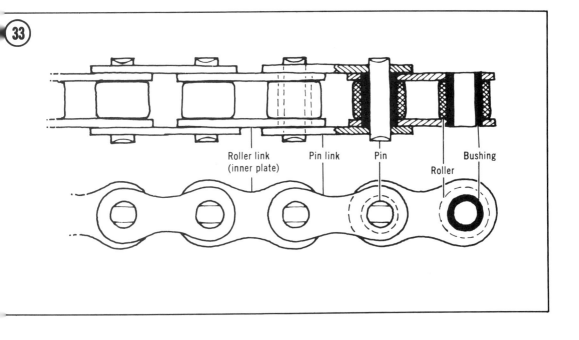

Roller link   Pin link   Pin   Bushing
(inner plate)   Roller

manufacturer's instructions. If a lubricant is not available use 10W/30 motor oil.

6. Reinstall the chain as described under *Drive Chain Lubrication* in this chapter.

7. Adjust the rear brake pedal free play as described in this chapter.

Drive Chain Guard and Rollers Replacment

The drive chain guard and rollers should be inspected and replaced as necessary. It is a good idea to inspect them prior to each race as this may just prevent chain damage. A chain that is too loosely adjusted will cause excessive wear and may cause damage to the rear swing arm.

1. To remove the chain guard on the swing arm pivot shaft (A, **Figure 34**), simply pull it off to the rear and remove it (it has a diagonal cut in it). Install by spreading it partially open and slipping it onto the swing arm. Spin it around a couple of times to make sure it is seated correctly.

2. Remove the screws (B, **Figure 34**) securing the chain guard on top of the swing arm and remove it. Install a new guard and tighten the screws securely.

3. Remove the bolt and nut securing the chain roller(s) (C, **Figure 34**) and remove them. Install new roller(s) and tighten the bolts securely.

4. On models with an aluminum swing arm, remove the screws (**Figure 35**) securing the chain guard to the rear of the swing arm and remove it. Install a new guard and tighten the screws securely.

> *NOTE*
> *Prior to installing the new chain guard, make sure the metal backing plate behind the chain guard is not bent. If bent, it must be straightened or replaced as it will cause the chain to wear prematurely. Remove the bolts (**Figure 36**) securing it, remove the plate and straighten or replace with a new one. **Figure 36** is shown with the swing arm removed for clarity; it is not necesary to remove it to perform this step.*

Front Brake Lever Adjustment

The front brake lever should be adjusted to suit your own personal preference, but should

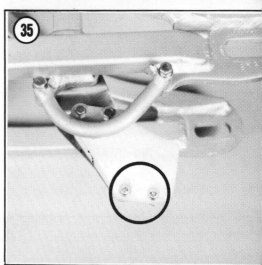

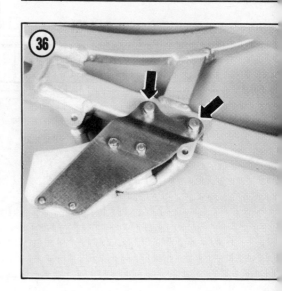

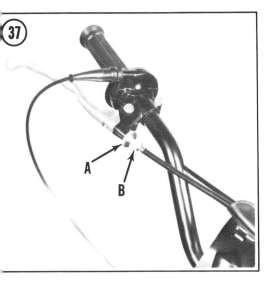

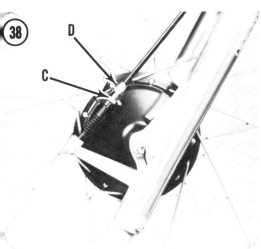

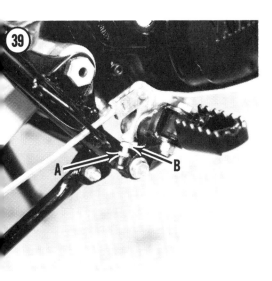

maintain a minimum cable slack of 0.2-0.32 in. (5-8 mm). The brake lever should travel this amount before the brake shoes come in contact with the drum, but it must not be adjusted so closely that the brake shoes contact the drum with the lever relaxed. The primary adjustment should be made at the hand lever.

1. Slide back the rubber boot.
2. Loosen the locknut (A, **Figure 37**) and turn the adjusting barrel (B, **Figure 37**) in or out to achieve the correct amount of free play. Tighten the locknut.

NOTE
Use the adjusting barrel closest to the hand grip for the primary adjustment.

3. Because of normal brake wear, this adjustment will eventually be "used up." It is then necessary to loosen the locknut (A) and screw the adjusting barrel (B) all the way in toward the hand grip. Tighten the locknut (B).
4. At the adjuster on the brake panel, loosen the locknut (C, **Figure 38**) and turn the adjuster nut (D, **Figure 38**) until the brake lever can be used once again for the fine adjustment. Be sure to tighten the locknut (C).

NOTE
The front brake on model YZ465G has a double leading shoe arrangement. This adjustment procedure is correct for this model also.

5. If proper adjustment cannot be achieved by the use of these adjustment points the cable has stretched and must be replaced; refer to Chapter Ten.

Rear Brake Pedal
Height Adjustment

The position of the pedal should be adjusted to your own personal preference.

1. Place the bike on the side stand.
2. Check that the brake pedal is in the at-rest position.
3. To change height position, loosen the locknut (A, **Figure 39**) and turn the adjuster (B, **Figure 39**). Looking at the adjuster head, turn it *clockwise* to lower the pedal and *counterclockwise* to raise the pedal.

4. Tighten the locknut (A) and adjust the pedal free play as described in the following procedure.

Rear Brake Pedal Adjustment

Adjust the brake pedal to the desired height as described earlier. Turn the adjustment nut on the end of the brake rod (**Figure 40**) until the pedal has 0.8-1.2 in. (20-30 mm) of free play (**Figure 41**). Free play is the distance the pedal travels from the at-rest position to the applied position when the pedal is lightly depressed by hand.

Rotate the rear wheel and check for brake drag. Also operate the pedal several times to make sure it returns to the at-rest position immediately after release.

Clutch Adjustment—Mechanism

The clutch should be adjusted at the intervals indicated in **Table 1**.

1. Drain the transmission oil as described under *Transmission Oil—Checking and Draining* in this chapter.

2. Remove the left-hand foot peg (A, **Figure 42**), shift lever (B, **Figure 42**) and the left-hand crankcase cover (C, **Figure 42**).

3. Completely loosen the locknut (A, **Figure 43**) on the cable inline adjuster and screw in the adjuster (B, **Figure 43**) all the way until it is tight.

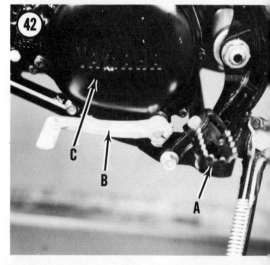

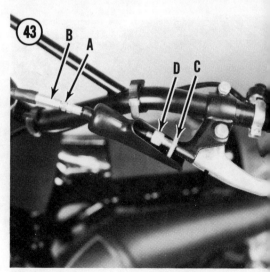

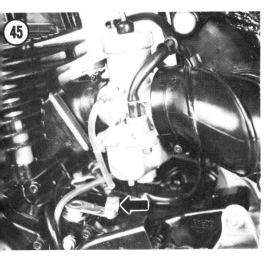

4. Loosen the locknut (C, **Figure 43**) on the hand lever and screw the adjuster barrel (D, **Figure 43**) in all the way.

5. Loosen the clutch mechanism locknut (A, **Figure 44**).

6. On 1976-1979 models, push the push lever (**Figure 45**) toward the front of the engine until it stops. Hold it in this position and turn the adjuster (B, **Figure 43**) in until the center of the push lever aligns with the match mark on the crankcase (**Figure 46**). Tighten the locknut to 6 ft.-lb. (8 N.m).

7. On models since 1980, turn the cable inline adjuster (B) until the edge of the push lever and the mark on the crankcase align. Tighten the cable locknut (A). Tighten the mechanism adjuster (B, **Figure 44**) until resistance is felt, tighten the locknut (A) to 6 ft.-lb.(8 N.m). Tighten the cable inline adjuster (A, **Figure 43**).

8. Install the left-hand crankcase cover, shift lever, and left-hand foot peg. Refill the transmission with the correct amount and type oil as described in this chapter.

Clutch Adjustment—Lever Free Play

Clutch lever free play should be rider preference but a minimum cable slack of 0.08-0.12 in. (2-3 mm) should be maintained; refer to **Figure 47**.

1. Adjust the mechanism first as previously described.

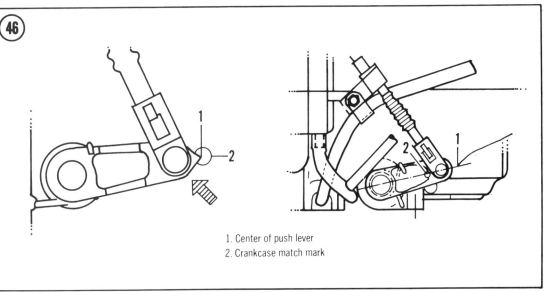

1. Center of push lever
2. Crankcase match mark

2. Loosen the locknut (A, **Figure 48**) and turn the adjusting barrel (**Figure 48**) in or out to obtain the correct amount of free play. Tighten the locknut (B).

> *NOTE*
> *There are 2 adjustment locations on the cable. The one on the hand lever and the cable length adjuster. Either or both of these adjusters can be used for this procedure.*

3. If the proper amount of clutch cable free play cannot be achieved using these adjustment points the cable has stretched to the point that it needs replacing. Refer to *Clutch Cable Removal/Installation* in Chapter Five for the complete procedure.

Throttle Adjustment and Operation

The throttle grip should have 0.12-0.20 in. (3-5 mm) rotational free play at the grip flange (**Figure 49**). If adjustment is necessary, loosen the locknut (A, **Figure 50**) and turn the adjuster (B, **Figure 50**), on top of the carburetor, in or out to achieve proper free play rotation. Tighten the locknut (A).

Check the throttle cable from grip to carburetor. Make sure it is not kinked or chafed. Replace as necessary.

Make sure the throttle grip rotates freely from a fully closed to fully open position. Check with the handlebar at center and at full right and full left. If necessary, remove the throttle grip and apply a lithium base grease to it.

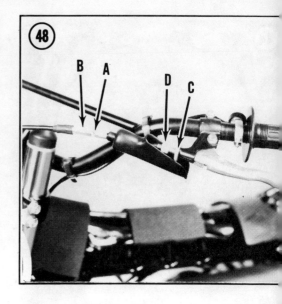

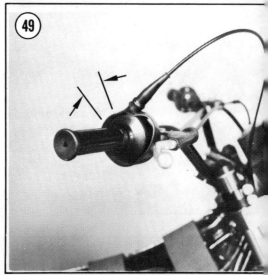

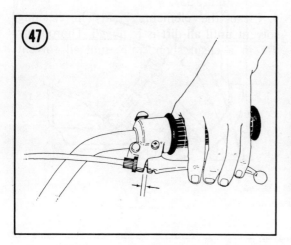

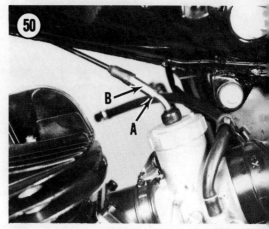

Air Cleaner

The air cleaner element should be removed, cleaned, and re-oiled at intervals indicated in **Table 1**.

The air cleaner removes dust and abrasive particles from the air before it enters the carburetor and engine. Very fine particles that may enter into the engine will cause rapid wear to the piston rings, cylinder and bearings and may clog small passages in the carburetor. Never run the YZ without the air cleaner element installed.

Proper air cleaner servicing can do more to insure long service from your engine than any other single item.

It is a good idea to have a second air cleaner element on hand, and ready to be installed, to replace the first unit between races.

Servicing

NOTE
Due to the number of models covered in this book, the following is a basic procedure using one model as a guide. Removal of side plates and any additional panels will vary slightly on your specific model.

1. Remove the screw(s) securing the cover (**Figure 51**) and remove it.
2. Pull the element out from the air box. On some models, remove the wing nut (**Figure 52**) securing the element.
3. Separate the double elements from the holder (**Figure 53**).
4. Clean the elements gently in cleaning solvent until all dirt is removed. Thoroughly dry in a clean shop cloth until all solvent residue is removed. Let it dry for about one hour. Some models are equipped with an additional small foam element (**Figure 54**); clean this element also.

NOTE
*Inspect the elements (**Figure 55**); if they are torn or broken in any area they should be replaced. Do not run with a damaged element as it may allow dirt to enter the engine.*

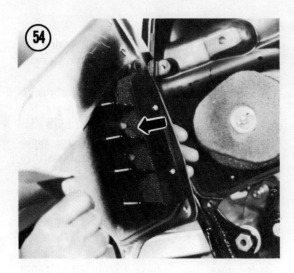

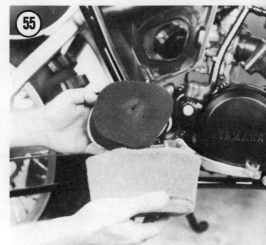

5. Pour a small amount of 30W engine oil or air filter oil onto the elements and work it thoroughly into the porous foam material. Do not oversaturate the elements as too much oil will restrict air flow. The elements will be discolored by the oil and should have an even color indicating that the oil is distributed evenly. Let it dry for another hour prior to installation. If installed too soon, the chemical carrier in the special filter oil will be drawn into the engine and may cause damage.

6. Wipe out the interior of the air box (**Figure 56**) with a shop rag and cleaning solvent. Make sure the drain plug in the bottom of the air box is clean and open.

7. Install the elements onto the holder. Apply a light coat of wheel bearing grease to the sealing edges of the element to provide a good airtight seal between the element and the air box.

8. Install the element assembly into the air box. Make sure it seats properly against the air box.

> *CAUTION*
> *An improperly installed air cleaner element will allow dirt and grit to enter the carburetor and engine, causing expensive engine damage.*

9. Install any holders and install the cover.

> *NOTE*
> *Clean off the inside surface of the side panel prior to installing it.*

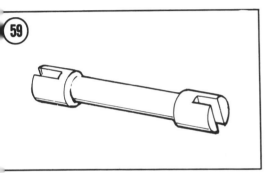

uel Line Inspection

Inspect the condition of the fuel line from he fuel tank to the carburetor (**Figure 57**). If is cracked or starting to deteriorate it must e replaced. Make sure the small hose clamps re in place and holding securely. Also make ure that the overflow tubes are in place **Figure 58**).

> *WARNING*
> *A damaged or deteriorated fuel line presents a very dangerous fire hazard to both the rider and the machine if fuel should spill onto a hot engine or exhaust pipe.*

Wheel Bearings

The wheel bearings should be checked as ndicated in **Table 1** or after crossing small vers or creeks. Refer to Chapters Eight and line for complete service procedures.

Steering Head Adjustment Check

The steering head is fitted with either roller bearings or loose ball bearings, depending on the model. It should be checked prior to each race or weekend ride.

Place the bike up on wood blocks or a milk crate so that the front wheel is off the ground.

Hold onto the front fork tubes and gently rock the fork assembly back and forth. If you can feel looseness, refer to *Steering Head Adjustment* in Chapter Eight.

Wheel Hubs, Rims, and Spokes

Check wheel hubs and rims for bends and other signs of damage. Check both wheels for broken or bent spokes. Replace damaged or broken spokes as described under *Wheels* in Chapter Eight. Pluck each spoke with your finger like a guitar string or tap each one lightly with a small hammer. All spokes should emit the same sound. A spoke that is too tight will have a higher pitch than the others; one that is too loose will have a lower pitch. If only one or two spokes are slightly out of adjustment, adjust them with a spoke wrench made for this purpose (**Figure 59**). If more are affected, the wheel should be removed and trued. Refer to *Spoke Adjustment* in Chapter Eight.

Check the rim locks (**Figure 60**) for tightness.

Front Suspension Check

1. Apply the front brake and pump the forks up and down as vigorously as possible. Check for smooth operation and check for any oil leaks.

2. Make sure the upper and lower fork bridge bolts (**Figure 61**) are tight.

3. Make sure the front axle pinch bolt(s) (**Figure 62**) are tight on models with this type of fork. On all models make sure the front axle nut is tight and the cotter pin is in place.

> *CAUTION*
> *If any of the previously mentioned bolts and nuts are loose, refer to Chapter Eight for correct procedures and torque specifications.*

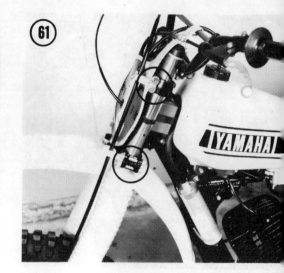

Rear Suspension Check

1. Place wooden blocks or a milk crate under the engine to raise the rear wheel off the ground.

2. Push hard on the rear wheel (sideways) to check for side play in the rear swing arm bushings. Remove the blocks from under the engine.

3. Check that the mounting bolts (or pins) securing the monoshock to the swing arm (**Figure 63** or **Figure 64**) are tight.

4. Make sure the rear axle nut is tight and the cotter pin is in place (**Figure 65**) on models so equipped.

5. Check the tightness of the rear brake torque arm bolts (**Figure 66**).

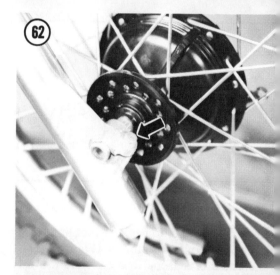

> *CAUTION*
> *If any of the previously mentioned nuts are loose, refer to Chapter Nine for correct procedures and torque specifications.*

Nuts, Bolts, and Other Fasteners

Constant vibration can loosen many of the fasteners on the motorcycle. Check the tightness of all fasteners, especially those on:

   a. Engine mounting hardware
   b. Engine crankcase covers
   c. Handlebar and front forks
   d. Gearshift lever
   e. Kickstarter lever
   f. Brake pedal and lever
   g. Exhaust system

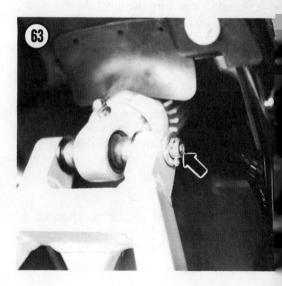

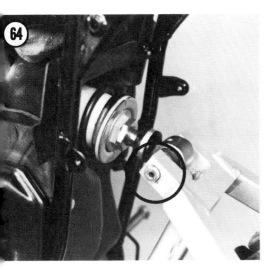

ENGINE TUNE-UP

The number of definitions for the term "tune-up" is probably equal to the number of people defining it. For the purposes of this book, a tune-up is generally adjustment and maintenance to insure peak engine performance.

The following paragraphs discuss each facet of a proper tune-up which should be performed in the order given. Unless otherwise specified, the engine should be thoroughly cool before starting any tune-up procedure.

Have the new parts on hand before you begin.

To perform a tune-up on your Yamaha YZ, you will need the following tools and equipment:

    a. 14 mm spark plug wrench
    b. Socket wrench and assorted sockets
    c. Phillips head screwdriver
    d. Allen wrench (some models only)
    e. Spark plug wire feeler gauge and gapper tool
    f. Dial indicator
    g. Flywheel puller

Cylinder Head Nuts

The engine must be at room temperature for this procedure.

1. Place support blocks under the frame to hold the bike securely.
2. Remove the seat.
3. Turn the fuel shutoff valve to the OFF position and remove the fuel line to the carburetor.
4. Remove the 2 bolts (A, **Figure 67**) and unhook the rubber strap (B, **Figure 67**) securing the rear of the fuel tank. Pull the tank to the rear and remove it.
5. Tighten each nut equally in a crisscross pattern to 18 ft.-lb. (25 N.m); refer to **Figure 68**. Some models have one bolt in place of one of the nuts; tighten to the same torque value.

Leave the seat and fuel tank off for the next procedures.

Correct Spark Plug Heat Range

Spark plugs are available in various heat ranges, hotter or colder than the plugs originally installed at the factory.

Select plugs of the heat range designed for the loads and conditions under which the YZ will be run. Use of incorrect heat ranges can cause a siezed piston, scored cylinder wall, or damaged piston crown.

In general, use a hot plug for low speeds and low temperatures. Use a cold plug for high speeds, high engine loads, and high temperatures. The plug should operate hot enough to burn off unwanted deposits, but not so hot that they burn themselves or cause preignition. A spark plug of the correct heat range will show a light tan color on the portion of the insulator within the cylinder after the plug has been in service.

The reach (length) of a plug is also important. A longer than normal plug could interfere with the piston, causing permanent and severe damage; refer to **Figure 69**.

The standard heat range spark plug for the various models is listed in **Table 12**.

Spark Plug Removal/Cleaning

1. Grasp the spark plug lead (**Figure 70**) as near the plug as possible and pull it off the plug. If it is stuck to the plug, twist it slightly to break it loose.
2. Blow away any dirt that has accumulated in the spark plug well.

> *CAUTION*
> *The dirt could fall into the cylinder when the plug is removed, causing serious engine damage.*

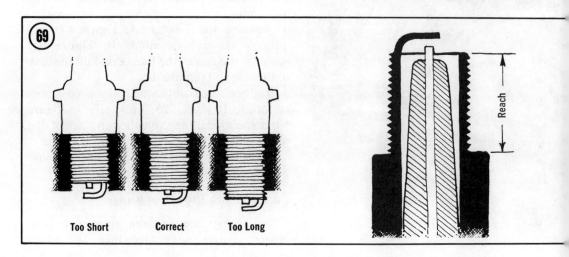

Too Short   Correct   Too Long

Reach

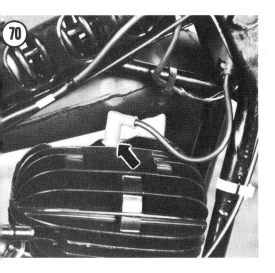

3. Remove the spark plug with a 14 mm spark plug wrench.

NOTE
If the plug is difficult to remove, apply penetrating oil, like WD-40 or Liquid Wrench, around the base of the plug and let it soak in about 10-20 minutes.

4. Inspect the plug carefully. Look for a broken center procelain, ecessively eroded electrodes, and excessive carbon or oil fouling. If deposits are light, the plug may be cleaned in solvent with a wire brush or cleaned in a special spark plug sandblast cleaner.

Gapping and Installing the Plug

A new spark plug should be carefully gapped to ensure the reliable, consistant spark. You must use a special spark plug gapping tool and a wire feeler gauge.

1. Remove the new spark plug from the box. Screw on the small piece that is loose in the box (**Figure 71**).

2. Insert a wire feeler gauge between the center and side electrode (**Figure 72**). The correct gap is listed in **Table 12**. If the gap is correct, you will feel a slight drag as you pull the wire through. If there is no drag, or the gauge won't pass through, bend the side electrode with a gapping tool (**Figure 73**) to set the proper gap.

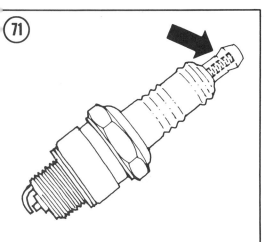

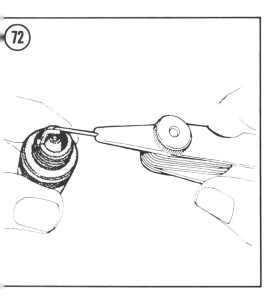

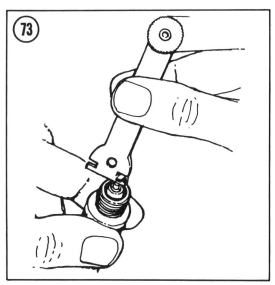

(74)

SPARK PLUG CONDITION

NORMAL

GAP BRIDGED

CARBON FOULED

OVERHEATED

OIL FOULED

SUSTAINED PREIGNITION

3. Put a small drop of oil on the threads of the spark plug.

4. Screw the spark plug in by hand until it seats. Very little effort is required. If force is necessary, you have the plug cross threaded; unscrew it and try again.

5. Use a spark plug wrench and tighten the plug an additional 1/4 to 1/2 turn after the gasket has made contact with the head. If you are installing an old, regapped plug and reusing the old gasket, only tighten an additional 1/4 turn.

NOTE
Do not overtighten. This will only squash the gasket and destroy its sealing ability.

6. Install the spark plug wire; make sure it is on tight.

Reading Spark Plugs

Much information about engine and spark plug performance can be determined by careful examination of the spark plug. This information is only valid after performing the following steps.

1. Ride the bike a short distance at full throttle in any gear.

2. Turn off the kill switch before closing the throttle and simultaneously pull in the clutch or shift to neutral; coast and brake to a stop.

3. Remove the spark plug and examine it. Compare it to **Figure 74**.

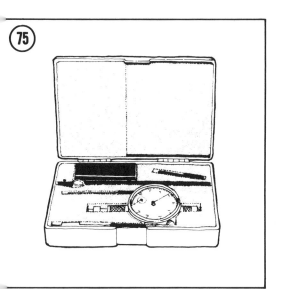

If the insulator is white or burned, the plug is too hot and should be replaced with a colder one.

A too-cold plug will have sooty or oily deposits.

If the plug has a light tan or gray colored deposit and no abnormal gap wear or electrode erosion is evident, the plug and the engine are running properly.

If the plug exhibits a black insulator tip, a damp and oily film over the firing end, and a carbon layer over the entire nose it is oil fouled. An oil fouled plug can be cleaned, but it is better to replace it.

Magneto

The engine mounted magneto generates electricity for the CDI unit and spark plug. It works similarly to a generator or alternator on an automobile, but is more compact and is attached directly to the crankshaft.

Chapter Seven explains how the magneto works in more detail.

Ignition Timing

The Yamaha YZ 100-465 cc bikes are equipped with a capacitor discharge ignition (CDI). This system uses no breaker points and greatly simplifies ignition timing and makes the ignition system much less susceptible to failures caused by dirt and moisture.

Since there are no components to wear, adjusting the ignition timing is only necessary after the engine has been disassembled or if the base plate screws have worked loose.

This procedure requires the use of a special tool called a dial indicator (**Figure 75**). These can be purchased from either a Yamaha dealer, motorcycle or auto supply store, or mail order supply house. A dial indicator, dial indicator tool stand and gauge needle are needed.

NOTE
Before starting this procedure, check all electrical connections related to the ignition system. Make sure all connections are tight and free of corrosion and that all ground connections are tight.

Model YZ465G

1. Start the engine and let it reach normal operating temperature.

2. Remove the screws securing the ignition cover and remove it (**Figure 76**).

3. Connect a portable tachometer and timing light to the engine following the manufacturer's instructions.

> *CAUTION*
> *The exhaust system is HOT; protect yourself accordingly!*

4. Restart the engine and let it idle at 2,000 rpm; adjust as necessary as described under *Carburetor Idle Speed Adjustment* in this chapter.

5. Direct the timing light to the timing marks on the magneto flywheel. The timing is correct if the magneto flywheel mark aligns with the fixed mark on the crankcase (**Figure 77**).

6. If timing is incorrect, remove the magneto rotor as described under *Magneto Removal/Installation* in Chapter Four.

7. Loosen the screws (A, **Figure 78**) securing the base plate and rotate it until the marks on the base plate align with the mark on the crankcase (B, **Figure 78**). Tighten the screws securely, making sure the base plate does not move while doing this.

8. Install the magneto rotor and repeat Steps 4 and 5.

9. If necessary repeat Steps 6 and 7 until timing is correct.

10. Disconnect the timing light and portable tachometer.

11. Install the ignition cover and gasket.

Model YZ400F, E, D, C

1. Remove the front muffler assembly (A, **Figure 79**) as described under *Muffler Assembly Removal/Installation* in Chapter Six.

2. Remove the spark plug.

3. Remove the screws securing the ignition cover (B, **Figure 79**) and remove it and the gasket.

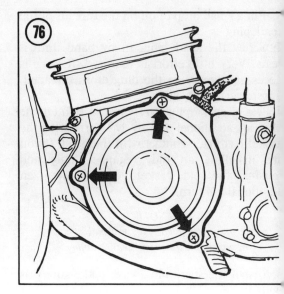

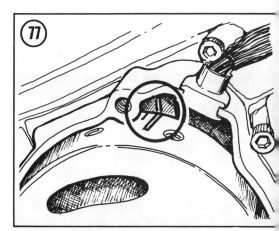

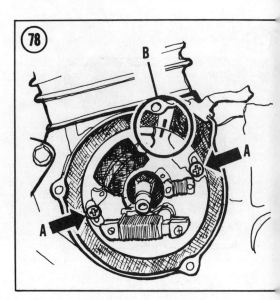

all the dial indicator assembly (**Figure**

te the magneto rotor until the piston is
dead center (TDC). Tighten the set
on the dial indicator to secure it
in the cylinder head.

the dial gauge face exactly with the
edle. Rotate the rotor back and forth
e that the gauge does not go past zero.
if necessary.

g at TDC rotate the magneto rotor
until the dial reads the dimension
able 13 for your specific model.

that the timing mark on the
rotor aligns with the fixed mark on
ase (**Figure 81**).

g is incorrect, remove the magneto
described under *Magneto*
Installation in Chapter Four.

10. Loosen the screws (A, **Figure 82**)
securing the base plate and rotate it until the
marks on the base plate align with the mark on
the crankcase (B, **Figure 82**). Tighten the
screws securely, making sure the base plate
does not move while doing this.

11. Install the magneto rotor and repeat Steps
7 and 8.

12. If necessary repeat Steps 9 and 10 until
timing is correct.

13. Unscrew the dial indicator assembly and
install the spark plug.

14. Install the ignition cover and gasket and
the muffler assembly.

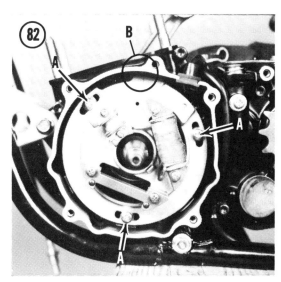

Model YZ100, YZ125, YZ175 and YZ250

1. Remove the front muffler assembly as described under *Muffler Assembly Removal/Installation* in Chapter Six.
2. Remove the spark plug.
3. Remove the screws securing the ignition cover (A, **Figure 83**) and remove it and the gasket.

> *NOTE*
> *Push down on the rear brake pedal (B,*
> ***Figure 83****) in order to remove the cover.*

4. Install the dial indicator assembly (**Figure 84**).
5. Rotate the magneto rotor until the piston is at top dead center (TDC). Tighten the set screw on the dial indicator to secure it properly in the cylinder head.
6. Align the dial gauge face exactly with the gauge needle. Rotate the rotor back and forth to be sure that the gauge does not go past zero. Readjust if necessary.
7. Starting at TDC rotate the magneto rotor *clockwise* if the magneto is on the left-hand side or *counterclockwise* if the magneto is on the right-hand side. Rotate until the dial reads the dimension given in **Table 13** for your specific model.
8. Check that the timing mark on the magneto rotor aligns with the fixed mark on the magneto stator (A, **Figure 85**).
9. If timing is incorrect, loosen the screws (B, **Figure 85**) securing the magneto stator and rotate it until the marks align (A). Tighten the screws securely, making sure the magneto stator does not move.
10. Remove the dial indicator assembly, and install the spark plug.
11. Install the ignition cover and muffler assembly.

Idle Speed Adjustment

Before starting this procedure the air cleaner must be clean, otherwise this procedure cannot be done properly.
1. Turn the pilot air screw (**Figure 86**) in until it lightly seats.

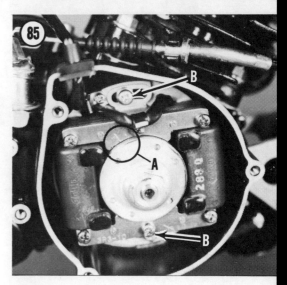

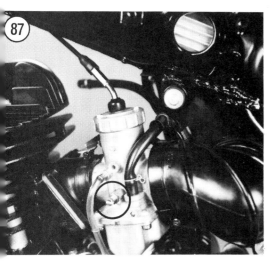

desired idle speed. This speed should be set to your own personal preference.

5. Turn the pilot air screw in or out to achieve the highest engine rpm.

6. Turn the idle stop screw in or out again to achieve the desired idle speed. Tighten the locknut (**Figure 87**).

NOTE
After this adjustment is completed, test ride the bike. Throttle response from idle should be rapid and without any hesitation. If there is any hesitation, turn the pilot air screw in or out in 1/4 turn increments until this problem is solved.

WARNING
With the engine idling, move the handlebar from side to side. If idle speed increases during this movement, the throttle cable needs adjusting or it may be incorrectly routed through the frame. Correct this problem immediately. Do not ride the bike in this unsafe condition.

Decarbonizing

The carbon deposits should be removed from the piston, cylinder head, exhaust port and muffler as indicated in **Table 1**. If it is not cleaned off it will cause preignition (ping), overheating, and high fuel consumption.

Engine Decarbonizing

1. Remove the cylinder head and cylinder as described under *Cylinder Removal/Installation* in Chapter Four.

2. Gently scrape off carbon deposits from the top of the piston and cylinder head (**Figure 88**) with a dull screwdriver or end of a hacksaw blade (**Figure 89**). Do not scratch the surface. Stuff a shop cloth into the opening in the crankcase to keep any residue from entering into it.

3. Wipe the surfaces clean with a cloth dipped in cleaning solvent.

4. Scrape off the carbon in the exhaust port (**Figure 90**) with a dull screwdriver or end of a hacksaw blade. Do not scratch the surface.

5. Install the cylinder and cylinder head.

. Back it out the following number of turns:
a. YZ465H, G: 1-1/2 turns
b. YZ400F: 1-3/4 turns
c. YZ400E, D: 1-1/2 turns
d. YZ400C: 1 turn
e. YZ250G: 2.0 turns
f. YZ250H, F, E, D, C: 1-1/2 turns
g. YZ125G, F, C: 1-1/2 turns
h. YZ125E: 1-3/4 turns
i. YZ125D,X: 1 turn
j. YZ100H, G, F, E, D, C: 1-1/2 turns
k. YZ100G, F, E, D, C: 1-1/2 turns

. Start the engine and let it reach normal operating temperature.

. Loosen the locknut and turn the idle stop screw (**Figure 87**) in or out to achieve the

Exhaust System Decarbonizing

1. Remove the exhaust pipe assembly as described under *Exhaust System Removal/Installation* in Chapter Six.
2. Gently scrape off carbon deposits from the interior of the head pipe where it attaches to the cylinder.
3. Clean out the rest of the interior of the expansion chamber by running a piece of used motorcycle drive chain around in it. Another way is to chuck a length of wire cable, with one end frayed, in an electric drill. Run it around in the front portion a couple of times. Shake out all loose carbon. Also tap on the outer shell of the exhaust pipe assembly with a plastic mallet to break any additional carbon loose.
4. Blow out the expansion chamber with compressed air.
5. Clean out the interior of the silencer.
6. Visually inspect the entire exhaust pipe assembly, especially in the many areas of welds, for cracks or other damage. Replace if necessary.
7. Install the assembly.

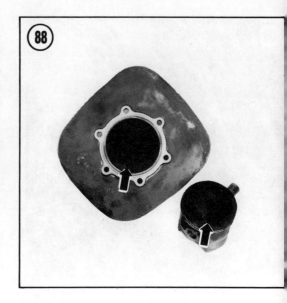

STORAGE

Several months of inactivity can cause serious problems and a general deterioration of the YZ's condition. This is especially true in areas of weather extremes. During the winter months it is advisable to specially prepare the bike for lay-up.

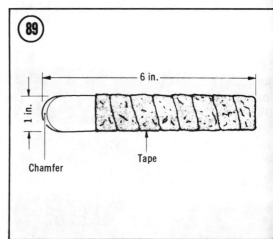

Selecting a Storage Area

Most cyclists store their bikes in their home garages. If you do not have a home garage, facilities suitable for long-term motorcycle storage are readily available for rent or lease in most areas. In selecting a building, consider the following points.

1. The storage area must be dry, free from dampness and excessive humidity. Heating is not necessary, but the building should be well insulated to minimize extreme temperature variations.
2. Buildings with large window areas should be avoided, or such windows should be masked (also a good security measure) if direct sunlight can fall on the bike.

3. Buildings in industrial areas, where factories are liable to emit corrosive fumes, are not desirable, nor are facilities near bodies of salt water.

4. The area should be selected to minimize the possibility of loss from fire, theft, or vandalism. The area should be fully insured, perhaps with a package covering fire, theft, vandalism, weather, and liability. The advice of your insurance agent should be solicited on these matters. The building should be fireproof and items such as the security of doors and windows, alarm facility, and proximity of police should be considered.

Preparing Bike for Storage

Careful preparation will minimize deterioration and make it easier to restore the bike to service later. Use the following procedure.

1. Wash the bike completely. Make certain to remove all dirt in all the hard to reach parts like the cooling fins on the head and cylinder. Completely dry all parts of the bike to remove all moisture. Wax all painted and polished surfaces, including any chromed areas.

2. Run the bike for about 20-30 minutes to warm up the oil in the clutch and transmission. Drain the oil, regardless of the time since the last oil change. Refill with the normal quantity and type of oil.

3. Drain all gasoline from the fuel tank, interconnecting hose, and the carburetor. Leave the fuel shutoff valve in the ON position. As an alternative, a fuel preservative may be added to the fuel. This preservative is available from many motorcycle shops and marine equipment suppliers.

4. Lubricate the drive chain and control cables; refer to specific procedures in this chapter.

5. Remove the spark plug and add about one teaspoon of SAE 10W/30 motor oil into the cylinder. Reinstall the spark plug and turn the engine over to distribute the oil to the cylinder walls and piston. Depress the engine kill switch while doing this to prevent it from starting.

6. Tape or tie a plastic bag over the end of the muffler to prevent the entry of moisture.

7. Check the tire pressure, inflate to the correct pressure and move the bike to the storage area. Place it securely on a milk crate or wood blocks with both wheels off the ground.

8. Cover the bike with a tarp, blanket or heavy plastic drop cloth. Place this cover over the bike mainly as a dust cover—do not wrap it tightly especially any plastic material, as it may trap moisture causing condensation. Leave room for air to circulate around the bike.

Inspection During Storage

Try to inspect the bike weekly while in storage. Any deterioration should be corrected as soon as possible. For example, if corrosion of bright metal parts is observed, cover them with a light coat of grease or silicone spray after a thorough polishing.

Turn the engine over a couple of times—don't start it, use the kickstarter and hold the kill switch on. Pump the front forks to keep the seals lubricated.

Restoring Bike to Service

A bike that has been properly prepared and stored in a suitable area requires only light maintenance to restore it to service. It is advisable, however, to peform a spring tune-up.

1. Before removing the bike from the storage area, reinflate the tires to the correct pressures. Air loss during storage may have nearly flattened the tires, and moving the bike can cause damage to tires, tubes, and rims.

2. When the bike is brought to the work area, turn the fuel shutoff valve to the OFF position, and refill the fuel tank with the correct fuel/oil mixture. Remove the main jet cover on the base of the carburetor, turn the fuel shutoff valve to the ON position, and allow several cups of fuel to pass through the fuel system. Turn the fuel shutoff valve to the OFF position and install the main jet cover.

WARNING
Place a metal container under the carburetor to catch all expelled fuel—this presents a real fire danger if allowed to drain onto the bike and the floor. Dispose of the fuel properly.

NOTE
If a fuel preservative was used, drain and properly dispose of the fuel.

3. Remove the spark plug and squirt a small amount of fuel into the cylinder to help remove the oil coating.
4. Install a fresh spark plug and start up the engine.
5. Perform the standard tune-up as described earlier in this chapter.

6. Check the operation of the engine kill switch. Oxidation of the switch contacts during storage may make it inoperative.
7. Clean and test ride the motorcycle.

WARNING
If any type of preservative (Armor All or equivalent) has been applied to the tire treads be sure the tires are well "scrubbed-in" prior to any fast riding or cornering on a hard surface. If not they will slip right out from under you.

Table 1   MAINTENANCE SCHEDULE*

Piston	
Clean and inspect	Every race
Replace	Every 5th race
Piston rings	
Replace	Every 2nd race
Cylinder head	
Inspect	Every race
Clean and retighten	Every race
Cylinder	
Clean and inspect	Every race
Retighten	Every race
Crankshaft main bearing	
Inspect	Every 5th race
Replace	As required
Piston wrist pin	
Inspect	Every 5th race
Replace	As required
Magneto rotor nut	
Retighten	Every 5th race
Kickstarter idle gear	
Inspect and replace	As required
Clutch	
Adjust	Every 3rd race
Inspect	Every race
Replace	As required
Transmission	
Change oil	Every 5th race
Inspect gears and shift forks	As required
Exhaust system	
Inspect	Every race
Decarbonize	Every 5th race
Carburetor	
Inspect and adjust	Every race
Clean and retighten	Every race
Fuel shutoff valve	
Clean	As required

(continued)

Table 1 MAINTENANCE SCHEDULE* (continued)

Air filter	
Clean and oil	Every race
Replace	As required
Spark plug	
Inspect and clean	Every race
Replace	As required
Drive chain	
Clean and lubricate	Every race
Check tension and alignment	Every race
Replace	As required
Chain guards and rollers	
Inspect and replace	As required
Frame	
Clean and inspect	Every race
Front fork	
Change oil	After initial 5 races, every 10th race thereafter
Replace oil seal	As required
Check and adjust air pressure	Every race
Monoshock	
Inspect and adjust	Every race
Lubricate	Every race
Steering head	
Inspect adjustment	Every race
Clean and lubricate	Every 5th race
Replace bearings	As required
Swing arm	
Inspect	Every race
Lubricate	Every race
Wheels and tires	
Check pressure, runout, and spoke tension	Every race
Inspect wheel bearings	Every race
Lubricate oil seals	Every 3rd race
Replace wheel bearings	As required
Throttle control	
Lubricate	Every race
Control cables	
Check routing and connections	Every race
Inspect and lubricate	Every race
Clutch and brake hand lever pivot points	
Lubricate	Every race
Retighten	Every race
Brakes	
Clean, inspect, adjust	Every race
Lubricate pivots	Every race
Replace linings	As required
Miscellaneous bolts and fasteners	
Inspect and tighten	Every race

*This Yamaha Factory maintenance schedule should be considered as a guide to general maintenance and lubrication intervals. Harder than normal use and exposure to mud, water, sand, high humidity, etc. will naturally dictate more frequent attention to most maintenance items.

Table 2   CORRECT FUEL/OIL MIXTURE

Initial break-in oil (either a new bike or rebuilt engine)	12:1 to 16:1
Normal mixture / premium gasoline	20:1

Table 3   TIRE INFLATION PRESSURE

Tire Size	Air Pressuure
Front	
3.00-21-4PR	14 psi (1.0 kg/cm^2)
Rear	
4.10-18-4PR	18 psi (1.2 kg/cm^2)
4.50-18-4PR	15 psi (1.1 kg/cm^2)
5.10-18-4PR	14 psi (1.0 kg/cm^2)

Table 4 RECOMMENDED LUBRICANTS AND FUEL

Engine oil	Yamaha Yamalube "R"
	Shell Super M
	Castrol R30
Transmission oil	SAE 10W/30 "SE" motor oil
Front forks	SAE10W/20, SAE15, SAE10, or special fork oil
Air filter	SAE10W/30 motor oil
Drive chain	Chain lube or 10W/30 motor oil
Control cables	Cable lube or 10W/30 motor oil
Control lever pivots	10W/30 motor oil
Steering head, wheel bearings, swing arm	Medium weight wheel bearing grease Water proof type
Brake cam	Lithium base
Fuel	Premimum grade—research octane 90 or higher

Table 5 FUEL CAPACITIES

Model	U.S. Gal.	Liters
YZ465	2.4	9.0
YZ400	2.0	7.6
YZ250	2.0	7.6
YZ175	1.5	5.8
YZ125	1.5	5.8
YZ100	1.4	5.2

Table 6 TRANSMISSION OIL CAPACITY

Model	Drain/Refill	Rebuild
YZ465H, G*	700-800 cc	750-850 cc
YZ400F	750-850 cc	800-900 cc
YZ400E, D, C	1,050-1,150 cc	1,150-1,250 cc
YZ250H, G*	700-800 cc	750-850 cc
YZ250F, E	750-850 cc	800-900 cc
YZ250D, C	1,050-1,150 cc	1,150-1,250 cc
YZ175C	650 cc	750 cc
YZ125 (all)	600 cc	700 cc
YZ100 (all)	600-700 cc	700-800 cc

* Note — add an additional 150 ± 50 cc to the affected models. Refer to the text for specific engine serial numbers involved.

Table 7 FRONT FORK OIL CAPACITY AND MEASUREMENT

Model	Capacity		Measurement	
	oz.	cc	in.	mm
Y465G	13.1	387	7.87	200
YZ400F	12.31	364	8.35	212
YZ400E, D	11.4	338	7.19	182
YZ400C	14.0	415	8.1	205
YZ250G	13.1	387	7.87	200
YZ250F	12.31	364	8.35	212
YZ250E, D	11.4	338	7.19	182
YZ250C	14.0	415	8.1	205
YZ175C	13.3	394	5.94	151
YZ125 (all)	6.1	180	8.3	212
YZ100G	8.9	262	–	–
YZ100F, E, D, C	6.1	180	–	–

Table 8 FRONT FORK CAP TORQUE SPECIFICATIONS

Model	Foot pounds (ft.lb.)	Newton meters (N•m)
YZ465G	16.5	23
YZ400F	16.5	23
YZ400E, D, E	18	25
YZ250G, F	16.5	23
YZ250E, D, C	18	25
YZ175	14	25
YZ125 (all)	14	20
YZ100G	14	20
YZ100F, E, D, C	22-29	30-40

Table 9 FRONT FORK AIR PRESSURE

Model	psi	kg/cm^2
YZ465G	0	0
YZ400F	12.8	0.9
YZ400E, D	14.0	1.0
YZ400C		
High-pressure chamber	56	2.9
Low-pressure chamber	29	2.0
YZ250G	0	0
YZ250F	11.2	0.8
YZ250D, E	14.0	1.0
YZ250C		
High-pressure chamber	56	2.9
Low-pressure chamber	29	2.0
YZ175C		
High-pressure chamber	45	3.1
Low-pressure chamber	23	1.6
YZ125G	0	0
YZ125F	12.8	0.9
YZ125D, E	14.0	1.0
YZ125X		
High-pressure chamber	45	3.1
Low-pressure chamber	23	1.6
YZ125C	Non air type	
YZ100	Non air type	

3

Table 10 DRIVE CHAIN SLACK

Model	Inches	Millimeters
YZ465H, G	0.4-0.6	10-15
YZ400F, E	0.4-0.6	10-15
YZ400D*	2.6-3.0	65-75
YZ400C*	2.2-2.6	55-65
YZ250H, G, F	0.4-0.6	10-15
YZ250E	1.4-1.6	35-40
YZ250D*	2.6-3.0	65-75
YZ250C*	2.2-2.6	55-65
YZ175C	1.5-1.7	40-45
YZ125G, F	0.4-0.6	10-15
YZ125E*	2.2-2.6	55-60
YZ125D, C, X	2.6-3.0	65-75
YZ100G, F, E, D	0.4-0.6	10-15
YZ100C	0.8-1.0	20-25
YZ100H	1.6-1.8	40-45

* Push down on chain tensioner unitl it is free from the drive chain for these models.

Table 11 DRIVE CHAIN REPLACEMENT NUMBERS

Model	Type	Number of Links
YZ465G	DK 520 TR	108
YZ400F	DK 520 TR	107
YZ400E	DID 520 TR	108
YZ400D	DK 520 TR	106
YZ400C	DK 520 T	106
YZ250G	DK 520 DS	106
YZ250F, D	DK 520 TR	107
YZ250E	DK 520 TR	105
YZ250C	DK 520 T	106
YZ175C	DK 530 T	98
YZ125G	DID 520 TR	102
YZ125F	DK 520 TR	101
YZ125E	DID 520 TR	103
YZ125D	DK 520 TR	100
YZ125C, X	DK 4268 HD	110
YZ100G, E	DK 520 TR	98
YZ100F	DK 520 TR	97
YZ100D, C	DK 520 T	90

Table 12 SPARK PLUG TYPE AND GAP

Model	Type	Gap In.	(mm)
YZ465G	Champion N-3	0.024-0.028	(0.6-0.7)
YZ400F	Champion N-3	0.024-0.028	(0.6-0.7)
YZ400D, C	Champion N-3G	0.024-0.028	(0.6-0.7)
YZ250 (all)	Champion N-2G	0.018-0.022	(0.45-0.55)
YZ175C	Champion N-596	0.020-0.023	(0.5-0.6)
YZ125 (all)	Champion N-59 G	0.024-0.028	(0.6-0.7)
YZ100 (all)	Champion N-59 G	0.024-0.028	(0.6-0.7)

Table 13 TIMING DIMENSIONS (WITH DIAL INDICATOR)*

Model	in.	mm
YZ465G	Does not apply (check dynamically)	
YZ400F	0.122	3.1
YZ400E, D, C	0.10	2.7
YZ250G	0.024	0.61
YZ250F	0.054	1.37
YZ250E	0.067	1.7
YZ250D, C	0.09	2.3
YZ175C	0.083	2.1
YZ125G	0.102	2.6
YZ125F	0.043	1.1
YZ125E, D, C, X	0.047	1.2
YZ100G, F	0.03	0.8
YZ100E, D, C	0.08	2.0

*All dimensions taken before top dead center (BTDC).

3

CHAPTER FOUR

ENGINE

The engines covered in this manual for the YZ series range from the YZ100 cc to the YZ465 cc. This chapter contains information for removal, inspection, service, and reassembly of the engine. Although the clutch and transmission are located within the engine they are covered in Chapter Five to simplify this material.

Service procedures for the different models are basically the same except for splitting and disassembling the crankcases. Where it would be too confusing to cover all models in one procedure it is split into the different type or models and covered separately. When differences occur within one procedure they are identified.

Prior to removing the engine or any major assembly, clean the entire engine and frame with a good grade commercial degreaser, like Gunk Cycle Degrease, or equivalent. It is easier to work on a clean engine and you will do a better job.

Make certain that you have all the necessary tools available, especially any special tool(s), and purchase replacement parts prior to disassembly. Also make sure you have a clean place to work.

It is a good idea to identify and mark parts as they are removed so that errors will be avoided during assembly and installation.

Clean all parts thoroughly upon removal, then place them in trays or boxes with their associated mounting hardware. Do not rely on memory alone as it may be days or weeks before you complete the job.

Refer to **Tables 1 and 2** at the end of this chapter for details on engine specifications and torque values. **Tables 1-3** are at the end of the chapter.

ENGINE PRINCIPLES

Figure 1 explains how the engine works. This will be helpful when troubleshooting or repairing the engine.

ENGINE LUBRICATION

Lubrication for the engine is provided by the fuel/oil mixture used to power the engine. There is no oil supply in the crankcase as it would be drawn into the cylinder causing the spark plug to foul. There is sufficient oil in the mixture to lubricate the crankshaft bearings as it is drawn into the crankcase (the clutch and transmission have their own oil supply).

ENGINE COOLING

Cooling is provided by air passing over the cooling fins on the engine cylinder head and cylinder. Therefore it is very important to

①

2-STROKE
OPERATING PRINCIPLES

The crankshaft in this discussion is rotating in a counterclockwise direction.

As the piston travels downward, it uncovers the exhaust port (A) allowing the exhaust gases, that are under pressure, to leave the cylinder. A fresh fuel/air charge, which has been compressed slightly, travels from the crankcase into the cylinder through the transfer port (B). Since this charge enters under pressure, it also helps to push out the exhaust gases.

While the crankshaft continues to rotate, the piston moves upward, covering the transfer (B) and exhaust (A) ports. The piston is now compressing the new fuel/air mixture and creating a low pressure area in the crankcase at the same time. As the piston continues to travel, it uncovers the intake port (C). A fresh fuel/air charge, from the carburetor (D), is drawn into the crankcase through the intake port, because of the low pressure within it.

Now, as the piston almost reaches the top of its travel, the spark plug fires, thus igniting the compressed fuel/air mixture. The piston continues to top dead center (TDC) and is pushed downward by the expanding gases.

As the piston travels down, the exhaust gases leave the cylinder and the complete cycle starts all over again.

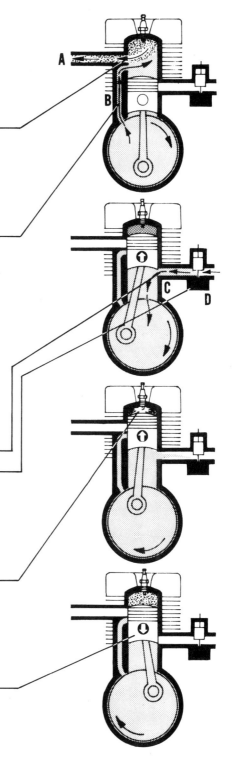

4

keep these fins free from buildup of dirt, oil, grease, and other foreign matter. Brush out the fins with a whisk broom or small stiff paint brush.

> *CAUTION*
> *Remember, these fins are thin, in order to dissipate heat, and may be damaged if struck too hard.*

SERVICING ENGINE IN FRAME

Some of the components can be serviced while the engine is mounted in the frame (the bikes frame is a great holding fixture—especially for breaking loose stubborn bolts and nuts):

   a. Cylinder head
   b. Cylinder
   c. Piston
   d. Carburetor
   e. Magneto
   f. Clutch

ENGINE

Removal/Installation

1. Place a milk crate or wood block(s) under the frame to support the bike securely.
2. Turn the fuel shutoff valve to the OFF position (**Figure 2**) and remove the fuel line to the carburetor.
3. Remove the seat and both side covers (**Figure 3**).

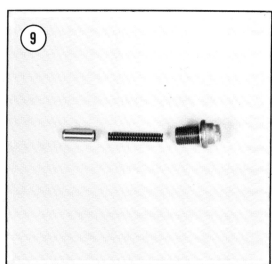

4

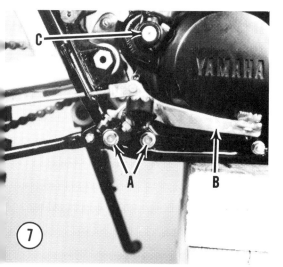

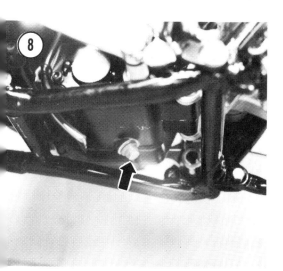

4. Pull the fuel fill cap vent tube free from the steering head area (A, **Figure 4**).

5. Remove the bolts (B, **Figure 4**) securing the front of the fuel tank. Pull up and unhook the strap (C, **Figure 4**) securing the rear of the tank. Pull the tank toward the rear and remove it.

6. Remove the exhaust system (A, **Figure 5**) as described under *Exhaust System Removal/Installation* in Chapter Six.

7. Remove the carburetor (B, **Figure 5**) as described under *Carburetor Removal/ Installation* in Chapter Six.

8. Remove the gearshift lever (A, **Figure 6**) and drive sprocket cover (B, **Figure 6**).

9. Remove the right-hand foot peg (A, **Figure 7**) and the rear brake pedal assembly (B, **Figure 7**).

10. Remove the kickstarter lever (C, **Figure 7**).

11. Remove the master link on the drive chain and remove it and the drive chain.

12. Remove the drain plug (**Figure 8**) for the clutch and transmision oil and allow the oil to completely drain.

NOTE
*On some models the drain plug is also the shift drum neutral locator. Don't lose the parts in the oil pan (**Figure 9**).*

13. Remove the clutch assembly as described under *Clutch Removal/Installation* in Chapter Five.

NOTE
If you are only removing the engine assembly and do not intend to disassemble it do not perform Steps 13-15; proceed to Step 16.

14. Remove the magneto as described under *Magneto Removal/Installation* in Chapter Seven.

15. Remove the cylinder head, cylinder, and piston as described in this chapter.

16. On models YZ465 to YZ250, remove the engine mounting bolts and nuts (**Figure 10**) and remove the crankcase assembly.

NOTE
Do not completely remove the long rear mounting bolt as the rear swing arm will fall off.

17. On models YZ175, YZ125 and YZ100, remove the engine mounting bolts and nuts (**Figure 11**) and remove the crankcase assembly.

NOTE
*After the engine has been removed, reinstall the long rear mounting bolt in one side and a long drift or socket extension in the other side of the rear swing arm pivot (**Figure 12**). This will keep the rear swing arm in place.*

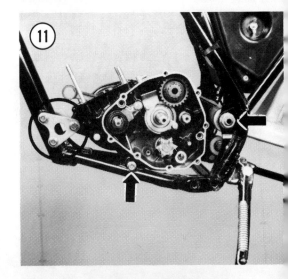

18. On models YZ465 to YZ250, inspect the condition of the rear engine mounting bracket. This part takes a lot of engine torque and will wear and become loose in the area indicated in **Figure 13**. Replace the assembly if it is worn or loose.

19. Install by reversing these removal steps.

20. Fill the clutch/transmission with the correct type and quantity oil; refer to Chapter Three.

21. Adjust the clutch, drive chain and rear brake pedal as described in Chapter Three.

22. Start the engine and check for leaks.

CYLINDER HEAD

Removal/Installation

CAUTION
To prevent warpage and damage to any component, remove the cylinder head only when the engine is at room temperature.

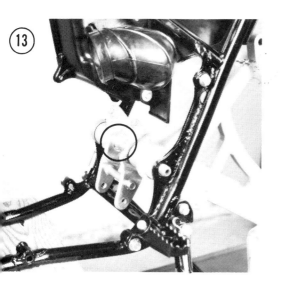

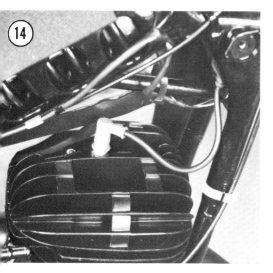

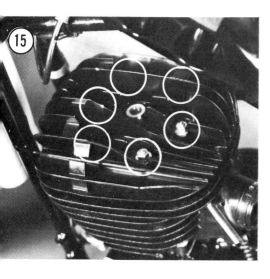

1. Remove the seat, side covers, and fuel tank.

2. Disconnect the spark plug wire and remove the spark plug (**Figure 14**).

3. Remove the exhaust system as described under *Exhaust System Removal/Installation* in Chapter Six.

4. Remove the cylinder head holding bracket on models so equipped.

5. Remove the nuts and washers (**Figure 15**) securing the cylinder head in a crisscross pattern. The number of nuts varies from 4 to 6 between the different models.

6. Loosen the head by tapping around the perimeter with a rubber or plastic mallet. If necessary, *gently* pry the head loose with a broad tipped screwdriver.

> *CAUTION*
> *Remember, the cooling fins are fragile and may be damaged if tapped or pried on too hard. Never use a metal hammer.*

> *NOTE*
> *Sometimes it is possible to loosen the head with engine compression. Rotate the engine with the kickstarter (reinstall the spark plug). As the piston reaches TDC on the compression stroke, it will pop the head loose.*

7. Remove the cylinder head by pulling straight up and off the cylinder studs.

8. Remove the cylinder head gasket and discard it.

9. Clean the cylinder head as described under *Engine Decarbonizing* in Chapter Three.

10. Lightly coat both surfaces of the new cylinder head gasket with grease and install it (**Figure 16**).

11. Install the cylinder head and install the washers; screw the nuts on finger-tight.

12. Tighten the nuts (**Figure 17**) in a crisscross pattern to the torque values in **Table 2** at the end of this chapter.

13. Install all items removed.

CYLINDER

Removal

1. Remove the cylinder head as described under *Cylinder Head Removal/Installation* in this chapter.

2. Remove the carburetor as described under *Carburetor Removal/Installation* in Chapter Six.

3. Remove the special long inner nuts (A, **Figure 18**) and outer nuts (B, **Figure 18**). The type of nuts varies with each model. Loosen and remove them in a crisscross pattern.

> *NOTE*
> *On models YZ250D, C and YZ400D, C, there are sealing washers under each of the special long nuts—don't lose them as they must be reinstalled.*

4. Loosen the cylinder by tapping around the perimeter with a rubber or plastic mallet. If necessary, *gently* pry the cylinder loose with a broad tipped screwdriver.

5. Rotate the engine so the piston is at the bottom of its stroke. Pull the cylinder straight up and off the crankcase studs and piston.

> *CAUTION*
> *Remember the cooling fins are fragile and may be damaged if tapped or pried on too hard. Do not use a metal hammer.*

6. Remove the cylinder base gasket and discard it. Install a piston holding fixture under the piston (**Figure 19**) to protect the piston skirt from damage. This fixture may be purchased or may be a homemade unit of wood. See **Figure 20**.

Inspection

The following procedure requires the uses of highly specialized and expensive measuring

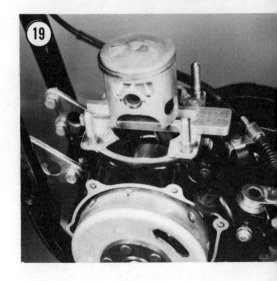

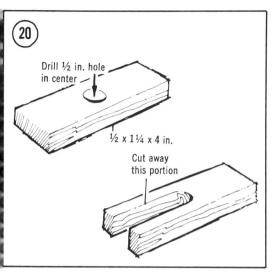

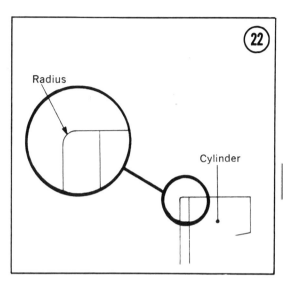

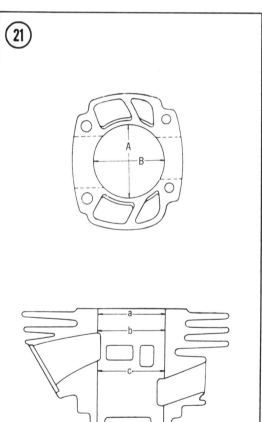

instruments. If such equipment is not readily available, have the measurements performed by a dealer or machine shop.

Measure the cylinder bore with a cylinder gauge or inside micrometer, at the points shown in **Figure 21**.

Measure in 2 axes–in line with the wrist pin and at 90 degrees to the pin. If either the taper or the out-of-round is not within the wear limit specification in **Table 1**, the cylinder must be rebored to the next oversize and a new piston installed.

NOTE
*The new piston should be obtained first before the cylinder is bored so that the piston can be measured; slight manufacturing tolerances must be taken into account in order to determine the actual size and working clearance indicated in **Table 1**.*

After the cylinder has been bored, the edges of the ports must be radiused with a fine file or grinder to prevent them from snagging the rings (**Figure 22**).

Inspect the condition of the transfer ports and the exhaust port (**Figure 23**). Clean the exhaust port as described under *Engine Decarbonizing* in Chapter Three.

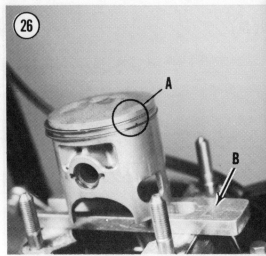

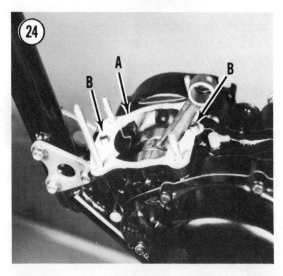

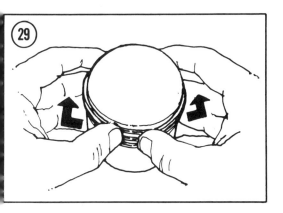

Installation

1. Check that the top surface of the crankcase and the bottom surface of the cylinder are clean prior to installation.
2. Install a new base gasket (A, **Figure 24**) and the 2 locating dowels.

NOTE
*The locating dowels are located on the centerline of the crankcase on the YZ100 and YZ125 (B, **Figure 24**) or on the studs (**Figure 25**) on the YZ250 through YZ465.*

3. Make sure the end gaps of the piston rings are lined up with the locating pins in the ring grooves (A, **Figure 26**). Lightly oil the piston rings and the inside of the cylinder bore. Rotate the crankshaft to bring the piston in contact with the piston holding fixture (B, **Figure 26**).
4. Start the cylinder down over the piston *with the exhaust port facing forward.* See **Figure 27**.
5. Compress each ring, with your fingers, as the cylinder starts to slide over it.

NOTE
Make sure the rings are still properly aligned with the locating pins in the piston.

5. Slide the cylinder down until it bottoms on the piston holding fixture.
7. Remove the piston holding fixture and slide the cylinder into place on the crankcase.
8. Install the special long inner nuts (A, **Figure 18**) and outer nuts (B, **Figure 18**). The type of nuts varies with each model. Tighten them in a crisscross pattern (**Figure 28**) to the torque values in **Table 2** at the end of this chapter.

CAUTION
On models YZ250D, C and YZ400D, C, make sure the sealing washers are in place under the special long nuts. If not installed the nuts will bottom out on the crankcase studs and the cylinder will not seal properly. This will cause an air leak which will result in poor engine performance and the leaning out of the fuel/air mixture resulting in severe damage to the engine.

9. Install the cylinder head as described under *Cylinder Head Removal/Installation* in this chapter.
10. Install the carburetor as described under *Carburetor Removal/Installation* in Chapter Six.
11. Follow the *Break-in Procedure* in this chapter if the cylinder was rebored or honed.

PISTON, PISTON PIN AND PISTON RINGS

The piston used in the YZ series is made of an aluminum alloy. The piston pin is a precision fit and is held in place by a clip at each end. A caged needle bearing is used on the small end of the connecting rod.

The piston can be removed with the engine in the frame.

Piston Removal

1. Remove the cylinder head and cylinder as described under *Cylinder Removal* in this chapter.
2. First remove the top ring by spreading the ends with your thumbs just enough to slide it up over the piston (**Figure 29**). Repeat for the other ring.
3. Before removing the piston, hold the rod tightly and rock the piston as shown in **Figure 30**. Any rocking motion (do not confuse with the normal sliding motion) indicates wear on the piston pin, needle bearing, piston pin bore or more likely a combination of all three.
4. Remove the clips from each side of the piston pin bore (**Figure 31**) with a small screwdriver or scribe. Hold your thumb over one edge of the clip when removing it to prevent it from springing out.

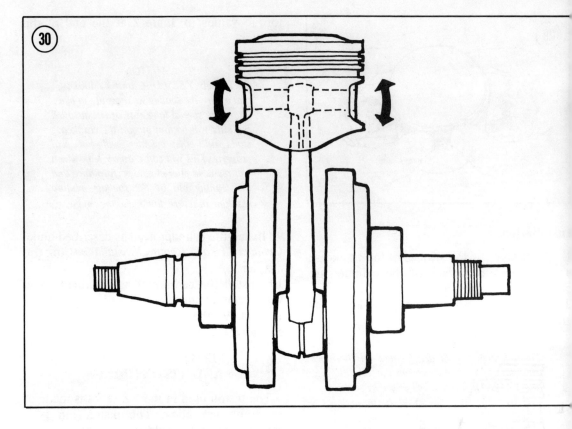

NOTE
Wrap a clean shop cloth under the piston
so that the clip will not fall into the
crankcase.

5. Use a proper size wooden dowel or socket extension and push out the piston pin.

CAUTION
Exercise care when removing the pin to
avoid damaging the connecting rod
needle bearing. If it is necessary to
gently tap the pin to remove it, be sure
that the piston is properly supported so
lateral shock is not transmitted to the
lower connecting rod bearing or rod as
bearing damage may occur.

6. If the piston pin is still difficult to remove, heat the piston and pin with a butane torch. The pin will probably push right out. Heat the piston to only about 140° F (60° C), i.e., until it is too warm to touch, but not excessively hot. If the pin is still difficult to push out, use a homemade tool as shown in **Figure 32**.

7. Lift the piston off the connecting rod.
8. Remove the needle bearing from the connecting rod (**Figure 33**).
9. If the piston is going to be left off for some time, place a piece of foam insulation tube (**Figure 34**) over the end of the rod to protect it

Inspection

1. Clean the needle bearing in solvent and dry it thoroughly. Use a magnifying glass and inspect the condition of the bearing cage for cracks at the corners of the needle slot (**Figure 35**) and inspect the needle themselves for cracking. If any cracks are found, the bearing must be replaced.
2. Wipe the bore in the connecting rod (**Figure 36**) with a clean rag and check it for galling, scratches, or any other signs of wear or damage. If any of these conditions exist replace as described under *Crankshaft and Crankcase* in this chapter.
3. Oil the needle bearing and pin and install them in the connecting rod. Slowly rotate the

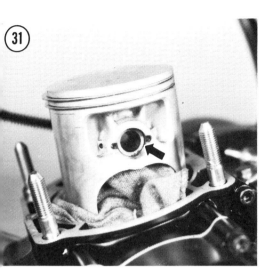

4

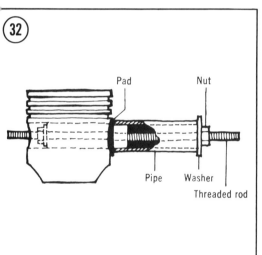

Pad   Nut

Pipe   Washer

Threaded rod

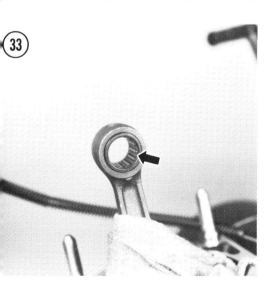

pin and check for radial and axial play (**Figure 37**). If any play exists, the pin and bearing should be replaced, providing the rod bore is in good condition. If the condition of the rod bore is in question, the old pin and bearing can be checked with a new connecting rod.

4. Carefully check the piston for cracks at the top edge of the transfer cutaways (**Figure 38**) and replace if found. Check the piston skirt for brown varnish buildup. More than a slight amount is an indication of worn or sticking rings which should be replaced.

5. Check the piston skirt for galling and abrasion which may have resulted from piston seizure. If light galling is present, smooth the affected area with No. 400 emery paper and oil or a fine oilstone. However if galling is severe or if the piston is deeply scored, replace it.

6. Measure each ring for wear as shown in **Figure 39**. Place each ring, one at a time, into the cylinder and push it in about 3/4 in. (20 mm) with the crown of the piston to ensure that the ring is square in the cylinder bore. Measure the gap with a flat feeler gauge and compare to dimensions in **Table 1**. If the gap is greater than specified, the rings should be replaced. When installing new rings, measure their end gap in the same manner as for old ones. If the gap is less than specified, carefully file the ends with a fine file until the gap is correct.

7. Carefully remove all carbon buildup from the ring grooves. Inspect the grooves carefully for burrs, nicks, or broken and cracked lands. Recondition or replace the piston if necessary.

8. Roll each ring around its piston groove as shown in **Figure 40** to check for binding. Minor binding may be cleaned up with a fine cut file.

9. Measure the side clearance of each ring in its groove with a flat feeler gauge (**Figure 41**) and compare to dimensions given in **Table 1**. If the clearance is greater than specified, the rings must be replaced, and if the clearance is still excessive with the new rings, the piston must also be replaced.

10. Measure the outside diameter of the piston across the skirt (**Figure 42**) at right angles to the piston pin. Because the piston skirt on most models is cut away for intake

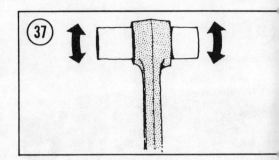

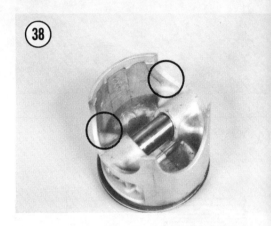

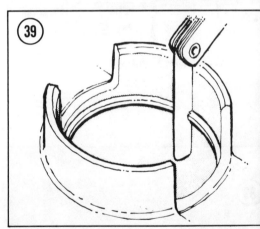

Do not use   Incorrect

4

passageway, use **Table 3** to determine the dimension up from the bottom of the piston skirt for the correct measuring point (**Figure 43**).

NOTE
*Do not measure from one of the intake fingers to the exhaust skirt (**Figure 44**) as the piston will appear to measure undersize. This is not correct due to the way the piston is ground during manufacturing.*

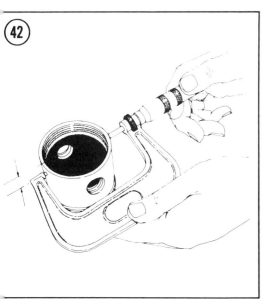

11. The measurement taken in Step 10 is to be used with the cylinder dimension taken in *Cylinder Inspection* in this chapter, to establish the piston to cylinder clearance.

12. Piston clearance is the difference between the maximum piston diameter and the minimum cylinder diameter. For a run-in (used) piston and cylinder, subtract the dimension of the piston from the cylinder dimension. If the clearance exceeds the dimension in **Table 1**, the cylinder should be rebored to the next oversize and a new piston installed.

13. To establish a final overbore dimension with a new piston, add the piston skirt measurement to the specified clearance. This will determine the dimension for the cylinder overbore size.

Piston Installation

1. Lightly oil the needle bearing and install it in the connecting rod (**Figure 45**).

2. Oil the piston pin and install it in the piston until the end of its extends slightly beyond the inside of the boss (**Figure 46**).

3. Place the piston over the connecting rod with the arrow on the piston crown pointing forward (**Figure 47**). Line up the pin with the bearing and push the pin into the piston until it is even with the piston pin clip grooves.

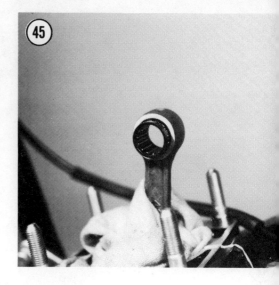

> *CAUTION*
> *If it is necessary to tap the piston pin into the connecting rod, do so gently with a block of wood or soft-faced hammer. Make sure you support the piston to prevent the lateral shock from being transmitted to the lower connecting rod bearing.*

4. Install new piston pin clips in the ends of the pin boss. Make sure they are seated in the grooves.

> *NOTE*
> *Install the clips with the gap away from the cutout in the piston (**Figure 48**) on models with this type of piston.*

5. Check the installation by rocking the piston back and forth around the pin axis and from side to side along the axis. It should rotate freely back and forth but not from side to side.

6. Install the piston rings—first the bottom one, then the top—by carefully spreading the ends of the ring with your thumbs and slipping the ring over the top of the piston. Make sure that the marks on the piston rings are toward the top of the piston.

7. Make sure the rings are seated completely in the grooves, all the way around the circumference, and that the ends are aligned with the locating pins (**Figure 49**).

8. Follow the *Break-in Procedure* in this chapter if a new piston or rings have been installed.

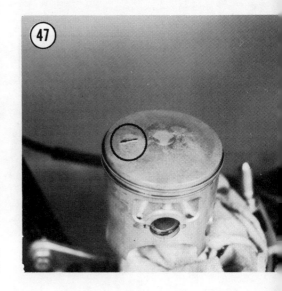

Break-in Procedure

If the rings were replaced, a new piston installed or the cylinder rebored, the engine must be run in at moderate speeds and loads for no less than 2 hours.

Don't exceed 75 percent of normal allowable rpm during run in. After the first

half hour, remove the spark plug and check its condition. The electrode should be dry and clean and the color of the insulation should be light to medium tan. If the insulation is white (indicating a too lean fuel/air mixture) or if it is dark and oily (indicating a too rich fuel/air mixture ratio), correct the condition with a main jet change; both incorrect conditions produce excessive engine heat and can lead to damage to the rings, piston, and cylinder before they have had a chance to seat in.

Refer to Chapter Three for further information on how to read a spark plug and to Chapter Six for carburetor jet change.

MAGNETO

Removal/Installation

Refer to *Magneto* in Chapter Seven for complete details on magneto removal, inspection, and installation. There are 2 different types of magnetos—outer rotor and inner rotor and Chapter Seven explains which type are used in the various models.

REED VALVE ASSEMBLY

All YZ models are equipped with a power reed valve assembly that is installed in the intake port of the cylinder. The smaller displacement engines (YZ100, YZ125 and YZ175) have 2 reeds per side (4) while the larger displacement engines (YZ250 through YZ465) have 3 per side (6).

Particular care must be taken when handling and repairing the reed valve assembly. A malfunctioning reed valve will cause severe performance loss as well as contribute to early engine failure due to a too lean mixture.

Removal/Installation

1. Remove the cylinder head and cylinder as described under *Cylinder Removal/Installation* in this chapter.
2. Remove the Allen or hex head bolts (**Figure 50**) securing the reed valve assembly to the cylinder and remove it.
3. Carefully remove the reed valve assembly from the cylinder. If the assembly is difficult to remove, use a drift or broad tipped screwdriver and gently tap the side of the

assembly to help break it loose from the gasket and cylinder.

4. Inspect as described in the following procedure.

5. Install a new gasket (**Figure 51**) and insert the reed valve assembly into the cylinder (**Figure 52**). The assembly is not marked or indexed as to a top or bottom so it can be installed either way with no problems.

6. Install the rubber intake manifold with the carburetor locating notch (**Figure 53**) facing UP. Tighten the bolts securely.

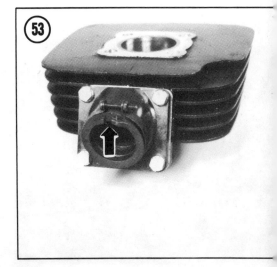

Inspection

Refer to **Figure 54** for basic reed valve construction. Stainless steel reeds (a) open and close the inlet port in response to crankcase pressure changes allowing the fuel/air mixture to enter and then close off to allow the crankcase to pressurize. The reed stops (d) are the stops or limiters of the reeds to prevent them from opening too far.

1. Carefully examine the reed valve assembly (**Figure 55**) for visible signs of wear, distortion or damage.

2. If reed stops are not equally spaced from the reed plate, pad the jaws of a wide jaw pair of pliers and gently bend reed stops as necessary.

3. Use a flat feeler gauge and check the clearance between the reed plate and the

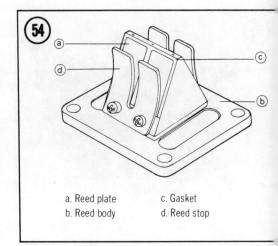

a. Reed plate   c. Gasket
b. Reed body   d. Reed stop

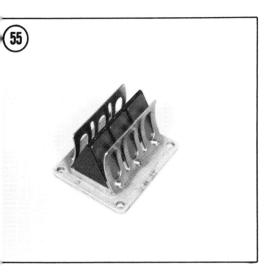

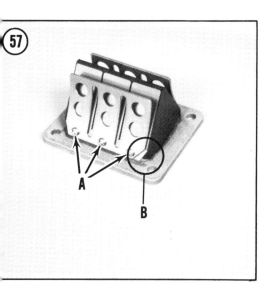

gasket (**Figure 56**). The service limit is as follows:

    a. Models YZ465-YZ250: 0.024 in. (0.6 mm)

    b. Models YZ175-YZ100: 0.012 in. (0.3 mm)

If the clearance exceeds this dimension the reed plate(s) must be replaced.

> *CAUTION*
> *Steel reeds can be turned over when out of tolerance; however, bear in mind an out of tolerance condition is caused by metal fatigue. It is suggested that steel reeds not be turned over more than once. Metal fatigue may cause one of the reeds to break off and enter the engine resulting in serious and expensive damage.*

4. Remove the screws (A, **Figure 57**) securing the reed stop to the reed body. Be careful that the screwdriver does not slip off and damage the reed plate.

5. Carefully examine the reed plate, reed stop, and gasket. Check for signs of cracks, metal fatigue, distortion, or foreign matter damage. Pay particular attention to the rubber gasket seal. The reed stops and reed plates are available as replacement parts but if the rubber gasket seal is damaged the entire assembly should be replaced.

6. Reassemble the unit; install the reed plate and reed stop with the cut off corner (B, **Figure 57**) in the lower right-hand corner. Apply Loctite Lock N' Seal to the threads prior to installation and tighten to 5-6 ft.-lb. (7-8 N•m).

> *NOTE*
> *Make sure that all parts are clean and free of any small dirt particles or lint from a shop cloth as they may cause a small amount of distortion in the reed plate.*

7. Reinstall the reed valve assembly as previously described.

CRANKCASE AND CRANKSHAFT

Disassembly of the crankcase—splitting the cases—and removal of the crankshaft assembly require that the engine be removed from the frame. However, the cylinder head, cylinder and all other attached assemblies should be removed with the engine in the frame.

The crankcase is made in 2 halves of precision diecast aluminum alloy and is of the "thin-walled" type. To avoid damage to them do not hammer or pry on any of the interior or exterior projected walls (**Figures 58 and 59**). These areas are easily damaged if stressed beyond what they are designed for.

They are assembled without a gasket; only gasket cement is used as a sealer while dowel pins align the crankcase halves when they are bolted together.

The crankshaft assembly is made up of 2 full-circle flywheels pressed together on a hollow crankpin. The connecting rod big end bearing on the crankpin is a needle bearing assembly (**Figure 60**). The crankshaft assembly is supported in 2 ball bearings in the crankcase. Service to the crankshaft is limited to removal and replacement.

The procedure which follows is presented as a complete, step-by-step major lower end rebuild that would be followed if an engine is to be completely reconditioned. However, if you're replacing a part that you know is defective, the disassembly should be carried out only until the failed part is accessible; there is no need to disassemble the engine beyond that point so long as you know the remaining components are in good condition and that they were not affected by the failed part.

In the 5 years that the Yamaha YZ has been a "monoshocker" there have been 4 different basic engines. The upper end is basically the same on all with the exception of a larger cylinder, piston, and cylinder head. The lower end is different in all models. The kickstarter, shift mechanism (external and internal), and transmission are all different in some way. Because of this, crankcase disassembly and assembly are coverd in different procedures and are placed into groups (Type I, II, III, IV). Inspection, and bearing and oil seal replacement are basically the same on all models and are covered in one procedure. Variations between different models are identified where they occur.

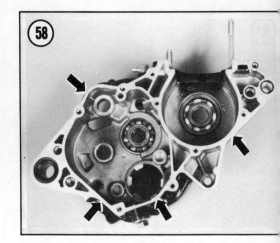

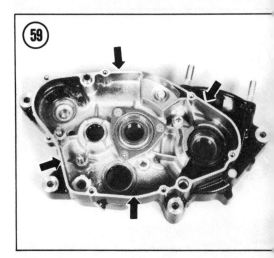

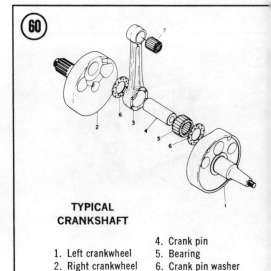

**TYPICAL
CRANKSHAFT**

1. Left crankwheel
2. Right crankwheel
3. Connecting rod
4. Crank pin
5. Bearing
6. Crank pin washer
7. Bearing

4

Crankcase Disassembly (Type I)

The Type I crankcase is found in the following models:
YZ465G
YZ400F
YZ250G, F, E

1. Remove all exterior engine assemblies as described in this chapter and other related chapters.

NOTE
Drain the clutch/transmission oil as described in Chapter Three.

2. Remove the drive sprocket by straightening the tab on the lockwasher.
3. Unscrew the locknut and remove it and the lockwasher (**Figure 61**).
4. Remove the drive sprocket (**Figure 62**) and collar (**Figure 63**).
5. On 1979 models (and 1978 YZ250) only, remove the shift drum external plug (**Figure 64**), circlip, and flat washer (**Figure 65**).

NOTE
On models since 1980 there is no external shift drum plug, washer and circlip.

6. Loosen all bolts securing the crankcase halves together one-quarter turn. To prevent warpage, loosen them in a crisscross pattern. It is easier to loosen tight screws with the engine still in the frame.

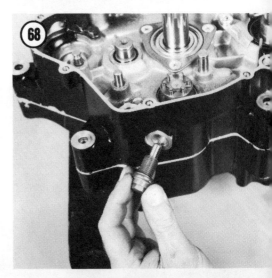

7. Remove the engine from the frame as described under *Engine Removal/Installation* in this chapter.

> *NOTE*
> *Set the engine on 2 wood blocks or fabricate a holding fixture of 2 X 4 inch wood as shown in **Figure 66**.*

8. Remove all bolts loosened in Step 6; refer to **Figure 67**. Be sure to remove all of them.

> *NOTE*
> *To prevent loss and to ensure proper location during assembly, draw the case outline on cardboard, then punch holes to correspond with screw locations. Insert the screws in their appropriate locations. Also record the position of any clips that hold electrical wires or drain tubes.*

. Unscrew the clutch/transmission drain
lug and neutral locator (**Figure 68**). Don't
ose the spring and plunger within it.

NOTE
On models since 1980 this is only a drain
plug and does not serve the dual purpose
as the neutral locator.

0. Hold onto the right-hand crankcase
nd/or studs and tap on the right-hand end of
ie crankshaft and transmission shaft with a
lastic or rubber mallet until the crankshaft
nd crankcase separate.

CAUTION
Perform this operation over and close
down to the workbench as the crankcase
halves may easily separate. DO NOT
hammer on the crankcase halves as they
will be damaged.

11. If the crankcase and crankshaft will not
separate using the method in Step 10, proceed
with the following method using a special tool.
12. Remove the crankshaft oil seal retainer
(A, **Figure 69**) and the plug (B, **Figure 69**).
13. Install the crankcase separating tool,
Yamaha special tool (part No. 90890-01135)
into the right-hand crankcase. Tighten the
securing bolts into the crankcase, making sure
the tool body is parallel with the crankcase. If
necessary, back out one of the bolts.
14. Screw the puller *clockwise* until both cases
begin to separate.

CAUTION
While tightening the puller make sure the
body is kept parallel to the crankcase
*surface during this operation (**Figure 70**).*
Otherwise it will put an uneven stress on
the case halves and may damage them.

4

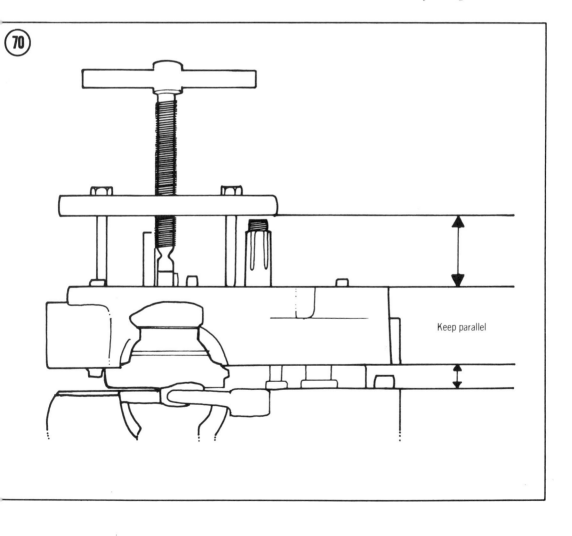

70

Keep parallel

15. Use a plastic or rubber mallet and tap the crankcase half and transmission shaft to help during separation.

> *CAUTION*
> *Crankcase separation requires only hand pressure on the puller screw. If extreme pressure seems to be needed, or if both halves will not remain parallel, STOP IMMEDIATELY. Check for crankcase screws not removed, or any part that is still attached, or transmission shafts hung up in a bearing. Relieve puller pressure immediately.*

> *NOTE*
> *Never pry between case halves. Doing so may result in oil leaks, requiring replacement of the case halves.*

16. Don't lose the 2 locating dowels.

17. Unscrew the crankcase separator tool and reinstall the crankcase plug.

18. The transmission assemblies and the crankshaft assemblies will usually stay in the left-hand crankcase half.

19. Lift up and carefully remove the transmission and shift drum assemblies (**Figure 71**).

20. Do not remove the crankshaft assembly from the left-hand crankcase half. This operation should be entrusted to a Yamaha dealer who can remove it and install a new one if necessary.

21. Inspect the crankcase halves and crankshaft as described under *Crankcase and Crankshaft Inspection—All Models* later in this chapter.

Crankcase Assembly (Type I)

1. Lightly oil the inner race of all bearings in the crankcase half that does not have the installed transmission assemblies.

2. On models since 1980, install the transmission assemblies, shift shafts, and shift drum in the right-hand crankcase half and lightly oil all shaft ends (**Figure 72**). Refer to Chapter Five for the correct procedure for your specific model.

3. On models prior to 1980, install the transmission assemblies, shift shafts, and shift drum in the left-hand crankcase half and lightly oil all shaft ends. Refer to Chapter Five for the correct procedure for your specific model.

> *NOTE*
> *On models prior to 1980, DO NOT install the shift drum neutral locator at this time. The spring pressure will push the shift drum over just enough to misalign the free end with the bearing in the right-hand crankcase during assembly.*

> *NOTE*
> *Set the crankcase assembly on 2 wood blocks or a wood holding fixture shown in the disassembly procedure.*

4. Apply a light coat of non-hardening liquid gasket (Yamabond No. 4, 4-Three Bond or equivalent) to the mating surfaces of both crankcase halves. Install the 2 locating dowel (**Figure 73**).

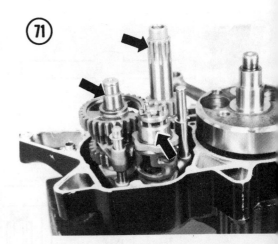

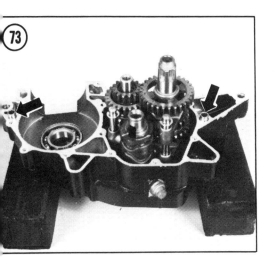

NOTE
Make sure the mating surfaces are clean and free of all old gasket material. This is to make sure you get a leak free seal.

5. Set the upper crankcase half over the one on the blocks. Push it down squarely into place until it reaches the crankshaft bearing (**Figure 74**), usually with about 1/2 inch left to go.

6. Lightly tap the case halves together with a plastic or rubber mallet (**Figure 75**) until they seat.

CAUTION
Crankcase halves should fit together without force. If the crankcase halves do not fit together completely, do not attempt to pull them together with the crankcase screws. Separate the crankcase halves and investigate the cause of the interference. If the transmission shafts were disassembled, recheck to make sure that a gear is not installed backwards. Also check that the shift drum neutral detent is not installed—it must be removed during this procedure (models prior to 1980 only). Crankcase halves are a matched set and are very expensive. Do not risk damage by trying to force the cases together.

7. Install all the crankcase screws and tighten only finger tight at first. Place any clips (**Figure 76**) under the screws in the locations recorded in Step 8, *Removal*.

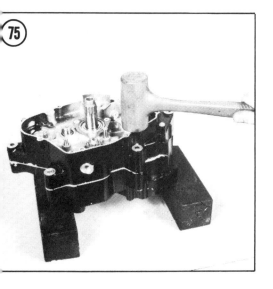

8. Securely tighten the screws in 2 stages in a crisscross pattern until they are firmly hand tight.

9. After the crankcase halves are completely assembled, rotate the crankshaft and transmission shafts to make sure there is no binding. If any is present, disassemble the crankcase and correct the problem.

10. Install the engine in the frame and tighten the mounting bolts and nuts to the torque values in **Table 2** at the end of this chapter.

11. On models prior to 1980, push on the right-hand end of the shift drum and install the washer and circlip (**Figure 77**). Without pushing on the shift drum it is impossible to correctly install the circlip. Install the shift drum external plug (**Figure 64**).

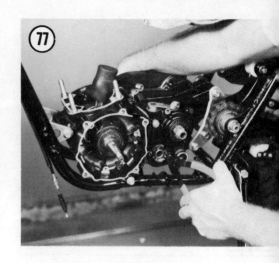

NOTE
On models since 1980 the shift drum is not
secured in this manner.

12. On models prior to 1980, install the clutch/transmission drain plug and neutral locator. On models since 1980 install the drain plug.

13. Install the collar, drive sprocket, and new lockwasher. Install a new lockwasher after at least the second removal or when the lockwasher begins to look like the one on the left in **Figure 78**.

14. Attach a "Grabbit" to the drive sprocket (**Figure 79**) and tighten the nut to the torque value in **Table 2** at the end of this chapter.

15. Bend over the tab on the lockwasher (**Figure 80**).

16. Install all exterior engine assemblies as described in this chapter and other related chapters.

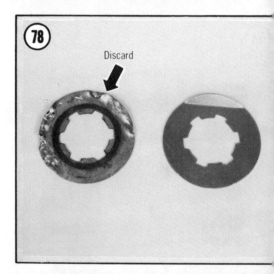

Discard

Crankcase Disassembly (Type II)

The Type II crankcase is found in the following models:
   YZ400E, D, C
   YZ250D, C

1. Remove all exterior engine assemblies as described in this chapter and other related chapters.

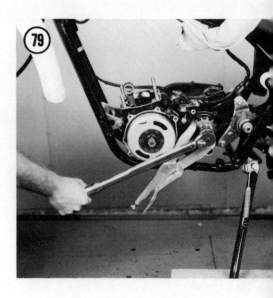

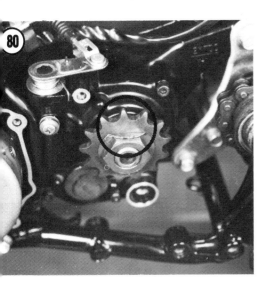

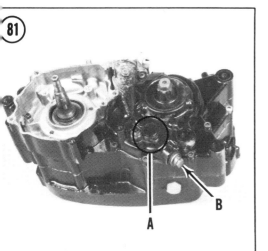

A B

NOTE
Drain the clutch/transmission oil as described in Chapter Three.

2. Remove the drive sprocket by straightening the tab on the lockwasher.

3. Unscrew the locknut and remove it and the lockwasher.

4. Remove the drive sprocket and collar.

5. Remove the shift drum external plug (A, **Figure 81**) and circlip and flat washer.

NOTE
Figure 81 is shown with the engine removed from the frame for clarity.

6. Loosen all bolts securing the crankcase halves together one-quarter turn. To prevent warpage, loosen them in a crisscross pattern. It is easier to loosen tight screws with the engine still in the frame.

7. Remove the engine from the frame as described under *Engine Removal/Installation* in this chapter.

NOTE
*Set the engine on 2 wood blocks or fabricate a holding fixture of 2 X 4 inch wood as shown in **Figure 66**.*

8. Remove all bolts loosened in Step 6; refer to **Figure 82**. Be sure to remove all of them.

NOTE
To prevent loss and to ensure proper location during assembly, draw the case outline on cardboard, then punch holes to correspond with screw locations. Insert the screws in their appropriate locations. Also record the position of any clips that hold electrical wires or drain tubes.

9. Unscrew the shift drum neutral locator (B, **Figure 81**). Don't lose the spring and plunger within it.

10. Hold onto the right-hand crankcase and/or studs and tap on the right-hand end of the crankshaft and transmission shaft with a plastic or rubber mallet until the crankshaft and crankcase separate.

CAUTION
Perform this operation over and close down to the workbench as the crankcase halves may easily separate. DO NOT hammer on the crankcase halves as they will be damaged.

11. If the crankcase and crankshaft will not separate using the method in Step 10, proceed with the following method using a special tool.
12. Remove both crankcase oil seal retainers (**Figure 83**).
13. Install the crankcase separating tool, Yamaha special tool (part No. 90890-01135) into the right-hand crankcase. Tighten the securing bolts into the crankcase, making sure the tool body is parallel with the crankcase. If necessary, back out one of the bolts.
14. Screw the puller *clockwise* until both cases begin to separate.

CAUTION
*While tightening the puller make sure the body is kept parallel to the crankcase surface (**Figure 70**). Otherwise it will put an uneven stress on the case halves and may damage them.*

15. Use a plastic or rubber mallet and tap the crankcase half and transmission shaft to help during separation.

CAUTION
Crankcase separation requires only hand pressure on the puller screw. If extreme pressure seems to be needed, or if both

halves will not remain parallel, STOP IMMEDIATELY. Check for crankcase screws not removed, or any part that is still attached, or transmission shafts hung up in a bearing. Relieve puller pressure immediately.

NOTE
Never pry between case halves. Doing so may result in oil leaks, requiring replacement of the case halves.

16. Don't lose the 2 locating dowels.
17. Unscrew the crankcase separator tool an reinstall the crankcase oil seal retainers.
18. The transmission assemblies and th crankshaft assemblies will usually stay in th left-hand case half.
19. Lift up and carefully remove th transmission and shift drum assemblie (**Figure 84**).
20. Do not remove the crankshaft assembl from the left-hand crankcase half. Th operation should be entrusted to a Yamah dealer who can remove it and install a new on if necessary.
21. Inspect the crankcase halves an crankshaft as described under *Crankcase an Crankshaft Inspection—All Models* later in th chapter.

Crankcase Assembly (Type II)

1. Lightly oil the inner race of all bearings i the crankcase half that does not have th installed transmission assemblies.

, Install the transmission assemblies, shift hafts, and shift drum in the left-hand rankcase half and lighly oil all shaft ends (Figure 84). Refer to Chapter Five for the orrect procedure for your specific model.

NOTE
DO NOT install the shift drum neutral detent at this time. The spring pressure will push the shift drum over just enough to misalign the free end with the bearing in the right-hand crankcase during assembly.

NOTE
Set the crankcase assembly on 2 wood blocks or a wood holding fixture shown in the disassembly procedure.

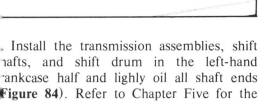

, Apply a light coat of non-hardening liquid asket (Yamabond No. 4, 4-Three Bond or quivalent) to the mating surfaces of both rankcase halves. Install the 2 locating dowels.

NOTE
Make sure the mating surfaces are clean and free of all old gasket material. This is to make sure you get a leak free seal.

, Set the upper crankcase half over the one n the blocks. Push it down squarely into lace until it reaches the crankshaft bearing (Figure 85), usually about 1/2 inch left to go.
, Lightly tap the case halves together with a lastic or rubber mallet until they seat.

CAUTION
Crankcase halves should fit together without force. If the crankcase halves do not fit together completely, do not attempt to pull them together with the crankcase screws. Separate the crankcase halves and investigate the cause of the interference. If the transmission shafts were disassembled, recheck to make sure that a gear is not installed backwards. Also check that the shift drum neutral detent is not installed—it must be removed during this procedure. Crankcase halves are a matched set and are very expensive. Do not risk damage by trying to force the cases together.

6. Install all the crankcase screws and tighten only finger tight at first. Place any clips (Figure 86) under the screws in the locations recorded in Step 8, *Removal.*
7. Securely tighten the screws in 2 stages in a crisscross pattern until they are firmly hand tight.
8. After the crankcase halves are completely assembled, rotate the crankshaft and transmission shafts to make sure there is no binding. If any is present, disassemble the crankcase and correct the problem.
9 Install the engine in the frame and tighten the mounting bolts and nuts to the torque values in **Table 2** at the end of this chapter.
10. Push on the right-hand end of the shift drum and install the washer and circlip.

Without pushing on the shift drum it is impossible to correctly install the circlip.

11. Install the shift drum external plug (A, **Figure 81**).

12. Install the collar, drive sprocket, and new lockwasher. Install a new lockwasher after at least the second removal or when the lockwasher begins to get chewed up around the edges.

13. Attach a "Grabbit" to the drive sprocket (**Figure 79**) and tighten the nut to the torque value in **Table 2** at the end of this chapter.

> *NOTE*
> *Figure 79 is shown on a Type I engine—the application is the same for Type II.*

14. Bend over the tab on the lockwasher.

15. Install all exterior engine assemblies as described in this chapter and other related chapters.

Crankcase Disassembly (Type III)

The Type III crankcase is found on the YZ125.

1. Remove all exterior engine assemblies as described in this chapter and other related chapters.

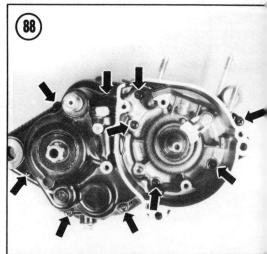

> *NOTE*
> *Drain the clutch/transmission oil as described in Chapter Three.*

2. Remove the drive sprocket by straightening the tab on the lockwasher.

3. Unscrew the lock nut and remove it and the lockwasher (**Figure 87**).

4. Remove the drive sprocket and collar.

5. Loosen all bolts securing the crankcase halves together one-quarter turn. To prevent warpage, loosen them in a crisscross pattern. It is easier to loosen tight screws with the engine still in the frame.

6. Remove the engine from the frame as described under *Engine Removal/Installation* in this chapter.

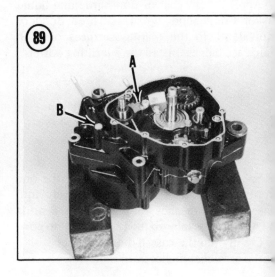

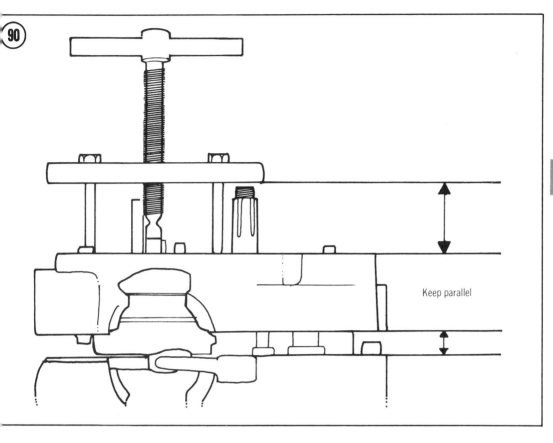

Keep parallel

NOTE
Set the engine on 2 wood blocks or fabricate a holding fixture of 2 X 4 inch wood as shown in **Figure 66**.

Remove all bolts loosened in Step 5; refer **Figure 88**. Be sure to remove all of them.

NOTE
To prevent loss and to ensure proper location during assembly, draw the case outline on cardboard, then punch holes to correspond with screw locations. Insert the screws in their appropriate locations. Also record the position of any clips that hold electrical wires or drain tubes.

Hold onto the left-hand crankcase and/or ds and tap on the left-hand end of the nkshaft and transmission shaft with a stic or rubber mallet until the crankshaft d crankcase separate.

CAUTION
Perform this operation over and close down to the workbench as the crankcase

halves may easily separate. DO NOT hammer on the crankcase halves as they will be damaged.

9. If the crankcase and crankshaft will not separate using the method in Step 8, proceed with the following method using a special tool.
10. Remove the crankcase oil seal retainer (A, **Figure 89**) and the plug (B, **Figure 89**).
11. Install the crankcase separating tool, Yamaha special tool (part No. 90890-01135) into the right-hand crankcase. Tighten the securing bolts into the crankcase, making sure the tool body is parallel with the crankcase. If necessary, back out one of the bolts.
12. Screw the puller *clockwise* until both cases begin to separate.

CAUTION
*While tightening the puller make sure the body is kept parallel to the crankcase surface during this operation (***Figure 90***). Otherwise it will put an uneven stress on the case halves and may damage them.*

13. Use a plastic or rubber mallet and tap the crankcase half and transmission shaft to help during separation.

> *CAUTION*
> *Crankcase separation requires only hand pressure on the puller screw. If extreme pressure seems to be needed, or if both halves will not remain parallel, STOP IMMEDIATELY. Check for crankcase screws not removed, or any part that is still attached, or transmission shafts hung up in a bearing. Relieve puller pressure immediately.*

> *NOTE*
> *Never pry between case halves. Doing so may result in oil leaks, requiring replacement of the case halves.*

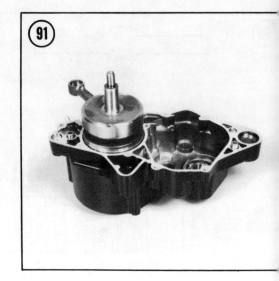

14. Don't lose the 2 locating dowels.

15. Unscrew the crankcase separator tool and reinstall the crankcase plug.

16. The transmission assemblies and the crankshaft assemblies will usually stay in the right-hand case half.

17. Lift up and carefully remove the transmission and shift drum assemblies.

18. Remove the kickstarter assembly from the left-hand crankcase; refer to the correct procedure at the end of this chapter.

19. Do not remove the crankshaft assembly (**Figure 91**) from the right-hand crankcase. This operation should be entrusted to a Yamaha dealer who can remove it and install a new one if necessary.

20. Inspect the crankcase halves and crankshaft as described under *Crankcase and Crankshaft Inspection—All Models* later in this chapter.

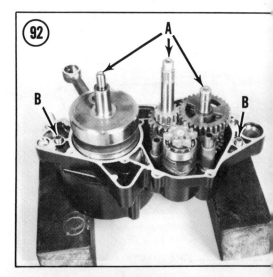

Crankcase Assembly (Type III)

1. Lightly oil the inner race of all bearings in the left-hand crankcase half.

2. Install the kickstarter assembly in the left-hand crankcase half. Refer to the kickstarter procedure at the end of this chapter for your specific model.

3. Install the transmission assemblies, shift shafts, and shift drum in the right-hand

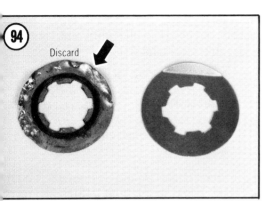

Discard

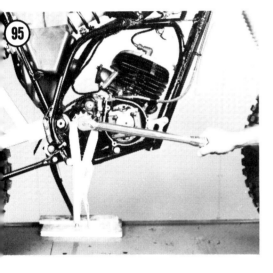

crankcase half and lightly oil all shaft ends (A, Figure 92). Refer to Chapter Five for the correct procedure for your specific model.

NOTE
Set the crankcase assembly on 2 wood blocks or a wood holding fixture shown in the disassembly procedure.

Apply a light coat of non-hardening liquid gasket (Yamabond No. 4, 4-Three Bond or equivalent) to the mating surfaces of both crankcase halves. Install the 2 locating dowels (B, Figure 92).

NOTE
Make sure the mating surfaces are clean and free of all old gasket material. This is to make sure you get a leak free seal.

Set the upper crankcase half over the one on the blocks. Push it down squarely into

place until it reaches the crankshaft bearing (usually with about 1/2 inch left to go).

6. Lightly tap the case halves together with a plastic or rubber mallet until they seat.

CAUTION
Crankcase halves should fit together without force. If the crankcase halves do not fit together completely, do not attempt to pull them together with the crankcase screws. Separate the crankcase halves and investigate the cause of the interference. If the transmission shafts were disassembled, recheck to make sure that a gear is not installed backwards. Crankcase halves are a matched set and are very expensive. Do not risk damage by trying to force the cases together.

7. Install all the crankcase screws and tighten only finger-tight at first.
8. Securely tighten the screws in 2 stages in a crisscross pattern until they are firmly hand tight.
9. After the crankcase halves are completely assembled, rotate the crankshaft and transmission shafts to make sure there is no binding. If any is present, disassemble the crankcase and correct the problem.
10. Install the engine in the frame and tighten the mounting bolts and nuts to the torque values in **Table 2** at the end of this chapter.
11. Install the collar (**Figure 93**), drive sprocket, and new lockwasher (**Figure 87**). Install a new lockwasher after at least the second removal or when the lockwasher begins to look like the one on the left in **Figure 94**.
12. Attach a "Grabbit" to the drive sprocket (**Figure 95**) and tighten the nut to the torque value in **Table 2** at the end of this chapter.
13. Bend over the tab on the lockwasher.
14. Install all exterior engine assemblies as described in this chapter and other related chapters.

Crankcase Disassembly (Type IV)

The Type IV crankcase is found in the following models:
YZ175C
YZ125F, E, D, C
YZ100G, F, E, D, C
YZ100X

4

1. Remove all exterior engine assemblies as described in this chapter and other related chapters.

NOTE
Drain the clutch/transmission oil as described in Chapter Three.

2. Remove the drive sprocket by straightening the tab on the lockwasher.
3. Unscrew the locknut and remove it and the lockwasher.
4. Remove the drive sprocket and collar.
5. Loosen all bolts securing the crankcase halves together one-quarter turn. To prevent warpage, loosen them in a crisscross pattern. It is easier to loosen tight screws with the engine still in the frame.
6. Remove the engine from the frame as described under *Engine Removal/Installation* in this chapter.

NOTE
Set the engine on 2 wood blocks or fabricate a holding fixture of 2 X 4 inch wood as shown in Figure 96.

7. Remove all bolts loosened in Step 5; refer to **Figure 97**. Be sure to remove all of them.

NOTE
To prevent loss and to ensure proper location during assembly, draw the case outline on cardboard, then punch holes to correspond with screw locations. Insert the screws in their appropriate locations.

8. Hold onto the right-hand crankcase and/or studs and tap on the right-hand end of the crankshaft and transmission shaft with plastic or rubber mallet until the crankshaft and crankcase separate.

CAUTION
Perform this operation over and close down to the workbench as the crankcase halves may easily separate. DO NOT hammer on the crankcase halves as they will be damaged.

9. If the crankcase and crankshaft will not separate using the method in Step 8, proceed with the following method using a special tool.
10. Remove the crankshaft oil seal retainer (A, **Figure 98**).
11. Install the crankcase separating tool Yamaha special tool (part No. 90890-01135) into the right-hand crankcase. Use the threaded holes (B, **Figure 98**). Tighten the securing bolts into the crankcase, making sure the tool body is parallel with the crankcase. necessary, back out one of the bolts.

NOTE
Figure 98 is shown with the crankcase disassembled for clarity.

12. Screw the puller *clockwise* until both cases begin to separate.

CAUTION
While tightening the puller make sure the body is kept parallel to the crankcase surface (Figure 90). Otherwise it will put an uneven stress on the case halves and may damage them.

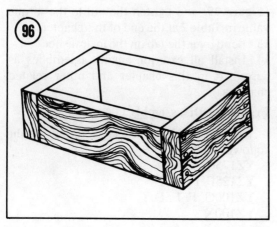

3. Use a plastic or rubber mallet and tap the crankcase half and transmission shaft to help during separation.

CAUTION
Crankcase separation requires only hand pressure on the puller screw. If extreme pressure seems to be needed, or if both halves will not remain parallel, STOP IMMEDIATELY. Check for crankcase screws not removed, or any part that is still attached, or transmission shafts hung up in a bearing. Relieve puller pressure immediately.

NOTE
Never pry between case halves. Doing so may result in oil leaks, requiring replacement of the case halves.

4. Don't lose the 2 locating dowels.
5. Unscrew the crankcase separator tool and reinstall the crankcase plug.
6. The transmission assemblies and the crankshaft assemblies will usually stay in the left-hand case half.
7. Remove the upper rear engine mount spacer assembly.
8. Lift up and carefully remove the transmission and shift fork assemblies.
9. Refer to Chapter Five for the correct procedure and remove the shift drum assembly.
10. Do not remove the crankshaft assembly from the left-hand crankcase. This operation should be entrusted to a Yamaha dealer who can remove it and install a new one if necessary.

21. Inspect the crankcase halves and crankshaft as described under *Crankcase and Crankshaft Inspection—All Models* later in this chapter.

Crankcase Assembly (Type IV)

1. Lightly oil the inner race of all bearings in both the left-hand and right-hand (**Figure 99**) crankcase halves.
2. Install the transmission assemblies, shift shafts, and shift drum in the right-hand crankcase half and lightly oil all shaft ends. Refer to Chapter Five for the correct procedure for your specific model.

NOTE
Set the crankcase assembly on 2 wood blocks or a wood holding fixture shown in the disassembly procedure.

3. Make sure the large dowel pin is in place (A, **Figure 100**) in the right-hand crankcase and install the upper rear engine mount spacer assembly (B, **Figure 100**).

NOTE
Make sure the O-ring seals are in good condition; replace if necessary.

4. Apply a light coat of non-hardening liquid gasket (Yamabond No. 4, 4-Three Bond or equivalent) to the mating surfaces of both crankcase halves.

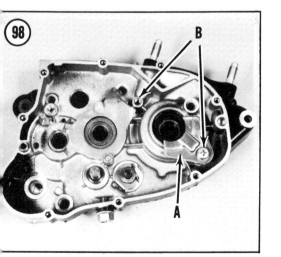

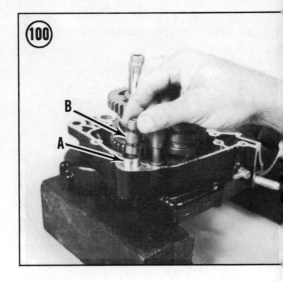

NOTE
Make sure the mating surfaces are clean and free of all old gasket material. This is to make sure you get a leak free seal.

5. Install the small dowel pin (**Figure 101**) at the front.

6. Set the left-hand crankcase half over the one on the blocks. Push it down squarely into place until it reaches the crankshaft bearing (usually with about 1/2 inch left to go).

7. Lightly tap the case halves together with a plastic or rubber mallet until they seat.

CAUTION
Crankcase halves should fit together without force. If the crankcase halves do not fit together completely, do not attempt to pull them together with the crankcase screws. Separate the crankcase halves and investigate the cause of the interference. If the transmission shafts were disassembled, recheck to make sure that a gear is not installed backwards. Crankcase halves are a matched set and are very expensive. Do not risk damage by trying to force the cases together.

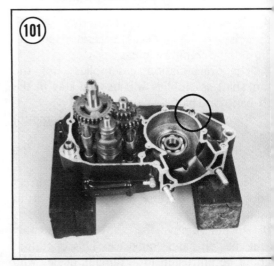

8. Install all the crankcase screws and tighten only finger-tight at first.

9. Securely tighten the screws in 2 stages in a crisscross pattern until they are firmly hand tight.

10. After the crankcase halves are completely assembled, rotate the crankshaft and transmission shafts to make sure there is no binding. If any is present, disassemble the crankcase and correct the problem.

11. Install the engine in the frame and tighten the mounting bolts and nuts to the torque values in **Table 2** at the end of this chapter.

12. Install the collar (**Figure 102**), drive sprocket, and new lockwasher. Install a new lockwasher after at least the second removal or when the lockwasher begins to get chewed up around the outside.

13. Attach a "Grabbit" to the drive srocket (**Figure 103**) and tighten the nut to the torque value in **Table 2** at the end of this chapter.

14. Bend over the tab on the lockwasher.

15. Install all exterior engine assemblies as described in this chapter and other related chapters.

Crankcase and Crankshaft Inspection (All Models)

The crankcases in the 4 different type engine groups (Type I, II, III, and IV) are all different in some way but the inspection procedure is basically the same for all. The following procedure will cover all models and the figures will represent components from the different models.

1. Clean both crankcase halves inside and out with cleaning solvent. Thoroughly dry with compressed air and wipe off with a clean shop cloth. Be sure to remove all traces of old gasket sealer from all mating surfaces.

2. Check the crankshaft main bearings (**Figure 104**) for roughness, pitting, galling, and play by rotating them slowly by hand. If any roughness or play can be felt in the bearing it must be replaced. Refer to *Bearing and Oil Seal Replacement* following in this chapter, for the correct procedure.

NOTE
*The bearing in the crankcase can be inspected with the crankshaft installed by turning the crankshaft by hand while holding onto the connecting rod to prevent damage to the surrounding crankcase opening (A, **Figure 105**). If this bearing is OK, apply a liberal coating of 2-stroke oil to the connecting rod big end (B, **Figure 105**) and into the crankshaft bearing delivery hole (C, **Figure 105**). Make sure that this bearing is well lubricated as it was washed in solvent and not exposed for thorough drying.*

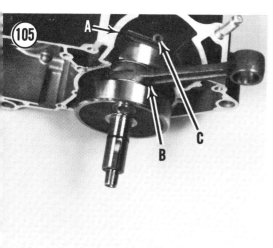

3. Inspect the condition of all the other bearings (**Figure 106**)—transmission and shift drum—as described in the previous step. Replace as necessary.

4. Carefully inspect the cases for cracks and fractures, especially in the lower areas (**Figure 107**); they are vulnerable to rock damage. Also check the areas around the stiffening ribs, around bearing bosses, and threaded holes. If any are found, have them repaired by a shop specializing in the repair of precision aluminum castings or replace them.

5. Check the condition of the connecting rod big end bearing by grasping the rod in one

hand and lifting up on it. With the heel of your other hand, rap sharply on the top of the rod. A sharp metallic sound, such as a click, is an indication that the bearing or crankpin or both are worn and the crankshaft assembly should be replaced.

6. Check the connecting rod to crankshaft side clearance with a flat feeler gauge (**Figure 108**). Compare to dimensions given in **Table 1** at the end of this chapter. If the clearance is greater than specified, the crankshaft assembly must be replaced.

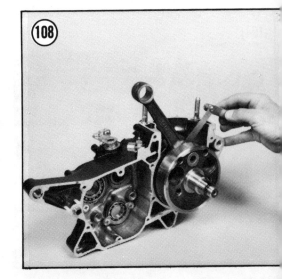

> *NOTE*
> *Other inspections of the crankshaft assembly involve accurate measuring equipment and should be entrusted to a Yamaha dealer or competent machine shop. The crankshaft assembly operates under severe stress and dimensional tolerances are critical. If any are off by the slightest amount it may cause a considerable amount of damage or destruction to the engine. The crankshaft assembly must be replaced as a unit as it cannot be serviced without the aid of a 10-12 ton (9,000-11,000 kilogram) capacity press, holding fixtures and crankshaft jig.*

7. Inspect the condition of the filler plugs in the crankshaft counter wheels (**Figure 109**), on models balanced this way. If they have holes in them or are damaged they should be replaced as this will change the compression

ratio (if they are damaged this will in affect increase the area of the crankcase volume—lowering the compression ratio). This operation is best left to a Yamaha dealer.

8. Remove all oil seals as they should be replaced each time the crankcase is disassembled. Refer to *Bearing and Oil Seal Replacement* following in this chapter.

Bearing and Oil Seal Replacement

1. Prior to removing the bearings, the oil seals should be removed. Remove the screw securing the oil seal retainer (**Figure 110**) on the crankshaft and remove the retainer.

2. Pry out the oil seals with a small screwdriver, taking care not to damage the crankcase bore. If the seals are old and difficult to remove, heat the cases as described later and use an awl and punch a small hole in the steel backing of the seal. Install a small sheet metal screw into the seal and pull the seal out with a pair of pliers.

CAUTION
Do not install the screw too deep or it may contact and damage the bearing behind it.

3. Remove the screws securing the bearing retainers (**Figures 111 and 112**) and remove them and the retainers.

4. The bearings are installed with a slight interference fit. The crankcase must be heated to a temperature of about 212 degrees F (100 degrees C) in an oven. As easy way to check to see that it is at the proper temperature is to drop tiny drops of water on the case; if they sizzle and evaporate immediately, the temperature is correct. Heat only one case at a time.

CAUTION
Do not heat the cases with a torch (propane or acetylene)—never bring a flame into contact with the bearing or case. The direct heat will destroy the case hardening of the bearing and will likely cause warpage of the case.

5. Remove the case from the oven and hold onto the 2 crankcase studs with a kitchen pot holder, heavy gloves, or heavy shop cloths—*it is hot.*

6. Remove the oil seals if not already removed.

7. Hold the crankcase with the bearing side down and tap it on a piece of soft wood. Continue to tap until the bearing(s) fall out. Repeat for the other half.

CAUTION
Be sure to tap the crankcase squarely on the piece of wood. Avoid damaging the surface of the crankcase as it forms an airtight seal when the halves are assembled.

8. If the bearings are difficult to remove, they can be gently tapped out with a socket or piece of pipe the same size as the bearing outer race.

NOTE
If the bearings and/or seals are difficult to remove or install, don't take a chance on expensive damage. Have the work performed by a Yamaha dealer or competent machine shop.

9. While heating up the crankcase halves, place the new bearings in a freezer if possible. Chilling them will slightly reduce their overall diameter while the hot crankcase is slightly larger due to heat expansion. This will make installation much easier.

10. While the crankcase is still hot, press the new bearing(s) into place in the crankcase by hand until it seats completely. Do not hammer it in. If the bearing will not seat, remove it and cool it again. Reheat the crankcase and install the bearing again.

11. Oil seals are best installed with a special tool, however a proper size socket or piece of pipe can be substituted. Make sure that the bearings and seals are not cocked in the hole and that they are seated properly.

KICKSTARTER

The kickstarters for the different engines are all basically the same but all have different components and are assembled differently. They are divided into different groups and given a type designation which relates to different models. With the exception of the Type V, all can be removed without splitting the crankcase.

The Type I kickstarter (**Figure 113**) is found in the following models:
YZ465G
YZ250G

The Type II kickstarter (**Figure 114**) is found in the following models:
YZ400F, E, D
YZ250F, E

The Type III kickstarter (**Figure 115**) is found in the following models:
YZ400C,
YZ250D, C

The Type IV kickstarter (**Figure 116**) is found in the following model:
YZ125G

The Type V kickstarter (**Figure 117**) is found in the following models:
YZ175C
YZ125F, E, D, C, G
YZ100F, D, C, G, E
YZ125X

The Type VI kickstarter (**Figure 118**) is found in the following models:
YZ125F, E, D, C
YZ100F, D, C
YZ125X

The previously described figures are exploded view drawings of each kickstarter mechanism. The following procedures on a Type II (external type) and Type V (internal type within the crankcase) represent a typical kickstarter removal, inspection, and installation sequence. Minor variations exist between models. Pay particular attention to the location and positioning of spacers, washers, and springs to make assembly easier.

Removal/Installation
(Type I, II, V)

NOTE
This procedure is shown on a Type II (YZ400F) with a few steps including the Type I and V. As previously mentioned there are differences with the different models.

1. Remove the clutch assembly as described under *Clutch Removal/Installation* for your specific model in Chapter Five.

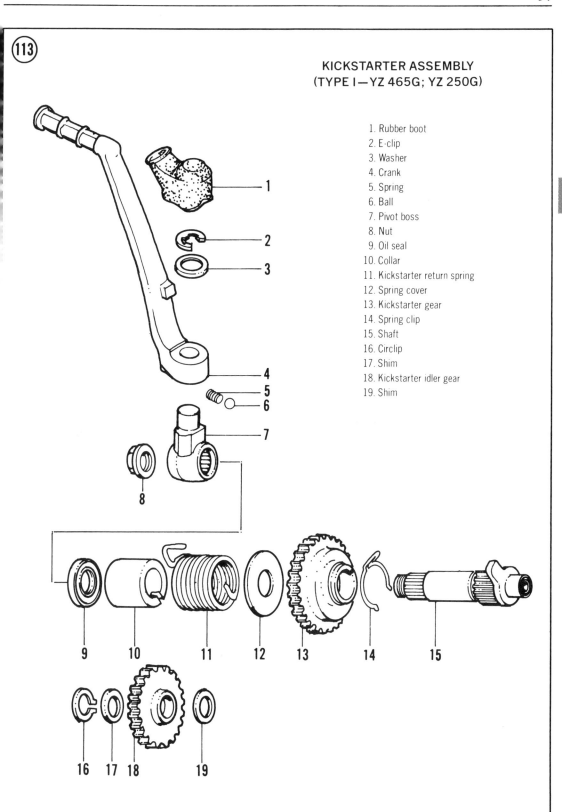

(113)

**KICKSTARTER ASSEMBLY
(TYPE I—YZ 465G; YZ 250G)**

1. Rubber boot
2. E-clip
3. Washer
4. Crank
5. Spring
6. Ball
7. Pivot boss
8. Nut
9. Oil seal
10. Collar
11. Kickstarter return spring
12. Spring cover
13. Kickstarter gear
14. Spring clip
15. Shaft
16. Circlip
17. Shim
18. Kickstarter idler gear
19. Shim

4

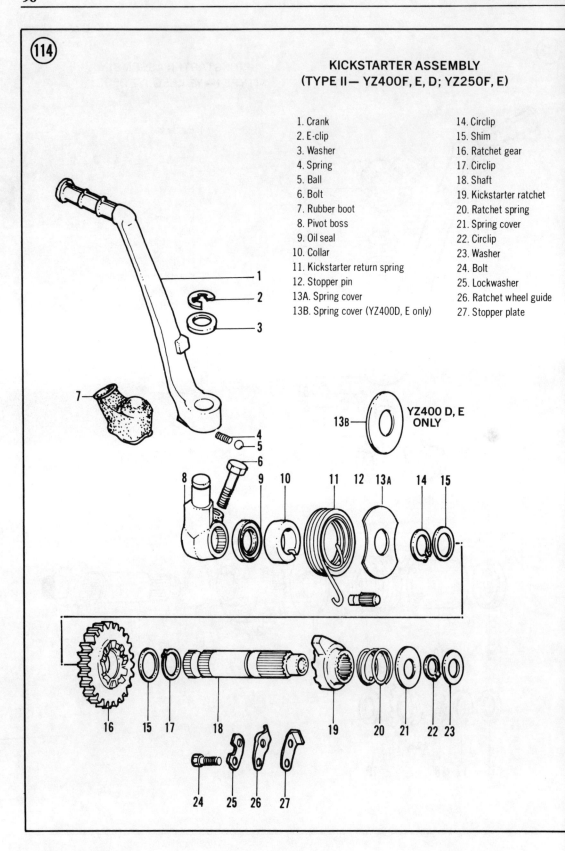

(114)

**KICKSTARTER ASSEMBLY
(TYPE II— YZ400F, E, D; YZ250F, E)**

1. Crank
2. E-clip
3. Washer
4. Spring
5. Ball
6. Bolt
7. Rubber boot
8. Pivot boss
9. Oil seal
10. Collar
11. Kickstarter return spring
12. Stopper pin
13A. Spring cover
13B. Spring cover (YZ400D, E only)

14. Circlip
15. Shim
16. Ratchet gear
17. Circlip
18. Shaft
19. Kickstarter ratchet
20. Ratchet spring
21. Spring cover
22. Circlip
23. Washer
24. Bolt
25. Lockwasher
26. Ratchet wheel guide
27. Stopper plate

13B   YZ400 D, E
       ONLY

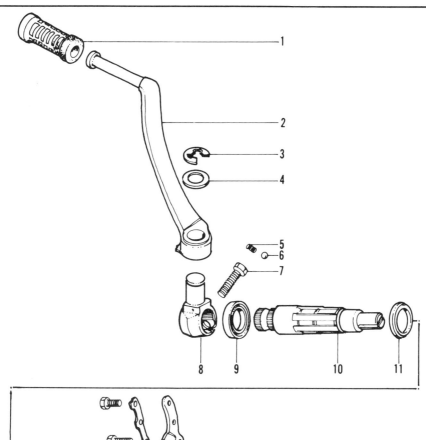

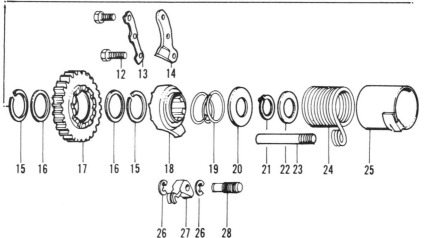

KICKSTARTER ASSEMBLY
(TYPE III — YZ400C; YZ 250D, C)

1. Cover	10. Shaft	19. Ratchet spring
2. Crank	11. Oil seal	20. Spring cover
3. E-clip	12. Bolt	21. Circlip
4. Washer	13. Lockwasher	22. Washer
5. Spring	14. Ratchet wheel guide	23. Stopper pin
6. Ball	15. Circlip	24. Kickstarter return pin
7. Bolt	16. Shim	25. Collar
8. Pivot boss	17. Kickstarter gear	26. E-clip
9. Oilseal	18. Kickstarter ratchet	27. Link
		28. Post

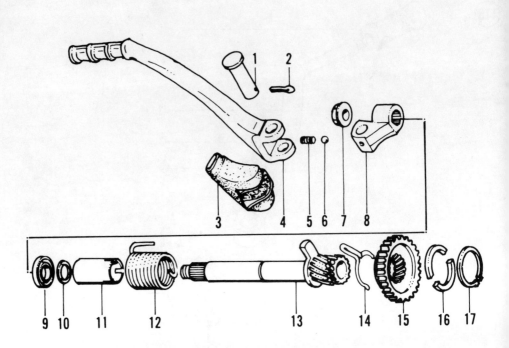

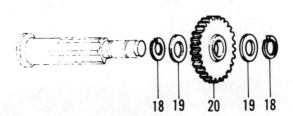

KICKSTARTER ASSEMBLY
(TYPE IV—YZ125G)

1. Pivot pin	11. Collar
2. Cotter pin	12. Kickstarter return spring
3. Rubber boot	13. Shaft
4. Crank	14. Spring clip
5. Spring	15. Kickstarter gear
6. Ball	16. Holders (2)
7. Nut	17. Circlip
8. Pivot boss	18. Circlip
9. Oil seal	19. Shim
10. Circlip	20. Kickstarter idle gear

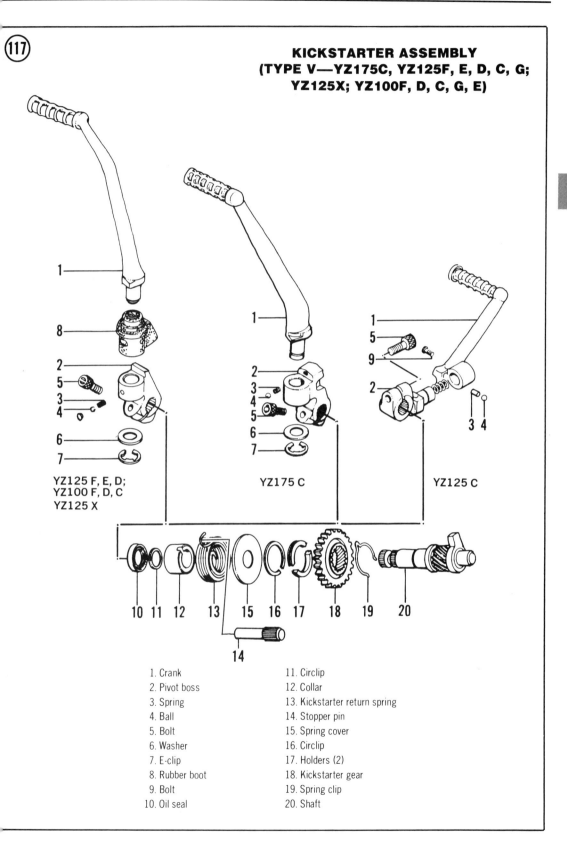

(117)

**KICKSTARTER ASSEMBLY
(TYPE V—YZ175C, YZ125F, E, D, C, G;
YZ125X; YZ100F, D, C, G, E)**

4

YZ125 F, E, D;
YZ100 F, D, C
YZ125 X

YZ175 C

YZ125 C

1. Crank	11. Circlip
2. Pivot boss	12. Collar
3. Spring	13. Kickstarter return spring
4. Ball	14. Stopper pin
5. Bolt	15. Spring cover
6. Washer	16. Circlip
7. E-clip	17. Holders (2)
8. Rubber boot	18. Kickstarter gear
9. Bolt	19. Spring clip
10. Oil seal	20. Shaft

2. Remove the kickstarter return spring from the pin (A, **Figure 118**) and pull the assembly (B, **Figure 118**) from the crankcase.

> *NOTE*
> *Don't lose the thin shim on the inside end of the shaft. Sometimes it will stick in the depression in the crankcase.*

3. On models with Type I and VI kickstarters, remove the spring end from the hole in the crankcase rib.

4. Remove the circlip and shim (A, **Figure 119**) securing the kickstarter idle gear.

Disassembly/Inspection/Assembly

1. Remove the collar, return spring and spring cover (**Figure 120**).

2. Turn the shaft over and remove the circlip, spring cover and spring (**Figure 121**).

3. Slide off the kickstarter ratchet (**Figure 122**).

4. Remove the circlip (A, **Figure 123**) and slide off the ratchet gear (B, **Figure 123**).

5. Check for broken, chipped, or missing teeth on the gear; replace if necessary.

6. Make sure the ratchet gear operates properly and smoothly on the shaft.

7. Check all parts for uneven wear; replace any that are questionable.

8. Apply assembly oil to the sliding surfaces of all parts.

9. Slide on the ratchet gear and install the circlip.

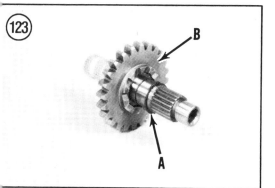

10. Install the kickstarter ratchet; align the punch mark (A, **Figure 124**) on the shaft with the straight portion of the kickstarter ratchet (B, **Figure 124**). This is necessary to maintain the proper spring-to-ratchet relationship.

11. Install the ratchet spring, spring cover and circlip.

NOTE
*Prior to installing the assembled unit in the crankcase, check with **Figure 125** for correct placement of all components.*

4

Installation

1. Install the inner shim (**Figure 126**) behind the kickstarter idle gear and install the idle gear.

2. Install the kickstarter idle gear and outer shim (**Figure 127**).

3. Install the circlip (A, **Figure 119**).

4. Install the shim (**Figure 120 or 129**) on the end of the shaft and install the assembled kickstarter unit into the crankcase.

> *NOTE*
> *Make sure the flat surface on the kickstarter ratchet is engaged behind the stopper plate attached to the crankcase (B, **Figure 119**).*

5. Pull the return spring into position with Vise Grips and place it on the stopper (**Figure 130**).

> *WARNING*
> *The spring is under pressure during this part of the procedure, protect yourself accordingly.*

6. On models equipped with a Type I or V kickstarter assembly, make sure the projection on the spring clip (**Figure 131**) is engaged into the notch in the crankcase (**Figure 132**). The spring hook goes into an opening in the edge of the crankcase rib (**Figure 133**).
7. Install the clutch assembly as described under *Clutch Removal/Installation* in Chapter Five.

Removal/Disassembly (Type IV)

1. Remove the engine as described under *Engine Removal/Installation* in this chapter.
2. Disassemble the crankcase as described under *Crankcase Disassembly/Assembly* in this chapter.

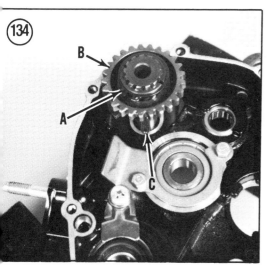

3. Remove the circlip securing the holders (A, **Figure 134**) and remove them and the kickstarter gear (B, **Figure 134**) and spring clip (C, **Figure 134**).

4. From the inside, remove the circlip (**Figure 135**) securing the collar.

Inspection

1. Check for broken, chipped, or missing teeth on the gear; replace if necessary.

2. Make sure the spirals within the kickstarter gear and on the outside of the shaft are in good condition with no burrs or rough spots; replace if necessary.

3. Check all parts for uneven wear; replace any that are questionable.

5. Using Vise Grips carefully pull the return sring up and out of the hole in the crankcase.
6. Slide off the return spring and collar from the inside and withdraw the shaft from the outside.

4. Apply assembly oil to the sliding surfaces of all parts.

Assembly/Installation

1. Insert the shaft from the outside and position the hole in the shaft up and down (**Figure 136**).

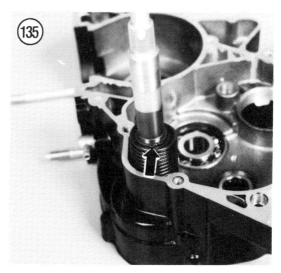

2. Install the return spring and insert the inside hook of the spring (A, **Figure 137**) into the hole in the shaft.

3. Slide on the spacer, align the slot (B, **Figure 137**) with the inside hook of the spring and push it all the way in.

4. Pull up on the outside hook with Vise Grips and install it in the hole (**Figure 138**) in the crankcase.

5. Install the circlip (**Figure 135**).

6. On the outside, slide on the spring clip and kickstarter gear.

7. Install the 2 holders and secure them with the circlip (A, **Figure 134**).

8. Assemble the crankcase halves and install the engine.

SERVICE AND ADJUSTMENT

When the engine has been assembled and installed in the bike and all is completed, walk around the bike and thoroughly double check all work. Do not be in a hurry to ride the bike. You have invested a lot of time, energy, and money so far so don't blow it now by forgetting some little item that may cost additional time and money. *Thoroughly* check and recheck all components, systems, and controls on the bike. Make sure all cables are correctly routed, adjusted, and secured and all bolts and nuts properly tightened. Position all electrical wires away from the exhaust system and control levers.

Refer to Chapter Three and perform all maintenance and lubrication procedures including all related adjustments.

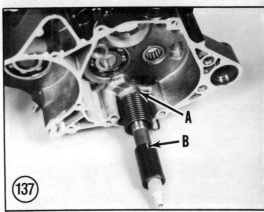

Table 1 ENGINE SPECIFICATIONS

Item	Specifications in. (mm)	Wear limit in. (mm)
Cylinder		
Bore and stroke		
YZ465	3.35 × 3.23 (85 × 82)	–
YZ400	3.23 × 2.95 (82 × 75)	–
YZ250	2.8 × 2.5 (70 × 64)	–
YZ175	2.59 × 1.97 (66 × 50)	–
YZ125	2.204 × 1.97 (56 × 50)	–
YZ100	1.97 × 1.97 (50 × 50)	–
Bore		
YZ465	3.346 (85)	3.35 (85.1)
YZ400	3.228 (82)	3.232 (82.1)
YZ250	2.75 (70)	2.76 (70.1)
YZ175	2.59 (66.0)	–
YZ125	2.204 (56.0)	–
YZ100	1.968 (50.0)	–
Taper limit		
YZ100	–	0.002 (0.05)
YZ125 and larger	–	0.003 (0.08)
Out of round		
YZ100	–	0.004 (0.01)
YZ125 and larger	–	0.002 (0.05)
Piston		
Piston/cylinder clearance		
YZ465	0.0020-0.0022 (0.050-0.055)	–
YZ400	0.0019-0.0022 (0.050-0.055)	–
YZ250	0.0018-0.0020 (0.045-0.050)	–
YZ175	0.0018-0.0020 (0.045-0.050)	–
YZ125	0.0018-0.0020 (0.045-0.050)	–
YZ100	0.0016-0.0018 (0.040-0.045)	–
Piston rings (top and second)		
Ring edn gap		
YZ465	0.012-0.019 (0.3-0.5)	–
YZ400	0.016-0.022 (0.4-0.55)	–
YZ250	0.012-0.019 (0.3-0.5)	–
YZ175	0.012-0.019 (0.3-0.5)	–
YZ125	0.012-0.019 (0.3-0.5)	–
YZ100	0.016-0.018 (0.40-0.45)	–
Ring side clearance		
YZ465		
Top	0.0016-0.0030 *0.04-0.08)	–
Second	0.0012-0.0028 (0.03-0.07)	–
YZ400	0.0028-0.0043 (0.07-0.11)	–
YZ250		
Top	0.0016-0.0030 (0.04-0.08)	–
Second	0.0012-0.0028 (0.03-0.07)	–
YZ175	0.0012-0.0019 (0.03-0.05)	–
YZ125		
Top	0.0016-0.0030 (0.04-0.08)	–
Second	0.0012-0.0019 (0.03-0.05)	–
YZ100	0.0012-0.0028 (0.03-0.07)	–
Crankshaft		
Deflection	–	0.0012 (0.03)
Big end side clearance	–	0.010-0.030 (0.25-0.75)

Table 2 ENGINE TORQUE SPECIFICATIONS

Item	ft.-lb.	N•m
Cylinder head		
Except YZ175C	18	25
YZ175C	14	20
Cylinder nuts	24	33
Cylinder stud bolts (YZ100, 125)	32	45
Clutch nut		
YZ250, YZ400, YZ465	54	75
YZ100-YZ125	36	50
YZ175	30	42
Drive sprocket		
YZ250, YZ400, YZ465	54	75
YZ100-YZ125	40	55
YZ175	47	65
Magneto		
Inner rotor		
YZ250, YZ400, YZ465	25	35
YZ100-YZ125	40	55
YZ175	28	40
Outer rotor	59	80

Table 3 PISTON MEASUREMENT LOCATION*

Model	Inches	Millimeters
YZ465G	1.18	30
YZ400G	1.34	34
YZ400E, D, C	1.18	30
YZ250G	1.22	31
YZ25F, E, F, C	1.18	30
YZ175C	0.70	18
YZ125 (all)	0.70	18
YZ100G, F, E, D	0.80	20
YZ100C	0.70	18

*Indicates dimension up from the bottom of the piston skirt at right angles to the wrist pin.

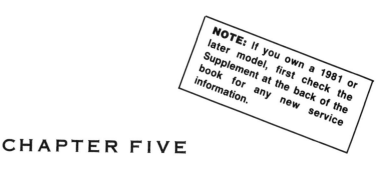

NOTE: If you own a 1981 or later model, first check the Supplement at the back of the book for any new service information.

CHAPTER FIVE

CLUTCH AND TRANSMISSION

This chapter contains removal, inspection and installation of the clutch, transmission, and shift mechanism (external and internal). There is basically one type of clutch mechanism, two transmissions (5-speed and 6-speed) and a variety of shift mechanisms used on the various Yamaha YZ models. Be sure to follow the correct procedure for your specific model.

CLUTCH

The clutch used on the Yamaha YZ is a wet multi-plate type which operates immersed in the oil supply it shares with the transmission. The clutch boss is splined to the transmission main shaft and the clutch housing can rotate freely on the main shaft. The clutch housing is geared to the primary drive gear attached to the crankshaft.

The clutch release mechanism is mounted within the top of the crankcase on the opposite side of the clutch mechanism. The mechanism consists of a push lever assembly, operated by the clutch cable. Pulling the clutch lever and cable pivots the push lever that in turn pushes the clutch pushrod. This actuates the pressure plate and disenages the clutch mechanism.

The clutch assembly used with the different engines is basically the same. Some have a different number of components (clutch plates and friction discs) and are assembled a little differently; where differences occur they are identified. Because of the minor variations, pay particular attention to the location and positioning of spacers and washers to make assembly easier.

The clutch can be removed with the engine in the frame.

Refer to **Table 1** at the end of this chapter for all clutch specifications and **Table 2** at the end of the chapter for clutch torque specifications.

Refer to **Figure 1** for the clutch assembly and release mechanism for the various models.

Removal/Disassembly

NOTE
This procedure is shown on a YZ400F with a few steps included from different models which are identified.

1. Place a milk crate or wood block(s) under the frame to support the bike securely.
2. Drain the clutch/transmission oil as described in Chapter Three.

1. Adjust screw
2. Locknut
3. Lockwasher
4. Washer
5. Pressure plate
6. Clutch bolt
7. Clutch spring
8. Pushrod (short)
9. Clutch nut
10. Lockwasher
11. Clutch plate
12. Friction discs
13. Clutch boss
14. Outer thrust washer
15. Clutch housing
16. Spacer
17. Inner thrust washer
18. Ball
19. Pushrod—All models except those listed below.
   X—Model YZ465G
   XX—Model YZ175C; YZ125F, E, D, C, X;
   YZ100G, F, E, D
20. Plug
21. Push lever assembly
22. Washer
23. Bolt
24. Return spring
25. Washer
26. Oil seal
27. Needle bearing

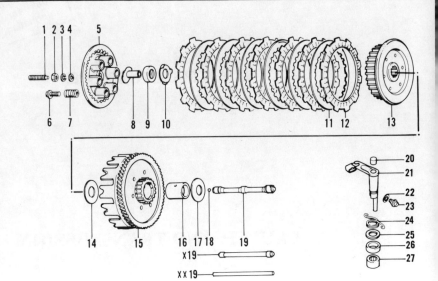

CLUTCH ASSEMBLY

①

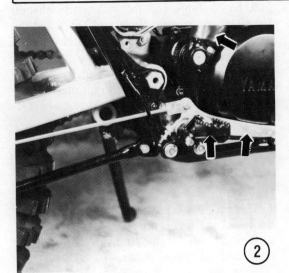

②

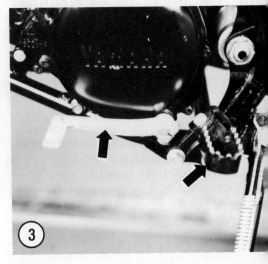

③

3. On all models except the YZ125G, remove the right-hand foot peg, rear brake pedal and kickstarter (**Figure 2**).

4. On model YZ125G, remove the gearshift lever and left-hand foot peg (**Figure 3**).

5. Remove the screws (**Figure 4, 5, or 6**) securing the clutch cover and remove it and the gasket. Don't lose the 2 locating dowels.

NOTE
Some of the following figures are shown with the engine partially disassembled. It is not necessary to do so for clutch removal.

6. Remove the clutch bolts (**Figure 7**) securing the pressure plate in a crisscross pattern.

NOTE
*If the primary drive gear is going to be removed, loosen the nut (**Figure 8**) at this time but don't remove it. You will*

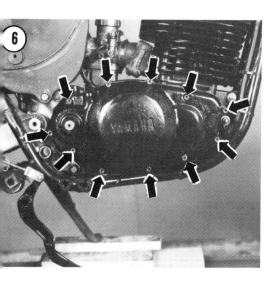

need the clutch housing to aid in removal. Place a broad tipped screwdriver or aluminum wedge between the primary drive and driven gear (located on the backside of the clutch housing) and loosen the nut. Don't try to use a shop cloth as the gears are bevel cut and will cut the cloth to shreds. Also watch your fingers as these gears are sharp, even on a well run in bike.

7. Remove the pressure plate and springs (**Figure 9**).

> *NOTE*
> *In Steps 6 and 7 there will be either 5 or 6 clutch bolts and springs depending on models.*

8. Remove all the clutch plates and friction discs (**Figure 10**).

9. Straighten out the locking tab on the clutch nut (**Figure 11**).

10. Remove the clutch nut and lockwasher. To keep the clutch boss from turning, attach a special tool like the "Grabbit" (**Figure 12**) to it.

> *NOTE*
> *The "Grabbit" (No. 969103) is available from Precision Sales and Manufacturing Co., P.O. Box 149, Clearwater, FL, 33517.*

> *CAUTION*
> *Do not insert a screwdriver or pry bar between the clutch housing and the clutch boss. The fingers on the clutch housing are fragile and can be tweaked out of alignment very easily.*

11. Remove the clutch boss, steel ball and pushrod.

12. Remove the outer thrust washer (A, **Figure 13**) and the clutch housing (B, **Figure 13**).

13. Remove the spacer and inner thrust washer (**Figure 14**).

14. Remove the primary drive gear nut (**Figure 15**) loosened in Step 6 and remove the lockwasher and gear (**Figure 16**).

15. Remove the Woodruff key (A, **Figure 17**) and the O-ring seal (B, **Figure 17**) on the crankshaft.

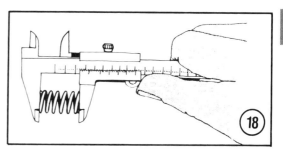

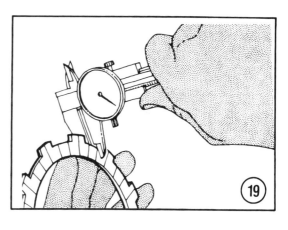

Inspection

NOTE
The following measurements apply to all models unless otherwise specified.

1. Clean all parts in a petroleum based solvent such as kerosene and thoroughly dry with compressed air.

2. Measure the free length of each clutch spring as shown in **Figure 18**. If any of the springs are 1.38 in. (35 mm) or less, replace all springs as a set.

3. Measure the thickness of each friction disc at several places around the disc as shown in **Figure 19**. A new friction disc measures 0.12

in. (3.0 mm). Replace any that measure 0.106 in. (2.7 mm) or less. For optimum performance, replace all discs as a set even though only one or more need replacement.

4. Check the clutch plates for warpage on a surface plate such as a piece of plate glass (**Figure 20**). Replace any that are warped 0.002 in. (0.05 mm) or more. For optimum performance, replace all plates as a set even though only one or two may require replacement.

5. Inspect the condition of the pushrod assembly (**Figure 21**) within the pressure plate. If the end is damaged, remove the nut, spring and plate washer (**Figure 22**) and remove the assembly.

6. Inspect the condition of the grooves in the pressure plate and clutch boss (**Figure 23** or **Figure 24**). If either shows signs of wear or galling (**Figure 25**) it should be replaced.

7. Inspect the condition of the inner splines (**Figure 26**) in the clutch boss; if damaged it should be replaced.

8. Inspect the condition of the teeth on the primary driven gear and kickstarter gear (**Figure 27**). Remove any small nicks on the gear teeth with an oil stone. If damage is severe as shown in **Figure 28** the clutch housing should be removed. This damage caused by the primary drive gear working loose from the crankshaft.

9. Inspect the condition of the slots in the clutch housing (**Figure 29**) for cracks, nicks, or galling where it comes in contact with the friction disc tabs. If any severe damage is evident (**Figure 30**), the housing must be replaced. This condition will cause erratic clutch operation.

10. Apply a light coat of oil to the clutch housing inner bushing (**Figure 31**) and insert the spacer. It should be a smooth finger-press fit and should rotate smoothly within the bushing. If rotation is rough or loose, replace either the spacer or the clutch housing.

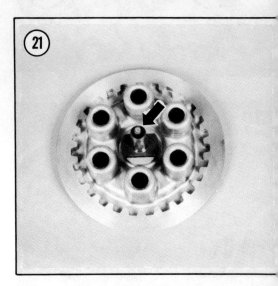

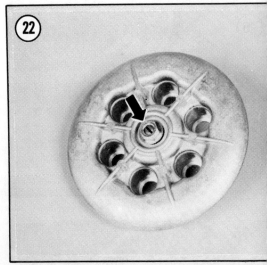

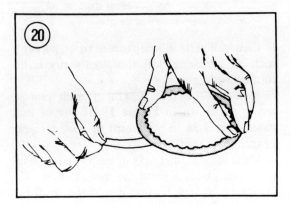

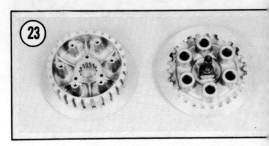

5

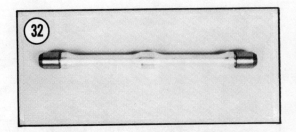

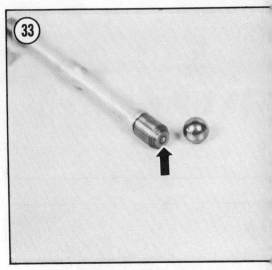

11. Roll the clutch pushrod (**Figure 32**) on a flat surface to check for bends or damage. Examine the end that rides against the ball (**Figure 33**); if a worn depression is evident it should be replaced as it will take up some of the clutch movement adjustment.

> *NOTE*
> *The clutch pushrod varies in length and construction with the different models as shown in **Figure 1**.*

12. Inspect the condition of the teeth on the primary drive gear. Remove any small nicks on the gear teeth with an oilstone. If damage is severe, the gear must be replaced.

Assembly/Installation

1. Install a new O-ring seal (**Figure 34**) on the crankshaft and install the Woodruff key (**Figure 35**). Make sure the key is seated correctly in the groove in the crankshaft.

2. Install the primary drive gear, lockwasher (**Figure 36**), and nut (**Figure 37**). Do not try to tighten the nut at this time.

3. Install the inner thrust washer and spacer (**Figure 14**).

4. Slide on the clutch housing and install the outer thrust washer (**Figure 13**).

5. Slide on the clutch boss and install a new lockwasher (**Figure 38**). Make sure the 3 locating tangs are installed into the holes in the clutch boss. Always replace the lockwasher at least every other time the clutch is disassembled or if it looks like the one on the left in **Figure 39**.

6. Install the clutch nut and tighten (**Figure 40**) to the torque specifications in **Table 2** at the end of this chapter. Use the same tool setup used in Step 10, *Removal/Disassembly.*

7. Bend down the locking tab of the lockwasher onto one of the flats on the clutch nut (**Figure 41**).

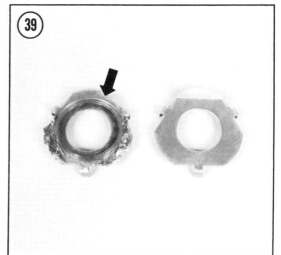

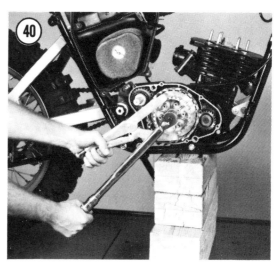

5

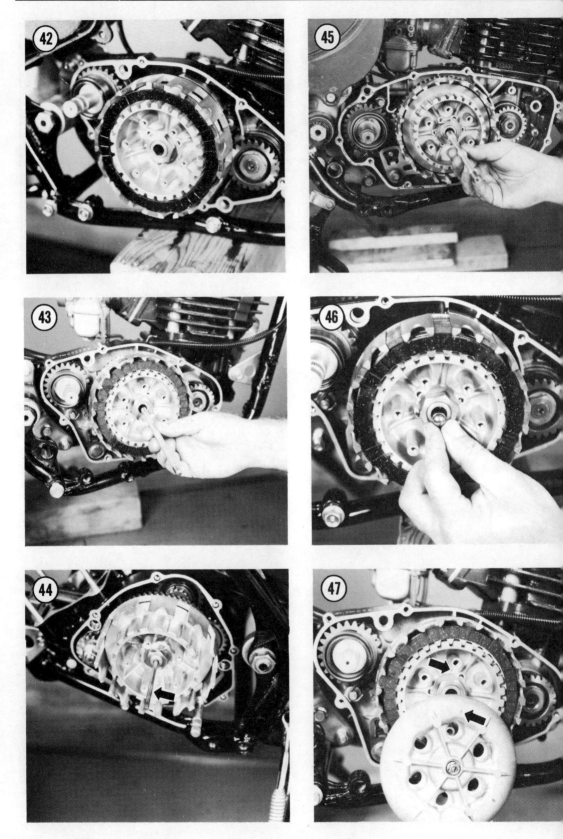

8. Install a friction disc first (**Figure 42**) and then a clutch plate. Continue to install a friction disc, then a clutch plate, until all are installed. Refer to **Table 1** for the exact amount of friction discs and clutch plates for your specific model.

CAUTION
If either or both friction and/or clutch plates have been replaced with new ones or cleaned, apply new clutch/transmission oil to all surfaces to avoid having the clutch lock up when used for the first time.

9. Install the clutch pushrod (**Figure 43, 44, or 45**). Apply a light coat of grease to the pushrod prior to installation.

10. Apply a light coat of grease to the ball and install it (**Figure 46**). Make sure it does not roll out.

NOTE
On models YZ100D and YZ125C, the clutch release mechanism was originally manufactured without a ball between the pushrods. This has caused most of these rods to wear and mushroom over, causing the clutch to drag. If your bike is without the ball it is a good idea to install the ball along with a new pushrod (Yamaha part No. 1W1-16357-00-00). If the ball is added the new shorter push rod must be installed as the old one will be too long.

11. On models so marked, align the arrows on the pressure plate with the arrows on the clutch boss (**Figure 47 or 48**) and install it. On models without the alignment arrows (**Figure 49**) alignment is not necessary.

12. Install the clutch springs (**Figure 50**) and bolts. Tighten the bolts (**Figure 51**) in a crisscross pattern in 2-3 stages.

13. Insert a broad tipped screwdriver or aluminum wedge between the primary drive and driven gear (located on the backside of the clutch housing) and tighten the nut (**Figure 52**). Don't try to use a shop cloth as the gears are bevel cut and will cut the cloth to shreads. Also watch your fingers as these gears are sharp, even on a well run in bike. Tighten to the torque value in **Table 2** at the end of this chapter.

14. Install the locating dowels and new cover gasket (**Figure 53, 54, or 55**).

15. Install the cover and tighten all screws.

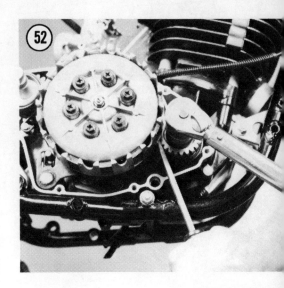

CLUTCH CABLE

Replacement

In time the clutch cable will stretch to the point that it is no longer useful and will have to be replaced.

1. Turn the fuel shutoff valve to the OFF position (**Figure 56**) and remove the fuel line to the carburetor.

2. Remove the seat.

3. Pull the fuel fill cap vent tube free from the steering head area (A, **Figure 57**).

4. Remove the bolts (B, **Figure 57**) securing the front of the fuel tank. Pull up and unhook the strap (C, **Figure 57**) securing the rear of the tank. Pull the tank toward the rear and remove it.

NOTE
Some of the following figures are shown with the engine partially disassembled for clarity. It is not necessary to remove these components for cable replacement.

5. Pull the protective boot away from the clutch lever and loosen the locknut and adjusting barrel (**Figure 58**).

6. Slip the cable end out of the hand lever.

7. At the top of the engine, pry open the locking tab (A, **Figure 59 or 60**) on the top of the push lever and remove the cable end.

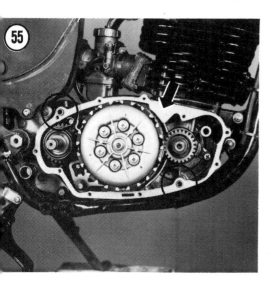

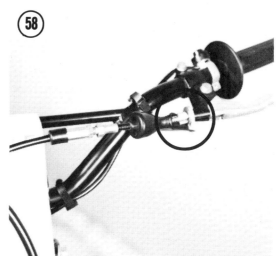

5

8. On models with the clutch release mechanism on the left-hand side, remove the bolt and clamp (B, **Figure 60**) securing the clutch cable to the top of the crankcase.

9. On models with the clutch release mechanism on the right-hand side, remove the cable from the clip (B, **Figure 59**) on the side of the cylinder.

NOTE
Prior to removing the cable make a drawing (or take a Polaroid picture) of the cable routing through the frame. It is very easy to forget how it was after it has been removed. Replace it exactly as it was, avoiding any sharp turns.

10. Pull the cable out of any retaining clips on the frame (**Figure 61**).

11. Remove the cable and replace it with a new one.

12. Install by reversing these removal steps. Be sure to bend over the locking tab (**Figure 62**) on the clutch push lever.

CLUTCH RELEASE (PUSH LEVER) MECHANISM

Removal/Installation

1. Perform Steps 5-9, *Clutch Cable, Replacement* in the preceding procedure.

2. Remove the locating bolt (**Figure 63**) securing the release mechanism in the crankcase.

3. Withdraw the push lever and remove the washer and spring.

4. Inspect the condition of the oil seal and roller bearing (**Figure 64**). Rotate the bearing with your finger; make sure it rotates smoothly with no signs of wear or damage. If the bearing has to be replaced, the crankcase must be split to gain access to it; refer to Chapter Four.

5. Install the push lever, spring and washer (**Figure 65**) into the crankcase. Install the locating bolt.

6. Install the clutch cable by reversing Steps 5-9, *Clutch Cable, Replacement* in the preceding procedure.

EXTERNAL SHIFT MECHANISM

The external shift mechanisms for the different engines are all basically the same but all have different components and are assembled differently. They are divided into different groups and given a type designation which relates to different models. The Type external shift mechanism is found in the following models:

YZ465G
YZ250G
YZ125G

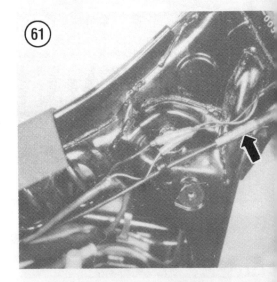

The Type II external shift mechanism is found in the following models:

YZ400F

YZ250F, E

The Type III external shift mechanism is found in the following models:

YZ400E, D, C

YZ250DC

The Type IV external shift mechanism is found in the following models:

YZ175C

YZ125F, E, D, C, X

YZ100H, G, F, D, C

The external shift mechanism is located on the same side of the crankcase as the clutch assembly and can be removed with the engine in the frame. To remove the shift drum and shift forks it is necessary to remove the engine and split the crankcases. This procedure is covered at the end of this chapter.

NOTE
The gearshift lever is subject to a lot of abuse under race conditions or very hard riding. If the motorcycle has been in a hard spill, the gearshift lever may have been hit and the shaft may have been bent. If the shaft is bent it is very hard to straighten without subjecting the crankcase to abnormal stress where the shaft enters the case.

If the shaft is bent enough to prevent it from being withdrawn from the crankcase, there is little recourse but to cut the shaft off with a hacksaw very close to the crankcase. It is much cheaper in the long run to replace the shaft than risk damaging a very expensive crankcase.

The following procedures are fairly short but are kept separate to avoid any confusion between the different models.

Removal/Installation (Type I)

NOTE
The following procedure is shown on a model with the clutch and external shift mechanism on the left-hand side. Other models have this mechanism on the right-hand side where the components are the same but are reversed.

1. Remove the clutch assembly as described under *Clutch Removal/Installation* for your specific model in this chapter.

2. Remove the gearshift lever (**Figure 66**).

3. Withdraw the gearshift lever assembly (A, **Figure 67**). See NOTE in the introduction to the procedure regarding a bent shaft if the assembly is difficult to remove.

4. Remove the flange bolt securing the shift pawl and spring (**Figure 68**) and remove them.

5. Remove the flat head screw (A, **Figure 69**) securing the shift cam and remove it and the flat key.

6. Inspect the condition of the spring. If broken or weak it must be replaced.

7. Inspect the gearshift lever assembly shaft for bending, wear or other damage; replace if necessary.

8. Install the flat key and shift cam. Apply Loctite Lock N ' Seal to the threads of the flat head screw prior to installing it. Tighten it securely.

9. Install the spring (B, **Figure 69**) as shown with the lower end in the relief in the crankcase.

10. Install the shift pawl, engaging it with the spring correctly and install the flange bolt (**Figure 68**). Tighen the flange bolt securely.

11. Install the gearshift lever asssembly. Make sure the return spring is correctly positioned onto the stopper plate bolt (B, **Figure 67**) and that it is engaged with the pins on the shift cam (C, **Figure 67**).

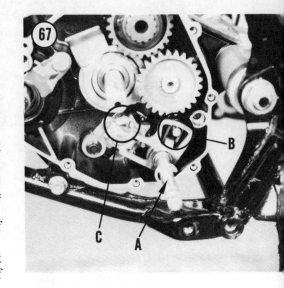

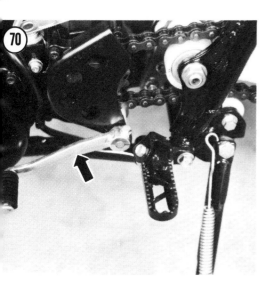

12. Install the shift lever and install the clutch assembly as described in this chapter.

Removal/Installation (Type II)

1. Remove the clutch assembly as described under *Clutch Removal/Installation* for your specific model in this chapter.

2. Remove the gearshift lever (**Figure 70**).

3. Withdraw the gearshift lever assembly (A, **Figure 71**). See NOTE in the introduction to the procedure regarding a bent shaft if the assembly is difficult to remove.

4. Remove the E-clip (**Figure 72**) securing the shift pawl assembly.

5. Push down on the inner leg of the shift pawl and slide off (**Figure 73**) the assembly.

6. Inspect the condition of the return spring (**Figure 74**). If broken or weak it must be replaced; replace the spacer also.

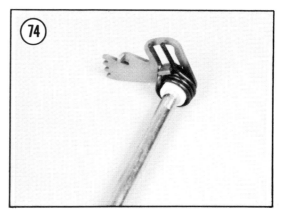

7. Inspect the shift pawl assembly spring (**Figure 75**). If broken or weak remove the E-clip and replace it.

8. Inspect the gearshift lever assembly shaft (**Figure 76**) for bending, wear or other damage; replace if necessary.

9. Install the shift pawl assembly and install the E-clip (**Figure 72**).

10. Install the gearshift lever assembly. Align the index mark on the shift pawl assembly with the center of the shift lever assembly (**Figure 77**). Make sure the return spring is correctly positioned onto the stopper plate bolt (B, **Figure 71**).

11. Install the shift lever and install the clutch assembly as described in this chapter.

Removal/Installation (Type III)

1. Remove the clutch assembly as described under *Clutch Removal/Installation* for your specific model in this chapter.

2. Remove the gearshift lever.

3. Withdraw the gearshift lever assembly (**Figure 78**). See NOTE in the introduction to the procedure regarding a bent shaft if the assembly is difficult to remove.

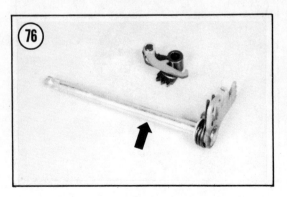

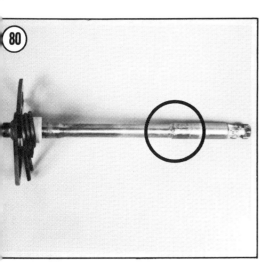

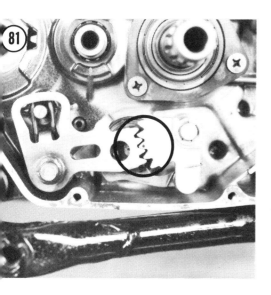

4. Remove the E-clip (**Figure 79**) securing the shift pawl assembly and slide off the assembly.

5. Inspect the condition of the return spring on the shift lever assembly. If broken or weak it must be replaced; replace the spacer also.

6. Inspect the shift pawl assembly spring. If broken or weak remove the E-clip and replace it.

7. Inspect the gearshift lever assembly shaft (**Figure 80**) for bending, wear or other damage; replace if necessary.

8. Install the shift pawl assembly and install the E-clip (**Figure 79**).

9. Install the gearshift lever assembly. Align the index mark on the shift pawl assembly with the center of the shift lever assembly (**Figure 81**). Make sure the return spring is correctly positioned onto the stopper plate bolt (**Figure 82**).

10. Install the shift lever and install the clutch assembly as described in this chapter.

Removal/Installation (Type IV)

1. Remove the clutch assembly as described under *Clutch Removal/Installation* for your specific model in this chapter.

2. Remove the gearshift lever.

3. Withdraw the gearshift lever shaft (**Figure 83**). See NOTE in the introduction to the procedure regarding a bent shaft if the assembly is difficult to remove.

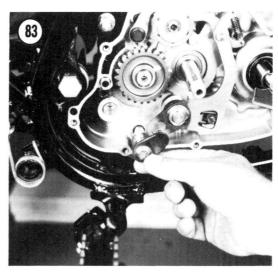

NOTE
Do not lose the small bushing on the backside of the engagement finger.

4. Push up on the upper part of the shift arm (**Figure 84**) and disengage it from the shift cam. Pull the shift arm assembly out and remove it.

5. Remove the return spring (A, **Figure 85**) and flange bolt (B, **Figure 85**) and remove the shift pawl (C, **Figure 85**).

6. Remove the E-clip (**Figure 86**) and remove the washer and shift cam.

7. Remove the shift cam pin (**Figure 87**).

8. Inspect the condition of the return spring on the shift arm assembly. If broken or weak it must be replaced.

NOTE
*On early production models of the YZ125D there is a Factory Technical Bulletin regarding a modification to the shift lever assembly for added shifting reliability. The window must be opened up a little at the lower right-hand corner to allow additional movement of the arm. Grind out 0.002-0.003 in. (0.05-0.07 mm) of material from this area (**Figure 88**). If you use a power grinder, do so slowly so as not to remove too much material. Scribe a line on first and work down to it slowly. Wear EYE PROTECTION if a power grinder is used. Also on this particular model the alignment of the lever to the shift drum is critical; refer to Steps 17-19. The engine serial numbers affected by this*

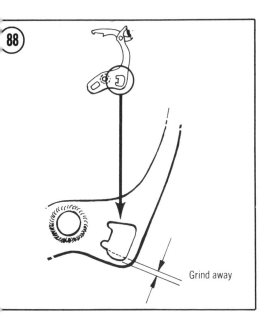

Grind away

modification are as follows: 1W1-000101 to -003179, 1W1-003531 to -004091, 1W1-006162 to -007770, and 1W1-009162 to -011709. Engine serial numbers not listed have already been modified by the factory.

9. Inspect the shift pawl return spring. If broken or weak it should be replaced.

10. Inspect the gearshift lever shaft for bending, wear or other damage; replace if necessary.

11. Install the shift cam pin.

12. Install the shift cam aligning the index mark on the cam with the one on the shaft (**Figure 89**).

13. Install the washer and the E-clip (**Figure 86**).

14. Install the shift pawl, flange bolt and return spring. Make sure the shift pawl roller is riding on the back portion of the shift cam as shown in **Figure 90**.

15. Push up on the upper part of the shift arm and push the shift arm assembly into place (**Figure 91**).

16. Shift the transmission into 1st gear.

17. The index mark on the shift cam and upper shift arm must align (**Figure 92**) for a proper shift progression from gear to gear.

18. If they do not align, remove the shift arm assembly and straighten the locking tab on the locknut. Loosen the locknut (A, **Figure 93**) and turn the eccentric screw (B, **Figure 93**) in or out for proper alignment. Reinstall the shift arm assembly and recheck alignment; repeat

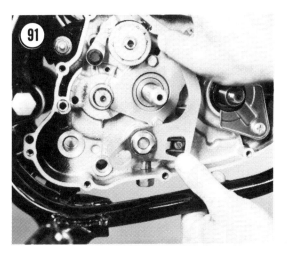

until correct. After alignment is correct tighten the locknut and bend up one side of the locking tab against it.

19. Reinstall the shift arm assembly.

20. Install the small bushing (**Figure 94**) into the backside of the engagement finger and install the shift lever shaft.

> *NOTE*
> *Make sure the return spring is properly engaged with the stopper bolt (eccentric screw). Refer to **Figure 95**.*

21. Make sure the finger is correctly installed into the elongated slot (**Figure 96**) in the shift arm assembly.

22. Install the shift lever and clutch assembly as described in this chapter.

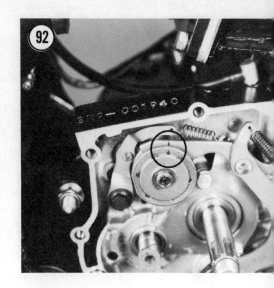

TRANSMISSION AND INTERNAL SHIFT MECHANISM

The transmission and internal shift mechanism (shift drum and forks) are all basically the same. The transmission is either a 5-speed or 6-speed unit; however, there are 6 different internal shift mechanisms all with major or minor differences. To gain access to the transmission and internal shift mechanism it is necessary to remove the engine and split the crankcase. Once the crankcase has been split removal of the transmission and shift drum and forks is a simple task of pulling the assemblies up and out of the crankcase. Installation is more complicated and is covered more completely than the removal sequence.

Because of the differences between models pay particular attention to the location of spacers, washers, and bearings during disassembly. Write down the order in which parts were removed to simplify assembly and ensure the correct placement of all parts.

> *NOTE*
> *If disassembling a used, well run-in engine for the first time by yourself, pay particular attention to any additional shims that may have been added by a previous owner. These may have been added to take up the tolerance of worn components and must be reinstalled in the same position since the shims have developed a wear pattern.*

If new parts are going to be installed these shims may be eliminated. This is something you will have to determine upon reassembly.

The transmission is either a 5-speed (Type or 6-speed (Type II) constant mesh type. The Type I transmission (**Figure 97**) is und in the following models:
YZ465G
YZ400F, E, D, C
YZ250C

Type II transmission (**Figure 98**) is found in e following models:
YZ250G, F, E, D
YZ175C
YZ125G, F, E, D, C, X
YZ100G, F, E, D, C

The internal shift mechanism is basically the same but differences do occur in all. They are separated into types that relate to different models and years.

The Type I internal shift mechanism (**Figure 99**) is found in the following models:
YZ465H, G
YZ250H, G
YZ125G

The Type II internal shift mechanism (**Figure 100**) is found in the following models:
YZ400F, E, D
YZ250F, E, D

The Type III internal shift mechanism (**Figure 101**) is found in the following models:
YZ400C
YZ250C

The Type IV internal shift mechanism (**Figure 102**) is found in the following models:
YZ125F, E, D
YZ100H, G, F, E

The Type V internal shift mechanism (**Figure 103**) is found in the following models:
YZ175C
YZ125C, X
YZ100D, C

The following procedures cover a typical 5-speed transmission and a typical 6-speed transmission. There are variations among different models using these different transmissions so pay particular attention to the location of spacers and washers during disassembly. Disassembly and inspection procedures for both the transmission and internal shift components are covered later in this chapter.

5-Speed Transmission and Internal Shift Mechanism Removal/Installation

1. Remove the engine and split the crankcase as described under *Crankcase Disassembly* for your specific model.
2. Pull the shift fork shafts up just enough to free them from their bearing holes in the crankcase.
3. Pivot them away from the shift drum (**Figure 104**) to allow room for the shift drum removal.

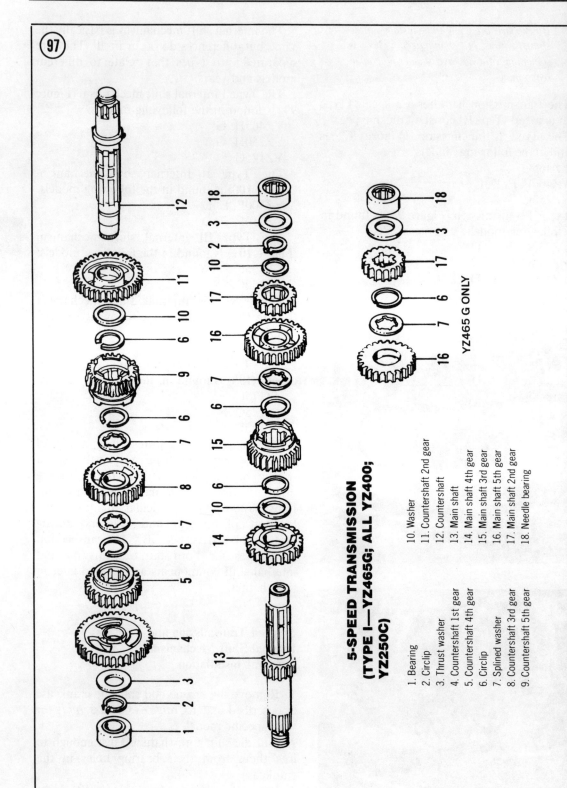

97

**5-SPEED TRANSMISSION
(TYPE I—YZ465G; ALL YZ400;
YZ250C)**

1. Bearing
2. Circlip
3. Thrust washer
4. Countershaft 1st gear
5. Countershaft 4th gear
6. Circlip
7. Splined washer
8. Countershaft 3rd gear
9. Countershaft 5th gear
10. Washer
11. Countershaft 2nd gear
12. Countershaft
13. Main shaft
14. Main shaft 4th gear
15. Main shaft 3rd gear
16. Main shaft 5th gear
17. Main shaft 2nd gear
18. Needle bearing

YZ465 G ONLY

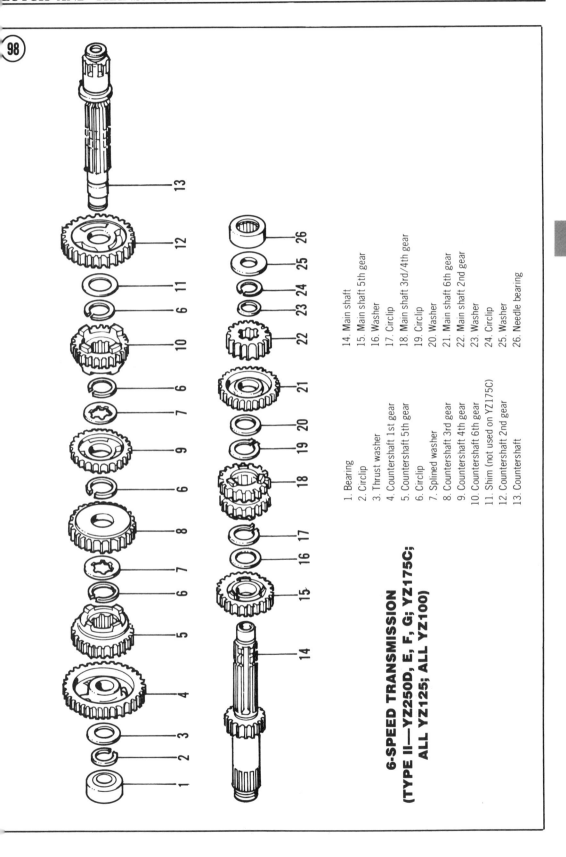

6-SPEED TRANSMISSION (TYPE II—YZ250D, E, F, G; YZ175C; ALL YZ125; ALL YZ100)

1. Bearing
2. Circlip
3. Thrust washer
4. Countershaft 1st gear
5. Countershaft 5th gear
6. Circlip
7. Splined washer
8. Countershaft 3rd gear
9. Countershaft 4th gear
10. Countershaft 6th gear
11. Shim (not used on YZ175C)
12. Countershaft 2nd gear
13. Countershaft
14. Main shaft
15. Main shaft 5th gear
16. Washer
17. Circlip
18. Main shaft 3rd/4th gear
19. Circlip
20. Washer
21. Main shaft 6th gear
22. Main shaft 2nd gear
23. Washer
24. Circlip
25. Washer
26. Needle bearing

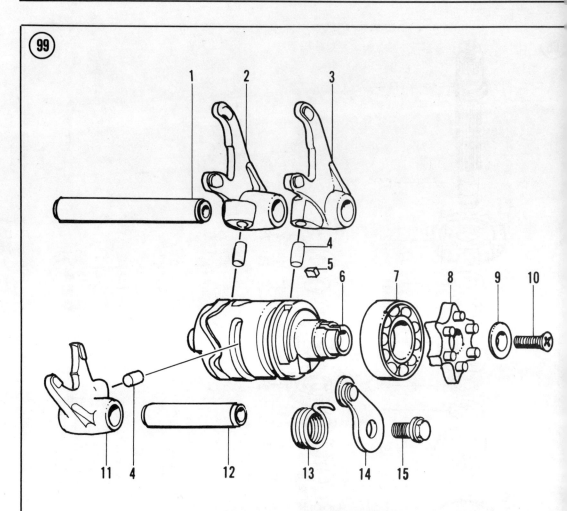

**INTERNAL SHIFT MECHANISM
(TYPE I—YZ465H, G;
YZ250H, G; YZ125G)**

1. Shift fork shaft (long)
2. Shift fork No. 3
3. Shift fork
4. Cam pin follower
5. Key
6. Shift drum
7. Bearing
8. Stopper plate
9. Washer
10. Screw
11. Shift fork No. 2
12. Shift fork shaft (short)
13. Spring
14. Shift pawl
15. Bolt

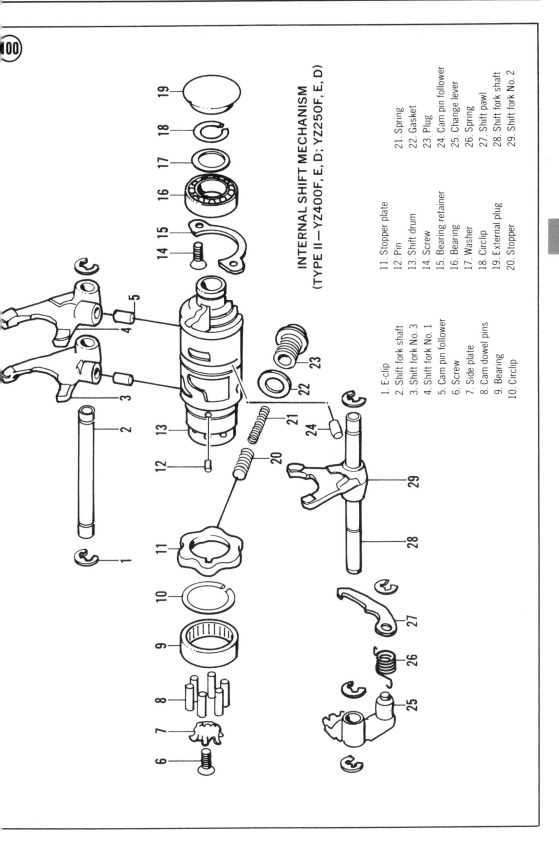

INTERNAL SHIFT MECHANISM
(TYPE II—YZ400F, E, D; YZ250F, E, D)

1. E-clip
2. Shift fork shaft
3. Shift fork No. 3
4. Shift fork No. 1
5. Cam pin follower
6. Screw
7. Side plate
8. Cam dowel pins
9. Bearing
10. Circlip
11. Stopper plate
12. Pin
13. Shift drum
14. Screw
15. Bearing retainer
16. Bearing
17. Washer
18. Circlip
19. External plug
20. Stopper
21. Spring
22. Gasket
23. Plug
24. Cam pin follower
25. Change lever
26. Spring
27. Shift pawl
28. Shift fork shaft
29. Shift fork No. 2

5

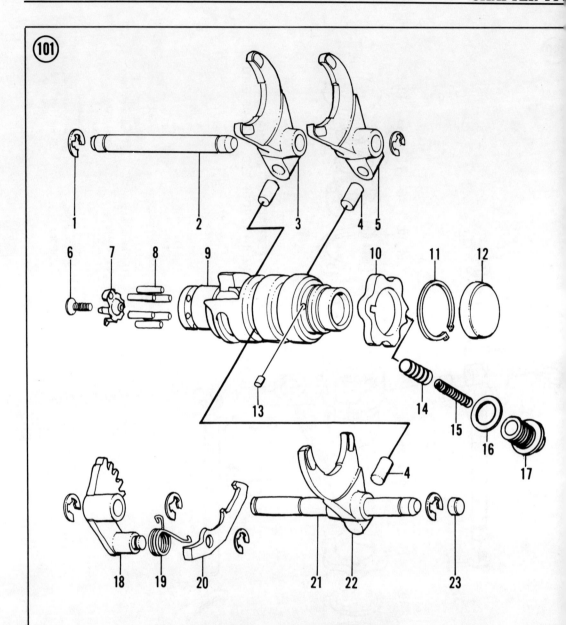

**INTERNAL SHIFT MECHANISM
(TYPE III—YZ400C; YZ250C)**

1. E-clip
2. Shift fork shaft
3. Shift fork
4. Cam pin follower
5. Shift fork
6. Screw
7. Side plate
8. Cam dowel pins

9. Shift drum
10. Stopper plate
11. Circlip
12. Plug
13. Pin
14. Stopper
15. Spring
16. Gasket

17. Plug
18. Change lever
19. Spring
20. Shift pawl
21. Shift fork shaft
22. Shift fork
23. Plug

(102)

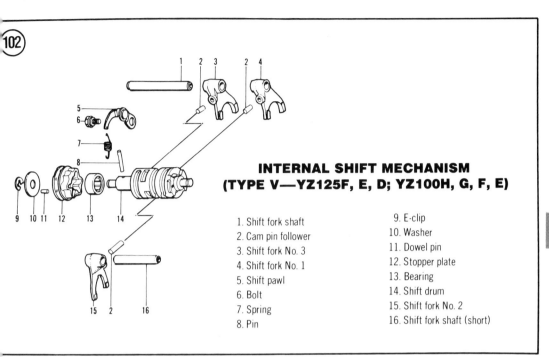

INTERNAL SHIFT MECHANISM
(TYPE V—YZ125F, E, D; YZ100H, G, F, E)

1. Shift fork shaft
2. Cam pin follower
3. Shift fork No. 3
4. Shift fork No. 1
5. Shift pawl
6. Bolt
7. Spring
8. Pin
9. E-clip
10. Washer
11. Dowel pin
12. Stopper plate
13. Bearing
14. Shift drum
15. Shift fork No. 2
16. Shift fork shaft (short)

5

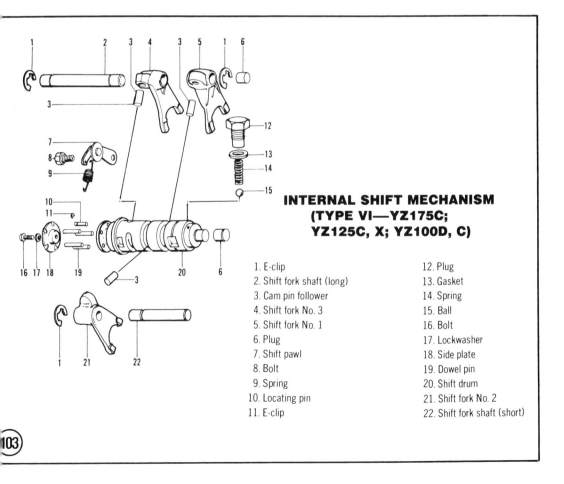

INTERNAL SHIFT MECHANISM
(TYPE VI—YZ175C;
YZ125C, X; YZ100D, C)

1. E-clip
2. Shift fork shaft (long)
3. Cam pin follower
4. Shift fork No. 3
5. Shift fork No. 1
6. Plug
7. Shift pawl
8. Bolt
9. Spring
10. Locating pin
11. E-clip
12. Plug
13. Gasket
14. Spring
15. Ball
16. Bolt
17. Lockwasher
18. Side plate
19. Dowel pin
20. Shift drum
21. Shift fork No. 2
22. Shift fork shaft (short)

(103)

4. Remove the shift drum.

5. Remove the shift forks and shafts (A, **Figure 105**) and remove both transmission assemblies (B, **Figure 105**).

6. Disassemble and inspect the shift forks and transmission assemblies as described later in this chapter.

7. Install by meshing the 2 transmission assemblies together in their proper relationship to each other. Install them in the left-hand crankcase. Hold the washer in place on the main shaft (**Figure 106**) and make sure it is still positioned correctly after the assemblies are completely installed (**Figure 107**). After both assemblies are installed, tap on the end of both shafts with a plastic or rubber mallet to make sure they are completely seated.

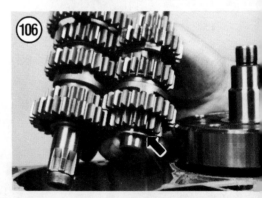

NOTE
If this washer does not seat correctly it will hold the transmission shaft up a little and prevent the crankcase halves from seating completely when assembled.

8. Install the rear shift forks and shaft. Engage the shift forks into the grooves in the gears (**Figure 108**) but *do not* insert the shift fork shaft into the bearing hole in the crankcase. Leave it pivoted away from the shift drum.

NOTE
*If the shift forks have been disassembled, make sure the identifying mark (**Figure 109**) on each fork is facing UP.*

9. Install the front shift fork and shaft. Pull up on the gear with the shift fork groove and

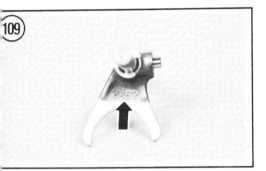

engage the shift fork into the groove (**Figure 110**). *Do not* insert the shift fork shaft into the bearing hole in the crankcase (**Figure 111**)—leave it pivoted away from the shift drum.

10. Coat all bearings and sliding surfaces of the shift drum with assembly oil and install it. Pivot each shift fork assembly into mesh with the shift drum. Make sure all 3 cam pin followers are in mesh with the shift drum grooves (**Figure 112**).

11. Spin the transmission shafts and shift through the gears using the shift drum. Make sure you can shift into all gears. This is the time to find that something may be installed incorrectly—not after the crankcase is completely assembled.

NOTE
This procedure is best done with the aid of a helper as the assemblies are loose and don't want to spin very easily. Have the helper spin the transmission shaft while you turn the shift drum through all the gears.

12. Assemble the crankcase as described under *Crankcase Assembly* for your specific model.

6-Speed Transmission and Internal Shift Mechanism Removal/Installation

This procedure uses 4 different models to show many of the special steps for an easy removal and installation sequence.

1. Remove the engine and split the crankcase as described under *Crankcase Disassembly* for your specific model.

2. Pull the shift fork shafts up just enough to free them from their bearing holes in the crankcase.

3. Pivot them away from the shift drum (**Figure 113**) to allow room for the shift drum removal.

> *NOTE*
> *On some later models the crankcases are smaller and do not have room to allow the pivoting of the shift forks. On these models pull the shift fork shafts (**Figure 114**) up and out of the shift forks.*

4. Remove the shift drum.

> *NOTE*
> *According to a Yamaha Technical Bulletin, some of the early model YZ250G and YZ125Gs were manufactured without sufficient thread locking compound on the screw securing the stopper plate to the shift drum. Remove the screw, washer and stopper plate. Clean the threads of the screw with a nonresidual cleaner (contact point cleaner) and dry thoroughly. Apply Loctite Stud N' Bearing Mount to the screw threads and reinstall all components. Tighten the screw to 5.8 ft.-lb. (8 N•m).*

5. Remove the shift forks and shafts (A, **Figure 115**) and remove both transmission assemblies (B, **Figure 115**).

> *NOTE*
> *Remove the shift forks (**Figure 116**) on models where the shift fork shafts have been removed.*

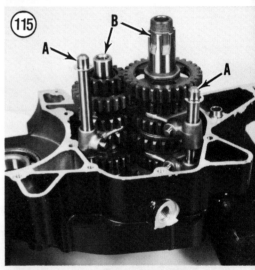

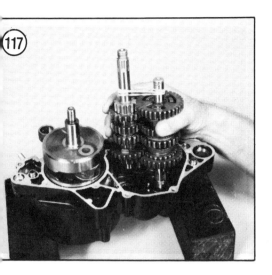

5

6. Disassemble and inspect the shift forks and transmission assemblies as described later in this chapter.

7. Install by meshing the 2 transmission assemblies together in their proper relationship to each other. Place a rubber band around the top end (**Figure 117**) of the shafts to hold them together. After they are installed, tap on the end of both shafts with a plastic or rubber mallet (**Figure 118**) to make sure they are completely seated.

NOTE
*On the YZ125 install the lower rear shift fork onto the transmission shaft (**Figure 119**) prior to installing the transmission assemblies. The surrounding area will be very tight to try to install it later (**Figure 120**).*

8. Install the rear shift forks and shaft. Engage the shift forks into the grooves in the gears but *do not* insert the shift fork shaft into the bearing hole in the crankcase. Leave it pivoted away from the shift drum.

NOTE
*If the shift forks have been disassembled, make sure the identifying mark (**Figure 121**) on each fork is facing UP.*

9. Install the front shift fork and shaft (**Figure 122**). *Do not* insert the shift fork shaft into the

bearing hole in the crankcase (**Figure 123**)—leave it pivoted away from the shift drum.

> *NOTE*
> *On some later models insert the shift forks into their proper position (**Figure 114**). DO NOT install the shift fork shafts at this time.*

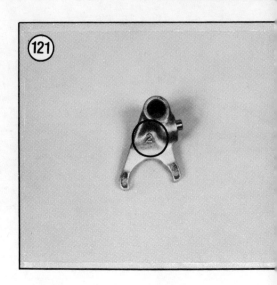

10. Coat all bearing and sliding surfaces of the shift drum with assembly oil and install it. Pivot each shift fork assembly into mesh with the shift drum.

> *NOTE*
> *On some later models pivot the shift forks into position and install the shift fork shafts. On the YZ125 it is necessary to slightly lift up on the upper 2 gears and shift fork (**Figure 124**) to install the shift fork pin follower into the shift drum.*

11. Make sure all 3 cam pin followers are in mesh with the shift drum grooves (**Figure 125**).
12. Spin the transmission shafts and shift through the gears using the shift drum. Make sure you can shift into all gears. This is the time to find that something may be installed incorrectly—not after the crankcase is completely assembled.

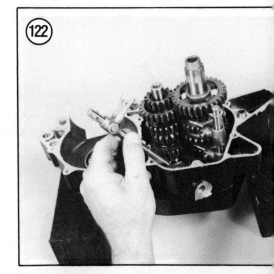

> *NOTE*
> *This procedure is best done with the aid of a helper as the assemblies are loose and don't want to spin very easily. Have the helper spin the transmission shaft while you turn the shift drum through all the gears.*

13. Assemble the crankcase as described under *Crankcase Assembly* for your specific model.

**Main Shaft Disassembly/
Inspection/Assembly
(5-Speed Transmission)**

Refer to **Figure 97** for this procedure.

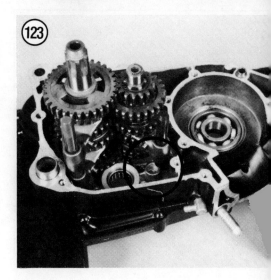

> *NOTE*
> *A helpful "tool" that should be used for transmission disassembly is a large egg flat (the type that restaurants get their eggs in). As you remove a part from the*

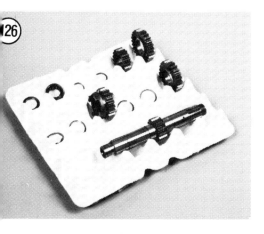

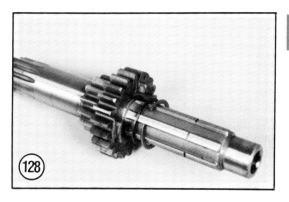

3. On all models except the YZ465G, remove the circlip and washer and slide off the 2nd and 5th gears.

NOTE
On YZ465G remove the 2nd gear (there is no circlip). Remove the circlip, splined washer and 5th gear.

4. Remove the splined washer, circlip and 3rd gear.

5. Remove the circlip, washer and 4th gear.

6. Check each gear for excessive wear, burrs, pitting or chipped or missing teeth. Make sure the lugs (**Figure 128**) on the gears are in good condition.

NOTE
Defective gears should be replaced, and it is a good idea to replace the mating gear on the countershaft even though it may not show as much wear or damage.

7. Make sure that all gears slide smoothly on the main shaft splines.

8. Slide on the 4th gear and install the washer and circlip (**Figure 128**).

*shaft set it in one of the depressions in the exact same position from which it was removed (**Figure 126**). This is an easy way to remember the correct relationship of all parts.*

Place the assembled shaft into a large can or ~stic bucket and thoroughly clean with vent and a stiff brush. Dry with compressed or let sit on rags to drip dry.

Remove the roller bearing and washer.

9. Slide on the 3rd gear and install the circlip and washer (**Figure 129**).

10. On all models except the YZ465G, slide on the 5th gear with the recessed side going on first (**Figure 130**).

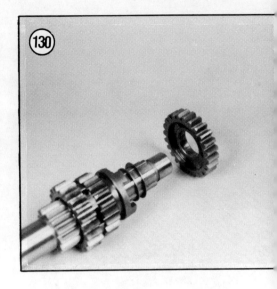

> *NOTE*
> *On YZ465G install the 5th gear with the flush side going on first followed by a thrust washer and circlip. Then install the 2nd gear (recessed side going on first), washer and the needle bearing.*

11. On all models except the YZ465G, install the 2nd gear with the recess (**Figure 131**) facing outward. Install the washer and circlip (**Figure 132**).

12. Install the washer and roller bearing (**Figure 133**).

13. After assembly is complete, refer to **Figure 134** for the correct placement of all gears. Make sure all circlips are seated correctly in the main shaft grooves. It is a good idea to replace all circlips every other time the transmission is disassembled as they take a beating in a competition machine.

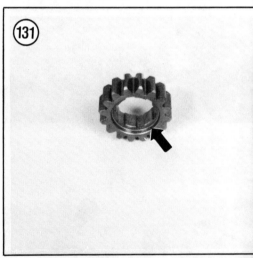

Countershaft Disassembly/ Inspection/Assembly (5-Speed Transmission)

Refer to **Figure 97** for this procedure.

> *NOTE*
> *Use the same large egg flat that was used on the main shaft disassembly for the countershaft (**Figure 135**). This is an easy way to remember the correct relationship of all parts.*

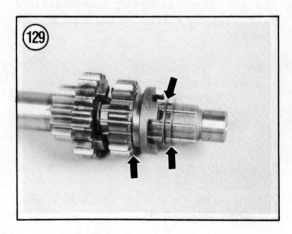

Place the assembled shaft into a large can or astic bucket and thoroughly clean with lvent and a stiff brush. Dry with compressed r or let sit on rags to drip dry.

Remove the circlip and washer and slide off e 1st and 4th gears.

Remove the circlip and splined washer, and de off the 5th gear.

(133)

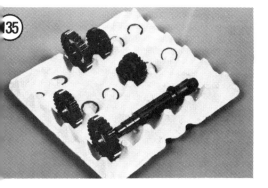

(135)

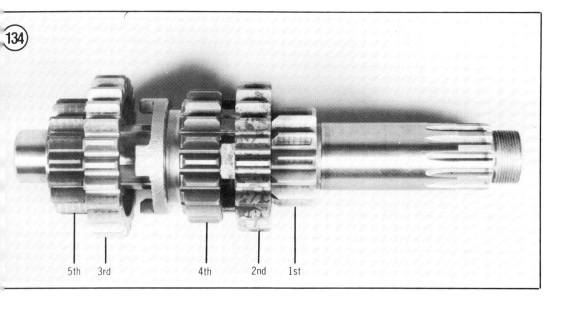

(134)

5th   3rd   4th   2nd   1st

4. Remove the circlip, washer and 2nd gear.

5. Check each gear for excessive wear, burrs, pitting, or chipped or missing teeth. Make sure the lugs (**Figure 127**) on the gears are in good condition.

NOTE
Defective gears should be replaced, and it is a good idea to replace the mating gear on the main shaft even though it may not show as much wear or damage.

6. Make sure that all gears slide smoothly on the countershaft splines.

7. Slide on the 2nd gear (flush side on first) and install the washer and circlip (**Figure 136**).

5

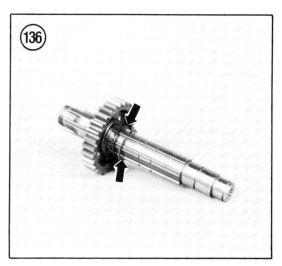

(136)

8. Slide on the 5th gear and install the circlip and washer (**Figure 137**).

9. Slide on the 3rd gear (recessed side on first); see **Figure 138**.

10. Install the splined washer and circlip and slide on the 4th gear (**Figure 139**).

11. Slide on the 1st gear (**Figure 140**).

12. Install the washer and circlip (**Figure 141**).

13. After assembly is complete refer to **Figure 142** for the correct placement of all gears. Make sure all circlips are seated correctly in the countershaft grooves. It is a good idea to replace all circlips every other time the transmission is disassembled as they take a beating in a competition machine.

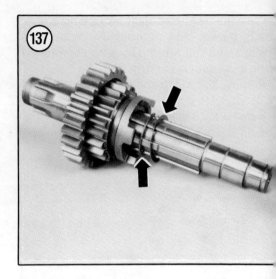

> *NOTE*
> *After both transmission shafts have been assembled, mesh the 2 assemblies together in the correct position (**Figure 143**). Check that all gears meet correctly. This is your last check prior to installing the assemblies into the crankcase to make sure they are correctly assembled.*

**Main Shaft Disassembly/
Inspection/Assembly
(6-Speed Transmission)**

Refer to **Figure 98** for this procedure.

> *NOTE*
> *A helpful "tool" that should be used for transmission disassembly is a large egg flat (the type that restaurants get their eggs in). As you remove a part from the shaft set it in one of the depressions in the exact same position from which it was removed (**Figure 144**). This is an easy way to remember the correct relationship of all parts.*

1. Place the assembled shaft into a large can or plastic bucket and thoroughly clean with solvent and a stiff brush. Dry with compressed air or let sit on rags to drip dry.

2. Remove the circlip and washer and slide off the 2nd and 6th gears.

> *NOTE*
> *On YZ125 and YZ100 models there is no washer. Just remove the circlip and slide off the 2nd and 6th gears.*

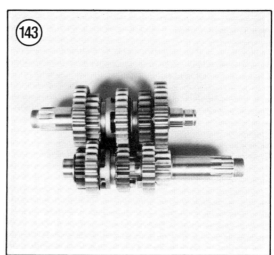

5

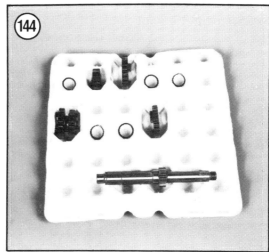

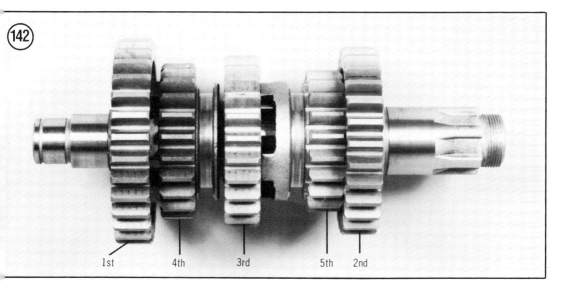

1st   4th   3rd   5th 2nd

3. Remove the washer, circlip and the 3rd/4th combination gear.

4. Remove the circlip, washer and 5th gear.

5. Check each gear for excessive wear, burrs, pitting, or chipped or missing teeth. Make sure the lugs (**Figure 145**) on the gears are in good condition.

> *NOTE*
> *Defective gears should be replaced, and it is a good idea to replace the mating gear on the countershaft even though it may not show as much wear or damage.*

6. Make sure that all gears slide smoothly on the main shaft splines.

7. Slide on the 5th gear and install the washer and circlip (**Figure 146**).

8. Slide on the 3rd/4th combination gear and install the circlip and washer (**Figure 147**).

9. Slide on the 6th gear (**Figure 148**).

10. Slide on the 2nd gear (**Figure 149**) and install the washer and circlip (**Figure 150**).

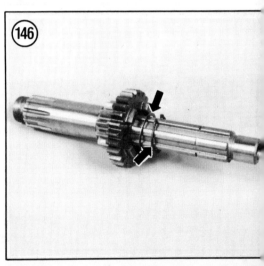

> *NOTE*
> *On YZ125 and YZ100 models there is no washer. Just install the circlip.*

11. After assembly is complete refer to **Figure 151** for the correct placement of all gears. Make sure all circlips are seated correctly in the main shaft grooves. It is a good idea to replace all circlips every other time the transmission is disassembled as they take a beating in a competition machine.

**Countershaft Disassembly/
Inspection/Assembly
(6-Speed Transmission)**

Refer to **Figure 98** for this procedure.

> *NOTE*
> *Use the same large egg flat that was used on the main shaft disassembly for the countershaft (**Figure 152**). This is an easy way to remember the correct relationship of all parts.*

1. Place the assembled shaft into a large can or plastic bucket and thoroughly clean with solvent and a stiff brush. Dry with compressed air or let sit on rags to drip dry.

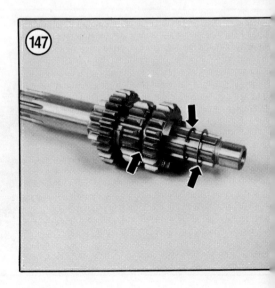

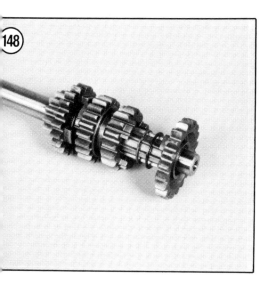

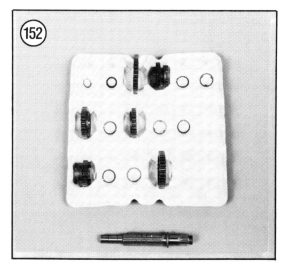

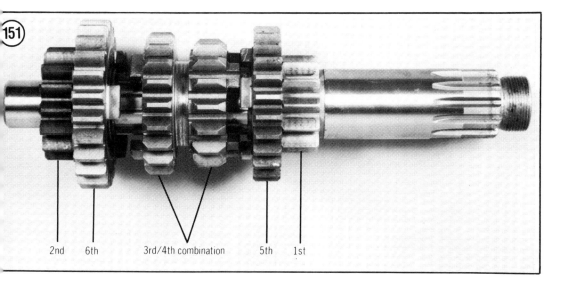

2nd   6th   3rd/4th combination   5th   1st

2. Remove the circlip and washer and slide off the 1st and 5th gears.

3. Remove the circlip and splined washer and slide off the 3rd gear.

4. Remove the circlip and slide off the 4th gear.

5. Remove the splined washer and circlip and slide off the 6th gear.

6. Remove the circlip and washer and slide off the 2nd gear.

7. Check each gear for excessive wear, burrs, pitting or chipped or missing teeth. Make sure the lugs (**Figure 154**) on the gears are in good condition.

NOTE
Defective gears should be replaced, and it is a good idea to replace the mating gear on the main shaft even though it may not show as much wear or damage.

8. Make sure that all gears slide smoothly on the countershaft splines.

9. Slide on the 2nd gear (flush side on first) and install the washer and circlip (**Figure 154**).

10. Slide on the 6th gear and install the circlip and washer (**Figure 155**).

11. Slide on the 4th gear (recessed side on first) for the YZ175, YZ125 and YZ100; refer to **Figure 156**. On YZ250 models install the 4th gear as shown in **Figure 157**. On all models install the circlip.

12. Install the 3rd gear (flush side on first) and install the splined washer and circlip (**Figure 158**).

13. Slide on the 5th and 1st gear (**Figure 159**) and install the washer and circlip (**Figure 160**).

14. After assembly is complete refer to **Figure 161** for the correct placement of all gears.

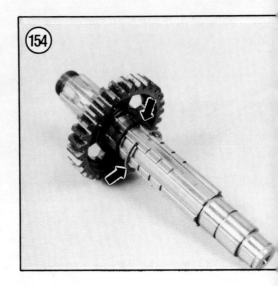

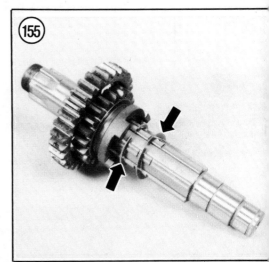

5

2nd   6th   4th   3rd   5th   1st

Make sure all circlips are seated correctly in the countershaft grooves. It is a good idea to replace all circlips every other time the transmission is disassembled as they take a beating in a competition machine.

> *NOTE*
> *After both transmission shafts have been assembled, mesh the 2 assemblies together in the correct position (**Figure 162**). Check that all gears meet correctly. This is your last check prior to installing the assemblies into the crankcase to make sure they are correctly assembled.*

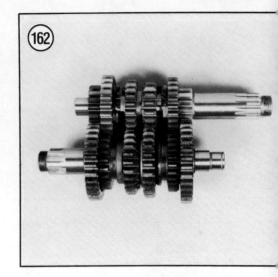

Internal Shift Mechanism Inspection

Refer to **Figures 100-104** for this procedure.

> *NOTE*
> *Due to the number of different internal shift mechanisms (Type I through V), components from all different types are not shown in the following procedure. Prior to removal or disassembly of any of the components, lay the assembly (**Figure 163**) down on a piece of paper or cardboard and carefully trace around it. Also write down the identifying marks or numbers (**Figure 164**) next to the item. Also mark where circlips, if any, are located. This will take a little extra time now but it may save some frustrating time later.*

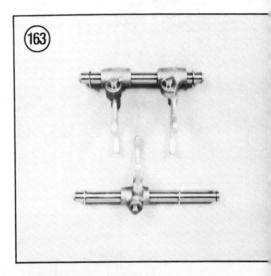

1. Inspect each shift fork for signs of wear or cracking. Check for bending and make sure each fork slides smoothly on its respective shaft (**Figure 165**).

> *NOTE*
> *Check for any arc-shaped wear or burned marks (**Figure 166**) on the shift forks. If this is apparent, the shift fork has come in contact with the gear, indicating that the fingers are worn beyond use and the fork must be replaced.*

2. Roll the shift fork shaft on a flat surface (a piece of plate glass) and check for any bending. If the shaft is bent, replace it.

3. Check the grooves in the shift drum (**Figure 167**) for wear or roughness. If any of the groove

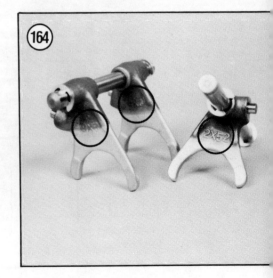

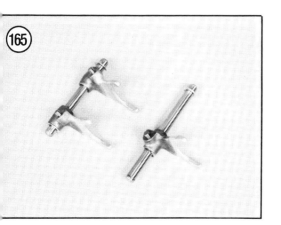

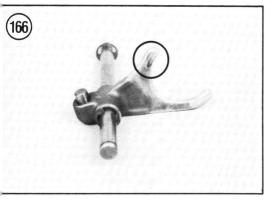

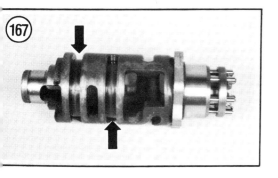

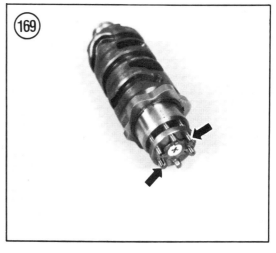

profiles have excessive wear or damage, replace the shift drum.

. On models with an integral bearing (**Figure 68**), check it for smooth operation. Make sure : spins with no signs of wear or damage. Replace if necessary.

. On Type II, III, IV, and VI, check the shift am dowel pins (**Figure 169**) and side plate wear, looseness or damage; replace any .efective parts.

. Check the cam pin followers (**Figure 170**) in ach shift fork. They should fit snug but not too tight. Check the end that rides in the shift drum for wear or burrs. Replace as necessary.

7. Inspect the condition of the ramps on the stopper plate (**Figure 171**) for wear or roughness. Also check the tightness of the screw securing the stopper plate. If it is loose, remove the screw, washer and stopper plate. Clean the threads of the screw with a nonresidual cleaner (contact point cleaner) and dry thoroughly. Apply Loctite Stud N' Bearing Mount to the screw threads and reinstall all components. Tighten the screw securely.

8. If shift fork assemblies have been disassembled, apply a light coat of oil to the shafts and inside bores of the fingers prior to installation.

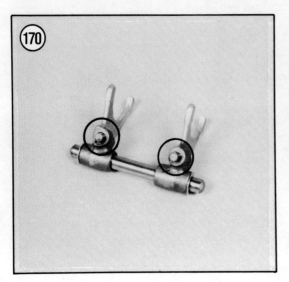

Table 1 CLUTCH SPECIFICATIONS

Item	Standard	Wear limit
Friction disc thickness	0.12 in. (3.0 mm)	0.106 in. (2.7 mm)
Clutch plate thickness		
(except YZ175-YZ100)	0.09 in. (2.3 mm)	0.002 in. (0.05 mm)
YZ175-YZ100)	0.047 in. (1.2 mm)	N.A.
Clutch plate warpage	–	0.002 in. (0.05 mm)
Clutch springs free		
length	1.42 in. (36.0 mm)	1.38 in. (35.0 mm)

	Items per model	
	Friction disc	Clutch plates
YZ465	7	6
YZ400	7	6
YZ250	6	5
YZ175	6	5
YZ125	5	4
YZ100	5	4

Table 2 CLUTCH TORQUE SPECIFICATION

Item	ft.-lb.	N•m
Clutch nut		
YZ250, YZ400, YZ465	54	75
YZ100, YZ125	36	50
YZ175	30	42
Clutch spring bolts		
YZ125, YZ100	5	6
All other models	6	8

CHAPTER SIX

FUEL AND EXHAUST SYSTEMS

6

The fuel system consists of the fuel tank, shutoff valve, and a single Mikuni carburetor and air cleaner. There are slight differences among the various models and they are noted in the various procedures.

The exhaust system consists of an exhaust pipe assembly and a silencer.

This chapter includes service procedures for all parts of the fuel system and exhaust system.

AIR CLEANER

The air cleaner must be cleaned frequently. Refer to Chapter Three for specific procedures and service intervals.

CARBURETOR OPERATION

For proper operation, a gasoline engine must be supplied with fuel and air mixed in proper proportions by weight. A mixture in which there is an excess of fuel is said to be rich. A lean mixture is one which contains insufficient fuel. A properly adjusted carburetor supplies the proper mixture to the engine under all operating conditions.

Mikuni carburetors consist of several major systems. A float and float valve mechanism maintain a constant fuel level in the float bowl. The pilot system supplies fuel at low speeds. The main fuel system supplies fuel at medium and high speeds. Finally a starter (choke) system supplies the very rich mixture needed to start a cold engine.

CARBURETOR SERVICE

Major carburetor service (removal and cleaning) should be performed after every moto or meet on a strictly competition bike. On a bike that is used for fun on weekends it should be performed whenever the engine is decarbonized or when poor engine performance, hesitation, and little or no response to mixture adjustment is observed. The service interval time will become natural to you after owning and running the bike for a period of time.

Carburetor Identification

Due to the many years and models covered in this manual and the slight differences in the specific carburetors the following will help identify your specific carburetor.

The Mikuni carburetor used on all of these models is basically the same and to help clarify this the carburetors are split into 4 types. Slight differences do occur between models, so it is important to pay particular attention to the location and order of parts during disassembly.

The Type I carburetor (**Figure 1**) is found in the following models:

YZ465H, G
YZ250H, G

The Type II carburetor (**Figure 2**) is found in the following models:

YZ400F, E, D, C
YZ250F, E, D, C
YZ175C

YZ125G, F, E, D
YZ125X

The Type III carburetor (**Figure 3**) is found in the following models:

YZ125C
YZ100G, F, E, D, C

Refer to **Table 1** at the end of this chapter for carburetor specifications.

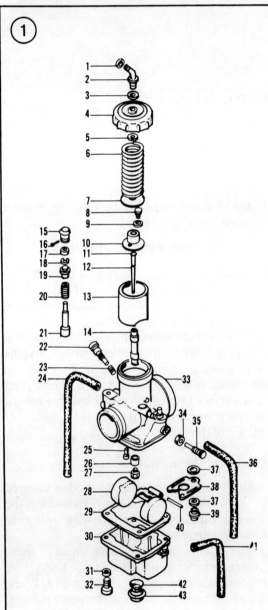

①

CARBURETOR ASSEMBLY
(TYPE I—YZ465G, H; YZ250G, H)

1. Nut
2. Cable guide
3. O-ring
4. Top cap
5. Clip
6. Throttle valve spring
7. Spring seat
8. Screw
9. Washer
10. Connector
11. Clip
12. **Jet needle**
13. Throttle valve (slide)
14. **Needle jet**
15. Holder
16. Cotter pin
17. Plunger cover
18. Clip
19. Plunger cap
20. Plunger spring
21. Plunger
22. Air screw

23. Spring
24. Overflow tube
25. Pilot jet
26. Main jet holder/washer
27. Main jet
28. Float
29. Gasket
30. Float bowl
31. Washer
32. Screw
33. **Carburetor body**
34. Locknut
35. Throttle set screw
36. Overflow tube
37. Washer
38. Plate
39. Needle valve assembly
40. Float pin
41. Drain tube
42. O-ring
43. Plug

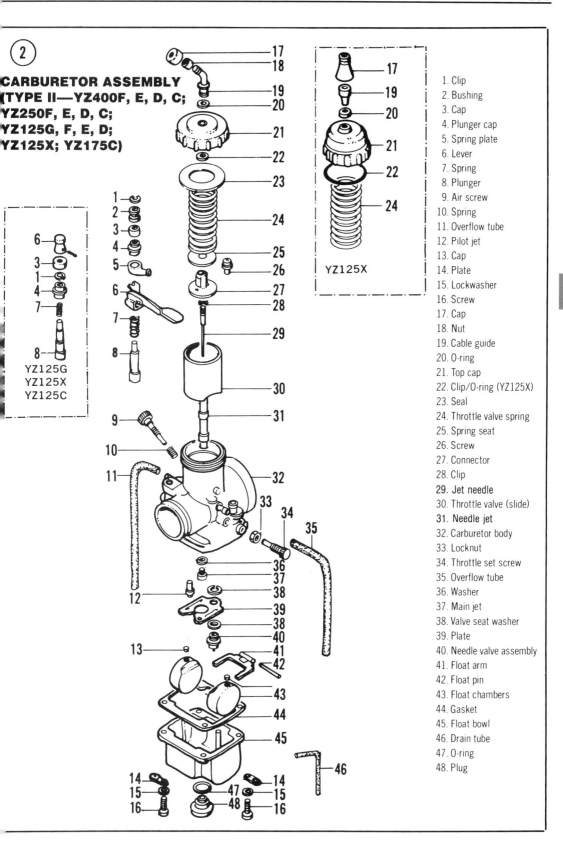

② CARBURETOR ASSEMBLY
(TYPE II—YZ400F, E, D, C;
YZ250F, E, D, C;
YZ125G, F, E, D;
YZ125X; YZ175C)

YZ125X

YZ125G
YZ125X
YZ125C

1. Clip
2. Bushing
3. Cap
4. Plunger cap
5. Spring plate
6. Lever
7. Spring
8. Plunger
9. Air screw
10. Spring
11. Overflow tube
12. Pilot jet
13. Cap
14. Plate
15. Lockwasher
16. Screw
17. Cap
18. Nut
19. Cable guide
20. O-ring
21. Top cap
22. Clip/O-ring (YZ125X)
23. Seal
24. Throttle valve spring
25. Spring seat
26. Screw
27. Connector
28. Clip
29. **Jet needle**
30. Throttle valve (slide)
31. **Needle jet**
32. Carburetor body
33. Locknut
34. Throttle set screw
35. Overflow tube
36. Washer
37. Main jet
38. Valve seat washer
39. Plate
40. Needle valve assembly
41. Float arm
42. Float pin
43. Float chambers
44. Gasket
45. Float bowl
46. Drain tube
47. O-ring
48. Plug

6

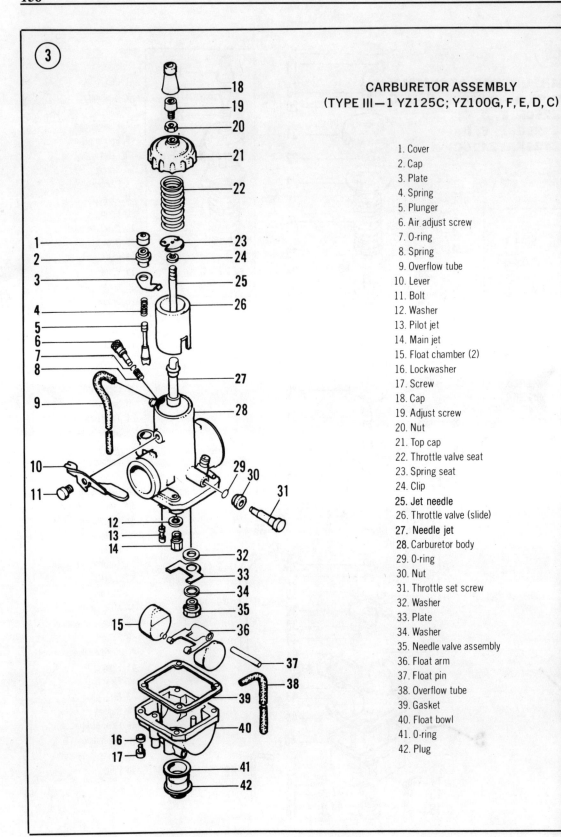

**CARBURETOR ASSEMBLY
(TYPE III—1 YZ125C; YZ100G, F, E, D, C)**

1. Cover
2. Cap
3. Plate
4. Spring
5. Plunger
6. Air adjust screw
7. O-ring
8. Spring
9. Overflow tube
10. Lever
11. Bolt
12. Washer
13. Pilot jet
14. Main jet
15. Float chamber (2)
16. Lockwasher
17. Screw
18. Cap
19. Adjust screw
20. Nut
21. Top cap
22. Throttle valve seat
23. Spring seat
24. Clip
25. Jet needle
26. Throttle valve (slide)
27. Needle jet
28. Carburetor body
29. O-ring
30. Nut
31. Throttle set screw
32. Washer
33. Plate
34. Washer
35. Needle valve assembly
36. Float arm
37. Float pin
38. Overflow tube
39. Gasket
40. Float bowl
41. O-ring
42. Plug

Carburetor Removal/Installation

All of the carburetors are basically the same even though minor variations exist among different models and years. This procedure is shown with a Type II carburetor on a YZ125G and YZ400F.

1. Place a milk crate or wood block(s) under the engine to support it securely.
2. Turn the fuel shutoff valve to the OFF position (**Figure 4**) and remove the fuel line to the carburetor.
3. Remove the seat.
4. Pull the fuel fill cap vent tube free from the steering head area (A, **Figure 5**).
5. Remove the bolts (B, **Figure 5**) securing the front of the fuel tank. Pull up and unhook the strap (C, **Figure 5**) securing the rear of the tank. Pull the tank toward the rear and remove it.
6. Loosen the locknut and adjuster on the throttle cable (A, **Figure 6**).

NOTE
Prior to removing the top cap, thoroughly clean the area around it so no dirt will fall into the carburetor.

7. Unscrew the carburetor top cap (B, **Figure 6**) and pull the throttle valve assembly up and out of the carburetor (**Figure 7**).

NOTE
If the top cover and slide assembly are not going to be removed from the cable for cleaning, wrap them in a clean shop cloth or place them in a plastic bag to help keep them clean.

8. Loosen the clamping screws (**Figure 8**) on both rubber boots. Slide off the clamps away from the carburetor.

9. Make sure all drain tubes are free (**Figure 9**).

10. Carefully work the carburetor free from the rubber boots and remove it.

11. Take the carburetor to workbench for disassembly and cleaning.

12. Install by reversing these removal steps, noting the following.

13. When installing the carburetor onto the engine side be sure to properly align the boss on the carburetor air horn with the groove in the rubber boot (**Figure 10**).

14. When installing the throttle valve assembly, make sure the groove in the slide aligns with the pin (**Figure 11**) in the carburetor body.

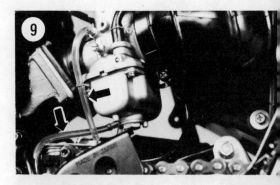

Disassembly/Cleaning/ Inspection/Assembly

Refer to **Figure 1, 2 or 3** for your specific carburetor for this procedure and to **Table 1** for carburetor specifications.

All of the carburetors are basically the same even though minor variations exist among different models and years. Where major differences occur they are identified.

1. Remove the screws (**Figure 12**) securing the float bowl and remove it.

2. On Type I carburetors, remove the float pin (**Figure 13**) and float assembly.

3. On Type I remove the float valve needle and seat (**Figure 14**).

4. On all other types the float arm pin (**Figure 15**) is wedged in place. Do not remove it unless you are sure the valve needle is faulty. If so, carefully push it out. Avoid damaging the posts that hold it in place. Remove the float lever, float valve needle, seat and washer and plate.

5. Remove the main jet (**Figure 16**).

6. Remove the main jet holder/washer (**Figure 17**).

7. Remove the needle jet (**Figure 18**).

8. Unscrew the pilot jet (**Figure 19**).

9. Remove the plastic drain tubes (A, **Figure 20**), choke assembly (B, **Figure 20**), and throttle adjust screw and spring (C, **Figure 20**).

10. Remove the plastic caps (A, **Figure 21**) securing the floats and remove them.

11. Remove the seal in the float bowl (B, **Figure 21**).

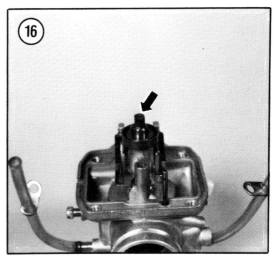

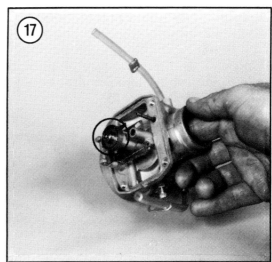

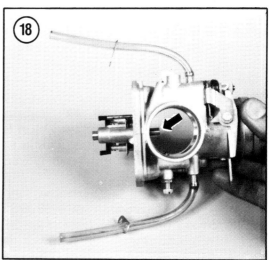

6

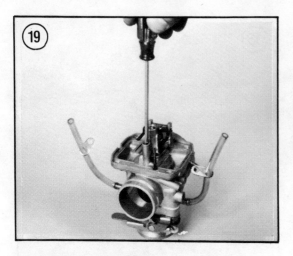

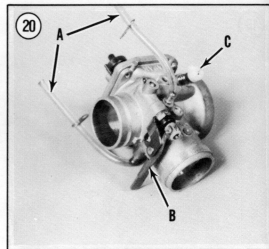

12. Remove the clip (**Figure 22**) securing the throttle cable in the slide assembly.

13. Remove the throttle cable from the throttle valve assembly (**Figure 23**) and remove it.

14. Remove the 2 screws (**Figure 24**) securing the jet needle into the throttle valve assembly and disassemble it (**Figure 25**).

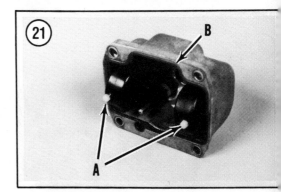

> *NOTE*
> *Further disassembly is neither necessary nor recommended. If throttle or choke shafts or butterflies are damaged, take the carburetor body to your dealer for replacement.*

15. Clean all parts, except rubber or plastic parts, in a good grade of carburetor cleaner. This solution is available at most automotive or motorcycle supply stores, in a small, resealable tank with a dip basket, for just a few dollars (**Figure 26**). If it is tightly sealed when not in use, the solution will last for several cleanings. Follow the manufacturer's instructions for correct soak time (usually about 1/2 hour).

16. Remove all parts from the cleaner and blow dry with compressd air. Blow out the jets with compressed air. *Do not* use a piece of wire to clean them as minor gouges in the jet can alter flow rate and upset the fuel/air mixture.

17. Be sure to clean out the overflow tube (**Figure 27**) from both ends.

18. Inspect the condition of the end of the float valve needle (**Figure 28**) for wear or damage; replace if necessary.

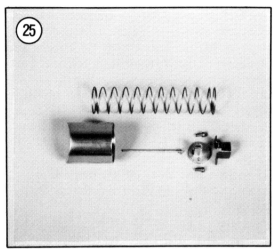

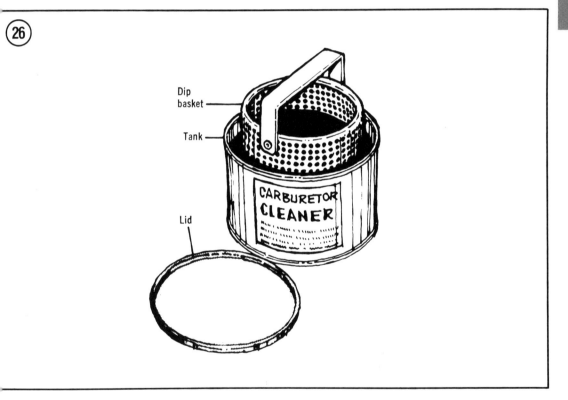

Dip
basket

Tank

Lid

19. O-ring seals tend to become hardened after prolonged use and heat and therefore lose their ability to seal properly. Inspect the condition of the O-ring seal on the float bowl plug.

20. Be sure to install the pilot jet as shown in **Figure 29**.

21. Install the jet needle clip in the correct groove; refer to **Table 1** at the end of this chapter.

22. Check the float height and adjust if necessary. Refer to *Float Adjustment* in this chapter.

23. After the carburetor has been disassembled adjust the pilot screw and the idle speed. Refer to *Pilot Screw and Idle Speed Adjustment* following in this chapter.

CARBURETOR ADJUSTMENTS

Float Adjustment

The carburetor assembly has to be removed and partially disassembled for this adjustment.

1. Remove the carburetor as described under *Carburetor Removal/Installation* in this chapter.

2. Remove the float bowl from the main body.

3. On Type I carburetors, measure the height of the float above the carburetor body (**Figure 30**). Use a float level gauge (**Figure 31**). Hold the carburetor so the float tang is just touching the float needle—not pushing it down. Refer to **Table 1** for the correct height.

4. On all other models, hold the carburetor so the float arm is just touching the float needle.

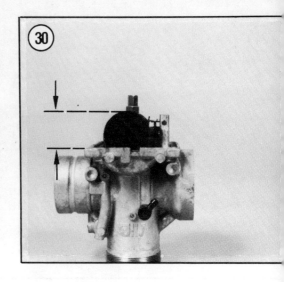

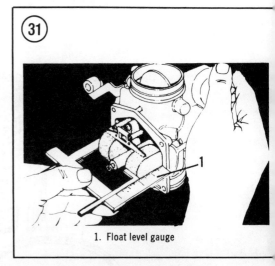

1. Float level gauge

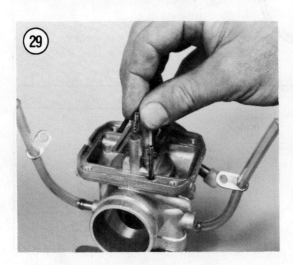

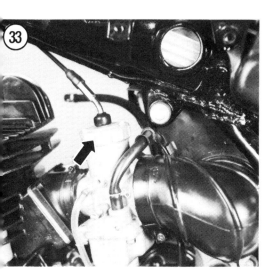

Use a float gauge and measure the distance from the carburetor body (without gasket) to the float arm (**Figure 32**). Refer to **Table 1** for the correct level.

5. Adjust by carefully bending the tang on the float arm.

NOTE
On all carburetors both float chambers must be at the same height.

6. If the float level is set too high, the result will be a rich fuel/air mixture. If it is set too low the mixture will be too lean.

7. Reassemble and install the carburetor.

Needle Jet Adjustment

The position of the needle jet can be adjusted to affect the fuel/air mixture for medium throttle openings.

The top of the carburetor must be removed for this adjustment. It is easier to perform this procedure with the fuel tank removed but it can be accomplished with it in place.

1. Unscrew the carburetor top cap (**Figure 33**) and pull the throttle valve assembly up and out of the carburetor.

NOTE
Prior to removing the top cap, thoroughly clean the area around it so no dirt will fall into the carburetor.

2. Withdraw the spring (**Figure 34**) out of the throttle valve assembly.

3. Remove the clip (**Figure 35**) securing the throttle cable in place. Slide the cable out and remove the throttle valve assembly.

4. Remove the 2 screws (**Figure 36**) securing the needle jet to the connector and remove it.

5. Slide the needle jet out of the connector and note the position of the clip. Raising the needle (lowering the clip) will enrich the mixture during mid-throttle opening, while lowering it (raising the clip) will lean the mixture. Refer to **Figure 37**.

6. Refer to **Table 1** for standard clip position for all models.

7. Reassemble and install the top cap.

Pilot Screw and Idle Speed Adjustment

Before starting this procedure the air cleaner must be clean, otherwise this procedure cannot be done properly.

1. Turn the pilot air screw (**Figure 38**) in until it lightly seats.

2. Back it out the following number of turns:
   a. YZ465H, G: 1-1/2 turns
   b. YZ400F: 1-3/4 turns
   c. YZ400E, D: 1-1/2 turns
   d. YZ400C: 1 turn
   e. YZ250G: 2 turns
   f. YZ175C: 1-1/2 turns
   g. YZ250H, F, E, D, C: 1-1/2 turns
   h. YZ125G, F, C: 1-1/2 turns
   i. YZ125E: 1-3/4 turns
   j. YZ125D, X: 1 turn
   k. YZ100H, G, F, E, D, C: 1-1/2 turns

3. Start the engine and let it reach normal operating temperature.

4. Loosen the locknut and turn the idle stop screw (**Figure 39**) in or out to achieve the desired idle speed. This speed should be set to your own personal preference.

5. Turn the pilot air screw in or out to achieve the highest engine rpm.

6. Turn the idle stop screw in or out again to achieve the desired idle speed. Tighten the locknut (**Figure 39**).

NOTE
After this adjustment is completed, test ride the bike. Throttle response from idle should be rapid and without any hesitation. If there is any hesitation, turn the pilot air screw in or out in 1/4 turn increments until this problem is solved.

WARNING
With the engine idling, move the handlebar from side to side. If idle speed increases during this movement, the throttle cable needs adjusting or it may be incorrectly routed through the frame. Correct this problem immediately. Do not ride the bike in this unsafe condition.

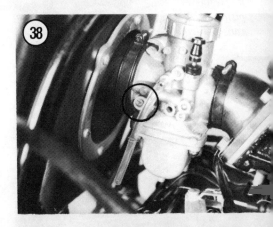

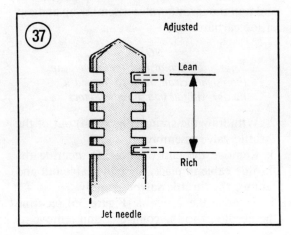

Jet needle

High Elevation Adjustment
(Main Jet Replacement)

If the bike is going to be raced or ridden for any sustained period of time at high elevations (above 5,000 feet—1,500 m), the main jet should be changed to a one-step smaller jet; never change the jet by more than one size at a time without test riding the bike and running a spark plug test. Refer to *Reading Spark Plugs* in Chapter Three.

The carburetor is set with the standard jet for normal sea level conditions. But if the bike is run at higher elevation or under heavy load—deep sand or mud—the main jet should be replaced or it will run too rich and carbon up quickly.

> *CAUTION*
> *If the bike has been rejetted for high elevation operation (smaller jet), it must be changed back to the standard main jet if it is ridden at elevation below 5,000 ft. (1,500 m). Engine overheating and piston seizure will occur if the engine runs too lean with the smaller jet.*

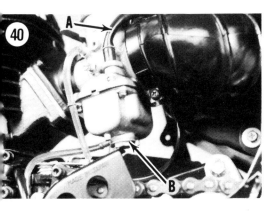

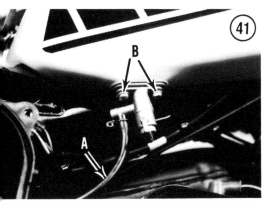

Refer to **Table 1**, at the end of this chapter, for standard main jet size.

1. Turn the fuel shutoff valve to the OFF position and disconnect the fuel line from the carburetor (A, **Figure 40**).
2. Loosen the 2 screws on the clamping bands on each side of the carburetor; pivot the carburetor to one side.
3. Loosen the main jet cover (B, **Figure 40**).

> *WARNING*
> *Place a metal container under the cover to catch the fuel that will flow out. Do not let it drain out onto the engine or the bike's frame as it presents a real fire danger. DO NOT PERFORM THIS PROCEDURE WITH A HOT ENGINE. Dispose of the fuel properly; wipe up any that may have spilled on the bike and the floor.*

4. Remove the main jet cover.
5. The main jet is directly under the cover; remove it and replace it with a different one—remember only one jet size at a time.
6. Install the main jet cover; tighten it securely.
7. Pivot the carburetor back to its original position; make sure it indexes into the slot in the rubber intake tube.
8. Tighten the clamping band screws and reinstall the carburetor fuel line.

FUEL SHUTOFF VALVE

Removal/Installation

1. Turn the fuel shutoff valve to the OFF position and remove the flexible fuel line to the carburetor (A, **Figure 41**).
2. Place the loose end into a clean, sealable, metal container. This fuel can be reused if kept clean.
3. Open the valve to the ON position and remove the fuel filler cap. This will allow air to enter the tank and speed up the flow of fuel. Drain the tank completely.
4. Remove the screws (B, **Figure 41**) securing the fuel shutoff valve to the tank and remove it.
5. After removing the valve, insert a corner of a clean shop rag into the opening in the tank to stop the dribbling of fuel onto the engine and frame.

6. Remove the screw above the handle and disassemble the valve. Clean all parts in solvent with a medium soft toothbrush, then dry. Check the condition of the small O-ring within the valve and the O-ring gasket; replace if they are starting to deteriorate or get hard. Make sure the spring is not broken or getting soft; replace if necessary.

7. Reassemble the valve and install it on the tank. Don't forget the O-ring gasket between the valve and the tank.

FUEL TANK

Removal/Installation

1. Place a milk crate or wood block(s) under the frame to support it securely.

2. Turn the fuel shutoff valve to the OFF position (**Figure 42**) and remove the fuel line to the carburetor.

3. Remove the seat.

4. Pull the fuel fill cap vent tube free from the steering head area (A, **Figure 43**).

5. Remove the bolts (B, **Figure 43**) securing the front of the fuel tank. Pull up and unhook the strap (C, **Figure 43**) securing the rear of the tank. Pull the tank toward the rear and remove it.

FUEL FILTER

The Yamaha YZ is not fitted with a fuel filter, not even in the shutoff valve as on some bikes. Due to dirt and residue that is found in today's "more expensive" gasoline it is a good idea to install an inline fuel filter to help keep the carburetor clean.

A good quality inline fuel filter (A.C.—GF453 or equivalent) is available at most auto and/or motorcycle supply stores. Just cut the flexible fuel line from the fuel tank to the carburetor and install it. You may have to cut out a section of the fuel line the length of the filter, so the fuel line does not get kinked and restrict fuel flow.

EXHAUST SYSTEM

The exhaust system on a 2-stroke motorcycle engine is much more than a means of routing the exhaust gases to the rear of the bike. It's a vital performance component and

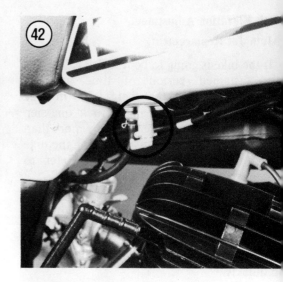

frequently, because of its design, it is a vulnerable piece of equipment. Check the exhaust system for deep dents and fractures and repair them as described under *Exhaust System Repairs* at the end of this chapter. Check the expansion chamber frame mounting flanges for fractures and loose bolts and bushings. Check the cylinder mounting flange or collar for tightness. A loose headpipe connection will not only rob the engine of power, it could also damage the piston and cylinder.

The exhaust system on the YZ consists of an exhaust pipe assembly (head pipe and expansion chamber) and a silencer. This system varies slightly with different models and

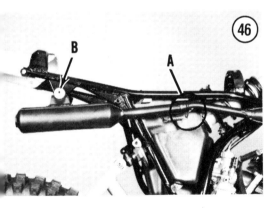

years. All attachments and springs are basically the same but they all vary a little. This procedure shows 2 different models—one on the right-hand side and the other on the left.

Removal/Installation

1. Remove the seat, fuel tank, and the side cover/number plate next to the exhaust pipe side (**Figure 44**).

2. Place the bike on a milk crate or wood blocks to support it securely.

3. To remove the silencer, loosen the clamping screws (A, **Figure 45**) or springs (A, **Figure 46**) securing the silencer to the exhaust pipe assembly.

4. Remove the bolt and washer (B, **Figure 45** or B, **Figure 46**) and remove the silencer.

5. Loosen the bolts and washers (**Figure 47**) securing the expansion chamber to the frame.

6. Use Vise Grips and remove the springs (**Figure 48** or **49**) securing the head pipe to the cylinder exhaust port.

7. Remove the bolts and washers loosened in Step 5 and remove the exhaust pipe assembly.

8. Inspect the condition of the gaskets at all joints; replace as necessary.

9. Install the exhaust pipe assembly into position and install the frame bolts and washers only finger-tight at this time until the head pipe springs are installed. This will minimize an exhaust leak at the cylinder.

10. Install the head pipe springs using Vise Grips. The springs on some models are under a lot of tension during installation—protect yourself accordingly. Make sure the head pipe inlet is correctly seated in the exhaust port.

11. Tighten the frame bolts securely.

12. Install the silencer and tighten the clamps securely or install the springs. Tighten the frame bolt(s) securely.

13. Install the fuel tank, seat and side cover/number plate.

14. After installation is complete, make sure there is no exhaust leak.

EXHAUST SYSTEM DECARBONIZING

Refer to Chapter Three for complete details on engine and exhaust system decarbonization.

EXHAUST SYSTEM REPAIR

A dent in the headpipe or expansion chamber of a 2-stroke exhaust system will alter the system's flow characteristics and degrade performance. Minor damage can be easily repaired if you have welding equipment, some simple body tools and a bodyman's slide hammer.

Small Dents

1. Drill a small hole in the center of the dent Screw the end of the slide hammer into the hole.

2. Heat the area around the dent evenly with a torch.

3. When the dent is heated to a uniform orange-red color, operate the slide hammer to raise the dent.

4. When the dent is removed, unscrew the slide hammer and weld or braze the drilled hole closed.

Large Dents

Large dents that are not crimped can be removed with heat and a slide hammer as previously described. However, several holes must be drilled along the center of the dent so that it can be pulled out evenly.

If the dent is sharply crimped along the edges, the affected section should be cut out with a hacksaw, straightened with a body dolly and hammer and welded back into place.

Before cutting the exhaust pipe apart, scribe alignment marks over the area where the cuts will be made to aid correct alignment when the pipe is rewelded.

After the welding is completed, wire brush and clean up all welds. Paint the entire pipe with a high-temperature paint to prevent rusting.

Table 1 CARBURETOR SPECIFICATIONS

	YZ465G	YZ400F	YZ400E YZ400D
Model No.	VM38ss	VM38ss	VM38ss
I.D. mark	3R500	2X500	1W400
Main jet	400	420	370
Needle jet	Q-2	Q-4	Q-0
Pilot jet	50	85	60
Jet needle	6F16	6F8	6F16
Clip position	2	2	3
Float level	1.06 in.	0.71 in.	0.71 in.
	(27 mm)	(18.1 mm)	(18.1 mm)
	YZ400C	**YZ250G**	**YZ250F**
Model No.	VM38ss	VM38ss	VM38ss
I.D. mark	51001	3R400	2X400
Main jet	380	370	400
Needle jet	P-4	P-8	Q-0
Pilot jet	60	60	50
Jet needle	6F16	6F8	6F16
Clip position	3	3	4
Float level	0.71 in.	1.06 in.	0.71 in.
	(18.1 mm)	(27 mm)	(18.1 mm)
	YZ250E	**YZ250D**	**YZ250C**
Model No.	VM38ss	VM38ss	VM38ss
I.D. mark	2K700	1W300	50903
Main jet	380	360	390
Needle jet	Q-0	P-6	Q-0
Pilot jet	60	60	60
Jet needle	6F16	6F15	6F16
Clip position	3	2	3
Float level	0.71 in.	0.71 in.	0.71 in.
	(18.1 mm)	(18.1 mm)	(19.1 mm)
	YZ175C	**YZ125G**	**YZ125F**
Model No.	VM34ss	VM32ss	VM32ss
I.D. mark	1L800	3R300	2X300
Main jet	380	300	320
Needle jet	P-8	P-8	P-8
Pilot jet	60	60	60
Jet needle	6F15	6F22	6F22
Clip position	3	3	3
Float level	0.93 in.	0.93 in.	0.93 in.
	(23.5 mm)	(23.5 mm)	(23.5 mm)

(continued)

6

Table 1 CARBURETOR SPECIFICATIONS (continued)

	YZ125E	YZ125D	YZ125C
Model No.	VM32ss	VM32ss	VM30ss
I.D. mark	2K600	1W101	53700
Main jet	280	270	210
Needle jet	P-8	P-8	P-4
Pilot jet	60	60	60
Jet needle	6F22	6F22	6DP1
Clip position	3	3	3
Float level	1.44 in.	0.93 in.	0.59 in.
	(36.5 mm)	(23.5 mm)	(15 mm)
	YZ125X	**YZ100G**	**YZ100F**
Model No.	VM34ss	VM32ss	VM32ss
I.D. mark	1G800	3R300	2X300
Main jet	310	300	320
Needle jet	P-8	P-8	P-8
Pilot jet	60	60	50
Jet needle	6F15	6F22	6F22
Clip position	2	3	3
Float level	0.93 in.	0.65 in.	0.65 in.
	(23.5 mm)	(16.4 mm)	(16.4 mm)
	YZ100E	**YZ100D**	**YZ100C**
Model No.	VM30ss	VM32ss	VM30ss
I.D. mark	2K500	1W101	1J400
Main jet	190	270	190
Needle jet	Q-2	P-8	Q-2
Pilot jet	40	60	40
Jet needle	6DP10	6F22	6DP10
Clip position	2	3	3
Float level	0.65 in.	0.65 in.	0.65 in.
	(16.4 mm)	(16.4 mm)	(16.4 mm)

NOTE: If you own a 1981 or later model, first check the Supplement at the back of the book for any new service information.

CHAPTER SEVEN

ELECTRICAL SYSTEM

The electrical system on the Yamaha YZ consists only of an ignition circuit. This consists of a magneto, CDI unit, ignition coil and a spark plug. The type of magneto varies with the different models and years. The larger displacement models have the outer rotor type which allows for a heavier flywheel, while the smaller displacement models have the inner rotor type. Both types operate the same way in generating electricity.

Table 1 is at the end of the chapter.

CAPACITOR DISCHARGE IGNITION

All models are equipped with a capacitor discharge ignition (CDI) system. This solid state system, unlike conventional ignition systems, uses no breaker points or other moving parts.

Alternating current from the magneto is rectified and used to charge the capacitor. As the piston approaches the firing position, a pulse from the pulser coil is rectified, shaped, and then used to trigger the silicone controlled rectifier. This in turn allows the capacitor to discharge quickly into the primary circuit of the ignition coil, where the voltage is stepped up in the secondary circuit to a value sufficient to fire the spark plug.

CDI Cautions

Certain measures must be taken to protect the capacitor discharge system. Instantaneous damage to the semiconductors in the system will occur if the following precautions are not observed.

1. Never disconnect any of the electrical connections while the engine is running.
2. Keep all connections between the various units clean and tight. Be sure that the wiring connectors are pushed together firmly to help keep out moisture.
3. Do not substitute another type of ignition coil.
4. The CDI unit is mounted within a rubber vibration isolator. Always be sure that the isolator is in place when replacing the unit.

CDI Troubleshooting

Problems with the capacitor discharge system fall into one of the following categories. See **Table 1**.
  a. Weak spark
  b. No spark

CDI Testing

Tests may be performed on the CDI unit but a good one may be damaged by someone unfamiliar with the test equipment. To play it safe, have the test made by a Yamaha dealer or substitute a known good unit for a suspected one.

The CDI unit is located either along side the steering head (**Figure 1**) or under the seat (**Figure 2**). This location varies with different models and years.

SPARK PLUG

The spark plug recommended by the factory is usually the most suitable for your machine. If riding conditions (other than racing) are mild, it may be advisable to go to a spark plug one step hotter than normal. Unusually severe riding conditions may require a slightly colder plug. See Chapter Three for details.

MAGNETO—OUTER ROTOR (TYPE I)

The Type I magneto is found in the following models:
YZ465G
YZ400F, E, D, C

Rotor Removal/Installation

Refer to **Figure 3** for this procedure.
1. Place a milk crate or wood block(s) under the frame to support it securely.
2. Turn the fuel shutoff valve (**Figure 4**) to the OFF position and remove the fuel line to the carburetor.
3. Remove the seat.
4. Remove the bolts (**Figure 5**) securing the front of the fuel tank. Pull up and unhook the strap (**Figure 6**) securing the rear of the tank. Pull the tank toward the rear and remove it.
5. Remove the shift lever (A, **Figure 7**) and the magneto cover (B, **Figure 7**).
6. Remove the nut (**Figure 8**) securing the magneto rotor (flywheel) in place.

> *NOTE*
> *If necessary use a strap wrench (**Figure** 9) to keep the rotor from turning while removing the nut.*

7. Remove the lockwasher and plain washer.
8. Screw in a flywheel puller (**Figure 10**) until it stops. Use the Yamaha puller (part No.

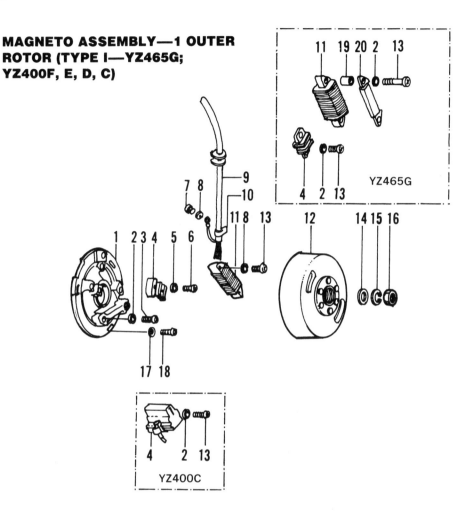

MAGNETO ASSEMBLY—1 OUTER ROTOR (TYPE I—YZ465G; YZ400F, E, D, C)

YZ465G

YZ400C

1. Base plate
2. Washer
3. Bolt
4. Pulser coil
5. Lockwasher
6. Screw
7. Screw
8. Lockwasher
9. Electrical wire harness
10. Clamp
11. Source coil
12. Lockwasher
13. Screw
14. Washer
15. Lockwasher
16. Rotor nut
17. Lockwasher
18. Screw
   Items listed below for YZ465G only
19. Spacer
20. Source coil

7

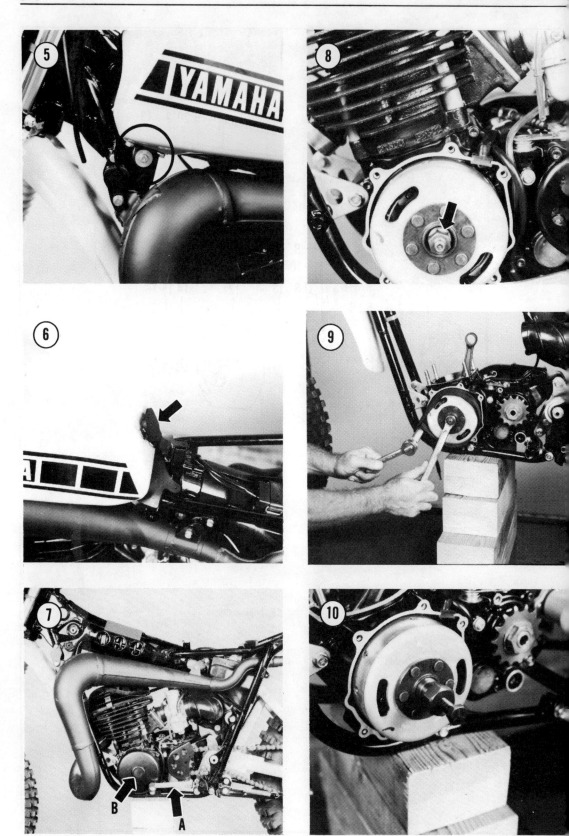

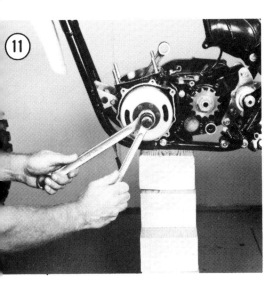

90890-01189), or a K & N puller (part No. T-100/1) or equivalent.

CAUTION
Many aftermarket types of pullers are available from most motorcycle dealers. The cost of these pullers is about $10 and they make an excellent addition to any mechanic's tool box. If you can't buy or borrow one, have a dealer remove the rotor. Don't try to remove the rotor without a puller; any attempt to do so will ultimately lead to some form of damage to the engine and/or rotor.

9. Hold the puller with a wrench and gradually tighten the center bolt (**Figure 11**) until the rotor disengages from the crankshaft.

NOTE
If the flywheel is difficult to remove, strike the puller center bolt with a hammer a few times. This will usually break it loose.

CAUTION
If normal rotor removal attempts fail, do not force the puller as the threads may be stripped out of the rotor causing expensive damage. Take it to a Yamaha dealer and have them remove it.

10. Remove the rotor and puller. Don't lose the Woodruff key on the crankshaft.

CAUTION
Carefully inspect the inside of the rotor for small bolts, washers or other metal "trash" that may have been picked up by the magnets. These small metal bits can cause severe damage to the magneto stator plate components.

11. Install by reversing these removal steps, noting the following.
12. Make sure the Woodruff key (**Figure 12**) is in place and align the keyway in the rotor with the key when installing the rotor.
13. Be sure to install the flat washer and lockwasher (**Figure 13**) prior to installing the rotor nut.
14. Tighten the rotor nut to specifications. See **Table 2**.

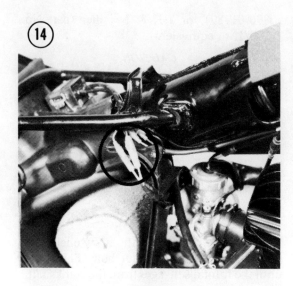

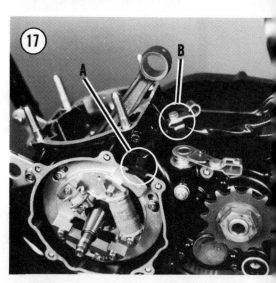

Stator Assembly
Removal/Installation

1. Remove the magneto rotor as previously described.

2. Disconnect the electrical wire connectors (**Figure 14**) from the magneto to the CDI unit.

3. Prior to removing the stator assembly, make a mark on the crankcase just above the timing mark (**Figure 15**) on the backing plate. This will assure correct ignition timing when the assembly is installed (providing it was correct prior to removal).

4. Remove the screws (**Figure 16**) securing the stator plate.

5. Carefully pull the electrical harness out along with the rubber grommet (A, **Figure 17**) from the crankcase and any holding clips (B, **Figure 17**) on the engine.

6. Remove the stator assembly.

7. Install by reversing these removal steps, noting the following.

8. When installing the stator assembly align the mark made in Step 3 for preliminary ignition timing.

9. Route the electrical wire the same way it was. Make sure to keep it away from the exhaust system.

10. Adjust the ignition timing as described in Chapter Three.

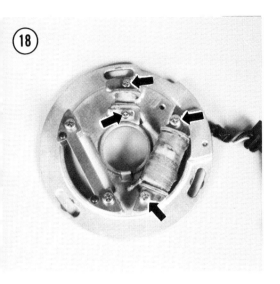

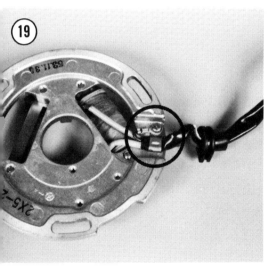

Charge and Pulser Coil Replacement

1. Remove the magneto stator assembly as previously described.

2. Remove the screws (**Figure 18**) securing the charge and pulser coils to the stator plate.

3. Turn the stator plate over and disconnect the screw (**Figure 19**) securing the clip and the ground connector.

4. Carefully remove the coils and wire harness.

5. Install by reversing these removal steps.

6. Make sure all electrical connections are tight and free from corrosion. This is absolutely necessary with a CDI ignition system.

MAGNETO—INNER ROTOR (TYPE II, III, IV)

The Type II magneto (**Figure 20**) is found in the following models:
  YZ250G, F, E
  YZ125G, F, E
  YZ100G, F

The Type III magneto (**Figure 21**) is found in the following models:
  YZ250C, D
  YZ175C
  YZ100E, D, C
  YZ125X

The Type IV magneto (**Figure 22**) is found in the the YZ125C.
  YZ360B
  YZ250B
  YZ125C

Rotor Removal/Installation

All of the inner rotor magnetos are basically the same even though minor variations exist between different models and years. This procedure is shown with a Type II magneto on a YZ125G.

1. Place a milk crate or wood block(s) under the frame to support it securely.

2. Remove the seat.

3. Turn the fuel shutoff valve to the OFF position and remove the fuel line to the carburetor.

4. Remove the bolts (**Figure 23**) securing the front of the fuel tank. Pull up and unhook the strap securing the rear of the tank. Pull the tank toward the rear and remove it.

5. Remove the shift lever (A, **Figure 24**), the magneto cover (B, **Figure 24**), and drive chain cover (C, **Figure 24**).

6. Remove the drive chain as described under *Drive Chain Removal/Installation* in Chapter Nine.

7. Shift the transmission into 4th gear.

NOTE
*To keep the rotor from turning while removing the nut, install a special tool (**Figure 26**) on the driven sprocket. The*

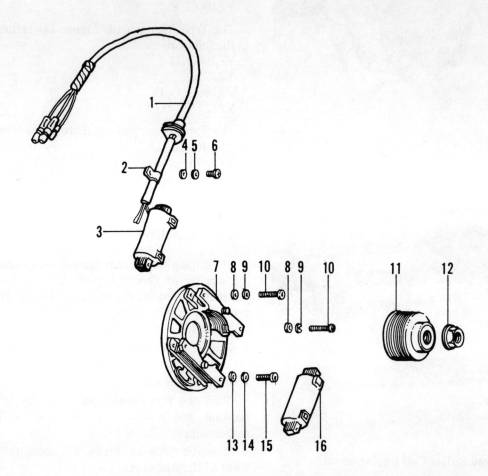

MAGNETO ASSEMBLY—INNER ROTOR
(TYPE II—YZ250G, F, E; YZ125G, F, E; YZ100G, F)

1. Electrical wire harness
2. Clip
3. Charge coil No. 2
4. Washer
5. Lockwasher
6. Screw
7. Baseplate
8. Washer
9. Lockwasher
10. Screw
11. Inner rotor
12. Rotor nut
13. Washer
14. Lockwasher
15. Screw
16. Charge coil No. 1

(21)

MAGNETO ASSEMBLY—INNER ROTOR
(TYPE III—YZ250D, C; YZ175C; YZ125X; YZ100E, D, C)

7

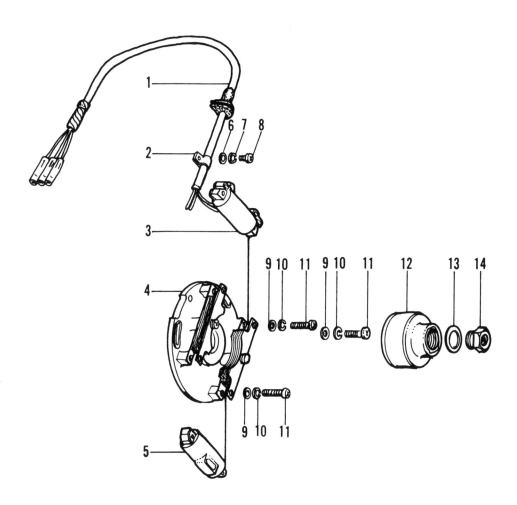

1. Electrical wire harness
2. Clip
3. Charge coil No. 2
4. Base plate
5. Charge coil No. 1
6. Washer
7. Lockwasher
8. Screw
9. Washer
10. Lockwasher
11. Screw
12. Inner rotor
13. Washer
14. Rotor nut

㉒

MAGNETO ASSEMBLY—INNER ROTOR
(TYPE IV—YZ125C)

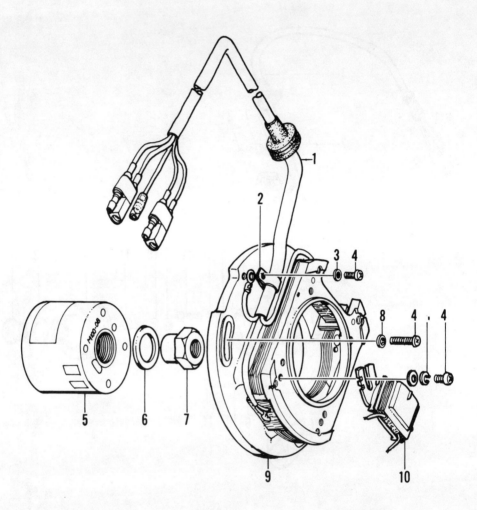

1. Electrical wire harness
2. Clip
3. Lockwasher
4. Screw
5. Inner rotor
6. Washer
7. Rotor nut
8. Lockwasher
9. Base plate
10. Pulser coil

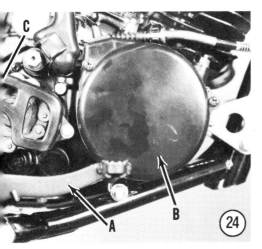

a. Type II and III—part No. 2K7-85555-00
b. Type IV—part No. 90109-20405-00

CAUTION

Many aftermarket types of pullers are available from most motorcycle dealers. The cost of these pullers is about $10 and they make an excellent addition to any mechanic's tool box. If you can't buy or borrow one, have a dealer remove the rotor. Don't try to remove the rotor without a puller; any attempt to do so will ultimately lead to some form of damage to the engine and/or rotor.

special tool is called the "Grabbit" (part No. 969103) and is available from Precision Manufacturing and Sales Co., P.O. Box 149, Clearwater, FL 33517.

Screw in a flywheel puller until it stops. Use uller with a 18 mm X 1.5 thread pitch or a naha puller as follows:

10. Gradually tighten the puller (**Figure 27**) until the rotor disengages from the crankshaft.

7

Tap the end of the wrench with your hand or rubber mallet to break it loose.

> *NOTE*
> *If the flywheel is difficult to remove, strike the puller center bolt with a hammer a few times. This will usually break it loose.*

> *CAUTION*
> *If normal rotor removal attempts fail, do not force the puller as the threads may be stripped out of the rotor causing expensive damage. Take it to a Yamaha dealer and have them remove it.*

11. Remove the rotor and puller. Don't lose the Woodruff key on the crankshaft.

> *CAUTION*
> *Carefully inspect the rotor for small bolts, washers or other metal "trash" that may have been picked up by the magnets. These small metal bits can cause severe damage to the magneto stator assembly.*

12. Install by reversing these removal steps, noting the following.

13. Make sure the Woodruff key (**Figure 28**) is in place and align the keyway in the rotor with the key when installing the rotor.

14. Be sure to install the flat washer on Type III and IV models prior to installing the rotor nut.

15. Tighten the rotor nut to the specifications in **Table 2**.

Stator Assembly
Removal/Installation

1. Remove the magneto rotor as previously described.

2. Disconnect the electrical wire connectors (**Figure 29**) from the magneto to the CDI unit.

3. Prior to removing the stator assembly, make a mark on the stator base plate that lines up with the center line of each of the attachment screws. This will assure correct ignition timing when the assembly is installed (providing it was correct prior to removal).

4. Remove the screws (**Figure 30**) securing the stator plate.

5. Carefully pull the electrical harness out along with the rubber grommet (A, **Figure 31**) from the crankcase and any holding clips (B, **Figure 31**) on the engine.

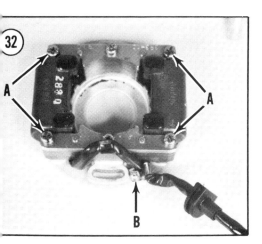

6. Remove the stator assembly.

7. Install by reversing these removal steps, noting the following.

8. When installing the stator assembly align the mark made in Step 3 for preliminary ignition timing.

9. Route the electrical wire the same way it was. Make sure to keep it away from the exhaust system.

10. Adjust the ignition timing as described in Chapter Three.

Charge Coil Replacement

1. Remove the magneto stator assembly as previously described.

2. Remove the screws (A, **Figure 32**) securing each of the charge coils to the stator plate.

3. Remove the screw (B, **Figure 32**) securing the clip.

4. Carefully remove the coils and wire harness.

5. Install by reversing these removal steps.

6. Make sure all electrical connections are tight and free from corrosion. This is absolutely necessary with a CDI ignition system.

IGNITION COIL

**Removal/Installation
(All Models)**

1. Remove the seat and fuel tank (**Figure 33**).

2. Disconnect the electrical wires to the ignition coil.

3. Disconnect the screws securing the ignition coil to the frame and remove it; refer to **Figure 34 or 35**.

4. Install by reversing these removal steps. Make sure all electrical connectors are tight and free of corrosion.

Testing

The ignition coil is a form of transformer which develops the high voltage required to jump the spark plug gap. The only maintenance required is that of keeping the electrical connectors clean and tight, and occasionally checking to see that the coil is mounted securely.

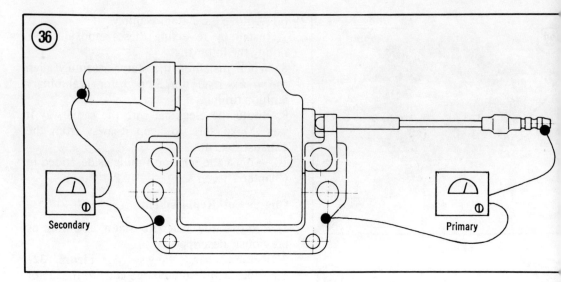

If the coil condition is doubtful, there are several checks which may be made.

First as a quick check of coil condition, disconnect the high voltage lead from the spark plug, then hold it about 1/4 in. (6 mm) away from the cylinder head.

Kick the engine over with the kickstarter. If a fat blue spark occurs the coil is in good condition; if not proceed as follows.

> *WARNING*
> *Hold the spark plug wire with an insulated screwdriver as the high voltage generated by the CDI could produce a serious or fatal shock.*

Refer to **Figure 36** for this procedure.

Disconnect the ignition coil wires before testing.

1. Measure the coil primary resistance using an ohmmeter set at R X 1. Measure the resistance between the primary terminal and the mounting flange. The value should be between 0.6-1.0 ohms +/- 10%.
2. Measure the secondary resistance, using an ohmmeter set at R X 1. Measure the resistance between the secondary lead (spark plug lead) and the mounting flange. The value should be 5.9-6.2 K ohms +/- 20%.
3. If the coil resistance does not meet these specifications, the coil must be replaced. If the coil exhibits visible damage, it should be replaced.

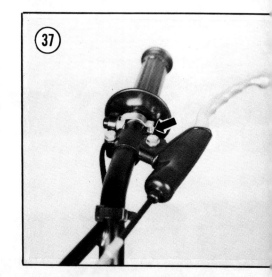

ENGINE
KILL SWITCH

Testing

1. Disconnect the electrical connectors fr the engine kill switch.
2. Use an ohmmeter set at R X 1 and conn the 2 leads of the ohmmeter to the 2 electr wires of the switch.
3. Push the kill switch button—if the switc good there will be continuity (resistance).
4. If the needle does not move continuity) the switch is faulty and must replaced. Remove the screw (**Figure** securing the switch and replace it with known good one.

Table 1 CDI TROUBLESHOOTING

Symptoms	Probable cause	Possible solution
Weak spark	Poor connections	Clean and retighten
	High voltage leak	Replace defective wire
	Defective coil	Replace ignition coil
No spark	Wiring broken	Replace wire
	Defective ignition	Replace coil
	Defective pulser coil in magneto	Replace coil

Table 2 TIGHTENING TORQUES

Item	ft.-lb.	N•m
Magneto		
Inner rotor		
YZ250, YZ400, YZ465	25	35
YZ100, YZ125	40	55
YZ175	28	40
Outer rotor	59	80

7

NOTE: If you own a 1981 or later model, first check the Supplement at the back of the book for any new service information.

CHAPTER EIGHT

FRONT SUSPENSION AND STEERING

This chapter describes repair and maintenance on the front wheel, forks, and steering components.

All models are equipped with dampened telescopic forks. The dampening rate can be changed by the viscosity of the fork oil and the spring rate can be changed by replacing the original springs with 2 different sets of factory springs that are available for most forks in the Yamaha YZ series. One additional variable is the addition of air pressure forks on some models. The combinations of all of these will permit you to choose the precise suspension feel for the conditions of the track for that day's race.

Front fork air pressure procedure and fork oil change is covered in Chapter Three.

Refer to **Table 1** for torque specifications on the front suspension. **Tables 1 and 2** are at the end of the chapter.

FRONT WHEEL

Removal/Installation

1. Place a milk crate or wood block(s) under the frame to support it securely with the front wheel off the ground.
2. Slacken the brake cable at the hand lever (**Figure 1**).

3. Slacken the brake cable at the brake pl (A, **Figure 2**) and remove the cable end (**Figure 2**) from the brake arm.
4. Remove the cotter pin and axle nut (**Figure 2**).
5. On models so equipped, loosen the fro axle pinch bolt(s). See **Figure 3**.
6. Remove the front axle from the right-ha side. Twist the axle while pulling it out.
7. Carefully pull the wheel down and forwa to disengage the brake panel from the boss the front fork.

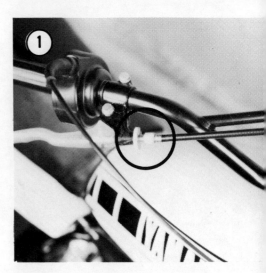

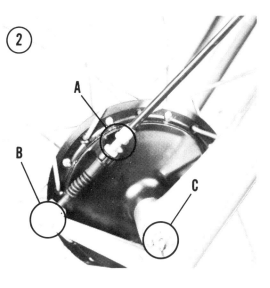

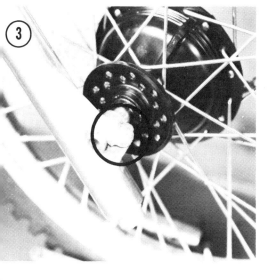

Inspection

Measure the radial and axial runout of the wheel rim with a dial indicator as shown in **Figure 4**. The standard value for both radial and axial runout is 0.02 in. (0.5 mm). The maximum permissible limit on both is 0.08 in. (2 mm).

Tighten or replace any bent or loose spokes. Refer to *Spoke Adjustment* or *Spoke Inspection and Replacement* in this chapter.

Check the axle runout as described under *Front Hub Inspection* in this chapter.

Installation

1. Make sure the axle bearing surfaces of the fork sliders and the axle are free from burrs and nicks.

2. Clean the axle and axle holders with solvent and thoroughly dry. Make sure all surfaces the axle comes in contact with are free from dirt prior to installation.

3. Apply a light coat of grease to the axle, bearings, and grease seals.

4. Position the wheel into place and insert the front axle in from the right-hand side.

NOTE
*Make sure the boss on the left-hand fork slider is properly engaged in the groove in the brake panel (**Figure 5**). This is necessary for proper brake operation.*

5. Tighten the axle nut and pinch bolt(s) — on models so equipped — to the torque values listed in **Table 1**.

8

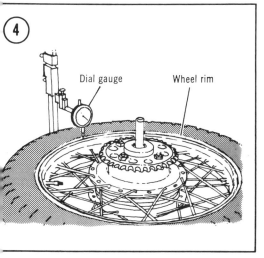

Dial gauge   Wheel rim

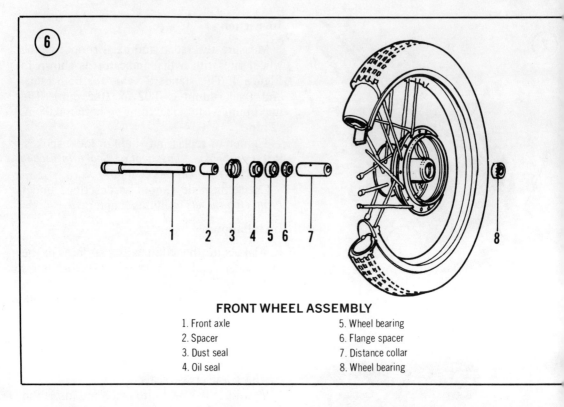

FRONT WHEEL ASSEMBLY

1. Front axle
2. Spacer
3. Dust seal
4. Oil seal
5. Wheel bearing
6. Flange spacer
7. Distance collar
8. Wheel bearing

6. Install a new cotter pin and bend it over completely.

7. Attach the front brake cable and adjust the brake as described under *Front Brake Adjustment* in Chapter Three.

8. After the wheel is installed, completely rotate it. Apply the brake several times to make sure it rotates freely and that the brake is operating correctly.

9. Remove the milk crate or wood blocks from under the frame.

FRONT HUB

Refer to **Figure 6** for this procedure.

Disassembly

1. Remove the front wheel as described under *Front Wheel Removal* in this chapter.

2. Pull the brake assembly straight up and out of the hub (**Figure 7**).

3. Remove the axle spacer (**Figure 8**) from the left-hand side.

4. Remove the dust seal (**Figure 9**).

5. Remove the right- and left-hand bearings (**Figure 10**) and distance collar. Insert a soft

aluminum or brass drift into one side of the hub. Push the distance collar over to one side and place the drift on the inner race of the lower bearing (**Figure 11**). Tap the bearing out of the hub, with a hammer, working around the perimeter of the inner race.

6. Remove the distance collar and tap out the opposite bearing.

Inspection

1. Thoroughly clean out the inside of the hub with solvent and dry with compressed air shop cloth.

NOTE
Avoid getting any greasy solvent residue on the brake drum during this procedure. If this happens, clean it off with a shop cloth and lacquer thinner.

2. Do not clean the sealed bearings. non-sealed bearings are installed, thoroughly clean them in solvent and thoroughly dry with compressed air. Do not let the bearing spin while drying.

3. Turn each bearing by hand (**Figure 12**) Make sure the bearings turn smoothly.

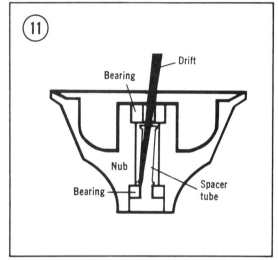

Drift

Bearing

Nub

Bearing

Spacer
tube

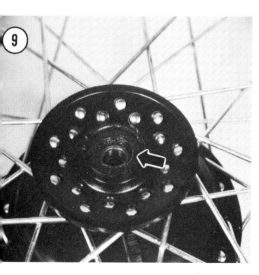

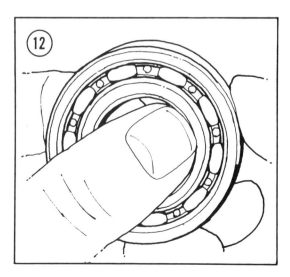

8

NOTE
Some axial play is normal, but radial play should be negligible. The bearing should turn smoothly.

4. On non-sealed bearings, check the balls for evidence of wear, pitting, or excessive heat (bluish tint). Replace bearing if necessary; always replace as a complete set. When replacing, be sure to take your old bearings along to ensure a perfect matchup.

NOTE
Fully sealed bearings are available from many good bearing specialty shops. Fully sealed bearings provide better protection from dirt and moisture that may get into the hub.

5. Check the axle for wear and straightness. Use V-blocks and a dial indicator as shown in **Figure 13**. If the runout is 0.008 in. (0.2 mm) or greater, the axle should be replaced.

Assembly

1. If cleaned, pack the bearings with a good quality bearing grease. Work the grease in between the balls thoroughly. Turn the bearing by hand a couple of times to make sure the grease is distributed evenly inside the bearing.
2. Pack the wheel hub and distance collar with multipurpose grease.
3. Install the left-hand bearing.
4. Press in the distance collar.
5. Install the right-hand bearing.

NOTE
Install the wheel bearing with the sealed side facing out.

CAUTION
*Tap the bearings squarely into place and tap on the outer race only. Use a socket (**Figure 14**) that matches the outer race diameter. Do not tap on the inner race or the bearing might be damaged. Be sure that the bearings are completely seated.*

6. Install a new grease seal. Lubricate it wi fresh multipurpose grease and tap it gent into place.
7. Install the front wheel as described und *Front Wheel Installation* in this chapter.

WHEELS

Wheels should be inspected prior to ea race or weekend ride in the boonies. This litt time spent will either help keep you in t race, or out on the trail longer on a weekend fun.

Wheel Balance

An unbalanced wheel is unsafe. Dependi on the degree of unbalance and the speed the bike, the rider may experience anythi from a mild vibration to a violent shimr which may even result in loss of control.

Balance weights are applied to the spokes the light side of the wheel to correct t condition.

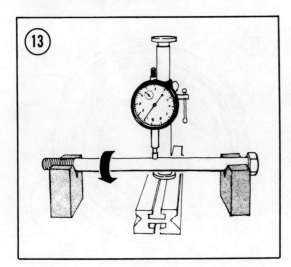

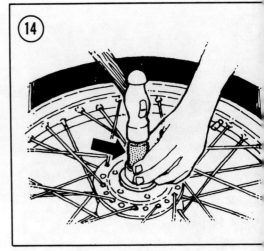

NOTE
When balancing the rear wheel do so with the final drive sprocket assembly attached as it affects the balance. The front brake panel does not rotate with the wheel so it should be removed from the front wheel.

Before you attempt to balance the wheel, check to be sure that the wheel bearings are in good condition and properly lubricated and that the brakes do not drag. The wheel must rotate freely.

. Remove the wheel as described under *Front or Rear Wheel Removal* in this chapter or Chapter Nine.

. Mount the wheel on a fixture such as the one shown in **Figure 15** so it can rotate freely.

. Give the wheel a spin and let it coast to a stop. Mark the tire at the lowest point.

. Spin the wheel several more times. If the wheel keeps coming to rest at the same point, it is out of balance.

. Attach a weight to the upper (or light) side of the wheel on the spoke (**Figure 16**). Weights come in 4 sizes: 5, 10, 15, and 20 grams. They are crimped onto the spoke with ordinary gas pliers.

. Experiment with different weights until the wheel, when spun, comes to rest at a different position each time. When this happens,

consider the wheel balanced and tighten the weights so they won't be thrown off.

Spoke Inspection and Replacement

Spokes loosen with use and should be checked prior to each race or a week end ride. The "tuning fork" method for checking spoke tightness is simple and works well. Tap each spoke with a spoke wrench or the shank of a screwdriver and listen for a tone. A tightened spoke will emit a clear, ringing tone, and a loose spoke will sound flat. All the spokes in a correctly tightened wheel will emit tones of similar pitch but not necessarily the same precise tone.

Bent or stripped spokes should be replaced as soon as they are detected, as they can cause the destruction of an expensive hub. Unscrew the nipple from the spoke and depress the nipple into the rim far enough to free the end of the spoke, taking care not to push the nipple all the way in. Remove the damaged spoke from the hub and use it to match a new spoke of identical length. If necessary, trim the new spoke to match the original and dress the end of the thread with a thread die. Install the new spoke in the hub and screw on the nipple; tighten it until the spoke's tone is similar to the tone of the other spokes in the

8

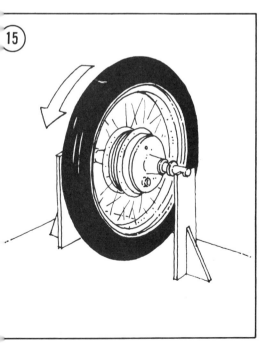

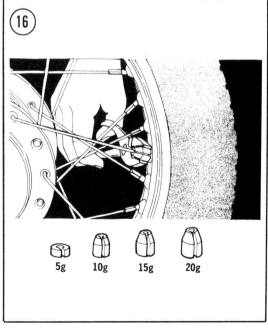

5g 10g 15g 20g

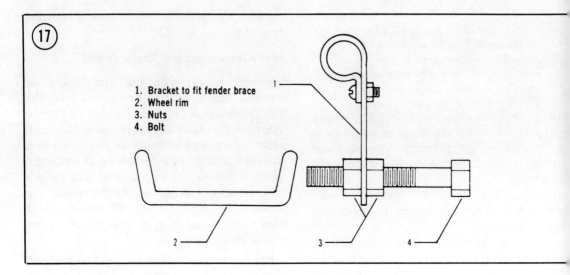

1. Bracket to fit fender brace
2. Wheel rim
3. Nuts
4. Bolt

wheel. Periodically check the new spoke; it will stretch and must be retightened several times before it takes its final set.

Spoke Adjustment

If all appear loose, tighten all spokes on one side of the hub, then tighten all spokes on the other side. One-half to one turn should be sufficient; do not overtighten.

After tightening the spokes, check rim runout to be sure you haven't pulled the rim out of shape.

One way to check rim runout is to mount a dial indicator on the front fork, or swing arm, so that it bears against the rim.

If you don't have a dial indicator, improvise one as shown in **Figure 17**. Adjust the position of the bolt until it just clears the rim. Rotate the rim and note whether the clearance increases or decreases. Mark the tire with chalk or light crayon at areas that produce significantly large or small clearance. Clearance must not change by more than 0.08 in. (2 mm).

To pull the rim out, tighten spokes which terminate on the same side of the hub and loosen spokes which terminate on opposite side of the hub (**Figure 18**). In most cases, only a slight amount of adjustment is necessary to true a rim. After adjustment, rotate the rim and make sure another area has not pulled out of true. Continue adjustment and checking until runout does not exceed 0.08 in. (2 mm).

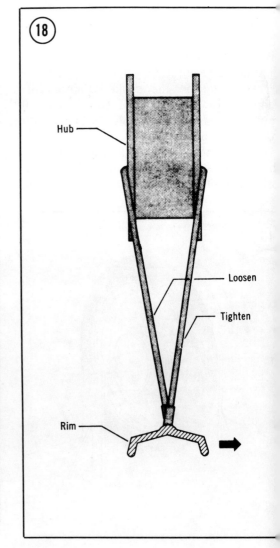

Hub

Loosen

Tighten

Rim

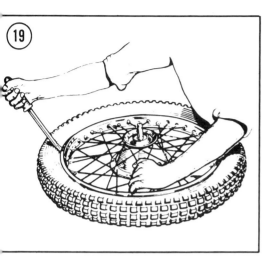

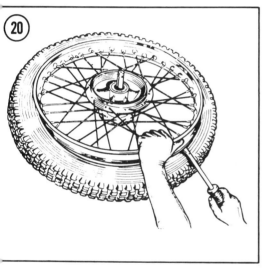

TIRE CHANGING

Removal

1. Remove the valve core and deflate the tire.
2. Press the entire bead on both sides of the tire into the center of the rim.
3. Lubricate the beads with soapy water.
4. Insert the tire iron under the bead next to the valve (**Figure 19**). Force the bead on the opposite side of tire into the center of the rim and pry the bead over the rim with the tire iron.
5. Insert a second tire iron next to the first to hold the bead over the rim. Then work around the tire with the first tire iron, prying the bead over the rim. Be careful not to pinch the inner tube with the tire irons.

6. Remove the valve from the hole in the rim and remove the tube from the tire.

NOTE
Step 7 is required only if it is necessary to completely remove the tire from the rim, such as for tire replacement.

7. Stand the tire upright. Insert the tire iron between the second bead and the side of the rim that the first bead was pried over (**Figure 20**). Force the bead on the opposite side from the tire iron into the center of the rim. Pry the second bead off of the rim, working around as with the first.

Installation

1. Carefully check the tire for any damage, especially inside. On the front tire carefully check the sidewall as it is very vulnerable to damage from rocks, motocross course stakes, and other riders footpegs.
2. A new tire may have balancing rubbers inside. These are not patches and should not be disturbed. A colored spot near the bead indicates a lighter point on the tire. This should be placed next to the valve or midway between the 2 rim locks.
3. Check that the spoke ends do not protrude through the nipples into the center of the rim to puncture the tube. File off any protruding spoke ends.
4. Be sure the rim rubber tape is in place with the rough side toward the rim.

NOTE
Refer to Chapter Twelve regarding replacing the rim rubber with duct tape and the use of a stronger heavy-duty inner tube.

5. Install the core into the inner tube valve. Put the tube in the tire and inflate just enough to round it out. Too much air will make installing it in the tire difficult, and too little will increase the chances of pinching the tube with the tire irons.
6. Lubricate the tire beads and rim with soapy water. Pull the tube partly out of the tire at the valve. Squeeze the beads together to hold the tube and insert the valve into the hole in the

rim (**Figure 21**). The lower bead should go into the center of the rim with the upper bead outside it.

7. Press the lower bead into the rim center on each side of the valve, working around the tire in both directions (**Figure 22**). Use a tire iron for the last few inches of the bead (**Figure 23**).

8. Press the upper bead into the rim opposite the valve. Pry the bead into the rim on both sides of the initial point with a tire iron, working around the rim to the valve (**Figure 24**).

9. Wiggle the valve to be sure the tube is not trapped under the bead. Set the valve squarely in it's hole before screwing on the valve nut to hold it against the rim.

10. Check the bead on both sides of the tire for even fit around the rim. Inflate the tire slowly to seat the beads in the rim. It may be necessary to bounce the tire to complete the seating. Inflate to the required pressure. Balance the wheel as described previously.

TIRE REPAIRS

This procedure is included in this chapter for the owners who do not race their YZ's but use them for off road fun only.

Every dirt rider eventually experiences trouble with a tire or tube. Repairs and replacement are fairly simple, and every rider should know the techniques.

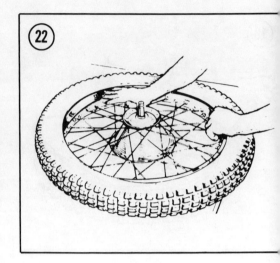

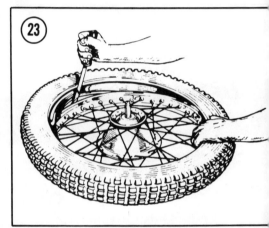

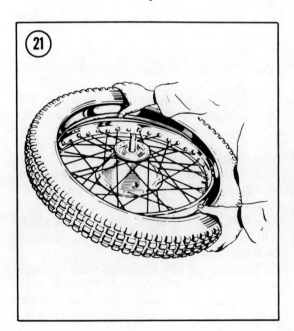

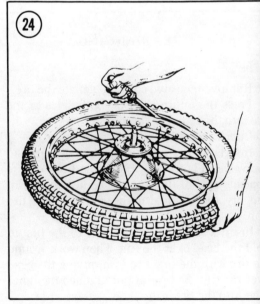

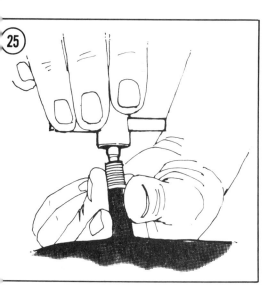

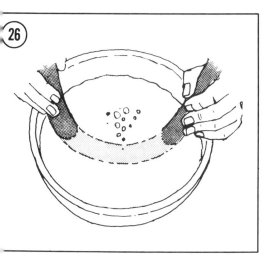

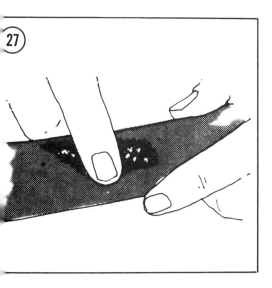

Patching a motorcycle tube is only a temporary fix, especially on a dirt bike. The tire flexes too much and the patch could rub right off. However, a patched tire will get you back to camp where you can replace the tube with the extra one that should be carried in your tool box or tow vehicle.

Tire Repair Kits

Tire repair kits can be purchased from motorcycle dealers and some auto supply stores. When buying, specify that the kit you want is for motorcycles.

There are 2 types of tire repair kits:

a. Hot patch
b. Cold patch

Hot patches are stronger because they actually vulcanize to the tube, becoming part of it. However, they are far too bulky to carry for trail repairs, and the strength is unnecessary for a temporary repair.

Cold patches are not vulcanized to the tube; they are simply glued to it. Though not as strong as hot patches, cold patches are still very durable. Cold patch kits are less bulky than hot and more easily applied under adverse conditions. A cold patch kit contains everything necessary and tucks easily in with your emergency tool kit.

Tube Inspection

1. Remove the inner tube as previously described.
2. Install the valve core into the valve stem (**Figure 25**) and inflate the tube slightly. Do not overinflate.
3. Immerse the tube in water a section at a time (**Figure 26**). Look carefully for bubbles indicating a hole. Mark each hole and continue checking until you are certain that all holes are discovered and marked. Also make sure that the valve core is not leaking; tighten it if necessary.

> *NOTE*
> *If you do not have enough water to immerse sections of the tube, try running your hand over the tube slowly and very close to the surface. If your hand is damp, it works even better. If you suspect a hole anywhere, apply some saliva to the area to verify it (**Figure 27**).*

4. Apply a cold patch using the techniques described under *Cold Patch Repair*, following.

5. Dust the patch area with talcum powder to prevent it from sticking to the tire.

6. Carefully check the inside of the tire casing for small rocks, sand or twigs which may have damaged the tube. If the inside of the tire is split, apply a patch to the area to prevent it from pinching and damaging the tube again.

7. Check the inside of the rim. Make sure the rim band (or duct tape) is in place, with no spoke ends protruding, which could puncture the tube.

8. Deflate the tube prior to installation in the tire.

Cold Patch Repairs

1. Remove the tube from the tire as previously described.

2. Roughen the area around the hole slightly larger than the patch, using a cap from the tire repair kit or pocket knife. Do not scrape too vigorously or you may cause additional damage.

3. Apply a small quantity of special cement to the puncture and spread it evenly with your finger (**Figure 28**).

4. Allow the cement to dry until tacky—usually 30 seconds or so is sufficient.

5. Remove the backing from the patch.

> *CAUTION*
> *Do not touch the newly exposed rubber with your fingers or the patch will not stick firmly.*

6. Center the patch over the hole. Hold patch firmly in place for about 30 seconds to allow the cement to set (**Figure 29**).

7. Dust the patched area with talcum powder to prevent sticking.

8. Install the tube as previously described.

HANDLEBAR

Removal/Installation

1. Remove the plastic straps on the engine kill switch wire (**Figure 30**).

2. Remove the screws securing the engine kill switch (A, **Figure 31**) and the clutch lever assembly (B, **Figure 31**) and remove them.

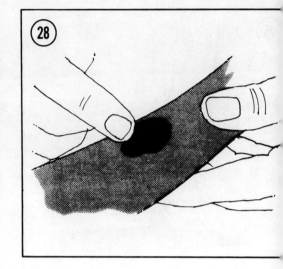

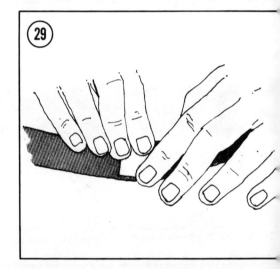

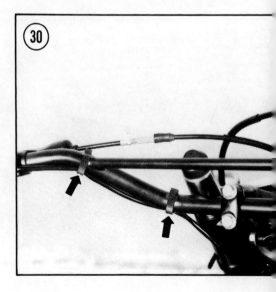

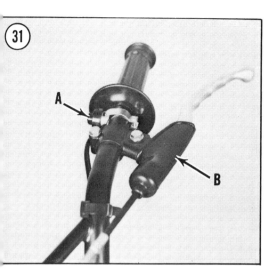

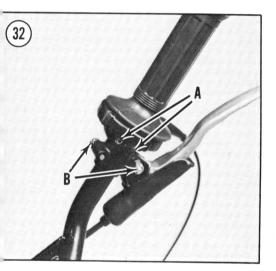

3. Remove the screws (A, **Figure 32**) securing the throttle assembly and slide it off.

NOTE
Carefully lay the throttle assembly and cable over the front fender, or back over the frame, so the cable does not get crimped or damaged.

4. Loosen the bolts (B, **Figure 32**) securing the front brake lever assembly and slide it off.

NOTE
Carefully lay the brake lever assembly and cable over the front fender, or back over the frame, so the cable does not get crimped or damaged.

5. Remove any plastic bands or number plate holder hardware from the fork.

6. Remove the bolts (**Figure 33**) securing the handlebar holders and remove them and the holders.

7. Remove the handlebar.

8. Install by reversing these removal steps noting the following.

9. To maintain a good grip in the handlebar and to prevent them from slipping down, clean the knurled section of the handlbar with a wire brush. It should be kept rough so it will be held securely by the holders. The holders should also be kept clean and free of any metal that may have been gouged loose by handlebar slippage.

10. Tighten the bolts securing the handlebar to the torque specifications listed in **Table 1**.

11. Apply a light coat of multipurpose grease to the throttle grip area on the handlebar prior to installation.

WARNING
After installation is completed, make sure the brake lever does not come in contact with the throttle grip assembly when it is pulled on fully.

12. Adjust the front brake and clutch as described in Chapter Three.

STEERING HEAD

There are 2 different types of steering head assemblies used on various models. One type uses assembled roller bearings while the other

8

uses loose balls. Refer to **Figure 34, 35, or 36** for this procedure.

One procedure is used to cover all models; where differences occur they are identified.

Disassembly

1. Remove the front wheel as described under *Front Wheel Removal* in this chapter.
2. Remove the handlebar as described under *Handlebar Removal/Installation* in this chapter.

3. Remove one fork leg as described under *Front Fork Removal/Installation* in this chapter. Leave one fork leg installed at this time.

NOTE
*Prior to removing the fork, measure and write down on a piece of masking tape attached to the fork, the distance from the top of the fork tube to the top of the upper fork bridge (**Figure 37**). This is not a standard dimension, but one derived from rider preference.*

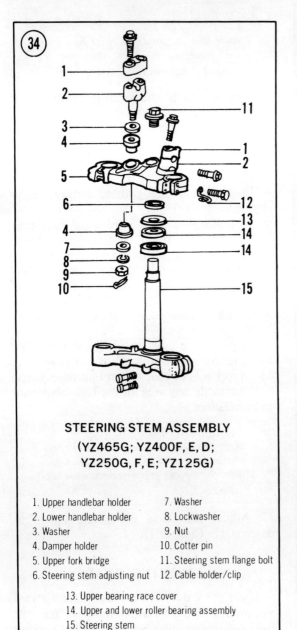

STEERING STEM ASSEMBLY (YZ465G; YZ400F, E, D; YZ250G, F, E; YZ125G)

1. Upper handlebar holder	7. Washer
2. Lower handlebar holder	8. Lockwasher
3. Washer	9. Nut
4. Damper holder	10. Cotter pin
5. Upper fork bridge	11. Steering stem flange bolt
6. Steering stem adjusting nut	12. Cable holder/clip

13. Upper bearing race cover
14. Upper and lower roller bearing assembly
15. Steering stem

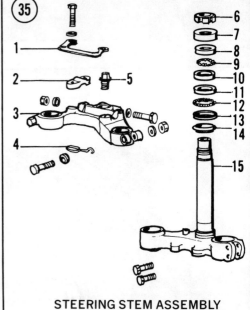

STEERING STEM ASSEMBLY (YZ400C; YZ250C; YZ125C, X; YZ100G, F, E, D, C)

1. Wire guide
2. Handlebar holder
3. Upper fork bridge
4. Cable holder/clip
5. Steering stem flange
6. Steering stem adjusting nut
7. Upper ball race cover
8. Outer ball race (upper)
9. Upper balls (3/16 in. — 22 total)
10. Inner ball race (upper)
11. Outer ball race (lower)
12. Lower balls (1/4 in. — 19 total)
13. Inner ball race (lower)
14. Dust seal
15. Steering stem

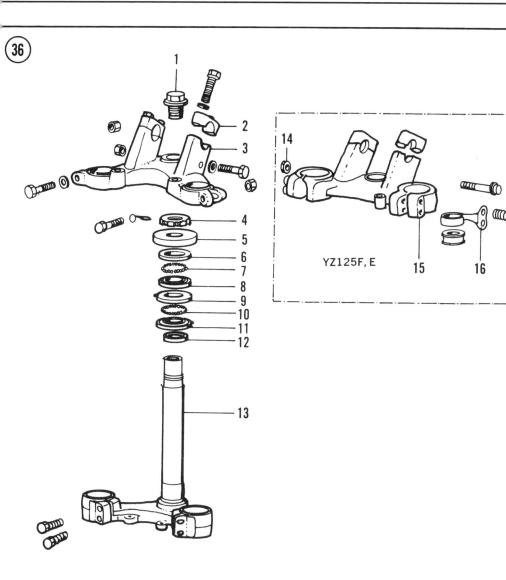

STEERING STEM ASSEMBLY
(YZ175C; YZ125F, E)

1. Steering stem flange bolt
2. Handlebar holder
3. Upper fork bridge
4. Steering stem adjusting nut
5. Upper ball race cover
6. Outer ball race (upper)
7. Upper balls (3/16 in. — 22 total)
8. Inner ball race (upper)
9. Outer ball race (lower)
10. Lower balls (1/4 in. — 19 total)
11. Inner ball race (lower)
12. Dust seal
13. Steering stem
14. Nut
15. Upper fork bridge (Model YZ125F,E)
16. Cable holder/clip

4. Loosen the upper fork bridge pinch bolt (A, **Figure 38**).

5. Loosen the steering stem flange bolt (B, **Figure 38**).

6. Remove the remaining fork leg assembly (C, **Figure 38**).

7. Remove the upper fork bridge assembly (**Figure 39**).

8. Remove the steering head adjusting nut (**Figure 40**). Use a large drift and hammer or use an easily improvised tool (**Figure 41**).

9. Lower the steering stem assembly down out of the steering head (**Figure 42**).

> *NOTE*
> *On models with loose ball bearings, have an assistant hold a large pan under the steering stem to catch the loose ball bearings and carefully lower the steering stem.*

10. On models with loose ball bearings, do not intermix the balls as they are different sizes and quantity. The upper bearing has 3/16 in. balls (quantity—22) and the lower has 1/4 in. balls (quantity—19).

11. Remove the upper bearing race cover (**Figure 43**).

12. Remove the upper roller bearing assembly (**Figure 44**) or loose ball bearings.

13. Remove the lower roller bearing assembly or loose ball bearings.

Inspection

1. Clean the bearing races in the steering head, the steering stem races, and the bearings with solvent.

2. Check the welds around the steering head for cracks and fractures. If any are found, have them repaired by a competent frame shop or welding service.

3. Check the balls or rollers for pitting, scratches, or discoloration indicating wear or corrosion. Replace them in sets if any are bad.

4. Check the races (**Figure 45**) for pitting or galling, and corrosion. If any of these conditions exist, replace the races as described under *Bearing Race Replacement* in this chapter.

5. Check the steering stem for cracks and check its race for damage or wear. If this race

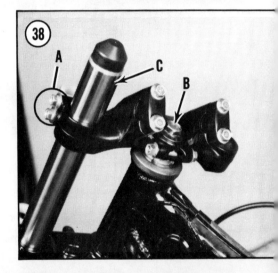

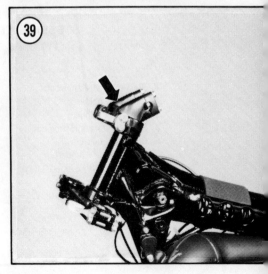

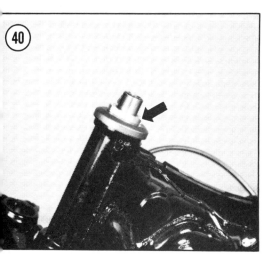

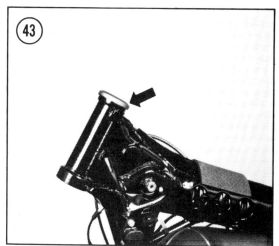

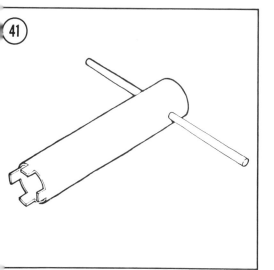

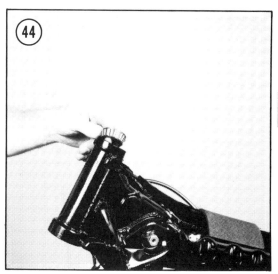

8

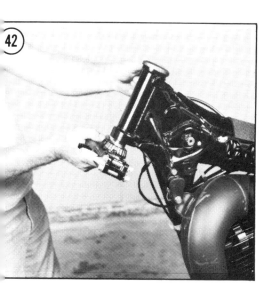

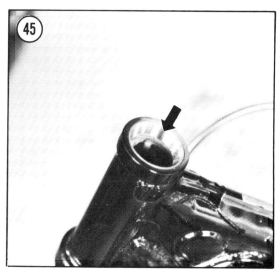

or any race is damaged, the bearings should be replaced as a complete bearing set. Take the old races and bearings to your dealer to ensure accurate replacement.

Bearing Race Replacement

The headset and steering stem bearing races are pressed into place. Because they are easily bent, do not remove them unless they are worn and require replacement.

To remove the headset race, insert a hardwood stick or soft punch into the head tube (**Figure 46**) and carefully tap the race out from the inside. To get it started there is a notch in the head tube (**Figure 47**) for the wood or punch to get a perch on the race. After it is started, tap around the race so that neither the race nor the head tube is damaged.

To install the headset race, tap it in slowly with a block of wood or suitable size socket or piece of pipe (**Figure 48**). Make sure they are squarely seated in the race bores before tapping them in. Tap them in until they are flush with the steering head.

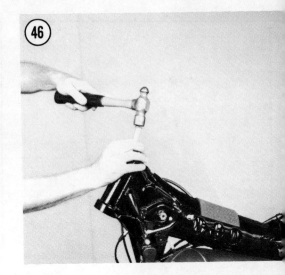

NOTE
The upper and lower bearings and races are not the same size (both the roller type and loose ball bearing type). Be sure that you install them at the proper ends of the head tube.

Steering Stem Race and Grease Seal Removal/Installation

To remove the steering stem race, try twisting and pulling it up by hand. If it will not come off, carefully pry it up with a screwdriver, while working around in a circle, prying a little at a time. Remove the race and the grease seal on models with loose ball bearings.

On models so equipped, install the grease seal. Slide the race over the steering stem with the bearing surface pointing up. Tap the race down with a piece of hardwood; work around in a circle so that the race will not be bent. Make sure it is seated squarely and all the way down.

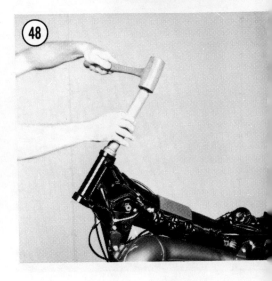

Steering Head Assembly

Refer to **Figure 34, 35, or 36** for this procedure.

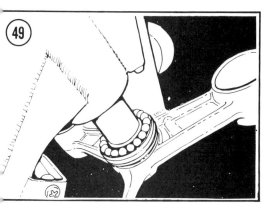

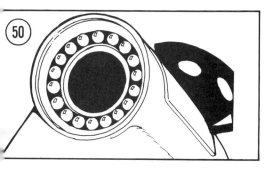

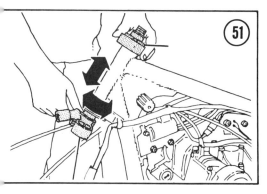

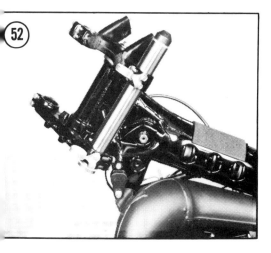

1. Make sure the steering head and stem races are properly seated.

2. On models with loose ball bearings, apply a coat of cold grease to the lower bearing race cone and fit 19 ball bearings around it (**Figure 49**).

NOTE
Remember the lower balls are the larger size—1/4 in. diameter.

3. Install the lower roller bearing assembly onto the steering stem on models so equipped.

4. On models with loose ball bearings, apply a coat of cold grease to the upper bearing race cone and fit 22 ball bearings around it (**Figure 50**).

NOTE
These are the smaller ball bearings—3/16 in. diameter.

5. Install the upper roller bearing assembly into the steering head.

6. Install the steering stem into the head tube (**Figure 42**) and hold it firmly in place.

7. Install the upper bearing race cover (**Figure 43**).

8. Install the steering stem adjusting nut (**Figure 40**) and tighten it until it is snug against the upper race, then back it off 1/8 turn.

NOTE
*The adjusting nut should be just tight enough to remove play, both horizontal and vertical (**Figure 51**), yet loose enough so that the assembly will turn to both lock positions under its own weight after an assist.*

9. Install the upper fork bridge and steering stem flange bolt—only finger-tight at this time.

NOTE
Steps 10-12 must be performed in order to assure proper upper and lower fork bridge to fork alignment.

10. Slide the fork tubes into position (**Figure 52**) and tighten the lower fork bridge bolts to the torque specifications in **Table 1**.

NOTE
Install the fork tube the same distance up from the top of the upper fork bridge; see NOTE after Step 3, Disassembly.

8

11. Tighten the steering stem flange bolt to torque specifications in **Table 1**.

12. Tighten the upper fork bridge bolts and pinch bolt to torque specifications in **Table 1**.

13. Continue assembly by reversing Steps 1-3, *Steering Stem Disassembly.*

14. After a few hours of riding, the bearings have had a chance to seat; readjust the free play in the steering stem with the steering stem adjusting nut (**Figure 53**). Refer to Step 8.

Steering Stem Adjustment

If play develops in the steering system, it may only require adjustment. However, don't take a chance on it. Disassemble the stem and look for possible damage. Then reassemble and adjust as described in Step 8, *Steering Head Assembly,* in the previous procedure.

FRONT FORK
(EXCEPT MODELS YZ400C,
YZ250C, YZ175C, YZ125X)

The fork on most Yamaha YZs have the assist of air pressure to change handling to suit any rider and track terrain. There are some precautions in regard to handling these forks that differ from the ordinary oil/spring type. The following WARNING must be adhered to for your own personal safety and that of others.

> *WARNING*
> *For pressurizing the fork use only compressed air or nitrogen. DO NOT USE ANY OTHER TYPE OF COMPRESSED GAS as an explosion may be lethal. NEVER heat the fork assembly with a torch or place it near an open flame or extreme heat as this will also result in an explosion. Always bleed off all air pressure from the forks prior to removal and disassembly.*

The front suspension is very basic in concept using a spring controlled, hydraulically damped telescopic fork plus the additional assist of air pressure. Before suspecting major trouble, drain the front

fork oil and refill with the proper type and quantity, refer to Chapter Three. If you still have trouble such as poor damping, tendency to bottom or top out, or leakage around the rubber seals, then follow the service procedures in this section.

To simplify fork service and to prevent the mixing of parts, the legs should be removed, serviced and installed individually.

Removal/nstallatiton

1. Remove the strap securing the front brake cable (**Figure 54**) to the left-hand fork.

2. Remove the front wheel as described under *Front Wheel Removal/Installation* in this chapter.

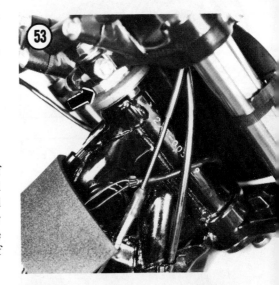

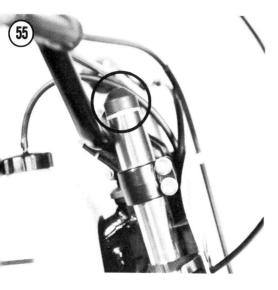

3. On models with an air assist fork, remove the top rubber cap (**Figure 55**). Remove the dust cap and *bleed off all air pressure* by depressing the valve stem.

NOTE
Release the air pressure gradually. If released too fast, oil will sprurt out with the air. Protect your eyes and clothing accordingly.

WARNING
Always bleed off all air pressure; failure to do so may cause personal injury when disassembling the fork assembly.

4. Remove the bolts securing the front fender and remove it.
5. Loosen the top cap bolt prior to removing the fork tube.
6. Loosen the upper and lower fork bridge bolts (**Figure 56**).

NOTE
*Prior to removing the fork, measure and write down on a piece of masking tape attached to the fork, the distance from the top of the fork tube to the top of the upper fork bridge (**Figure 57**). This is not a standard dimension, but one derived from rider preference.*

7. Remove the fork tube. It may be necessary to slightly rotate the fork tube while pulling it down and out.
8. Install by reversing these removal steps.
9. Install the fork tubes in the same position as noted in *Removal*, Step 6.
10. Tighten the bolts to the torque values in **Table 1**.

Disassembly

Refer to **Figure 58**. The following procedure represents a typical fork disassembly. Minor variations exist among different models and years. Pay particular attention to the location and positioning of spacers, washers and springs to make sure they are assembled in the correct location.

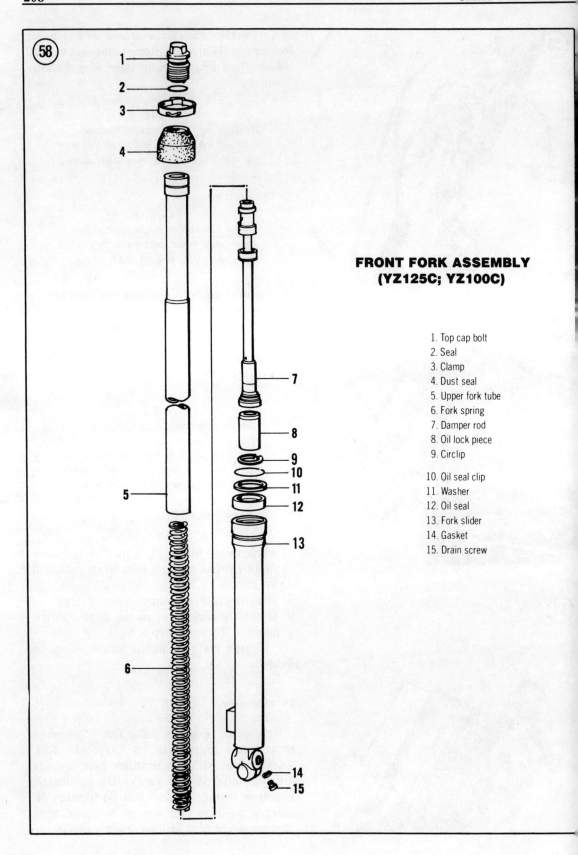

**FRONT FORK ASSEMBLY
(YZ125C; YZ100C)**

1. Top cap bolt
2. Seal
3. Clamp
4. Dust seal
5. Upper fork tube
6. Fork spring
7. Damper rod
8. Oil lock piece
9. Circlip

10. Oil seal clip
11. Washer
12. Oil seal
13. Fork slider
14. Gasket
15. Drain screw

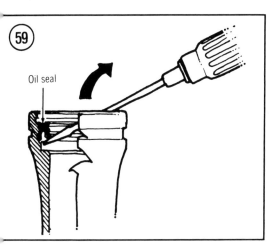

Oil seal

1. Hold the upper fork tube in a vise with soft jaws. Remove the top bolt, and spacer and spring seat (on models so equipped).
2. Remove the fork spring.
3. Remove the fork from the vise and pour the fork oil out and discard it. Pump the fork several times by hand to expel most of the remaining oil.
4. Clamp the slider in a vise with soft jaws.
5. Remove the Allen bolt and gasket from the bottom of the slider.

> *NOTE*
> *This bolt has been secured with Loctite and is very difficult to remove because the damper rod will turn inside the slider. It can be removed with an air impact driver or you just may be lucky and get it off easily. If you are unable to remove it, take the fork tubes to a dealer and have them remove the bolts.*

6. Pull the fork tube out of the slider.
7. Remove the oil lock piece, the damper rod and rebound spring.
8. If oil has been leaking from the top of the slider, remove the dust seal cover, dust seal, circlip and oil seal.

> *NOTE*
> *It may be necessary to slightly heat the area on the slider around the oil seal prior to removal.*

> *CAUTION*
> *Use a dull screwdriver blade to remove the oil seal (Figure 59). Do not damage the outer edge or inner surface of the slider.*

Inspection

1. Thoroughly clean all parts in solvent and dry. Check the fork tube for signs of wear or scratches.
2. Check the damper rod for straightness. **Figure 60** shows one method. The rod should be replaced if the runout is 0.008 in. (0.2 mm) or greater.
3. Carefully check the damper rod valve and piston (**Figure 61**) for wear or damage.
4. Inspect the oil seals for scoring and nicks and loss of resiliency. Replace if their condition is questionable.

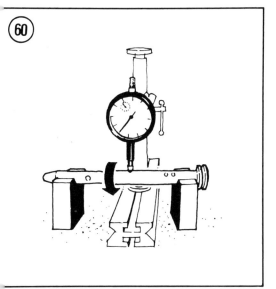

8

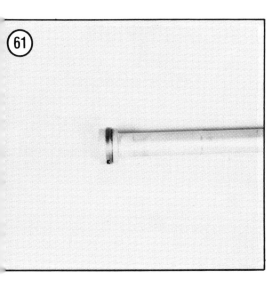

5. Check the upper fork tube for straightness. If bent or severely scratched, it should be replaced.

6. Check the lower slider for dents or exterior damage that may cause the upper fork tube to hang up during riding conditions. Replace if necessary.

7. Measure the uncompressed length of the main spring with a square as shown in **Figure 62**. The standard spring length for all models is listed in **Table 2**. Replace any spring that is about 1/2 inch shorter than these standard dimensions.

8. Any parts that are worn or damaged should be replaced. Simply cleaning and reinstalling unserviceable components will not improve performance of the front suspension.

Assembly

1. Install a new oil seal and circlip (**Figure 63**). Coat all parts with fresh fork oil prior to installation.

2. Insert the dust seal and dust seal cover (**Figure 64**).

3. Install the rebound spring onto the damper rod (on models so equipped); refer to **Figure 65**.

4. Insert them into the fork tube (**Figure 66**).

5. Temporarily install the fork spring and top cap bolt (**Figure 67**) to hold the damper rod in place.

6. Install the oil lock piece onto the damper rod (**Figure 68**) and install the upper fork assembly into the slider (**Figure 69**).

7. Make sure the gasket (**Figure 70**) is on the Allen bolt.

8. Apply Loctite Lock N' Seal to the threads of the Allen bolt prior to installation. Install it in the fork slider and tighten to specifications listed in **Table 1**.

9. Install the forks.

10. Remove the top cap bolt and spring and fill the fork tube with the correct type and quantity oil (**Figure 71**); refer to Chapter Three.

11. Install the fork spring, washer (**Figure 72**) and spacer (on models so equipped); refer to **Figure 73**.

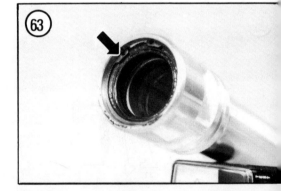

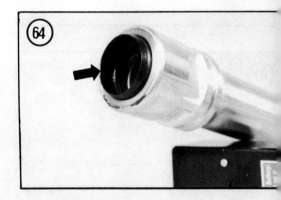

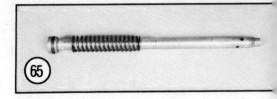

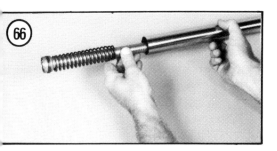

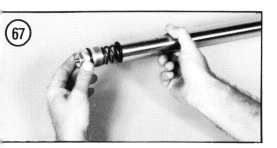

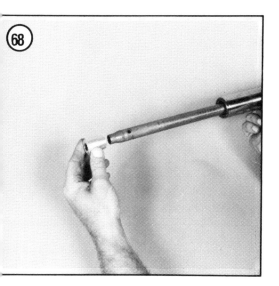

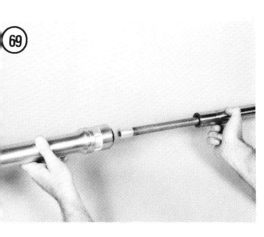

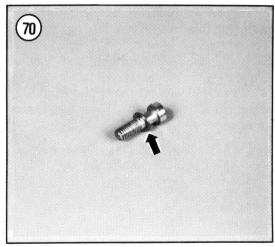

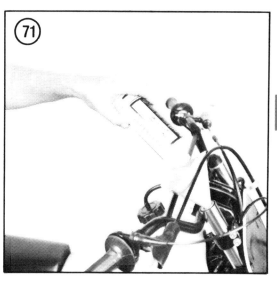

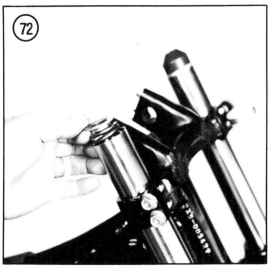

12. Inspect the condition of the O-ring seal on the top cap bolt (**Figure 74**); replace it if necessary.

13. Install the top cap bolt and tighten securely.

14. On models with air pressure assist, inflate to the correct air pressure. Refer to Chapter Three.

FRONT FORK
(MODELS YZ400C, YZ250C, YZ175C, YZ125X)

This particular fork was used only in 1976 on models YZ400C, YZ250C, YZ175C and YZ125X. This fork is quite unique in that compressed air takes the place of the typical fork spring. This was to provide unlimited tuning possibilities without the need of replacing fork springs.

There is a floating piston and a dual air pressure chamber—one low pressure and one high pressure—mounted on top of each fork (**Figure 75**). Each has its own air pressure valve. The low pressure chamber responds to small road shocks but under severe load or large road shock, the piston compresses the air in the upper or high pressure chamber for damping.

Changing fork oil and changing air pressure is different from all of the other fork assemblies—always refer to the correct procedure for your bike as outlined in Chapter Three.

There are some precautions in regard to handling this type fork that differ from the ordinary oil/spring type. The following WARNINGS must be adhered to for your own personal safety and that of others.

WARNING
For pressurizing the fork use only compressed air or nitrogen. DO NOT USE ANY OTHER TYPE OF COMPRESSED GAS as a lethal explosion could occur. NEVER heat the fork assembly with a torch or place it near an open flame or extreme heat as this will also result in an explosion. Always bleed off all air pressure from the forks prior to removal and disassembly.

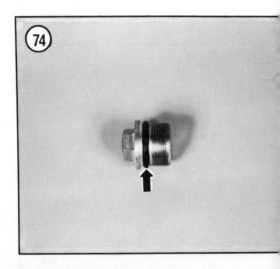

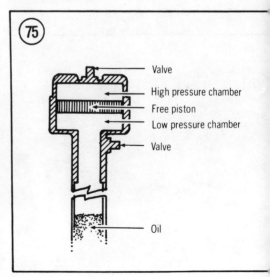

Valve

High pressure chamber

Free piston

Low pressure chamber

Valve

Oil

Removal/Installation

1. Remove the strap securing the front brake cable to the left-hand fork.

2. Remove the front wheel as described under *Front Wheel Removal/Installation* in this chapter.

3. Remove the rubber cap from the air valve on both the low and high pressure chambers. Depress the valve stem and expel all air pressure.

4. Place a drain pan under the fork and remove the drain screw (**Figure 76**). Allow the oil to drain for at least 5 minutes. *Never reuse the oil.*

> *CAUTION*
> *Do not allow the fork oil to come in contact with any of the brake components.*

5. Remove the safety wire securing each air chamber to the handebar.

6. Unscrew the air chamber from each fork.

> *WARNING*
> *Make sure all air pressure is expelled from the air chamber prior to removing it. Failure to do so may result in personal injury.*

7. Remove the bolts securing the front fender and remove it.

8. Loosen the upper and lower fork bridge bolts.

> *NOTE*
> *Prior to removing the fork, measure and write down on a piece of masking tape attached to the fork, the distance from the top of the fork tube to the top of the upper fork bridge. This is not a standard dimension, but one derived from rider preference.*

9. Remove the fork tube. It may be necessary to slightly rotate the fork tube while pulling it down and out.

10. Install by reversing these removal steps.

11. Install the fork tubes in the same position as noted in *Removal*, Step 8.

12. Tighten the bolts to the torque values in **Table 1**.

Disassembly

Refer to **Figure 77** for this procedure.

1. Clamp the slider in a vise with soft jaws (**Figure 78**).

2. Remove the Allen bolt and gasket (**Figure 79**) from the bottom of the slider.

> *NOTE*
> *This bolt has been secured with Loctite and is very difficult to remove because the damper rod will turn inside the slider. It can be removed with an air impact driver or you just may be lucky and get it off easily. If you are unable to remove it, take the fork tubes to a dealer and have them remove the bolts.*

3. Pull the fork tube out of the slider.

4. Remove the oil lock piece, the damper rod and rebound spring.

5. If oil has been leaking from the top of the slider, remove the circlip, washer and oil seal.

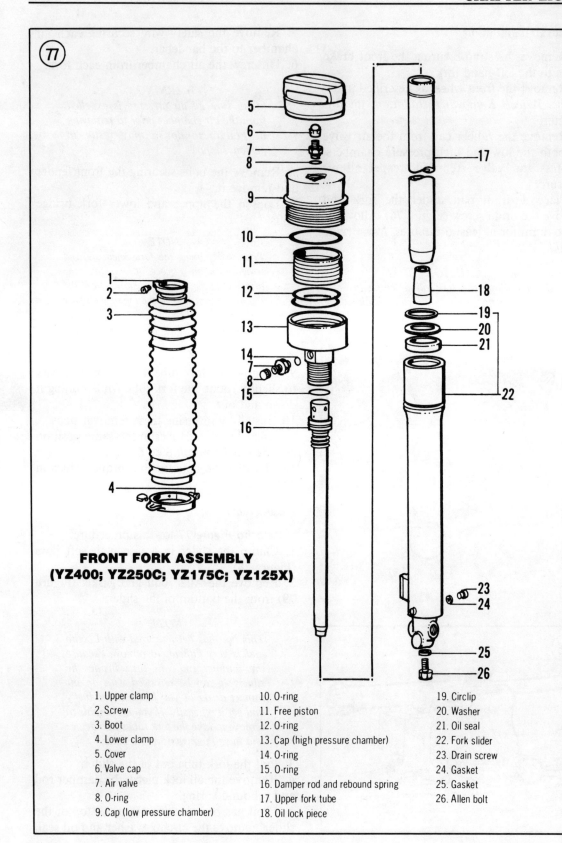

**FRONT FORK ASSEMBLY
(YZ400; YZ250C; YZ175C; YZ125X)**

1. Upper clamp
2. Screw
3. Boot
4. Lower clamp
5. Cover
6. Valve cap
7. Air valve
8. O-ring
9. Cap (low pressure chamber)

10. O-ring
11. Free piston
12. O-ring
13. Cap (high pressure chamber)
14. O-ring
15. O-ring
16. Damper rod and rebound spring
17. Upper fork tube
18. Oil lock piece

19. Circlip
20. Washer
21. Oil seal
22. Fork slider
23. Drain screw
24. Gasket
25. Gasket
26. Allen bolt

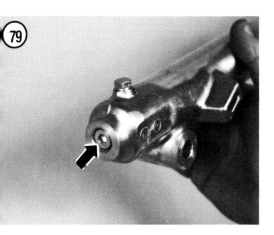

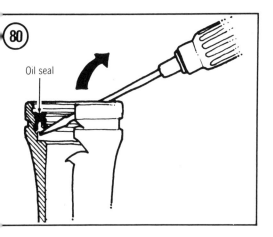

Oil seal

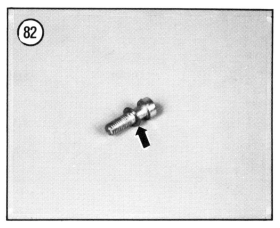

8

NOTE
It may be necessary to slightly heat the area on the slider around the oil seal prior to removal.

CAUTION
*Use a dull screwdriver blade to remove the oil seal (**Figure 80**). Do not damage the outer edge or inner surface of the slider.*

Inspection

Inspection is the same as with other models; refer the previous procedure covering all other models.

Assembly

Install a new oil seal, washer and circlip (**Figure**). Coat all parts with fresh fork oil prior to installation.

2. Install the rebound spring onto the damper rod, if removed.
3. Insert them into the fork tube.
4. Install the oil lock piece and install the upper fork assembly into the slider.
5. Make sure the gasket (**Figure 82**) is on the Allen bolt.
6. Apply Loctite to the threads of the Allen bolt prior to installation. Install it in the fork slider and tighten to specifications listed in **Table 1**.
7. Install the forks.
8. Install the air chambers onto the fork tube and tighten to 10-15 ft.-lb. (15-20 N•m).

NOTE
Inspect the condition of the O-ring seal on the air chamber prior to installing it; replace if necessary.

9. Safety wire the air chamber to the handlebar.
10. Refill the fork tube with fork oil and pressurize them; refer to Chapter Three.

Table 1 FRONT SUSPENSION TORQUE SPECIFICATIONS*

Models	YZ465G YZ400F YZ250G,F	YZ400E,D,C YZ250E,D,C	YZ175C YZ125C (all)	YZ100 (all)
Front axle nut	43 (60)	43 (60)	61 (85)	29 (40)
Front axle pinch nut(s)	14 (20)	11 (15)	——	——
Handle bar holder bolts	17 (23)	11 (15)	18 (25)	11 (15)
Fork bridge bolts				
Upper	16 (23)	11 (15)	25 (35)	25 (35)
Lower	16 (23)	11 (15)	15 (20)	15 (20)
Steering stem bolt	68 (95)	43 (60)	69 (95)	40 (55) YZ125E: 40 (55)
Steering stem nut	5 (7)	5 (7)	11 (15)	11(15)
Steering stem pinch bolt	17 (23)	11 (15)	15 (20)	15 (20)
Fork cap bolt	17 (23)	18 (25)	15 (20)	15 (20)

* Ft.-lb. (N•m)

Table 2 FRONT FORK SPRING FREE LENGTH*

Model	in.	mm
YZ465G	23.9	608
YZ400F	22.8	579
YZ400E, D	19.9	502
YZ400C	No spring used	
YZ250G	23.9	608
YZ250F	22.8	579
YZ250E, D	19.8	502
YZ250C	No spring used	
YZ175C	No spring used	
YZ125G	22.12	563
YZ125F	23.1	589.5
YZ125E	20.19	513
YZ125D	N.A.	N.A.
YZ125C	19.53	496
YZ125X	No spring used	
YZ100G	19.55	496.5
YZ100F	22.54	572.5
YZ100C	15.49	393.5
YZ100E, D	N.A.	N.A.

*N.A.=Information not available.

NOTE: If you own a 1981 or later model, first check the Supplement at the back of the book for any new service information.

CHAPTER NINE

REAR SUSPENSION

The rear suspension of the monoshock YZ series is basically the same on all models. The rear swing arm is either steel or aluminum and the monoshock is nestled up in the frame backbone out of the way. There are a variety of different spring preload and damping adjustments available to suit almost any combination of rider weight and track conditions. Each adjustment procedure varies among the different models and years so be sure to follow the correct one for your specific bike.

This chapter contains repair and replacement procedures for the rear wheel and hub and rear suspension components. Service to the rear suspension consists of periodically checking bolt tightness., replacing swing arm bushings, and checking the condition of the spring/gas monoshock units and replacing them as necessary.

Refer to **Table 1** for rear suspension torque specifications. **Tables 1 and 2** are at the end of the chapter.

REAR WHEEL

Removal/Installation

NOTE
This procedure is shown with 2 different models—one with the drive sprocket on the left-hand side and the other on the right.

1. Place a milk crate or wood block(s) under the frame so that the rear wheel is off the ground.
2. Remove the bolt and nut (**Figure 1**) securing the rear brake torque link. Let it pivot down out of the way.

NOTE
Some models have a cotter pin through the bolt, outside the nut. Be sure to remove it prior to trying to remove the nut.

3. Rotate the brake panel forward and unscrew the rear brake adjusting nut completely from the brake rod (**Figure 2**).

4. Withdraw the brake rod from the brake lever.

5. Remove the axle nut and lockwasher (**Figure 3**).

6. Remove the master link (**Figure 4**) from the drive chain and remove the chain from the drive sprocket.

7. Withdraw the axle (**Figure 5**) from the sprocket side of the wheel.

8. Pull the wheel to the rear; do not lose the wheel spacer (A, **Figure 6**).

9. Leave the axle adjusters (B, **Figure 6**) on the swing arm. If they are loose, remove them, tap the open end slightly with a hammer and reinstall on the swing arm.

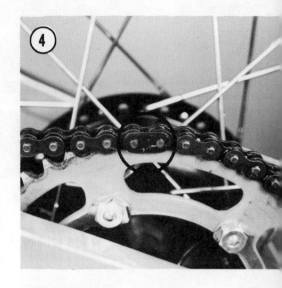

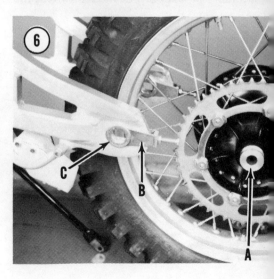

NOTE
*Don't lose the bushings (C, **Figure 6**) inside the axle adjusters.*

10. Install by reversing these removal steps.

11. Be sure to install all axle spacer on both sides of the wheel (**Figures 7 and 8**).

NOTE
These spacers vary with the different models but there should be one on each side of the wheel.

CAUTION
Rear wheel spacers should be routinely replaced. Frequent tightening of the rear axle nut causes the spacers to compress slightly. A compressed spacer alters swing arm to rear wheel clearance.

12. Install a new clip on the master link and install it so that the closed end of the clip is facing direction of chain travel; see **Figure 9**.

13. Install the axle from the drive sprocket side.

14. Adjust the drive chain tension as described under *Drive Chain Adjustment* in Chapter Three.

15. Tighten the axle nut and brake torque link nut to the torque values in **Table 1** at the end of this chapter.

NOTE
On models so equipped, install a new cotter pin on the brake torque link bolt.

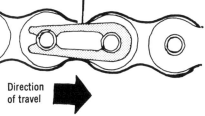

Master link clip

Direction of travel

16. After the wheel is completely installed, rotate it several times to make sure it rotates smoothly. Apply the brakes several times to make sure it operates correctly.

17. Adjust the rear brake as described under *Rear Brake Pedal Adjustment* in Chapter Three.

Inspection

Measure the radial and axial runout of the wheel rim with a dial indicator as shown in **Figure 10**. The standard value for both radial and axial runout is 0.02 in. (0.5 mm)

Tighten or replace any bent or loose spokes. Refer to *Spoke Inspection and Replacement* in Chapter Eight.

Check axle runout as described under *Rear Hub Inspection* in this chapter.

REAR HUB

Refer to **Figure 11** for this procedure.

NOTE
This procedure is shown with 2 different models—one with the drive sprocket on the left-hand side and the other on the right.

Disassembly

1. Remove the rear wheel as described under *Rear Wheel Removal/Installation* in this chapter.

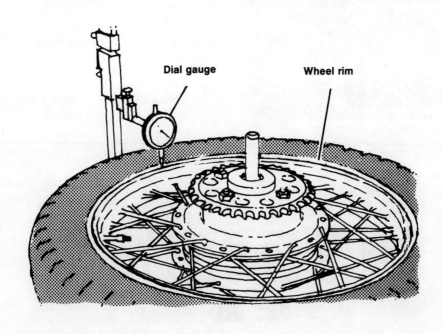

Dial gauge

Wheel rim

11

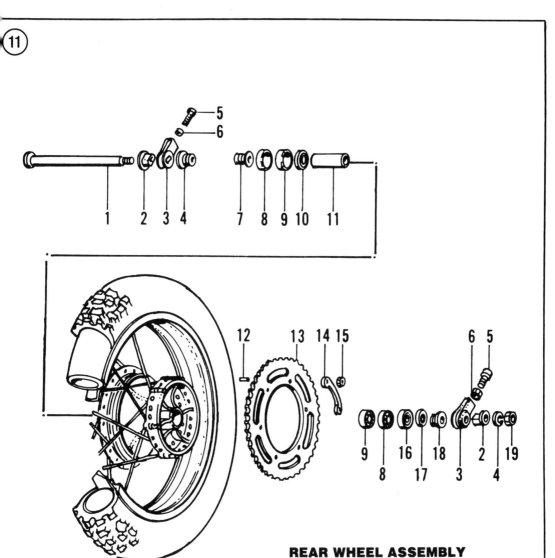

REAR WHEEL ASSEMBLY

1. Rear axle
2. Bushing
3. Axle adjuster
4. Seal
5. Adjuster bolt
6. Locknut
7. Seal
8. Bearing
9. Wheel bearing
10. Spacer flange
11. Distance collar
12. Bolt
13. Sprocket
14. Lockwasher
15. Nut
16. Oil seal
17. Dust seal
18. Seal
19. Axle nut

9

2. Remove the axle spacers from the wheel (**Figure 12, 13, or 14**).

3. Pull the brake assembly (**Figure 15**) straight up and out of the drum.

4. Remove the dust seal (**Figure 16**) on the side opposite the brake drum.

5. Remove the right- and left-hand bearings (**Figure 17**) and distance collar. Insert a soft aluminum or brass drift into one side of the hub. Push the distance collar over to one side and place the drift on the inner race of the lower bearing (**Figure 18**). Tap the bearing out of the hub, with a hammer, working around the perimeter of the inner race.

6. Remove the distance collar and tap out the opposite bearing.

Inspection

1. Thoroughly clean out the inside of the hub with solvent and dry with compressed air or shop cloth.

> *NOTE*
> *Avoid getting any greasy solvent residue on the brake drum during this procedure. If this happens, clean it off with a shop cloth and lacquer thinner.*

2. Do not clean the sealed bearings. If non-sealed bearings are installed; thoroughly clean them in solvent and thoroughly dry with compressed air. Do not let the bearing spin while drying.

3. Turn each bearing by hand (**Figure 19**). Make sure the bearings turn smoothly.

4. On non-sealed bearings, check the balls for evidence of wear, pitting, or excessive heat (bluish tint). Replace bearing if necessary; always replace as a complete set. When replacing, be sure to take your old bearings along to ensure a perfect matchup.

NOTE
Fully sealed bearings are available from
many good bearing speciality shops. Fully
sealed bearings provide better protection
from dirt and moisture that may get into
the hub.

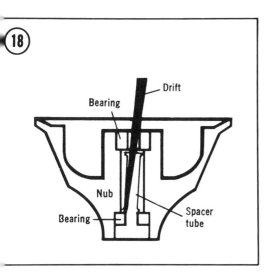

5. Check the axle for wear and straightness. Use V-blocks and a dial indicator as shown in **Figure 20**. If the runout is 0.008 in. (0.2 mm) or greater, the axle should be replaced.

Assembly

1. If cleaned, pack the bearings with a good quality bearing grease. Work the grease in between the balls thoroughly. Turn the bearing by hand a couple of times to make sure the grease is distributed evenly inside the bearing.
2. Pack the wheel hub with multipurpose grease.
3. Install the left-hand bearing.

9

Drift
Bearing
Nub
Bearing
Spacer
tube

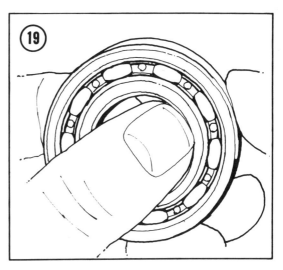

4. Press in the distance collar.
5. Install the right-hand bearing.

> *NOTE*
> *Install the wheel bearing with the sealed side facing out.*

> *CAUTION*
> *Tap the bearings squarely into place and tap on the outer race only. Use a socket (**Figure 21**) that matches the outer race diameter. Do not tap on the inner race or the bearing might be damaged. Be sure that the bearings are completely seated.*

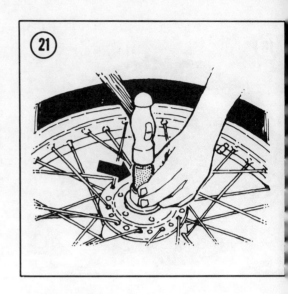

6. Install a new grease seal. Lubricate it with fresh multipurpose grease and tap it gently into place.
7. Install the rear wheel as described under *Rear Wheel Removal/Installation* in this chapter.

DRIVE SPROCKET

Disassembly/Assembly

The drive sprocket is held in place either with Allen bolts or hardened hex head bolts and lockwashers. This varies with different models and years.
1. Remove the rear wheel as described under *Rear Wheel Removal/Installation* in this chapter.
2. On models with right-hand drive chain, remove the brake panel assembly from the brake drum.

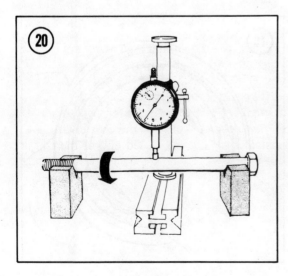

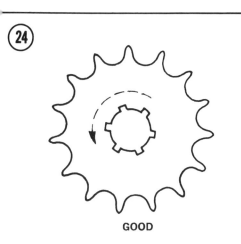

GOOD

Bent teeth   Bent teeth

Worn area   Worn area

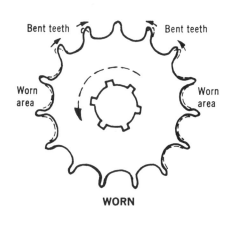

WORN

3. On models with Allen bolts, remove the Allen bolts (**Figure 22**) and remove the drive sprocket.

4. On models with hex bolts, straighten the locking tabs and remove the bolts (**Figure 23**). Remove the drive sprocket.

5. Assemble by reversing these disassembly steps, noting the following.

6. Tighten the bolts securely.

7. Install new locking tabs on models so equipped.

Inspection

Inspect the condition of the teeth on the sprocket. If they are visibly worn as shown in **Figure 24**, replace with a new one.

If the sprocket requires replacement, the drive chain is probably worn also and may need replacement. Refer to *Drive Chain/Cleaning, Inspection, and Lubrication* in Chapter Three.

DRIVE CHAIN

Removal/Installation

1. Place a milk crate or wood block(s) under the frame so the rear wheel is off the ground.

2. Turn the rear wheel and drive chain until the master link is accessible.

3. Remove the bolts securing the driven sprocket cover (**Figure 25**) and remove it.

NOTE
These covers vary in shape and amount of bolts securing them for the various models and years.

4. Remove the master link clip (**Figure 26**) and remove the master link.

5. Slowly rotate the rear wheel and pull the drive chain off the drive sprocket.

6. Install by reversing these removal steps.

7. Install a new clip on the master link and install it so that the closed end of the clip is facing the direction of chain travel (**Figure 27**).

Service and Inspection

For service and inspection of the drive chain, refer to *Drive Chain/Cleaning, Inspection, and Lubrication* in Chapter Three.

9

WHEEL BALANCING

For complete information refer to *Wheel Balancing* in Chapter Eight.

TIRE CHANGING AND TIRE REPAIRS

Refer to *Tire Changing* or *Tire Repairs* in Chapter Eight for complete procedures on tire changing and repairs.

REAR SWING ARM

The rear swing arm is manufactured either of aluminum or steel; this varies with different models and years. Due to the number of models covered in this manual, use the following information for swing arm identification. Because bearings and bushings greatly affect handling performance, they should be replaced when they become worn or damaged.

The Type I swing arm (**Figure 28**) is found on the following models:
YZ100C, D.
YZ125C, X.
YZ175C.

The Type II swing arm (**Figure 29**) is found on the following models:
YZ100E, F and G.

The Type III swing arm (**Figure 30**) is found on the following model:
YZ125D.

The Type IV swing arm (**Figure 31**) is found on the following models:
YZ125E, F.

The Type V swing arm (**Figure 32**) is found on the following model:
YZ125G.

The Type VI swing arm (**Figure 33**) is found on the following models:
YZ250C.
YZ400C.

The Type VII swing arm (**Figure 34**) is found on the following models:
YZ250D, E.
YZ400D, E.

The Type VIII swing arm (**Figure 35**) is found on the following models:
YZ250F, G.
YZ400F.
YZ465G.

Swing Arm Removal/Installation

NOTE
This procedure is shown with both types of swing arms.

1. Remove the rear wheel and drive chain as described under *Rear Wheel Removal/Installation* in this chapter.
2. Remove the cotter pin on the end of the upper mounting pin.
3. Remove mounting pin and nut(s) and gently let the swing arm pivot down (**Figure 36**).

NOTE
Don't lose the cover washers on each side of the monoshock rear mount.

4. After the upper end of the swing arm is disconnected grasp the rear end of it and try to move it from side to side in a horizontal arc. The maximum allowable side play is 0.04 in.

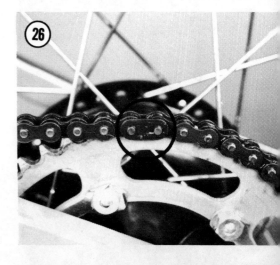

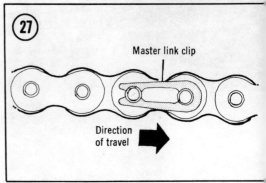

Master link clip

Direction of travel

㉘

REAR SWING ARM ASSEMBLY
(TYPE I-YZ100C, D; YZ125C, X
AND YZ175C)

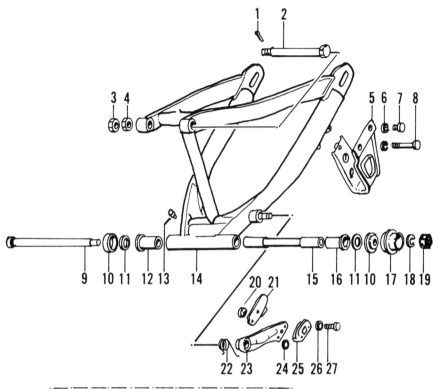

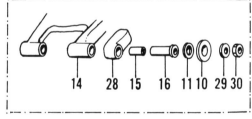

1. Cotter pin	11. Shim	21. Chain guide
2. Bolt	12. Bushing	22. Spring
3. Nut	13. Grease fitting	23. Tensioner arm
4. Nut	14. Swing arm assembly	24. Circlip
5. Chain guard	15. Bushing (long or short)	25. Tensioner
6. Lockwasher	16. Bushing	26. Lockwasher
7. Bolt	17. Chain roller	27. Bolt
8. Bolt	18. Lockwasher	28. Chain guard
9. Pivot bolt	19. Nut	29. Washer
10. Thrust cover	20. Nut	30. Nut

9

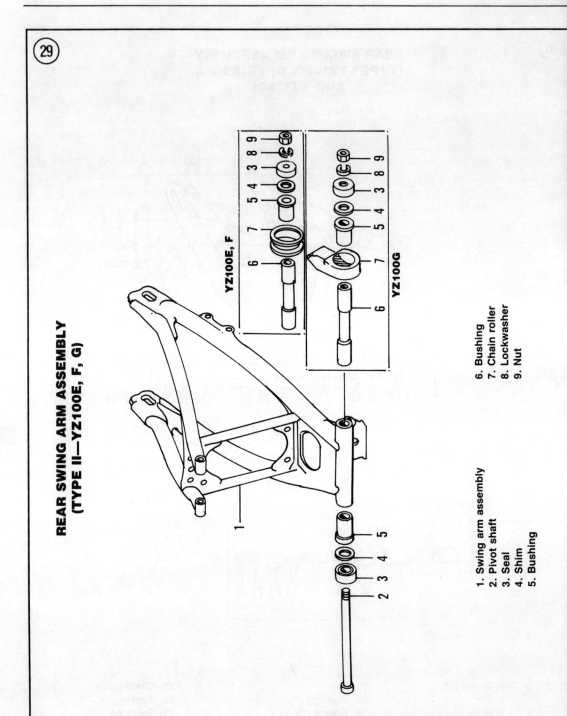

29

REAR SWING ARM ASSEMBLY
(TYPE II—YZ100E, F, G)

YZ100E, F

YZ100G

1. Swing arm assembly
2. Pivot shaft
3. Seal
4. Shim
5. Bushing
6. Bushing
7. Chain roller
8. Lockwasher
9. Nut

1 mm). If play is greater than this, and pivot bolt is tightened correctly, the bearings should be replaced.

5. Remove the lower pivot bolt retaining nut and lockwasher and withdraw the pivot bolt from the other side. It is not necessary to remove the engine to remove the swing arm.

6. Remove the swing arm assembly.

7. To install, position the swing arm into the lower mounting area. Align the holes in the swing arm with the hole in the engine rear mounting assembly. Insert a drift in from the side opposite where the bolt is to be inserted and align the holes.

NOTE
If the engine is installed it may be necessary to loosen the other engine mounting hardware to help align the swing arm holes. The lower portion of the bike's frame is very flexible and tends to move a little when major components are either removed or loosened.

8. After all holes are aligned, insert the pivot bolt from the opposite side and install the lockwasher and nut. Tighten the nut to the torque values in **Table 1** at the end of the chapter. Retighten engine mounting hardware if it was loosened in the previous step.

9. Install the cover washers on each side of the monoshock (**Figure 37**).

10. Insert the upper mounting pin from the left-hand side. Apply a light coat of grease to it prior to installing it.

11. Install fasteners, if so equipped, and a new cotter pin—never reuse a cotter pin as it may break and fall out. Hold the left-hand end of the pin with

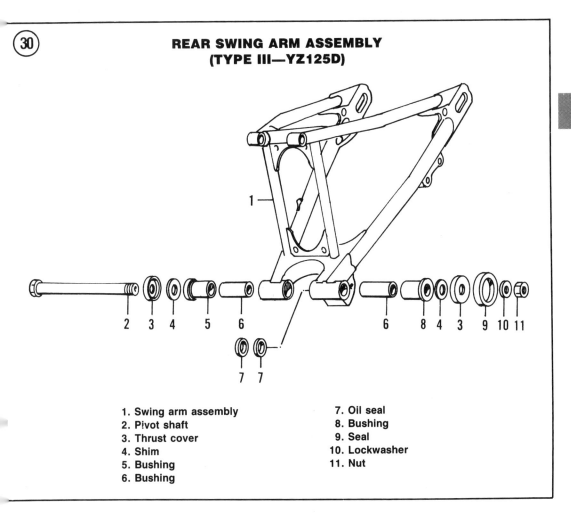

**REAR SWING ARM ASSEMBLY
(TYPE III—YZ125D)**

1. Swing arm assembly
2. Pivot shaft
3. Thrust cover
4. Shim
5. Bushing
6. Bushing
7. Oil seal
8. Bushing
9. Seal
10. Lockwasher
11. Nut

a wrench and bend over the end of the cotter pin completely (**Figure 38**).

> *NOTE*
> *Make sure that both cover washers (**Figure 39**) are installed. They are necessary to maintain the proper clearance between the monoshock and the swing arm. If they are slightly flattened out, replace them.*

12. Install the rear wheel as described under *Rear Wheel Removal/Installation* in this chapter.

Aluminum Swing Arm
Disassembly/Inspection/Assembly

Refer to the drawing for your model when servicing the swing arm assembly:
a. **Figure 32** (Type V).
b. **Figure 33** (Type VI).
c. **Figure 35** (Type VIII).

1. Remove the swing arm as previously described.
2. Secure the swing arm in a vise with soft jaws.
3. Carefully remove thrust cover (**Figure 40**).
4. Remove the flat bearing and oil seal.

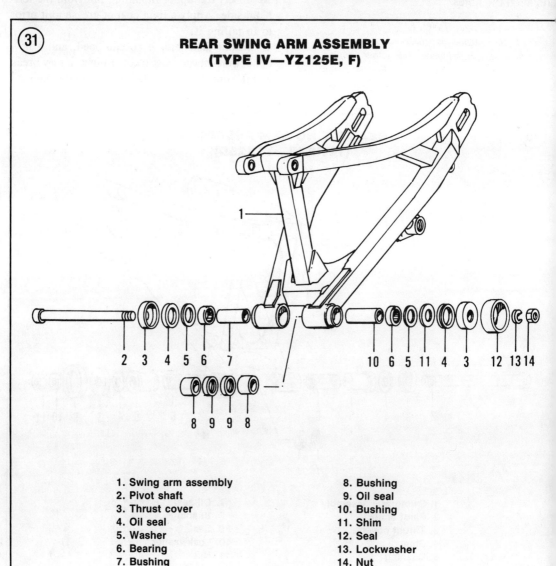

31

**REAR SWING ARM ASSEMBLY
(TYPE IV—YZ125E, F)**

1. Swing arm assembly
2. Pivot shaft
3. Thrust cover
4. Oil seal
5. Washer
6. Bearing
7. Bushing
8. Bushing
9. Oil seal
10. Bushing
11. Shim
12. Seal
13. Lockwasher
14. Nut

Tap out the long bushing (**Figure 41**) and inner and outer bearing (or bushing). Use a suitable size drift or socket and extension and carefully drive them out with a hammer.

CAUTION
Do not remove the bearings or bushings just for inspection as they are usually damaged during removal.

Remove the oil seal.

Wash all parts, including the inside of the swing arm pivot area, in solvent and thoroughly dry.

Apply a light coat of waterproof grease to all parts prior to installation. Oil the lips of the new oil seals (always replace the oil seals with new ones).

Install all parts in the reverse order of disassembly. Tap the bearings or bushings into place slowly and squarely with a block of wood and hammer. Make sure they are not cocked and that they are completely seated.

CAUTION
Never reinstall a bearing or bushing that has been removed. During removal it becomes slightly damaged and is no longer true to alignment. If installed, it will damage the long bushing and create an unsafe riding condition.

10. Inspect the condition of the drive chain sliders. Replace if necessary by removing attachment screws and/or bolts.

Steel Swing Arm Disassembly/Inspection/Assembly

Refer to the drawing for your model when servicing the swing arm assembly:
a. **Figure 28** (Type I).
b. **Figure 29** (Type II).

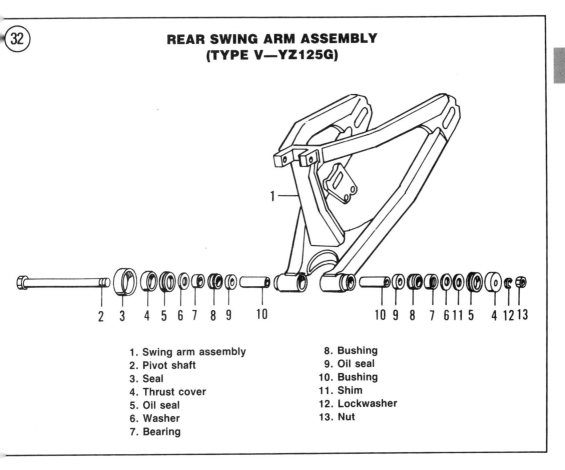

REAR SWING ARM ASSEMBLY (TYPE V—YZ125G)

1. Swing arm assembly
2. Pivot shaft
3. Seal
4. Thrust cover
5. Oil seal
6. Washer
7. Bearing
8. Bushing
9. Oil seal
10. Bushing
11. Shim
12. Lockwasher
13. Nut

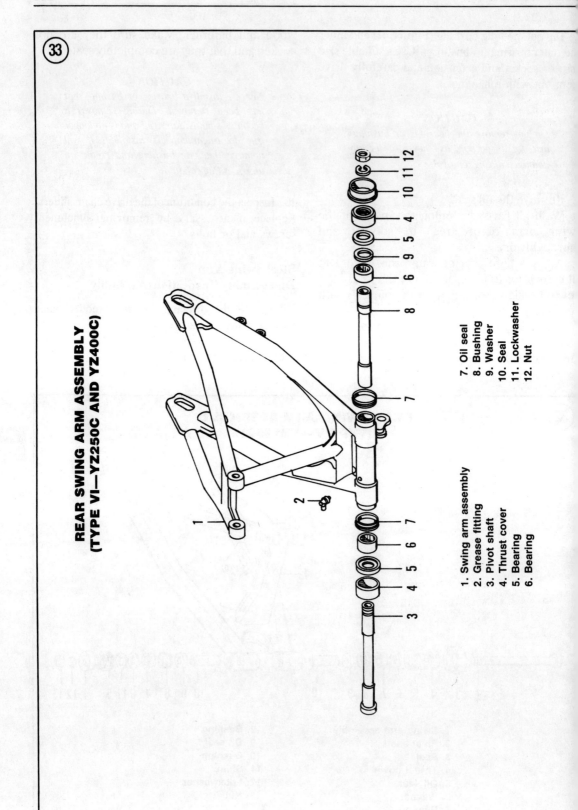

REAR SWING ARM ASSEMBLY
(TYPE VI—YZ250C AND YZ400C)

1. Swing arm assembly
2. Grease fitting
3. Pivot shaft
4. Thrust cover
5. Bearing
6. Bearing
7. Oil seal
8. Bushing
9. Washer
10. Seal
11. Lockwasher
12. Nut

c. **Figure 30** (Type III).
d. **Figure 31** (Type IV).
e. **Figure 34** (Type VII).

. Remove the swing arm as previously
described.
2. Secure the swing arm in a vise with soft
jaws.
3. Remove the chain guard/seal.
4. Remove the thurst cover/oil seal (A, **Figure 42**).

5. Remove the shim (B, **Figure 42**) and inner
bushing (C, **Figure 42**).

NOTE
*On some models there is one long inner
bushing that runs the width of the swing
arm pivot.*

6. Tap out the outer bushings. Use a suitable
size drift or socket and extension and carefully
drive them out with a hammer.

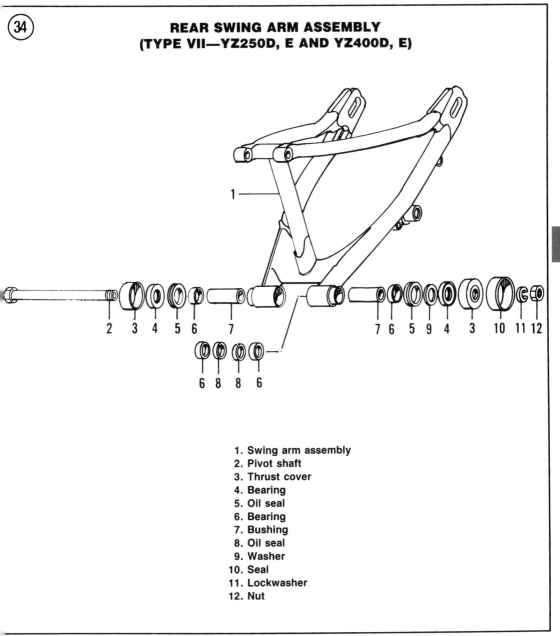

REAR SWING ARM ASSEMBLY
(TYPE VII—YZ250D, E AND YZ400D, E)

1. Swing arm assembly
2. Pivot shaft
3. Thrust cover
4. Bearing
5. Oil seal
6. Bearing
7. Bushing
8. Oil seal
9. Washer
10. Seal
11. Lockwasher
12. Nut

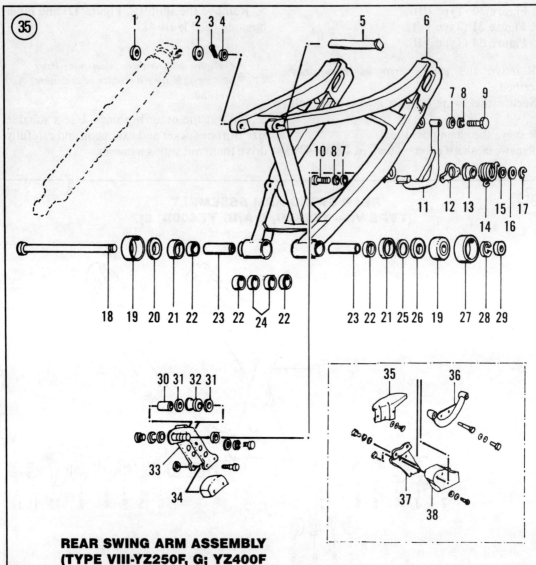

REAR SWING ARM ASSEMBLY (TYPE VIII-YZ250F, G; YZ400F AND YZ465G)

1. Monoshock thrust cover
2. Monoshock thrust cover
3. Cotter pin
4. Nut
5. Bolt
6. Swing arm
7. Washer
8. Lockwasher
9. Bolt
10. Bolt
11. Chain guard
12. Cover
13. Collar

14. Spring
15. Washer
16. Washer
17. E-clip
18. Pivot bolt
19. Thrust cover
20. Oil seal
21. Cover
22. Bearing
23. Bushing
24. Cover
25. Washer
26. Oil seal

27. Chain guard
28. Lockwasher
29. Pivot boltnut
30. Bushing
31. Washer
32. Bushing assembly
33. Bracket assembly
34. Chain support
35. Chain protector
36. Chain guard
37. Bracket
38. Chain support

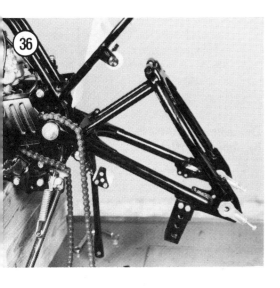

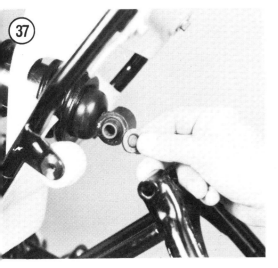

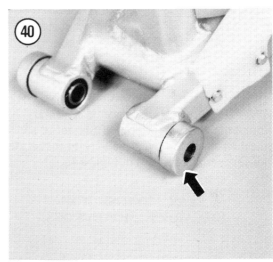

9

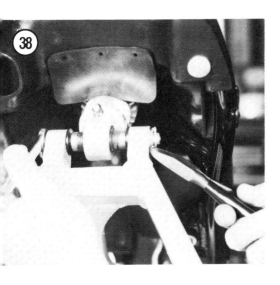

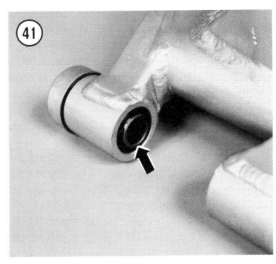

CAUTION
Do not remove the bushings just for inspection as they are usually damaged during removal.

7. Wash all parts, including the inside of the swing arm pivot area, in solvent and thoroughly dry.

8. Apply a light coat of waterproof grease to all parts prior to installation.

9. Install all parts in the reverse order of disassembly. Tap the bushings into place slowly and squarely with a block of wood and hammer. Make sure they are not cocked and that they are completely seated.

CAUTION
Never reinstall a bushing that has been removed. During removal it becomes slightly damaged and is no longer true to alignment. If installed, it will damage the inner bushing and create an unsafe riding condition.

10. Inspect the condition of the drive chain slider (**Figure 43**). Replace if necessary by removing attachment bolts. If the entire slider mechanism is removed, be sure to install the tension spring as shown in **Figure 43**.

REAR MONOSHOCK (DECARBON MONOCROSS SYSTEM)

The rear suspension on all YZs is basically the same. In 1977 the monoshock unit was improved to the DeCarbon Monocross System (except model YZ100 which was changed in 1978). The monoshock unit is tucked up in the frame's hollow back bone under the fuel tank. On some models since 1980 the nitrogen gas tank reservoir has been moved out from under the fuel tank and onto the side of the frame. This allows more rapid cooling to prevent shock fading.

All models offer a variety of damping and spring preload adjustments. The adjustment procedures vary with the different models and are covered separately.

Removal and installation is basically the same on all models and where differences occur they are noted.

NOTE
The unit used on the 1976 models is substantially different from the DeCarbon type and is covered separately at the end of the chapter.

DeCarbon Monocross System Operation

The monocross monoshock unit is a nitrogen charged, free piston shock constructed of a single cylinder (**Figure 44**). Inside the cylinder are an oil chamber and gas chamber which are kept separated by a free piston and O-ring which prevent the oil and gas from mixing. There is also a floating valve

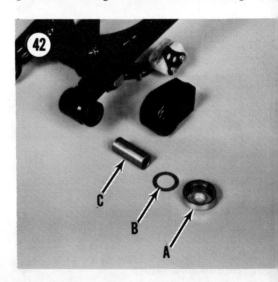

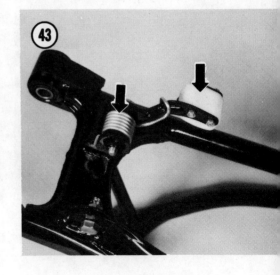

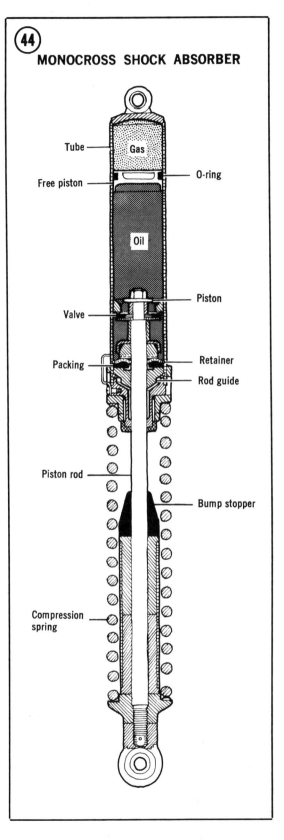

(44)

MONOCROSS SHOCK ABSORBER

Tube — Gas

Free piston — O-ring

Oil

Valve — Piston

Packing — Retainer

Rod guide

Piston rod — Bump stopper

Compression spring

which allows the oil to move freely around the piston. The floating valve is an improvement over older models, in that it responds more quickly to changes in the pressure in the gas chamber.

> *NOTE*
> *On some models since 1980, the nitrogen gas cylinder is now remote from the main shock body. Operation is still basically the same except that gas cooling is more rapid.*

Basically the monoshock unit works as follows:

In the stretch stroke, the oil is forced downward by the change in gas pressure. As the piston speed increases, the floating valve allows the oil to flow faster, creating friction and damping the stretch of the suspension. The damping amount is automatically controlled according to the speed of the piston movement.

In the compression stroke, the oil stored under the piston moves upward, compressing the nitrogen in the gas chamber. Again, as the piston moves faster, the floating valve reacts, allowing the oil to move faster, thus creating a damping force. The damping is controlled automatically by the speed of the piston.

> *WARNING*
> *The monoshock unit contains highly compressed nitrogen gas. Do not tamper with or attempt to open the damper/cylinder assembly (**Figure 45**).*

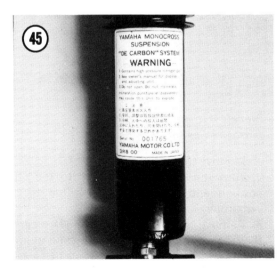

(45)

Do not place it near an open flame or other extreme heat. Do not weld on the frame near it. Do not dispose of the damper subassembly yourself. Take it to a Yamaha dealer where it can be deactivated and disposed of properly. Never attempt to remove the plug at the bottom of the nitrogen tank (Figure 46).

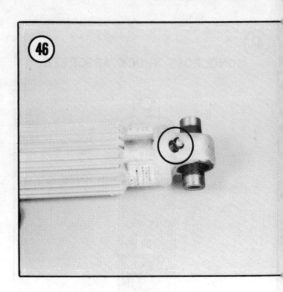

Damping Adjustment—1977 and Later (Except Model YZ100)

Models With Remote Nitrogen Gas Tank

1. Remove the side cover/number plate (**Figure 47**).

> *NOTE*
> *It is not necessary to remove the side cover/number plate but it will save a lot of cuts on the forearm from the sharp edges on the plastic.*

2. Turn the adjuster (**Figure 48**) to any of the 24 steps that are available. It is not necessary to remove the shock unit to perform this adjustment.
3. To make damping stiffer, turn the adjuster *clockwise* as looking from the rear. For softer damping, turn it *counterclockwise*.

> *NOTE*
> *This adjustment should be made one notch at a time and the bike test ridden each time. Turn the adjuster until it clicks into position. There are approximately 12 notches on either side of the standard position.*

> *WARNING*
> *Do not turn the adjuster when it becomes either light or heavy to turn.*

Models Without Remote Nitrogen Gas Tank

1. Remove the seat.
2. Turn the fuel shutoff valve to the OFF position and remove the fuel line to the carburetor.
3. Remove the bolts (A, **Figure 49**) securing the front of the fuel tank. Pull up and unhook the strap (B, **Figure 49**) securing the rear of

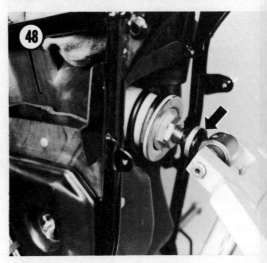

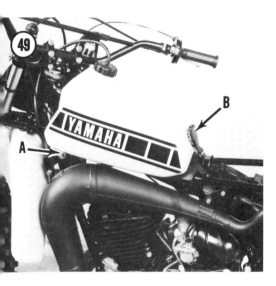

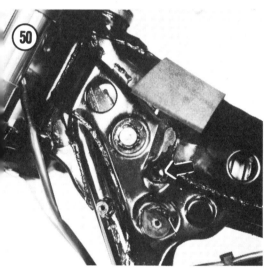

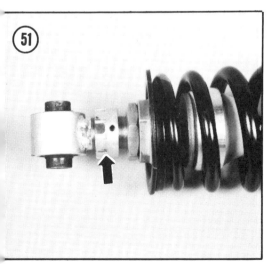

the tank. Pull the tank toward the rear and remove it.

NOTE
On some models it is unnecessary to remove the fuel tank to gain access to the adjustment hole in the frame. Check this out prior to removing your fuel tank.

4. Insert a slotted head screwdriver through the hole in the frame (**Figure 50**). Place the blade of the screwdriver into the notches in the adjuster (**Figure 51**). Turn it in either direction as shown in **Figure 52** to achieve a stiffer or softer damping. The hole in the frame may be either on the right- or left-hand side, depending on which model you have.

5. Turn the adjuster (**Figure 51**) to any of the 20-24 steps that are available. It is not necessary to remove the shock unit to perform this adjustment. **Figure 51** is shown with it removed for clarity.

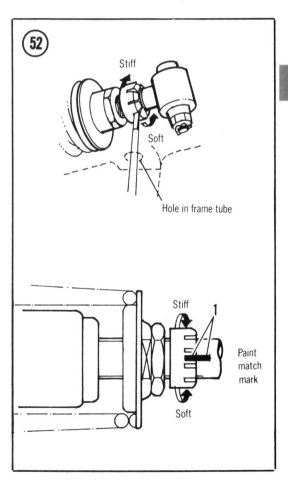

9

NOTE
*This adjustment should be made one notch at a time and the bike test ridden each time. Turn the adjuster until it clicks into position. There are approximately 10-12 notches on either side of the standard position. The standard position is marked with a paint stripe on both the shock and the adjuster (**Figure 53**).*

WARNING
Do not turn the adjuster when it becomes either light or heavy to turn.

Spring Pre-load—1977 and Later (Except Model YZ100)

Models With Remote Nitrogen Gas Tank

1. Remove the side cover/number plate (**Figure 47**).

NOTE
It is not necessary to remove the side cover/number plate but it will save a lot of cuts on the forearm from the sharp edges on the plastic.

2. Using the 32 mm wrench provided in the owners tool kit, loosen the locknut (A, **Figure 54**) and turn the adjuster (B, **Figure 54**). Tighten it to increase spring pre-load or loosen it to decrease it.

NOTE
Adjustments should be made in increments of 2 mm each time; test ride the bike after each adjustment.

3. The installed spring length (**Figure 55**) must be within the following range:
  a. Standard length—14.0 in. (356 mm)
  b. Minimum length—13.6 in. (345 mm)
  c. Maximum length—14.2 in. (360 mm)
4. After the adjustment is correct, tighten the locknut to 40 ft.-lb. (55 N.m).

Models Without Remote Nitrogen Gas Tank

1. Remove the monocross unit as described under *Monoshock Removal/Installation* in this chapter.

2. Using the 32 mm wrench provided in th owner's tool kit, loosen the locknut (A Figure 56), and turn the adjuster (B, **Figur** 56). Tighten it to increase spring pre-load o loosen it to decrease it.

NOTE
Adjustments should be made in increments of 2 mm each time; test ride the bike after each adjustment.

3. After the adjustment is correct, tighten th locknut to 40-43 ft.-lb. (55-60 N.m).
4. Install the monoshock unit as describe under *Monoshock Removal/Installation* in thi chapter.

Spring Pre-Load—Model 1978 and Later Model YZ100

Spring pre-load is the only adjustmen available for this type of monoshock—there i no damping adjustment.

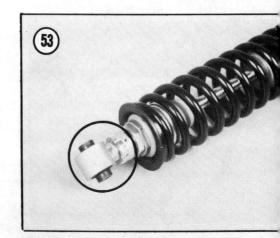

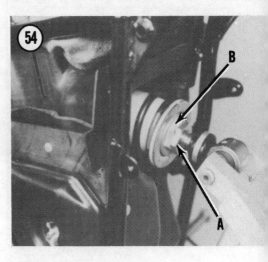

1. Remove the seat.

2. Unscrew the set screw (**Figure 57**) from the monoshock. The screw is secured to a piece of spring wire—do not remove it from this.

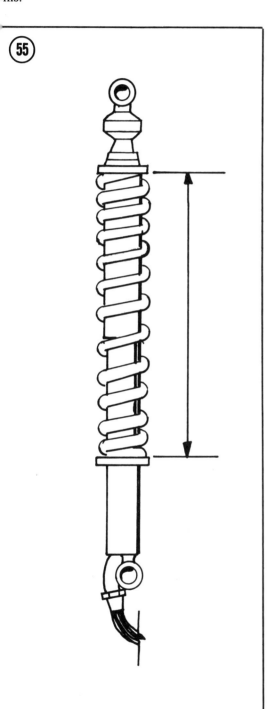

3. Use the ring nut wrench supplied in the owner's tool kit and turn the spring seat to the left-hand side to decrease spring pre-load or to the right to increase spring pre-load. Refer to **Table 2** for number of turn(s) required for each setting.

> *NOTE*
> *Adjustments should be made in increments of one adjusting position each time; test ride the bike after each adjustment.*

4. Install the set screw and tighten it securely.

Monoshock Removal/Installation

Models With Remote Nitrogen Gas Tank

1. Place a milk crate or wood block(s) under the frame, high enough to lift the rear wheel off the ground by at least 10-12 inches.

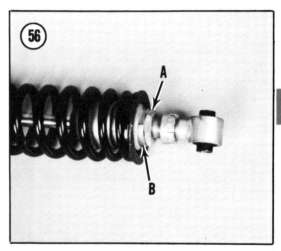

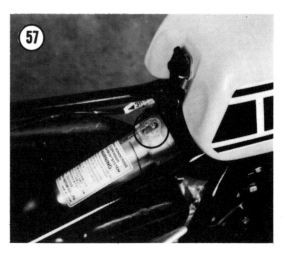

2. Remove the seat.

3. Turn the fuel shutoff valve to the OFF position and remove the fuel linc to the carburetor.

4. Remove the bolts (A, **Figure 58**) securing the front of the fuel tank. Pull up and unhook the strap (B, **Figure 58**) securing the rear of the tank. Pull the tank toward the rear and remove it.

5. Remove the screw (A, **Figure 59**) securing the band to the frame. Remove the band from the nitrogen gas tank.

NOTE
The nitrogen gas tank is mounted on different sides for different models.

6. Pull the nitrogen tank up and out of the rubber grommet (B, **Figure 59**) on the frame.

7. Remove the cotter pin and nut (**Figure 60**) securing the upper portion to the frame. Remove the bolt.

8. Remove the cotter pin and washer (**Figure 61**) securing the lower portion to the swing arm. Remove the pin.

9. Pivot down the rear wheel and swing arm. Do not lose the 2 cover washers on each side of the monoshock.

10. Carefully withdraw the monoshock assembly out through the rear of the frame, over the rear wheel. Be careful not to damage the nitrogen gas tank and its rubber hose.

NOTE
If you cannot withdraw the monoshock over the rear wheel, either block up the engine more or remove the rear wheel.

11. Install by reversing these removal steps, noting the followng.

12. Install the cover washers on each side of the monoshock.

13. Insert the mounting pin (**Figure 61**) from the left-hand side. Apply a light coat of grease to it prior to installing it.

14. Install the washer and a new cotter pin—never reuse a cotter pin as it may break and fall out. Hold the left-hand end of the pin with a wrench and bend over the end of the cotter pin completely.

NOTE
*Make sure that both cover washers (**Figure 62**) are installed. They are necessary to maintain the proper clearance between the monoshock and the swing arm. If they are slightly flattened out, replace them.*

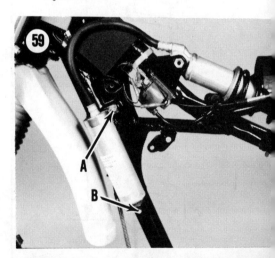

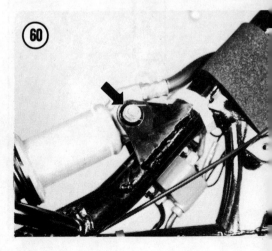

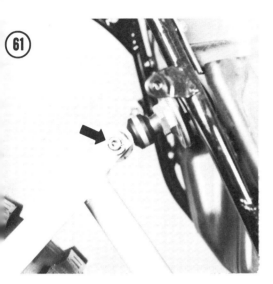

15. Install the bolt and nut securing the upper portion to the frame. Tighten the bolt and nut to 22 ft.-lb. (30 N.m). Install a new cotter pin—never reuse a cotter pin as it may break and fall out.

16. Make sure the nitrogen gas tank is secured properly in place, with the lower end positioned in the grommet. Tighten the screw on the band securely.

Models Without Remote Nitrogen Gas Tank (1977 and Later)

Removal/Installation

1. Place a milk crate or wood block(s) under the frame high enough to lift the rear wheel off the ground by at least 10 to 12 inches.

2. Remove the seat.

3. Turn the fuel shutoff valve to the OFF position and remove the fuel line to the carburetor.

4. Remove the bolts (A, **Figure 63**) securing the front of the fuel tank. Pull up and unhook the strap (B, **Figure 63**) securing the rear of the tank. Pull the tank toward the rear and remove it.

5. Remove the cotter pin and nut (**Figure 64**) securing the upper portion to the frame. Remove the bolt.

6. Remove the cotter pin and washer securing the lower portion to the swing arm. Remove the pin.

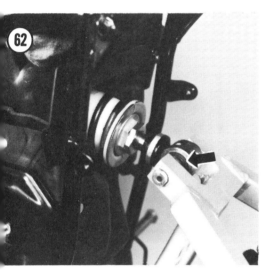

9

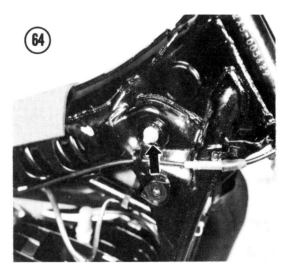

7. Pivot down the rear wheel and swing arm. Do not lose the 2 cover washers (**Figure 65**) on each side of the monoshock.

8. Carefully withdraw the monoshock assembly out through the rear of the frame, over the rear wheel.

> *NOTE*
> *If you cannot withdraw the monoshock over the rear wheel, either block up the engine more or remove the rear wheel.*

9. Install by reversing these removal steps, noting the followng.

10. Install the cover washers (**Figure 66**) on each side of the monoshock.

11. Insert the mounting pin from the left-hand side. Apply a light coat of grease to it prior to installing it.

12. Install the washer and a new cotter pin—never reuse a cotter pin as it may break and fall out. Hold the left-hand end of the pin with a wrench and bend over the end of the cotter pin completely (**Figure 67**).

> *NOTE*
> *Make sure that both cover washers are installed. They are necessary to maintain the proper clearance between the monoshock and the swing arm. If they are slightly flattened out, replace them.*

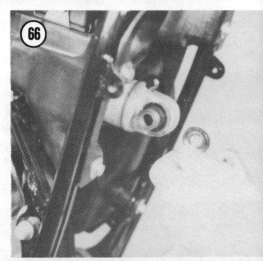

13. Install the bolt and nut securing the upper portion to the frame. Tighten the bolt and nut to 22 ft.-lb. (30 N.m). Install a new cotter pin—never reuse a cotter pin as it may break and fall out.

Monoshock—1977 and Later
(Except YZ100)
Disassembly/Inspection/Assembly

Refer to **Figure 68 or 69** for this procedure. The spring on these monoshocks are not under the same amount of pressure as those used on a dual-shock rear suspension. Therefore a spring compression tool is not needed for disassemby.

1. Remove the monoshock as described under *Monoshock Removal/Installation* in this chapter.

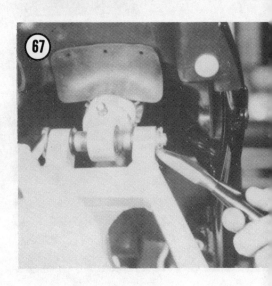

MONOSHOCK ASSEMBLY
(YZ465G; YZ250G; YZ125G)

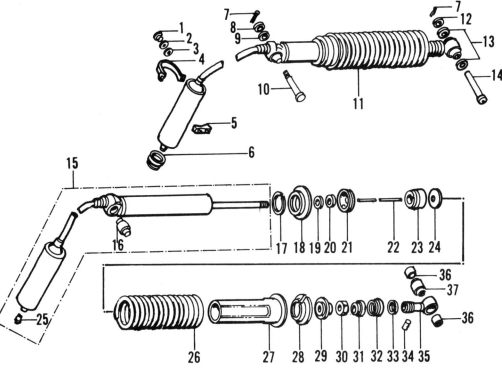

1. Screw	20. Seal ring housing
2. Lockwasher	21. Case cap
3. Washer	22. Pushrod
4. Remote tank band	23. Stopper
5. Tank damper	24. Stopper support
6. Tank grommet	25. Screw
7. Cotter pin	26. Spring
8. Nut	27. Spring guide
9. Washer	28. Spring seats (keepers)
10. Bolt	29. Upper spring seat
11. Monoshock assembly	30. Pre-load locknut
12. Washer	31. Cover
13. Thrust covers	32. Damping adjuster
14. Pin	33. Cover
15. Damper subassembly	34. Dowel pin
16. Bushing	35. Rear bracket subassembly
17. Circlip	36. Bushing
18. Lower spring seat	37. Bushing assembly
19. Dust seal	

9

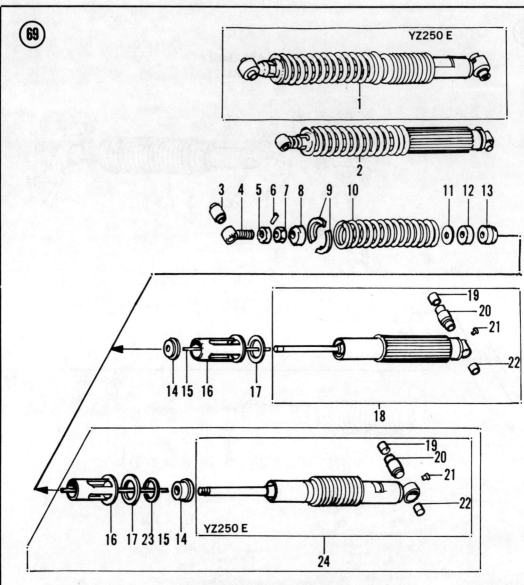

MONOSHOCK ASSEMBLY
(YZ400F, E, D; YZ250F, E; YZ125F, E, D)

 1. Monoshock assembly—YZ250E only
 2. Monoshock assembly—all models except YZ250E
 3. Bushing
 4. Frame bracket assembly
 5. Adjustment nut
 6. Dowel pin
 7. Locknut
 8. Upper spring seat
 9. Spring seats (keepers)
10. Spring
11. Stopper support
12. Cover
13. Stopper
14. Case clip
15. Pushrod
16. Spring guide
17. Lower spring seat
18. Damper subassembly—all models except YZ250E
19. Bushing
20. Bushing assembly
21. Screw
22. Bushing
23. Circlip
24. Damper subassembly—YZ250E only

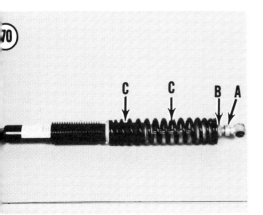

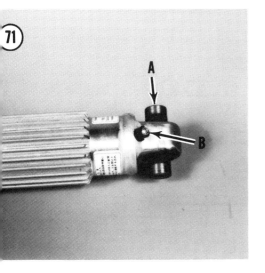

9

> *NOTE*
> *In order to maintain the same adjustments (damping and spring pre-load)record the number of turns of both of these adjusters as they are moved for removal.*

Turn the damping adjuster (A, **Figure 70**) the way toward the end.

Loosen the spring pre-load locknut and n it and the adjuster (B, **Figure 70**) all the y toward the end.

As the spring pre-load adjuster is turned ay from the spring the spring seats epers) will become loose; remove them if y have not already fallen out.

Slide off the spring and spring guide (C, ;ure 70).

Inspect the condition of the upper and ver mounting bushings (A, **Figure 71 and** . Replace if necessary.

7. Check the damper unit for leakage and make sure the damper rod is straight.

> *NOTE*
> *The damper unit cannot be rebuilt; it must be replaced as a unit.*

> *WARNING*
> *The monoshock unit contains highly compressed nitrogen gas. Do not tamper with or attempt to open the damper/cylinder assembly (**Figure 73**). Do not place it near an open flame or other extreme heat. Do not dispose of the damper subassembly yourself. Take it to a Yamaha dealer where it can be deactivated and disposed of properly. Never attempt to remove the plug at the bottom of the nitrogen tank (B, **Figure 71**).*

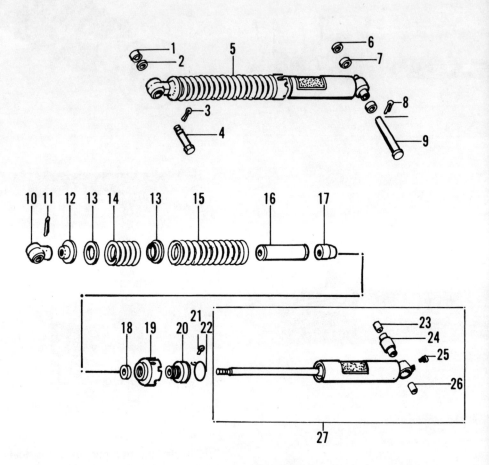

MONOSHOCK ASSEMBLY
(YZ100G, F, E)

1. Nut
2. Washer
3. Cotter pin
4. Bolt
5. Monoshock assembly
6. Washer
7. Thrust cover
8. Cotter pin
9. Pin
10. Upper bracket
11. Cotter pin
12. Upper bracket
13. Spring seat/guide
14. Spring (short)

15. Spring (long)
16. Sleeve
17. Stopper
18. Inner stopper
19. Lower spring seat
20. Case cap
21. Set screw
22. Spring clip retainer
23. Bushing
24. Bushing assembly
25. Screw
26. Bushing
27. Damper subassembly

Install the new spring—making sure all rts are in their correct position; refer to gure **68 or 69**.

NOTE
There are 2 additional factory springs available for the monoshock. One is stiffer and the other softer. The springs are color coded on the end of the spring for easy identification. Take the spring to a Yamaha dealer to choose the correct spring for your specific needs (combination of rider weight and track conditions).

Install the spring seats (keepers) and hten the spring pre-load adjuster. If the me spring (spring rate) is installed; return e adjuster to the same position as noted in

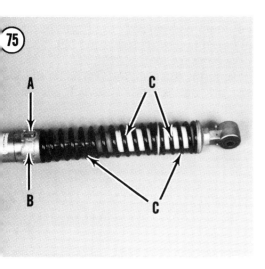

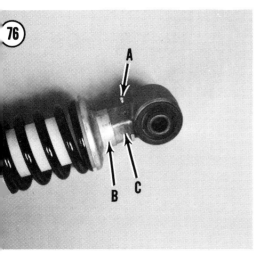

Step 1, NOTE. Screw in the locknut and tighten to 40-43 ft.-lb. (55-60 N.m).
10. Screw the damper adjuster to its original position as noted in Step 1, NOTE.

NOTE
*If a new spring with a different spring rate has been installed, readjust as described under **Spring Pre-Load** and **Damping Adjustment** in this chapter.*

11. Install the monoshock as described under *Monoshock Removal/Installation* in this chapter.

Monoshock—Model YZ100 (1978 and Later) Disassembly/Inspection/Assembly

Refer to **Figure 74** for this procedure. The springs on this monoshock are not under the same amount of pressure as those used on a dual-shock rear suspension. Therefore a spring compression tool is not needed for disassemby.

1. Remove the monoshock as described under *Monoshock Removal/Installation* in this chapter.

NOTE
In order to maintain the same spring pre-load adjustment record the number of turns of the adjuster as it is turned to its fully relaxed position.

2. Remove the set screw (A, **Figure 75**); leave it attached to the spring clip retainer.
3. Relieve the spring pressure by turning the spring preload adjuster (B, **Figure 75**) all the way *counterclockwise*. This direction is established by holding onto the damper portion of the monoshock with the spring pointed away from you.
4. Remove the cotter pin (A, **Figure 76**) from the upper bracket.
5. Hold the spring seat (B, **Figure 76**) with a wrench and loosen the upper bracket (C, **Figure 76**).
6. Unscrew the upper bracket and spring seat from the damper rod.
7. Slide off the 2 springs, spring guide, and sleeve (C, **Figure 75**).

8. Inspect the condition of the upper and lower mounting bushings; replace if necessary.

9. Check the damper unit for leakage and make sure the damper rod is straight.

NOTE
The damper unit cannot be rebuilt; it must be replaced as a unit.

WARNING
The monoshock unit contains highly compressed nitrogen gas. Do not tamper with or attempt to open the damper/cylinder assembly. Do not place it near an open flame or other extreme heat. Do not dispose of the damper subassembly yourself. Take it to a Yamaha dealer where it can be deactivated and disposed of properly. Never attempt to remove the plug at the bottom of the damper/cylinder.

10. Install the new springs, spring guide and sleeve—making sure all parts are in their correct position; refer to **Figure 74**.

NOTE
There are 2 additional factory springs available for the monoshock. One is stiffer and the other softer. The springs are color coded on the end of the spring for easy identification. Take the spring to a Yamaha dealer to choose the correct spring for your specific needs (combination of rider weight and track conditions).

11. Screw on the spring seat and upper bracket. Tighten the upper bracket to 43 ft.-lb. (60 N.m).

12. Install a new cotter pin—never install an old cotter pin as it may break and fall out.

13. If the same springs (spring rate) are installed; return the adjuster to the same position as noted in Step 1, NOTE. Screw in the set screw.

14. Turn the spring pre-load adjuster to its original position as noted in Step 1, NOTE.

NOTE
*If new springs with a different spring rate have been installed, readjust as described under **Spring Pre-Load Adjustment** in this chapter.*

15. Install the monoshock as described unde *Monoshock Removal/Installation* in thi chapter.

REAR SUSPENSION (MONOCROSS TYPE)

The monocross type rear suspension on th 1976 YZs (1977 for the YZ100) is a very basi unit without the adjustment features late adapted in the DeCarbon System. This un has no provisions for adjusting the dampin action or spring pre-load. The monoshock un is tucked up in the frame's hollow back bor under the fuel tank.

Removal/Installation

1. Place a milk crate or wood block(s) unde the frame high enough to lift the rear whee off the ground by at least 10 to 12 inches.

2. Remove the seat.

3. Turn the fuel shutoff valve to the OF position and remove the fuel line to th carburetor.

4. Remove the bolt securing the rear of th fuel tank. Pull the tank toward the rear ar remove it. Don't lose the 2 rubber damp pads on the frame; they will usually come o when the tank is removed.

5. Remove the cotter pin, pivot shaft nu washer and rubber damper (**Figure 77**).

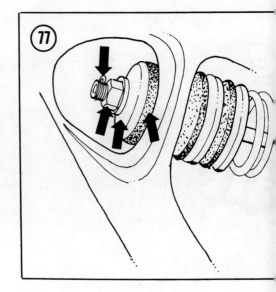

Remove the bolt and nut securing the membrane housing/damper unit at the rear to the swing arm. Don't lose the 2 washers.

Let the swing arm and rear wheel pivot down.

Withdraw the monoshock unit out through the rear.

Install by reversing these removal steps. Tighten the rear bolt and nut and the front nut to the torque specified in **Table 1**. Install a new cotter pin—never reuse an old one as it may break and fall out.

Disassembly/Inspection/Assembly

Refer to **Figure 79** for this procedure.

Remove the monoshock assembly as previously described.

Place the mounting surfaces of the membrane housing/damper unit in a vise with soft jaws. Mount it so the spring end is pointed up.

Remove the nut (7), 2 washers (8 and 9), 2 rubber dampers (10), collar (11), nutplate (12), and upper spring seat (13) from the damper rod.

Slide off the spring (14), lower spring seat (15) and washer (16).

Check the damper unit for leakage and make sure the damper rod is straight.

> *NOTE*
> *The damper unit cannot be rebuilt; it must be replaced as a unit.*

> *WARNING*
> *The monoshock unit contains highly compressed nitrogen gas. Do not tamper with or attempt to open the membrane housing/damper unit assembly. Do not place it near an open flame or other extreme heat. Do not dispose of the damper subassembly yourself. Take it to a Yamaha dealer where it can be deactivated and disposed of properly. Never attempt to remove the plug at the bottom of the damper/cylinder.*

6. Check the tightness of 2 items (**Figure 78**). Loosen the ring nut and tighten the cap case to 108 ft.-lb. (150 N•m). Retighten the ring nut to 146 ft.-lb. (200 N•m). This torque specification is correct even though it is large.

> *NOTE*
> *Tightening the ring nut requires a special tool. It is a Ring Nut Wrench and is available from Yamaha dealers.*

7. Install all items removed in Steps 3 and 4 in reverse order. Refer to **Figure 79** to make sure they are installed in the correct order.

> *NOTE*
> *There are 2 additional factory springs available for the monoshock. One is stiffer and the other softer. The springs are color coded on the end of the spring for easy identification. Take the spring to a Yamaha dealer to choose the correct spring for your specific needs (combination of rider weight and track conditions).*

8. Tighten the nut to 11 ft.-lb. (15 N•m).

9. Install the monoshock assembly as previously described.

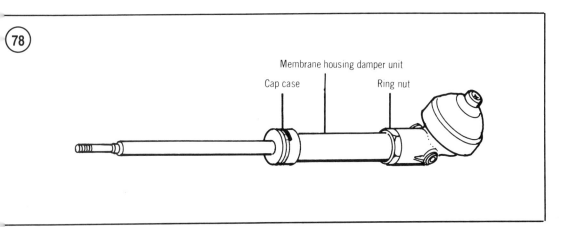

(78)

Membrane housing damper unit

Cap case Ring nut

9

⑦⑨

MONOSHOCK ASSEMBLY
(YZ400; YZ250; YZ175C; YZ125C; YZ125X; YZ100D)

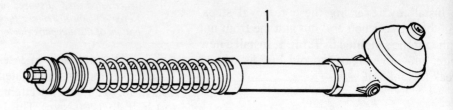

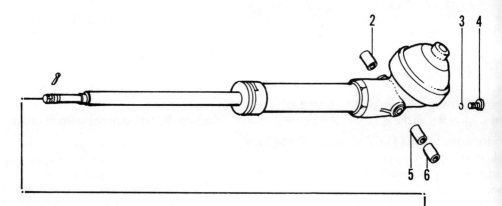

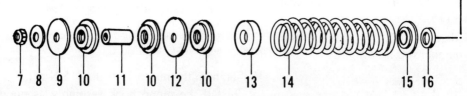

1. Monoshock assembly	9. Large washer
2. Bushing	10. Rubber damper
3. O-ring	11. Spacer
4. Screw	12. Nut plate
5. Collar	13. Upper spring seat
6. Bushing	14. Spring
7. Nut	15. Lower spring seat
8. Small washer	16. Washer

Table 1 REAR SUSPENSION TORQUE SPECIFICATIONS*

	YZ465G YZ400F YZ250G, F	YZ400E, YZ250E, D	YZ175C	YZ125	YZ100
Rear axle nut	58 (80)	58 (80)	61 (85	61 (85)	61 (85)
Monoshock bolt to frame	22 (30)	18 (25)	43 (60)	22 (30)	22 (30)
Monoshock adjust locknut	43 (60)**	43 (60)	43 (60)	43 (60)	none
Swing arm pivot nut	58 (80)	65 (90)	36 (50)	61 (85)	32 (45)

*ft.-lb. (Newton-meters)
**Applies to YZ400F and YZ250F only.

Table 2 MONOSHOCK SPRING LENGTH–INSTALLED

Models YZ465G and YZ250G only	
Standard length	14.0 in. (356 mm)
Minimum length	13.6 in. (345 mm)
Maximum length	14.2 in. (360 mm)

Table 3 MONOSHOCK SPRING PRE-LOAD SETTINGS MODELS YZ100 (1978 AND LATER)

	Soft	Standard	Hard				
Adjusting positions	1	–	1	2	3	4	5
Number of 1/2 turns	1/2	–	1/2	1	1 1/2	2	2

9

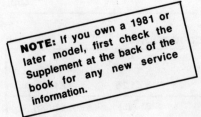

CHAPTER TEN

BRAKES

The brakes on both the front and rear are drum type. **Figure 1** illustrates the major components of the brake assembly. By activating the brake hand lever or foot pedal it pulls the cable or rod which in turn rotates the camshaft. This forces the brake shoes out into contact with the brake drum.

Lever and pedal free play must be maintained on both brakes to minimize brake drag and premature brake wear, and maximize braking effectiveness. Refer to *Front Brake Lever Adjustment* and *Rear Brake Pedal Free Play* in Chapter Three, for complete adjustment procedures.

The front brake cable must be inspected and replaced periodically as it will stretch with use and can no longer be properly adjusted.

Brake specifications (**Table 1**) are at the end of the chapter.

FRONT BRAKE

Disassembly

Refer to **Figure 1** for this procedure.

1. Remove the front wheel as described under *Front Wheel Removal/Installation* in Chapter Eight.
2. Pull the brake assembly (**Figure 2**) straight up and out of the brake drum.

NOTE
Prior to removing the brake shoes, measure them as described in the following procedure.

3. Remove the brake shoes from the backing plate by firmly pulling up on the center of each shoe as shown in **Figure 3**.

NOTE
Place a clean shop rag on the linings to protect them from oil and grease during removal.

4. Remove the return springs and separate the shoes.
5. Mark the position of the cam lever(s) the camshaft(s) so it (they) will be reinstalled in the same position.
6. On single leading shoe models, loosen the bolt securing the brake lever to the cam (**Figure 4**). Remove the lever, cam seal, and camshaft.
7. On double leading shoe models, loosen the bolts securing the upper and lower brake levers to the cams. Remove the levers, cam seals, return spring on lower lever, and camshafts.

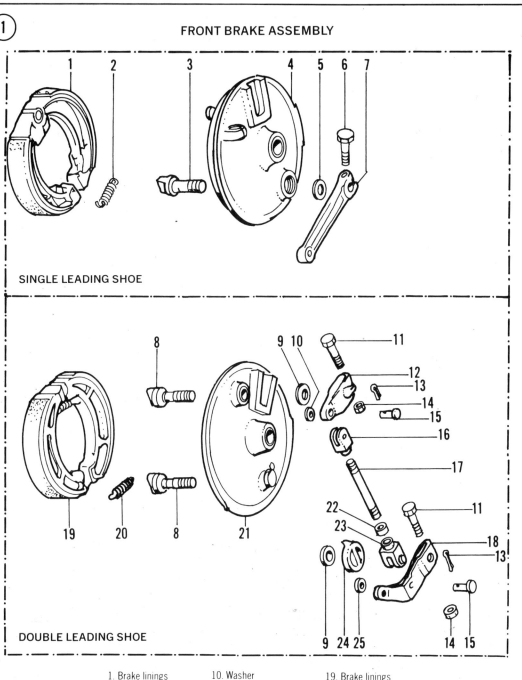

① **FRONT BRAKE ASSEMBLY**

SINGLE LEADING SHOE

DOUBLE LEADING SHOE

1. Brake linings	10. Washer	19. Brake linings
2. Return springs	11. Bolt	20. Return springs
3. Camshaft	12. Brake lever	21. Backing plate
4. Backing plate	13. Cotter pin	22. Nut
5. Seal	14. Nut	23. Rod end
6. Bolt	15. Pin	24. Return spring
7. Brake lever	16. Rod end	25. Washer
8. Camshaft	17. Connecting rod	
9. Camshaft seal	18. Brake lever	

Inspection

1. Thoroughly clean and dry all parts except the linings.

2. Check the contact surface of the drum (**Figure 5**) for scoring. If there are deep grooves, deep enough to snag a fingernail, the drum should be reground and new shoes fitted. This type of wear can be avoided to a great extent if the brakes are disassembled and thoroughly cleaned after the bike has been ridden in mud or deep sand, or after each race.

> *NOTE*
> *If oil or grease is on the drum surface, clean it off with a clean rag soaked in lacquer thinner—do not use any solvent that may leave an oil residue.*

3. Use vernier calipers (**Figure 6**) and check the inside diameter of the drum for out-of-round or excessive wear. Refer to **Table 1** for brake specifications.

4. If the drum is turned, the linings will have to be replaced and the new linings arced to the new drum contour.

5. Inspect the linings for imbedded foreign material. Dirt can be removed with a stiff wire brush. Check for traces of oil or grease. If they are contaminated, they must be replaced.

6. With the linings installed on the backing plate, measure the outside diameter in the locations shown in **Figure 7** with vernier calipers. Refer to **Table 1** for brake specifications. Replace as necessary.

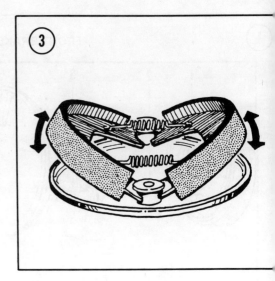

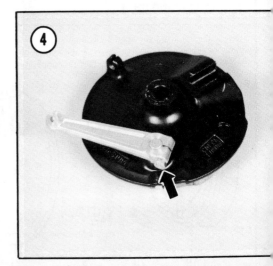

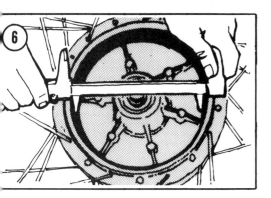

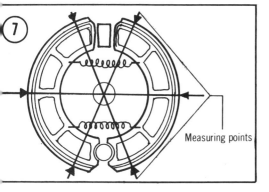

Measuring points

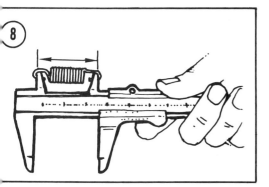

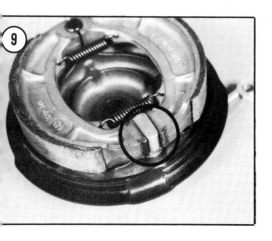

7. Inspect the cam lobe and the pivot pin area of the shaft for wear and corrosion. Minor roughness can be removed with a fine emery cloth.

8. Inspect the brake shoe return springs (**Figure 8**) with vernier calipers. Refer to **Table 1** for specifications. Replace as necessary. If they are stretched, they will not fully retract the brake shoes from the drum, resulting in a power-robbing drag on the drums and premature wear of the linings. Replace as necessary and always replace as a pair.

Assembly

1. Assemble the brake by reversing the disassembly steps.

2. Grease the shaft(s), cam(s), and pivot post (**Figure 9**) with a light coat of molybdenum disulfide grease (**Figure 10**); avoid getting any grease on the brake plate where the linings come in contact with it.

3. On double leading shoe models be sure to install the lever return spring, be sure that it is positioned correctly in the hole in the backing plate and onto the brake lever.

4. When installing the brake lever onto the brake camshaft, be sure to align the 2 parts with the 2 marks made in *Disassembly*, Step 5.

5. Hold the brake shoes in a V-formation with the return springs attached and snap them in

10

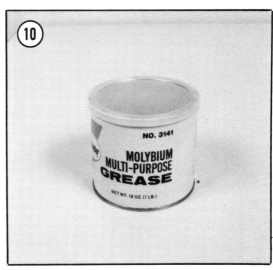

NO. 3141
MOLYBIUM
MULTI-PURPOSE
GREASE
NET WT. 16 OZ. (1 LB.)

place on the brake backing plate. Make sure they are firmly seated on it (**Figure 11**).

> *NOTE*
> *If new linings are being installed, file off the leading edge of each shoe a little (**Figure 12**) so that the brake will not grab when applied.*

6. Install the brake panel assembly into the brake drum.
7. Install the front wheel as described under *Front Wheel Removal/Installation* in Chapter Eight.

> *NOTE*
> *When installing the front wheel, be sure that the locating slot in the brake panel is engaged with the boss on the front fork leg (**Figure 13**). This is necessary for proper brake operation.*

8. Adjust the front brake as described under *Front Brake Lever Adjustment* in Chapter Three.

REAR BRAKE

Disassembly

Refer to **Figure 14** for this procedure.
1. Remove the rear wheel as described under *Rear Wheel Removal/Installation* in Chapter Nine.
2. Pull the brake assembly (**Figure 15**) straight up and out of the brake drum.

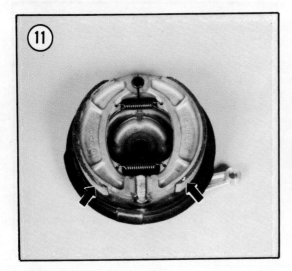

> *NOTE*
> *Prior to removing the brake shoes, measure them as described in the following procedure.*

3. Remove the brake shoes from the backing plate by firmly pulling up on the center of each shoe as shown in **Figure 3**.

> *NOTE*
> *Place a clean shop rag on the linings to protect them from oil and grease during removal.*

4. Remove the return springs and separate the shoes.
5. Mark the position of the cam lever to the camshaft so it will be reinstalled in the same position.
6. Loosen the bolt securing the brake lever to the cam (**Figure 16**). Remove the lever, cam, seal, and camshaft.

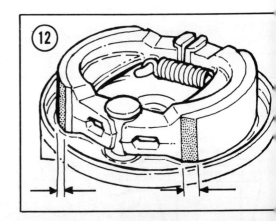

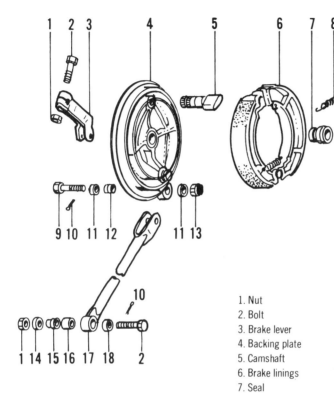

REAR BRAKE ASSEMBLY

1. Nut
2. Bolt
3. Brake lever
4. Backing plate
5. Camshaft
6. Brake linings
7. Seal
8. Return springs
9. Bolt
10. Cotter pin
11. Oil seal
12. Bushing
13. Nut
14. Washer
15. Bushing
16. Collar
17. Torque link arm
18. Bushing

10

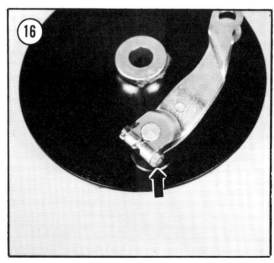

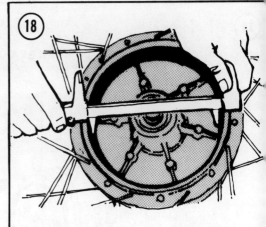

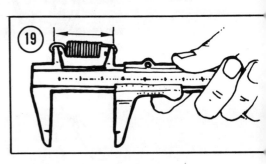

Inspection

1. Thoroughly clean and dry all parts except the linings.

2. Check the contact surface of the drum (**Figure 17**) for scoring. If there are deep grooves, deep enough to snag a fingernail, the drum should be reground and new shoes fitted. This type of wear can be avoided to a great extent if the brakes are disassembled and thoroughly cleaned after each race or if the bike has been ridden in mud or deep sand.

> *NOTE*
> *If oil or grease is on the drum surface, clean it off with a clean rag soaked in lacquer thinner—do not use any solvent that may leave an oil residue.*

3. Use vernier calipers (**Figure 18**) and check the inside diameter of the drum for out-of-round or excessive wear. Refer to **Table 1** for brake specifications.

4. If the drum is turned, the linings will have to be replaced and the new linings arced to the new drum contour.

5. Inspect the linings for imbedded foreign material. Dirt can be removed with a stiff wire brush. Check for traces of oil or grease. If they are contaminated, they must be replaced.

6. With the linings installed on the backing plate, measure the outside diameter in the locations shown in **Figure 7** with vernier calipers. Refer to **Table 1** for brake specifications. Replace as necessary.

7. Inspect the cam lobe and the pivot pin are of the shaft for wear and corrosion. Mine roughness can be removed with fine eme cloth.

8. Inspect the brake shoe return sprin (**Figure 19**) with vernier calipers. Refer **Table 1** for specifications. Replace necessary. If they are stretched, they will n fully retract the brake shoes from the drum resulting in a power-robbing drag on t drums and premature wear of the lining Replace as necessary and always replace as pair.

Assembly

1. Assemble the brake by reversing t disassembly steps.

2. Grease the shaft, cam, and pivot po (**Figure 20**) with a light coat of molybdenu disulfide grease; avoid getting any grease the brake plate where the linings come contact with it.

3. When installing the brake lever onto t brake camshaft, be sure to align the 2 pa with the 2 marks made in *Disassembly* Step 5.

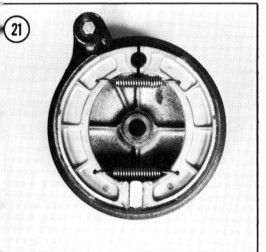

4. Hold the brake shoes in a V-formation with the return springs attached and snap them in place on the brake backing plate. Make sure they are firmly seated on it (**Figure 21**).

NOTE
*If new linings are being installed, file off the leading edge of each shoe a little (**Figure 12**) so that the brake will not grab when applied.*

5. Install the brake panel assembly into the brake drum.

6. Install the rear wheel as described under *Rear Wheel Removal/Installation* in Chapter Nine

7. Adjust the rear brake as described under *Rear Brake Pedal Adjustment* in Chapter Three.

FRONT BRAKE CABLE

Brake cable adjustment should be checked periodically as the cable stretches with use and increases brake lever free play. Free play is the distance that the brake lever travels between the released position and the point when the brake shoes come in contact with the drum.

If the brake adjustment, as described in Chapter Three, can no longer be achieved the cable must be replaced.

Replacement

1. At the hand lever, loosen the locknut (A, **Figure 22**) and turn the adjusting barrel (B, **Figure 22**) all the way toward the cable sheath.

2. At the brake assembly, loosen the locknut (A, **Figure 23**) and screw it all the way toward

10

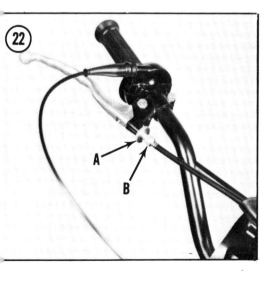

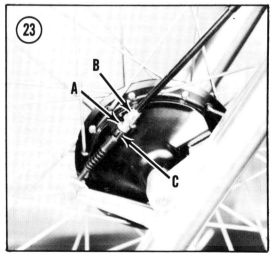

the cable sheath. Withdraw the pin from the end of the brake lever (B, **Figure 23**) and disconnect the cable from the receptacle on the backing plate (C, **Figure 23**).

3. Pull the hand lever all the way to the grip, remove the cable nipple from the lever and remove the cable.

4. Remove the band (**Figure 24**) securing the cable to the front fork leg.

5. Withdraw the cable from the plastic holders on the front fork clamps (**Figure 25**).

> *NOTE*
> *Prior to removing the cable, make a drawing (or take a Polaroid picture) of the cable routing through the frame. It is very easy to forget how it was once it has been removed. Replace it exactly as it was, avoiding any sharp turns.*

6. Install by reversing these removal steps.

7. Adjust the brake as described under *Fro Brake Lever Adjustment* in Chapter Three.

REAR BRAKE
PEDAL ASSEMBLY

Removal/Installation

1. Place a milk crate or wood blocks under t frame to hold the bike securely in place.

2. Unscrew the adjuster (A, **Figure 2** completely from the brake rod.

3. Pull the brake lever to the rear and pull t brake rod forward through the pivot p Remove the pivot pin (B, **Figure 26**).

4. Remove the bolts (**Figure 27**) securing t right-hand front footrest and remove it.

5. From under the frame, remove the E-c securing the brake lever pivot arm to

ame. Use a screwdriver to pry it out of the
lot.

Carefully unhook the return spring from un-
er the pedal, slide the pedal assembly out
rom the frame and remove it. instal the rear
oil spring, pivot pin and adjusting nut onto the
nd of the brake rod so they will not get lost.

7. Install by reversing these removal steps.
Apply grease to the pivot arm prior to installing it into the frame.

8. Make sure that the E-clip securing the pivot
arm is correctly in place so it will not fall off.

9. Adjust the rear brake as described under
Rear Brake Pedal Free Play in Chapter Three.

Table 1 BRAKE SPECIFICATIONS*

Item	YZ465 & YZ400	YZ250	YZ125 & YZ175	YZ100
Drum I.D. (new)				
Front	5.12 (130)	5.12 (130)	5.12 (130)	4.33 (110)
Rear	6.3 (160)	5.12 (130)	5.12 (130)	5.12 (130)
Brake shoe O.D. wear limit				
Front	4.96 (126)	4.96 (126)	4.96 (126)	4.17 (106)
Rear	6.14 (156)	4.96 (126)	4.96 (126)	4.96 (126)
Lining thickness wear limit				
Front and rear		all–0.08 (2)		
Shoe spring free length (new)				
Front	1.38 (35)	1.38 (35)	1.38 (35)	1.38 (35)
Rear	2.68 (68)	1.38 (35)	1.38 (35)	1.38 (35)

*Ft.-lb. (Newton-meters).

10

CHAPTER ELEVEN

FRAME AND REPAINTING

The frame does not require routine maintenance. However it should be inspected after each race or after a weekend of hard riding. All welds should be inspected immediately after any accident or severe spill, even a slight one.

This chapter describes procedures for completely stripping the frame. In addition, recommendations are provided for repainting the stripped frame.

This chapter also includes procedures for the kickstand and footpegs.

KICKSTAND (SIDE STAND)

Removal/Installation

1. Place the bike on a milk crate or wood blocks to support it securely.
2. Raise the kickstand and disconnect the return spring (A, **Figure 1**) from the pin on the frame with Vise Grips.
3. Remove the bolt and nut (B, **Figure 1**), and remove the kickstand from the frame.
4. Install by reversing these removal steps. Apply a light coat of multipurpose grease to the pivot surfaces of the frame tab and the kickstand yoke prior to installation.

FOOTPEGS

Replacement

Remove the bolts (**Figure 2**) securing the footpegs to the frame and remove them.

Make sure the spring is in good condition and not broken. Replace as necessary.

Lubricate the pivot points prior to installation. Tighten the bolts securely.

FRAME

The frame does not require routine maintenance. However it should be inspected after each race or after a weekend of hard riding. All welds should be inspected immediately after any accident or severe spill, even a slight one.

Component Removal/Installation

1. Remove the seat, side cover/number panels, and fuel tank.
2. Remove the engine as described in Chapter Four.
3. Remove the front wheel, steering and suspension components as described Chapter Eight.

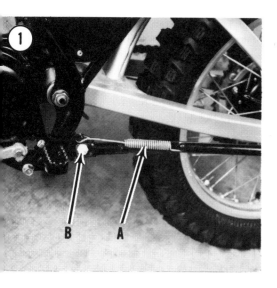

4. Remove the rear wheel, fender, Monoshock, and rear swing arm as described in Chapter Nine.

5. Remove the ignition coil and wiring harness as described in Chapter Seven.

6. Remove the kickstand and footpegs as described in this chapter.

7. Remove the steering head races from the steering head tube as described in Chapter Eight.

8. Inspect the frame for bends, cracks or other damage, especially around welded joints and areas that are rusted.

9. Assemble by reversing these removal steps.

Stripping and Painting

Remove all components from the frame. Thoroughly strip off all old paint. The best way is to have it sandblasted down to bare metal. If this is not possible, you can use a liquid paint remover and steel wool and a fine, hard wire brush.

NOTE
The side cover/number panels, fenders, air box and fuel tank are molded polypropylene which is a very slick and flexible plastic (Figure 3). Do not try to paint them as it is very difficult. Besides who wants to get rid of Yamaha Competition Yellow?

CAUTION
Do not use any liquid paint remover on these components as it will damage the surface. The color is an integral part of the component and cannot be removed.

When the frame is down to bare metal, have it inspected for hairline and internal cracks. Magnafluxing is the most common and complete process.

Make sure that the primer is compatible with the type of paint you are going to use for the final coat. Spray one or 2 coats of primer as smoothly as possible. Let it dry thoroughly and use a fine grade of wet sandpaper (400-600 grit) to remove any flaws. Carefully wipe the surface clean and then spray the final coat. Use either lacquer or enamel base paint and follow the manufacturer's instructions.

11

A shop specializing in painting will probably do the best job. However, you can do a surprisingly good job with a good grade of spray paint. Spend a few extra bucks and get a good grade of paint as it will make a difference in how well it looks and how long it will stand up. One trick in using spray paint is to first shake the can thoroughly—make sure the ball inside the can is loose; if it is not, return the can and get a good one. It is a good idea to make sure the ball is loose when you purchase the can of paint. Shake the can as long as is stated on the can. Then immerse the can *upright* in a pot or bucket of *warm water (not hot—not over 120 degrees F)*.

Leave the can in for several minutes. When thoroughly warmed, shake the can again and spray the frame. Be sure to get into all the crevasses where there may be rust problems.

Several light mist coats are better than one heavy coat. Spray painting is best done in temperatures of 70-80 degrees F; any temperature above or below this will give you problems.

After the final coat has dried completely, at least 48 hours, any overspray or orange peal may be removed with a *light application* of Dupont rubbing compound (red color) and finished with Dupont polishing compound (white color). Be careful not to rub too hard and go through the finish.

Finish off with a couple of good coats of wax prior to reassembling all the components.

It is a good idea to keep the frame touched up with fresh paint after it has been cleaned up after a race.

An alternative to painting is powder coating. The process involves spraying electrically charged particles of pigment and resin on the object to be coated, which is negatively charged. The charged powder particles adhere to the electrically grounded object until heated and fused into a smooth coating in a curing oven. Powder coated surfaces are more resistant to chipping, scratching, fading and wearing than other finishes. A variety of colors and textures are available.

Powder coating also has advantages over paint as no environmentally hazardous solvents are used.

SUPPLEMENT

1981 AND LATER SERVICE INFORMATION

The following supplement provides additional information for servicing the 1981-1984 Yamaha YZ100, YZ125, YZ250, YZ465 and YZ490.

The chapter headings in this supplement correspond to those in the main portion of this manual. If a chapter is not included in this supplement, then there are no changes in that chapter for 1981 and later models. If you are servicing a YZ490, use the information given for the YZ465 unless otherwise specified in this supplement.

If your bike is covered by this supplement, carefully read the supplement and then read the appropriate chapter in the basic book before beginning any work.

12

CHAPTER ONE

GENERAL INFORMATION

For the 1982 model year, the displacement of the YZ465 was increased to 490 cc. This was accomplished by increasing the bore from 85 mm (3.35 in.) to 87 mm (3.43 in.). Because the YZ465 and YZ490 are very similar the information on the YZ465 in Chapters One through Twelve of the main book can be used to service the YZ490 (also take note of the information found in this supplement).

SERIAL NUMBERS

Frame and engine serial numbers for 1981 and later models are listed in **Table 1**.

Table 1 ENGINE AND CHASSIS NUMBERS (1981-ON)

Model number	Engine serial No. (start to end)	Frame serial No. (start to end)
YZ465H	4V4-000101-*	4V4-000101-*
YZ490J	5X6-000101-*	5X6-000101-*
YZ490K	23X-000101*	23X-000101-*
YZ490L	4OT-000101-on	4OT-000101-on
YZ250H	4V3-000101-*	4V3-000101-*
YZ250J	5X5-000101-*	5X5-000101-*
YZ250K	24Y-000101-*	24Y-000101-*
YZ250L	39X-000101-on	39X-000101-on
YZ125H	4V2-000101-*	4V2-000101-*
YZ125J	5X4-000101-*	5X4-000101-*
YZ125K	24X-000101-*	24X-000101-*
YZ125L	39W-000101-on	39W-000101-on
YZ100H	3R2-020101-*	3R2-020101-*
YZ100J	5X3-000101-*	5X3-000101-*
YZ100K**	5X3-060101-on	5X3-060101-on

* Not available.
** Last year manufactured.

CHAPTER THREE

LUBRICATION, MAINTENANCE AND TUNE-UP

PERIODIC LUBRICATION

Engine Oil

Table 2 lists new fuel/oil recommendations for 1981 and later models that differ from 1980 models.

Fuel Capacity

Refer to **Table 3** for new fuel tank capacities.

Transmission Oil Checking and Changing

The procedures for checking and changing the transmission oil are the same as for 1980 and earlier models; some oil capacities have changed. See **Table 4**.

Front Fork Oil Change

Procedures for changing the front fork oil are the same as for 1980 models except that on all 1983 models you must remove the handlebars to gain access to the fork cap. See **Figure 1**. New fork oil capacity and measurement specifications are in **Table 5**.

Front Fork Air Pressure

New front fork air pressure specifications for 1981 and later models are in **Table 6**.

> *WARNING*
> *Use only compressed air or nitrogen—**do not** use any other type of compressed gas as an explosion may result. Never heat the front forks with a torch or place them near an open flame or extreme heat.*

PERIODIC MAINTENANCE

Monoshock Adjustment

Refer to the Chapter Nine section of this supplement for complete details.

Drive Chain Adjustment

On all 1981 and later models (except YZ100H), drive chain tension is checked on the top chain run as shown in **Figure 2**. **Table 7** lists drive chain slack specifications for 1981 and later models that are different from 1980 models. **Table 8** lists new drive chain replacement numbers for 1981 and later models that are different from 1980 models.

12

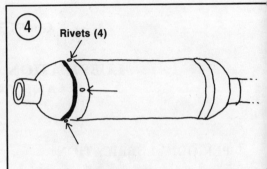

Rivets (4)

Sprocket Replacement
(YZ250K and YZ490K)

On these models, the position of the rear chain support (**Figure 3**) on the swing arm depends upon the size of the rear sprocket. When a sprocket size of 48-50 is used, the support should be mounted in the first and third hole positions. When a sprocket size of 44-46 is used, the support should be mounted in the second and fourth hole positions.

ENGINE TUNE-UP

Cylinder Head Nuts

Procedures for tightening the cylinder head nuts are the same as for 1980 and earlier models; some tightening torques have changed. See **Table 9**.

Correct Spark Plug
Heat Range and Gap

Standard replacement spark plugs for 1981 and later models are listed in **Table 10**.

Ignition Timing

Procedures for checking and adjusting the ignition timing for 1981-on models are the same as for 1980 models; some timing specifications have changed. See **Table 11**.

Idle Speed Adjustment

Refer to **Table 12** for new carburetor specifications. Procedures for adjusting the carburetor are the same as for 1980 models.

Decarbonizing (1984)

When carbon builds up in the silencer replace the internal fiber element as follows
1. Remove the silencer from the bike.
2. Remove the silencer end cap by drilling out the rivets with a 5/32 in. (4 mm) drill b
See **Figure 4**.
3. Remove the element and replace it with new fiber element.

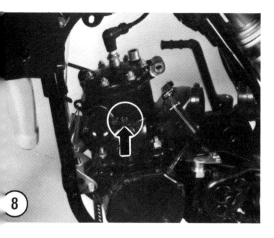

Coolant Type

Only a high quality ethylene glycol-based coolant compounded for aluminum engines should be used. The coolant should be mixed with water in a 50/50 ratio. Coolant capacity is listed in **Table 13**. When mixing antifreeze with water, make sure to use only soft or distilled water. Never use hard or salt water as this will damage engine parts. Distilled water can be purchased at supermarkets in gallon containers.

Coolant Level Check

Before every race, the coolant level in the radiator should be checked. With the engine cool, remove the radiator cap (**Figure 5**) and make sure the level is just below the overflow pipe. If not, add a sufficient amount of coolant in a 50/50 antifreeze-to-water ratio as described under *Coolant Type*.

Coolant Change

This procedure is shown on a YZ250K; other models are similar.
1. Place a large clean container under the engine.
2. Remove the radiator cap (**Figure 5**).

> *WARNING*
> *Do not remove the radiator cap when the engine is hot.*

3. Remove the water pump drain bolt (**Figure 6**) and the cylinder drain bolt (**Figure 8**) and allow the coolant to drain thoroughly.
4. Using a garden hose, pour water into the radiator and thoroughly flush the cooling system. Once the water flowing out through the water pump and cylinder drain bolts is clean, remove the garden hose and allow all water to drain. Reinstall the water pump drain bolt and the cylinder drain bolt.
5. Pour a 50/50 mixture of antifreeze and water into the radiator. See *Coolant Type*.
6. Start the engine and watch the level of coolant in the radiator. Continue to add coolant until its level is correct. See *Coolant Level Check*.
7. Install the radiator cap.

Install the end cap and secure with new rivets.
Install the silencer.

LIQUID COOLING SYSTEM SERVICE

The engine on the following models is liquid-cooled:
a. YZ125 1981-on.
b. YZ250 1982-on.

> *WARNING*
> *When performing any service work on the engine or cooling system, never remove the radiator cap (Figure 5) or coolant drain screws (Figure 6) or disconnect any hose (Figure 7) while the engine and radiator are hot. Scalding fluid and steam may be blown out under pressure and cause serious injury.*

12

Table 2 CORRECT FUEL/OIL MIXTURE*

	Yamalube "R"	Castrol R30
YZ490L, K, J	24:1	20:1
YZ465H	16:1	20:1
YZ250L, K, J	24:1	20:1
YZ250H	16:1	20:1
YZ125L, K, J	24:1	20:1
YZ125H	16:1	20:1
YZ100K, J	24:1	20:1
YZ100H	16:1	20:1

*Normal mixture with premium gasoline.

Table 3 FUEL CAPACITIES

Model	U.S. gal.	Liters
YZ490L, K	2.8	10.5
YZ250L, K, J	2.25	9.0
YZ125L	1.98	7.5
YZ125K	1.84	7.0
YZ125J	2.2	8.2
YZ125H	1.7	6.5
YZ100K, J	2.2	8.2

Table 4 TRANSMISSION OIL CAPACITY

Model	Drain/refill	Rebuild
YZ490L, K, J	750 cc	800 cc
YZ465H	700 cc	750 cc
YZ250L, K, J	850 cc	900 cc
YZ250H	750 cc	800 cc
YZ125L, K, J	800 cc	850 cc
YZ125H	700 cc	750 cc
YZ100K, J	550-650 cc	650-750 cc

Table 5 FRONT FORK OIL CAPACITY AND MEASUREMENT

Model	Capacity oz. (cc)	Measurement in. (mm)
YZ490L	18.6 (550)	
Standard		6.3 (160)
Minimum		5.91 (150)
Maximum		7.09 (180)
YZ490K	19.5 (578)	6.7 (170)
YZ490J	20.42 (606)	5.9 (150)
YZ465H	20.4 (604)	5.9 (150)
YZ250L	18.6 (550)	
Standard		6.3 (160)
Minimum		5.91 (150)
Maximum		7.09 (180)

(continued)

Table 5 FRONT FORK OIL CAPACITY AND MEASUREMENT (continued)

Model	Capacity oz. (cc)	Measurement in. (mm)
YZ250K	19.5 (578)	
Standard		6.7 (170)
Minimum		5.91 (150)
Maximum		7.9 (200)
YZ250J	20.42 (606)	5.9 (150)
YZ250H	20.40 (604)	5.9 (150)
YZ125L	17.59 (520)	
Standard		6.30 (160)
Minimum		4.92 (125)
Maximum		7.87 (200)
YZ125K	14.67 (434)	
Standard		6.34 (161)
Minimum		5.51 (140)
Maximum		8.66 (220)
YZ125J	15.3 (454)	5.9 (150)
YZ125H	13.9 (414)	7.9 (200)
YZ100K		
Standard		6.9 (170)
Minimum		5.91 (150)
Maximum		7.48 (190)
YZ100J	14.0 (340)	6.70 (170)
YZ100H	8.7 (258)	–

Table 6 FRONT FORK AIR PRESSURE

Model	psi	kg/cm^2
YZ490L, K, J	0-17	0-1.2
YZ465H	0-17	0-1.2
YZ250	0-17	0-1.2
YZ125	0-17	0-1.2
YZ100K, J	0-17	0-1.2
YZ100H	Non-air type	

12

Table 7 DRIVE CHAIN SLACK

Model	in.	mm
YZ490L	1.2-1.6	30-40
YZ490K	0.8-1.2	20-30
YZ490J	0.8-1.2	20-30
YZ250L, K	1.2-1.6	30-40
YZ250J	0.8-1.2	20-30
YZ125K	1.2-1.6	30-40
YZ125L, J	1.2-1.4	30-35
YZ125H	0.4-0.6	10-15
YZ100K, J	1.4	35
YZ100H	1.6-1.8	40-45

Table 8 DRIVE CHAIN REPLACEMENT NUMBERS

Model	Type	Number of links
YZ490L	DK520DS	113
YZ490K	DK520DS	111
YZ490J	DK520DS	110
YZ465H	DK520DS	107
YZ250L	DK520DS	111
YZ250K, J, H	DK520DS	109
YZ125L	DK520DS	109
YZ125K	DK520DS	105
YZ125J, H	DK520DS	104
YZ100K	DS520DS	105
YZ100J	DS520DS	106

Table 9 CYLINDER HEAD TIGHTENING TORQUES

Item	ft.-lb.	N•m
Stud bolt		
YZ490L, K	11	15
YZ250L	10	13
YZ250K	18	25
YZ250J	10	13
YZ125L, K	10	13
YZ125J	10	13
YZ100	18	25
Nut		
YZ490L, J	16	22
YZ250L, K	18	25
YZ250J	10	13
YZ125L, K, J, H	18	25

Table 10 SPARK PLUG TYPE AND GAP

Model	Type	Gap in.	Gap mm
YZ490L, K	Champion N-86	0.020-0.024	0.5-0.6
YZ250L, K, J	Champion N-86	0.020-0.024	0.5-0.6
YZ125L	Champion N-84	0.020-0.024	0.5-0.6
YZ125K	Champion N-86	0.020-0.024	0.5-0.6
YZ125J	Champion N-84	0.020-0.024	0.5-0.6
YZ125H	Champion N-59G	0.004-0.028	0.6-0.7
YZ100K, J	Champion N-84	0.020-0.024	0.5-0.6
YZ100H	Champion N-59G	0.020-0.024	0.5-0.6

Table 10 IGNITION TIMING (WITH DIAL INDICATOR)

Model	in.	mm
YZ490L, K, J	0.08	2.0
YZ465H	0.08	2.0
YZ250L, K	0.06	1.5
YZ250J	0.035	0.88
YZ250H	0.024	0.61
YZ125L, K, L	0.074	1.88
YZ125H	0.089	2.27
YZ100K, J, H	0.031	0.8

Table 12 CARBURETOR PILOT SCREW ADJUSTMENT*

Model	No. of turns
YZ490L	1
YZ490K, J	1 3/4
YZ465H	1 1/2
YZ250L	1 1/2
YZ250K, J	1 1/4
YZ250H	1 1/2
YZ125L	2.0
YZ125K, J	1 1/2
YZ125H	1 3/4
YZ100K, J, H	1 1/2

* Carburetor idle speed should be set to rider preference.

Table 13 COOLING SYSTEM SPECIFICATIONS

Coolant capacity	1.1 qt. (1.0 liters)
Coolant type	50/50 mixture of water and anti-freeze for aluminum engines

CHAPTER FOUR

ENGINE

While many of the 1981 and later model engine service procedures are very similar to 1980 models, the 1981 and later YZ125 and the 1982 and later YZ250 models use a completely new engine. On these models, the engine is liquid-cooled with a radiator mounted on the triple clamps behind the number plate (**Figure 9**) and a water pump mounted in the clutch cover (**Figure 10**). The cylinder head and cylinder are cast without the typical cooling fins found on air-cooled 2-stroke engines (**Figure 11**).

New engine specifications are in **Table 14**. New tightening torques are in **Table 15**.

CYLINDER HEAD

Removal/Installation
(Liquid-cooled Models)

This procedure is shown on a YZ250K; other liquid-cooled models are similar.

1. Remove the seat, side covers and fuel tank.
2. Disconnect the spark plug wire and remove it. Loosen the spark plug but do not remove it.
3. Drain the radiator as described under *Coolant Change* in the Chapter Three section of this supplement.
4. Disconnect the radiator hoses at the cylinder head. See **Figure 12**.
5. Disconnect the engine brace at the cylinder head (**Figure 13**), if so equipped.
6. Remove the nuts securing the cylinder head in a crisscross pattern.
7. Loosen the cylinder head by tapping around the perimeter with a rubber or plastic mallet. Never use a metal hammer.
8. Remove the cylinder head by pulling it straight up and off the cylinder studs.
9. Remove the O-rings or cylinder head gasket.

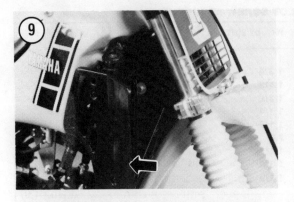

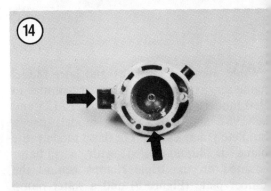

10. Cover the top of the cylinder with a clean shop rag until the cylinder head is reinstalled.

11. Clean the cylinder head as described under *Engine Decarbonizing* in Chapter Three of the main book.

12. Check the water passages in the cylinder head (**Figure 14**) and clean out any residue and sludge that may have collected.

13. Inspect all cylinder head and cylinder O-rings (if so equipped) and replace any that are worn or damaged.

14. Install the 2 O-rings or head gasket.

15. Place the cylinder head on the cylinde with the radiator hose coupling facing towar the rear. Screw on the nuts finger-tight.

16. Tighten the nuts in a crisscross pattern t specifications in **Table 15**.

17. Reinstall the radiator hoses at th cylinder head and tighten the hose clamp securely.

18. Fill the radiator as described und *Coolant Change* in the Chapter Three sectio of this supplement.

19. Install all items previously removed.

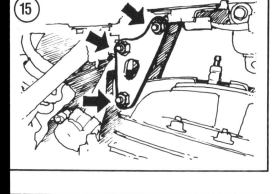

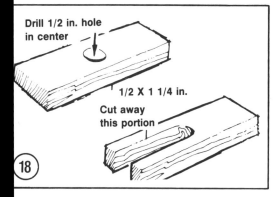

Drill 1/2 in. hole
in center

1/2 X 1 1/4 in.

Cut away
this portion

Removal/Installation
(1983-on YZ490)

These models are equipped with a cylinder head brace (**Figure 15**) to help steady the engine's top end during operation. When the cylinder head requires removal, the brace must be removed first by removing the 3 bolts and nuts. During installation, tighten the cylinder head-to-cylinder bolts first. Then tighten the cylinder head-to-brace bolts to the following torque specifications:

    a. Upper brace to frame: 22 ft.-lb. (30 N•m).

    b. Upper brace to cylinder head: 47 ft.-lb. (65 N•m).

CYLINDER

Removal/Installation
(Liquid-cooled Models)

1. Loosen the clutch cable adjuster at the handlebar. Pull the clutch cable out of its mounting bracket at the engine mounting position.

2. Drain the coolant and remove the cylinder head as described in this supplement.

3. Remove the carburetor as described in Chapter Six of the main book.

4. Disconnect the power valve assembly at the cylinder as described in this supplement.

5. Loosen and remove the cylinder mounting nuts (**Figure 16**).

6. Loosen the cylinder by tapping around the perimeter with a rubber or plastic mallet.

7. Rotate the engine so the piston is at the bottom of its stroke. Pull the cylinder straight up and off the crankcase studs and piston.

8. Remove the cylinder base gasket and discard it. Install a piston holding fixture under the piston (**Figure 17**) to protect the piston skirt from damage. This fixture may be purchased or may be a homemade unit of wood. See **Figure 18**.

9. Place a clean shop cloth into the crankcase opening to prevent the entry of foreign material. See **Figure 19**.

Inspection

Cylinder inspection procedures described in Chapter Four of the main book can be used

12

to inspect and measure the cylinder for wear. The additional procedures described in this section are unique to liquid-cooled engines.

1. Check inside the cylinder water jackets (**Figure 20**) for mineral sludge or rust. Remove with a blunt wooden scraper.

2. Examine the cylinder O-rings (if so equipped) for wear or damage and replace as required.

Installation

1. Check that the top surface of the crankcase and the bottom surface of the cylinder are clean prior to installation.

2. Install a new base gasket.

3. Make sure that the piston ring end gaps are lined up with the locating pins in the piston ring grooves. Lightly oil the piston rings and the inside of the cylinder bore. Rotate the crankshaft to bring the piston in contact with the piston holding fixture.

4. Start the cylinder down over the piston with the exhaust port facing forward.

NOTE
When installing the cylinder, make sure to pivot the cylinder so that it does not hang up on the hose guide on the front of the frame downtube.

5. Compress each ring with your fingers a the cylinder starts to slide over it.

NOTE
Make sure the rings are still properly aligned with the locating pins in the piston.

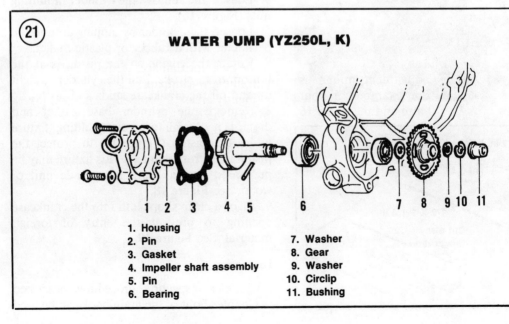

WATER PUMP (YZ250L, K)

1. Housing
2. Pin
3. Gasket
4. Impeller shaft assembly
5. Pin
6. Bearing
7. Washer
8. Gear
9. Washer
10. Circlip
11. Bushing

. Slide the cylinder down until it bottoms on
he piston holding fixture.
. Remove the piston holding fixture and
lide the cylinder into place on the crankcase.
ighten the cylinder nuts to specifications in
able 15.
. Connect the power valve assembly to the
ylinder as described in this supplement.
. Install the cylinder head as described in
his supplement.
). Install the carburetor as described in
hapter Six of the main book.
. Attach the clutch cable at the cylinder.
djust the clutch as described in Chapter
hree of the main book.

PISTON, PISTON PIN AND PISTON RINGS

Measurement

Some 1981 and later models use pistons
ith a large cutaway on the piston skirt.
ecause of the cutaway, piston measurement
described in Chapter Four of the main
ook is no longer possible. To measure the
ston on any 1981 or later model that
quires a partial adjustment specification
ee Table 16), perform the following:
Using a micrometer, measure across the
ston skirt at the height specified in Table
. Record this specification (which is
nsidered the partial measurement).
Add to the partial measurement (Step 1)
e adjustment amount (determined by
amaha) in Table 16. The total of the partial
easurement and the adjustment amount is
e piston diameter. For example, if your
ston measures 41.970 mm and the Table 16
justment amount is 0.025 mm, the piston
ameter is 41.970 + 0.025 = 41.995 mm.

WATER PUMP

A water pump is mounted in the clutch
ver on all liquid-cooled models. Under
rmal operating conditions, disassembly of
e water pump should not be necessary.
owever, if coolant appears in the
ansmission, if the engine overheats or if the
olant level changes, the water pump should
removed and examined. The water pump

is shown in **Figures 21-25**. Refer to the
appropriate drawing for your bike.

Removal/Installation

1. Drain the coolant as described under
Coolant Change in the Chapter Three section
of this supplement.
2. Drain the transmission oil. See Chapter
Three in the main body of this book.
3. Remove the coolant hoses at the water
pump cover. See **Figure 26** (typical).
4. Remove the clutch cover as described in
Chapter Five of the main book.

Disassembly/Inspection/Assembly

1. From the back of the clutch cover, remove
the spacer (if so equipped). Then remove the
circlip securing the impeller shaft gear to the
impeller shaft and remove the gear and all
washers. Remove the governor assembly
from the backside of the crankcase cover.
2. From the front side of the clutch cover,
remove the water pump cover and
disassemble the water pump as shown in the
appropriate drawing (**Figures 21-25**).
3. Lay out the impeller shaft assembly parts
as shown in **Figures 21-25**. Examine each part
for wear or damage. Also check the impeller
shaft for coolant crust and clean if necessary.
4. Examine the water pump bearing and seal
for damage. If necessary, replace as described
in this supplement.
5. Examine the impeller shaft bearing surface
in the case for damage. Remove small burrs
with fine grit sandpaper.
6. Lightly grease the impeller shaft and insert
through the cover.
7. When assembling the water pump and
installing the clutch cover, note the following:
8. *YZ125J and H and YZ250J models*:
   a. Align the impeller shaft and the pump
     drive gear serrations when meshing the
     parts together.
   b. Align the groove in the governor with
     the fork in the case cover and fit the
     governor to the case cover.
   c. Align the impeller shaft inside the clutch
     case cover with the pump drive gear by
     aligning their serrations.

12

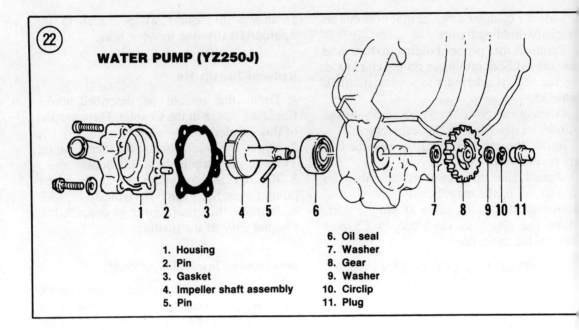

(22)

WATER PUMP (YZ250J)

1. Housing
2. Pin
3. Gasket
4. Impeller shaft assembly
5. Pin
6. Oil seal
7. Washer
8. Gear
9. Washer
10. Circlip
11. Plug

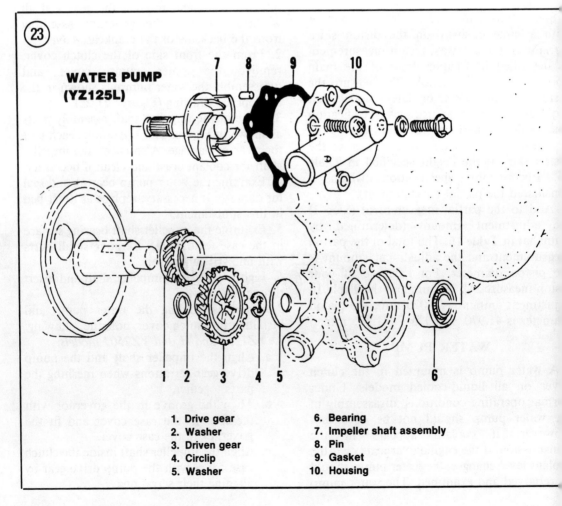

(23)

WATER PUMP (YZ125L)

1. Drive gear
2. Washer
3. Driven gear
4. Circlip
5. Washer
6. Bearing
7. Impeller shaft assembly
8. Pin
9. Gasket
10. Housing

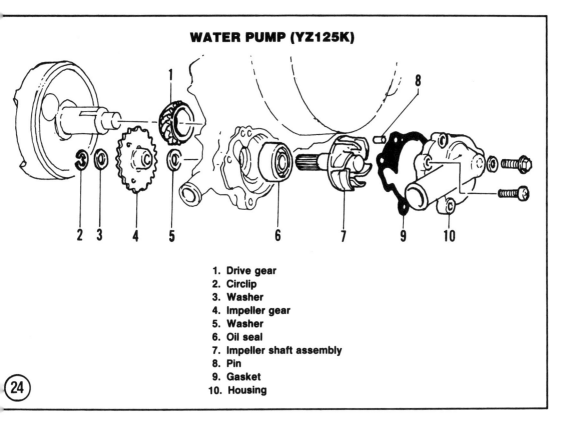

WATER PUMP (YZ125K)

1. Drive gear
2. Circlip
3. Washer
4. Impeller gear
5. Washer
6. Oil seal
7. Impeller shaft assembly
8. Pin
9. Gasket
10. Housing

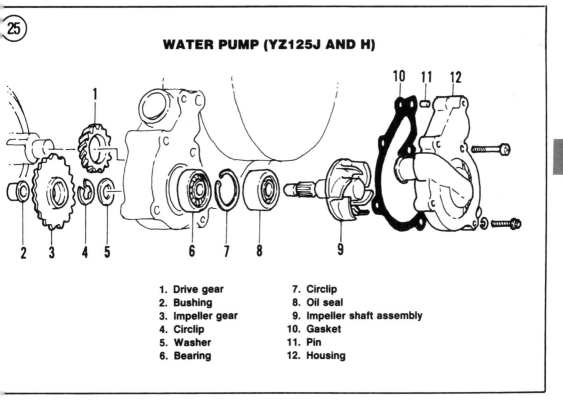

WATER PUMP (YZ125J AND H)

1. Drive gear
2. Bushing
3. Impeller gear
4. Circlip
5. Washer
6. Bearing
7. Circlip
8. Oil seal
9. Impeller shaft assembly
10. Gasket
11. Pin
12. Housing

12

9. *YZ125K and YZ250K:* Before installing the impeller shaft, apply a small amount of grease to the impeller shaft and oil seal. Turn the impeller shaft when installing it.

10. Replace the clutch cover gasket if damaged. Then install the clutch cover while turning the impeller shaft assembly to make sure the impeller gear meshes with the primary gear.

11. Install all parts previously removed.

12. Add the correct amount of transmission oil to the clutch case. See **Table 4**.

13. Fill the cooling system as described under *Coolant Change* in the Chapter Three section of this supplement.

Bearing and Oil Seal Replacement

The bearing and seal can be replaced as described under *Bearing and Oil Seal Replacement* in Chapter Four of the main book.

KICKSTARTER

Removal/Installation

YZ100H

The kickstarter is the same as that used on previous YZ100 models, except that the circlip installed between the oil seal and collar is not used. See Chapter Four of the main book for complete kickstarter service.

YZ100J and K

Figure 27 is an exploded view of the kickstarter mechanism used on all 1982-or YZ100 models. When servicing this kickstarter, refer to service procedures for the YZ125G kickstarter assembly described in Chapter Four of the main book.

26

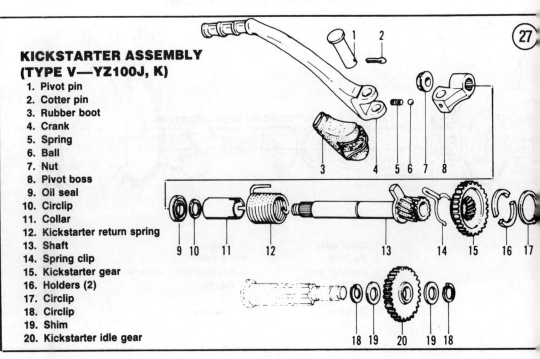

27

KICKSTARTER ASSEMBLY (TYPE V—YZ100J, K)
1. Pivot pin
2. Cotter pin
3. Rubber boot
4. Crank
5. Spring
6. Ball
7. Nut
8. Pivot boss
9. Oil seal
10. Circlip
11. Collar
12. Kickstarter return spring
13. Shaft
14. Spring clip
15. Kickstarter gear
16. Holders (2)
17. Circlip
18. Circlip
19. Shim
20. Kickstarter idle gear

Table 14 ENGINE SPECIFICATIONS

Item	Specifications in. (mm)
Cylinder	
Bore and stroke	
YZ490L, K, J	3.43 × 3.23 (87 × 82)
YZ250L, K	2.677 × 2.677 (68 × 68)
Bore	
YZ490L, K, J	3.43 (87)
YZ250L, K	2.6800-2.6808 (68.000-68.020)
Out of round	
YZ100K, J	0.0004 (0.01)
Piston	
Piston/cylinder clearance	
YZ490L, K, J	0.0031-0.0033 (0.080-0.085)
YZ465H	0.0028-0.0030 (0.070-0.075)
YZ250L, K, J	0.0024-0.0026 (0.060-0.065)
YZ250H	0.0022-0.0024 (0.055-0.060)
YZ125L	0.0026-0.0028 (0.065-0.070)
YZ125K	0.0022-0.0024 (0.055-0.060)
YZ125J	0.0028-0.0030 (0.070-0.075)
YZ125H	0.0024-0.0026 (0.060-0.065)
Piston rings	
Ring end gap	
YZ490L, K	0.014-0.020 (0.35-0.50)
YZ250L, K, J	0.014-0.020 (0.35-0.50)
YZ125L, K, J	0.014-0.020 (0.35-0.50)
YZ100K, J	0.008-0.014 (0.20-0.35)
Ring side clearance	
YZ490L, K	0.0012-0.0020 (0.03-0.05)
YZ250L, K, J	0.0016-0.0031 (0.04-0.08)
YZ125L, K, J, H	0.0012-0.0028 (0.03-0.07)
Crankshaft	
Big end side clearance	
YZ125L, J, H	0.008-0.028 (0.2-0.7)
YZ100K, J	0.008-0.028 (0.2-0.7)

Table 15 ENGINE TORQUE SPECIFICATION

Item	ft.-lb.	N•m
Cylinder head		
Stud bolt		
YZ490L, K, J	11	15
YZ250L	10	13
YZ250K	18	25
YZ250J	10	13
YZ125L, K	10	13
YZ125J	10	13
YZ100	18	25
Nut		
YZ490L, J	16	22
YZ250L, K	18	25
YZ250J	10	13
YZ125L, K, J, H	18	25
(continued)		

12

Table 15 ENGINE TORQUE SPECIFICATION (continued)

Item	ft.-lb.	N•m
Clutch nut		
YZ125L, K, J	58	80
YZ125H	38	53
YZ100K, J	58	80
YZ100K	40	55
Magneto		
YZ490L, K, J	61	85
YZ250L, K, J	30	40
YZ250H	26	35
YZ125L, K	30	40
YZ125J, H	26	35
YZ100K, J	27	38
YZ100H	36	50
Drive sprocket		
YZ125L, K	43	60
YZ125J	46	65
YZ100K, J	43	60

Table 16 PISTON MEASUREMENT LOCATION

Model	Measurement height* in. (mm)	Adjustement amount** in. (mm)
YZ490L, K, J	1.26 (32)	0
YZ465H	1.18 (30)	0
YZ250L, K	1.22 (31)	0
YZ250J, H	1.22 (31)	0.0004 (0.01)
YZ125L, K, J, H	0.75 (19)	0.0002 (0.005)
YZ100K, J	0.79 (20)	0.0001 (0.002)
YZ100H	0.79 (20)	0.0008 (0.020)

*Indicates dimension up from the bottom of the piston skirt @ right angles to the wrist pin.
**See text for details.

CHAPTER FIVE

CLUTCH AND TRANSMISSION

CLUTCH

Removal/Installation

An exploded view of the clutch assembly used on all 1981 and later YZ100 and YZ125 models is shown in **Figure 28**. Removal and installation procedures are the same as for 1980 models.

When removing and installing the clutch cover on liquid-cooled models, note the following changes:

a. Disconnect the power valve unit at th cylinder as described in the Chapter S section of this supplement.

b. Drain the coolant and disconnect th coolant hose at the water pump described under *Water Pump Remova Installation* in the Chapter Four sectic of this supplement.

c. When reinstalling the clutch cover, alig the water pump gears as describe during the water pump assemb

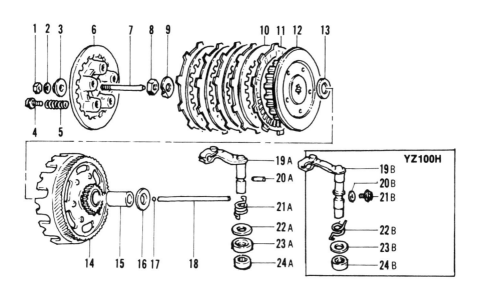

28

CLUTCH ASSEMBLY
(YZ100K, J AND H; YZ125K, J AND H)

1. Nut	9. Lockwasher		
2. Washer	10. Clutch plate	17. Ball	21B. Screw
3. Push plate	11. Friction disc	18. Pushrod	22A. Washer
4. Bolt	12. Clutch boss	19A. Push lever assembly	22B. Spring
5. Spring	13. Washer	19B. Push lever assembly	23A. Oil seal
6. Pressure plate	14. Primary driven gear	20A. Pin	23B. Washer
7. Pushrod	15. Spacer	20B. Washer	24A. Bearing
8. Nut	16. Washer	21A. Spring	24B. Bearing

12

procedure in the Chapter Four section of this supplement.

d. Connect the power valve unit to the cylinder as described in the Chapter Six section of this supplement.

EXTERNAL SHIFT MECHANISM

The shift shaft assembly used on all 1982 and later YZ100 models is the same as that used on all YZ125 models. Refer to Chapter Five of the main book for service procedures.

INTERNAL SHIFT MECHANISM

The following models have redesigned internal shift mechanisms:

a. YZ125L, K and YZ250L, K—**Figure 29**.
b. YZ490J, L, K—**Figure 30**.
c. YZ490J, YZ250J and YZ100K and J—**Figure 31**.

d. YZ250H—**Figure 32**.

Procedures for servicing the internal shift mechanism are the same as for 1980 and earlier models.

TRANSMISSION

Removal/Installation (YZ100 and YZ125)

Procedures for servicing the transmission are the same as for 1980 and earlier models as described in Chapter Five of the main book. However, these models do not use the main shaft washers No. 23 and No. 25; see **Figure 33**.

Removal/Installation (YZ250)

These models now use a 5-speed transmission. Refer to **Figure 34** (YZ250K and J) or **Figure 35** (YZ250H) for all service procedures.

Removal/Installation (YZ465 and YZ490)

These models use a 4-speed transmission. Refer to **Figure 36** for all service procedures.

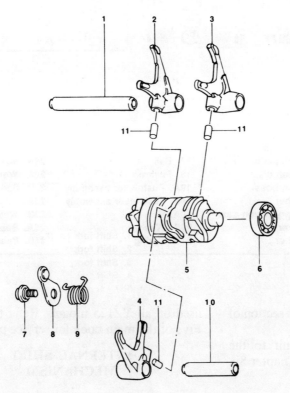

INTERNAL SHIFT MECHANISM (YZ250L, K AND YZ125L, K)

1. Shift fork shaft
2. Shift fork
3. Shift fork
4. Shift fork
5. Shift drum
6. Bearing
7. Bolt
8. Shift pawl
9. Spring
10. Shift fork shaft
11. Cam pin follower

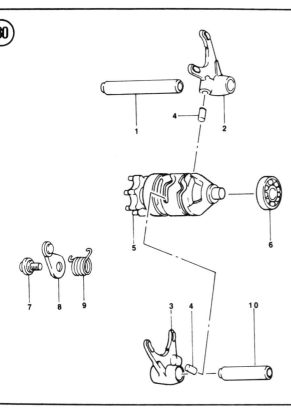

**INTERNAL SHIFT MECHANISM
(YZ490J, L, K)**

1. Shift fork shaft
2. Shift fork
3. Shift fork
4. Cam pin follower
5. Shift drum
6. Bearing
7. Bolt
8. Shift pawl
9. Spring
10. Shift fork shaft

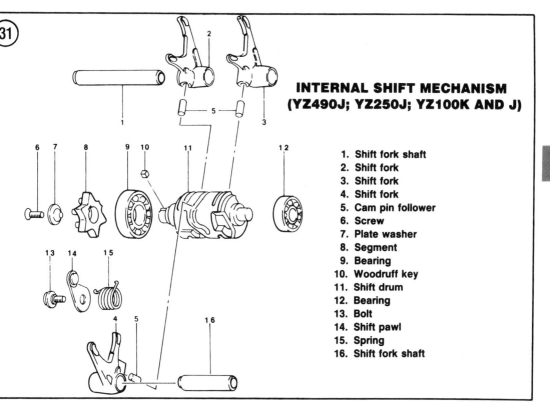

**INTERNAL SHIFT MECHANISM
(YZ490J; YZ250J; YZ100K AND J)**

1. Shift fork shaft
2. Shift fork
3. Shift fork
4. Shift fork
5. Cam pin follower
6. Screw
7. Plate washer
8. Segment
9. Bearing
10. Woodruff key
11. Shift drum
12. Bearing
13. Bolt
14. Shift pawl
15. Spring
16. Shift fork shaft

12

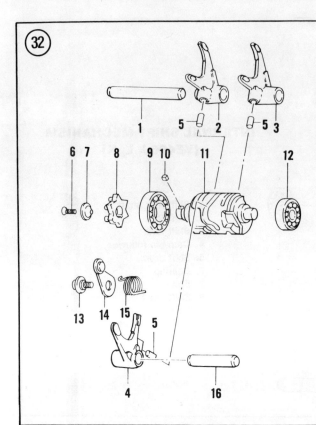

INTERNAL SHIFT MECHANISM (YZ250H)

1. Shift fork shaft
2. Shift fork
3. Shift fork
4. Shift fork
5. Cam pin follower
6. Screw
7. Plate washer
8. Segment
9. Bearing
10. Woodruff key
11. Shift drum
12. Bearing
13. Bolt
14. Shift pawl
15. Spring
16. Shift fork shaft

5-SPEED TRANSMISSION (YZ250K AND J)

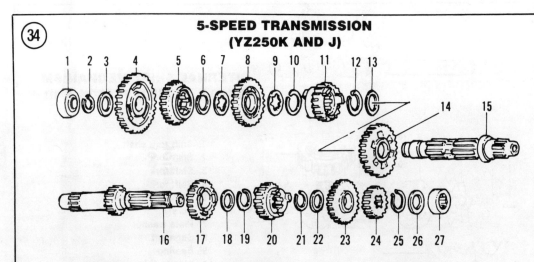

1. Bearing
2. Circlip
3. Spacer
4. Countershaft 1st gear
5. Countershaft 4th gear
6. Circlip
7. Washer
8. Countershaft 3rd gear
9. Washer
10. Circlip
11. Countershaft 5th gear
12. Circlip
13. Washer
14. Countershaft 2nd gear
15. Countershaft
16. Mainshaft/1st gear
17. Mainshaft 4th gear
18. Washer
19. Circlip
20. Mainshaft 3rd gear
21. Circlip
22. Washer
23. Mainshaft 5th gear
24. Mainshaft 2nd gear
25. Circlip
26. Washer (YZ250L, K models only)
27. Bearing

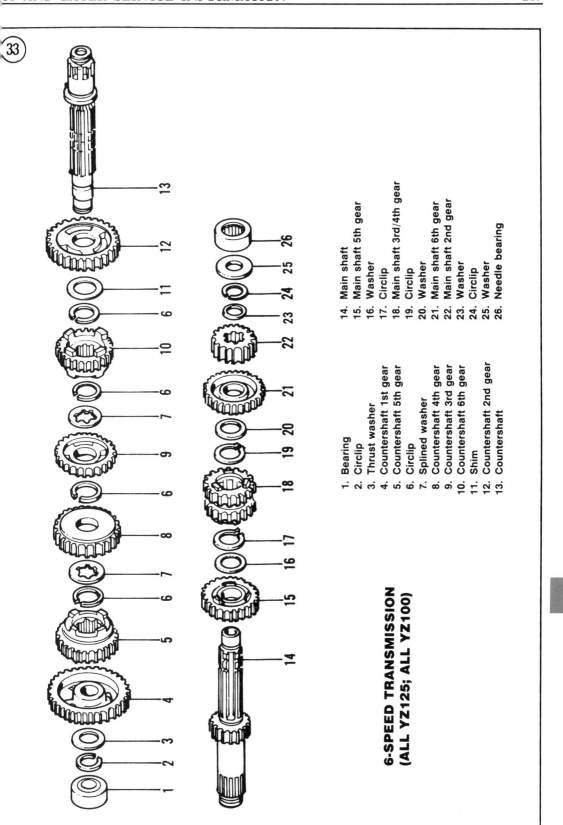

6-SPEED TRANSMISSION (ALL YZ125; ALL YZ100)

1. Bearing
2. Circlip
3. Thrust washer
4. Countershaft 1st gear
5. Countershaft 5th gear
6. Circlip
7. Splined washer
8. Countershaft 4th gear
9. Countershaft 3rd gear
10. Countershaft 6th gear
11. Shim
12. Countershaft 2nd gear
13. Countershaft

14. Main shaft
15. Main shaft 5th gear
16. Washer
17. Circlip
18. Main shaft 3rd/4th gear
19. Circlip
20. Washer
21. Main shaft 6th gear
22. Main shaft 2nd gear
23. Washer
24. Circlip
25. Washer
26. Needle bearing

12

5-SPEED TRANSMISSION (YZ250H)

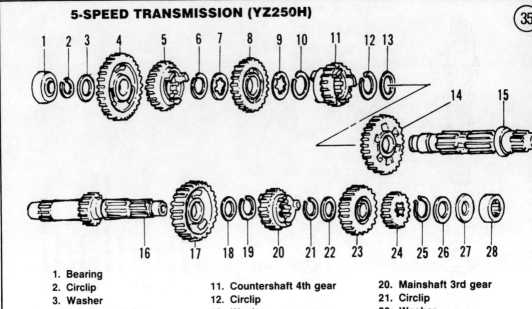

1. Bearing
2. Circlip
3. Washer
4. Countershaft 1st gear
5. Countershaft 5th gear
6. Circlip
7. Washer
8. Countershaft 3rd gear
9. Washer
10. Circlip
11. Countershaft 4th gear
12. Circlip
13. Washer
14. Countershaft 2nd gear
15. Countershaft
16. Mainshaft/1st gear
17. Mainshaft 5th gear
18. Washer
19. Circlip
20. Mainshaft 3rd gear
21. Circlip
22. Washer
23. Mainshaft 4th gear
24. Mainshaft 2nd gear
25. Washer
26. Circlip
27. Washer
28. Bearing

4-SPEED TRANSMISSION (YZ465H AND YZ490J AND K)

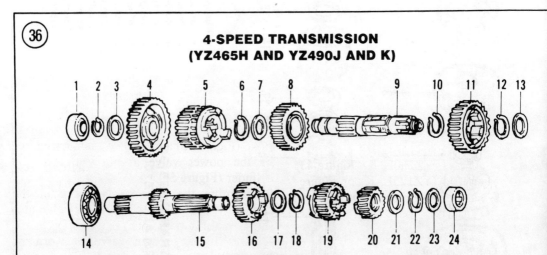

1. Bearing
2. Circlip
3. Washer
4. Countershaft 1st gear
5. Countershaft 4th gear
6. Circlip
7. Washer
8. Countershaft 3rd gear
9. Countershaft
10. Circlip
11. Countershaft 2nd gear
12. Circlip
13. Washer
14. Bearing
15. Main shaft/1st gear
16. Main shaft 4th gear
17. Washer
18. Circlip
19. Main shaft 3rd gear
20. Main shaft 2nd gear
21. Washer
22. Circlip
23. Washer (YZ490K models only)
24. Bearing

CHAPTER SIX

FUEL AND EXHAUST SYSTEMS

CARBURETOR

New carburetors are used on the following models:
a. YZ490L—**Figure 37**.
b. YZ490K and J; YZ250L, K and J—**Figure 38**.
c. YZ125L—**Figure 39**.
d. YZ125K, J and H—**Figure 40**.
e. YZ100K, J and H—**Figure 41**.

hen service to the carburetor is required, fer to Chapter Six of the main book and to **gures 37-41** as appropriate for your rticular model.

Carburetor specifications for all models are ted in **Table 17**.

POWER VALVE INDUCTION SYSTEM (MODELS YZ250K AND J AND YZ125K AND J)

Refer to **Figure 42** (YZ250L, K), **Figure 43** Z250J), **Figure 44** (YZ125L, K) or **Figure** (YZ125J) when performing this procedure.

NOTE
This procedure is shown on a YZ250K; other models are similar.

Remove the fuel tank.
Remove the power valve cover. See **Figure** (YZ250) or **Figure 47** (YZ125).
Insert a pin through the power valve lever d into the cylinder to lock the power valve ver. See **Figure 48**.
Using a socket, remove the nut securing e power valve lever.

5. Remove the pin and disconnect the power valve lever (**Figure 49**) from the cylinder. Remove the lever boss (**Figure 50**).

NOTE
Steps 1-5 are all that is required when the cylinder is to be removed. Steps 6-20 describe complete removal and installation of the power valve assembly.

6. Remove the holder screws (**Figure 51**) and remove the holder (**Figure 52**) from the left-hand (YZ250) or right-hand side (YZ125).
7. Using an Allen wrench (**Figure 53**), remove the Allen screw securing the power valve left- and right-hand sides. Then remove one half of the valve from the left-hand (YZ250) or right-hand side (YZ125). See **Figure 54**.
8. Working on the bike's right-hand (YZ250) or left-hand (YZ125) side, remove the thrust plate (**Figure 55**) and slide the remaining half of the power valve assembly out of the cylinder (**Figure 56**).
9. Examine the power valve bore in the cylinder (**Figure 57**) and the power valve unit (**Figure 58**) closely for signs or wear or seizure. If the power valve is worn or damaged, it must be replaced. If the power valve bore in the cylinder is worn or damaged, refer the cylinder to a Yamaha dealer for further examination.
10. Replace the power valve O-ring if worn or damaged.
11. Examine the bearing surface on the holder (**Figure 59**) for wear or damage. Replace it if necessary.

12

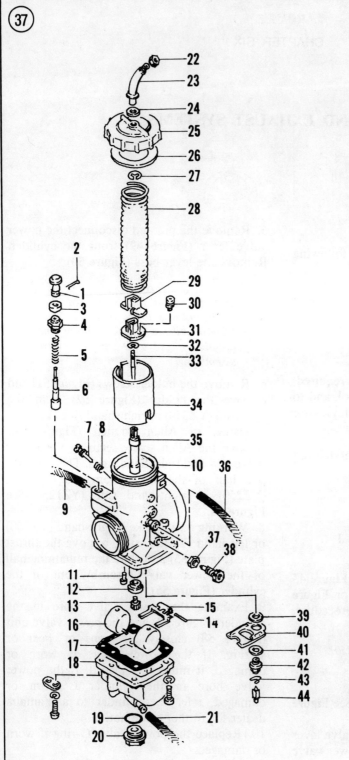

37

CARBURETOR (YZ490L)

1. Cover
2. Cotter pin
3. Cover
4. Plunger cap
5. Spring
6. Plunger
7. Air screw
8. Spring
9. Hose
10. Carburetor body
11. Pilot jet
12. Main jet washer
13. Main jet
14. Float pin
15. Float arm
16. Floats
17. Gasket
18. Float bowl
19. O-ring
20. Plug
21. Hose
22. Nut
23. Cable guide
24. Washer
25. Top cap
26. Seal
27. Circlip
28. Spring
29. Cable connector
30. Screw
31. Connector
32. Circlip
33. Jet needle
34. Throttle valve (slide)
35. Needle jet
36. Hose
37. Locknut
38. Throttle stop screw
39. Seal
40. Plate
41. Seal
42. Needle valve seat
43. Needle valve clip
44. Needle valve

38

CARBURETOR
(YZ490K AND J; YZ250L, K AND J)

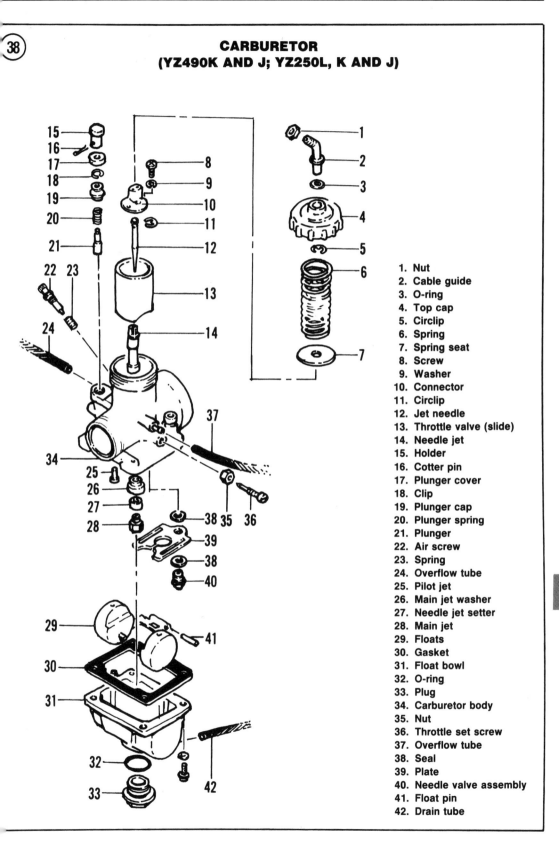

1. Nut
2. Cable guide
3. O-ring
4. Top cap
5. Circlip
6. Spring
7. Spring seat
8. Screw
9. Washer
10. Connector
11. Circlip
12. Jet needle
13. Throttle valve (slide)
14. Needle jet
15. Holder
16. Cotter pin
17. Plunger cover
18. Clip
19. Plunger cap
20. Plunger spring
21. Plunger
22. Air screw
23. Spring
24. Overflow tube
25. Pilot jet
26. Main jet washer
27. Needle jet setter
28. Main jet
29. Floats
30. Gasket
31. Float bowl
32. O-ring
33. Plug
34. Carburetor body
35. Nut
36. Throttle set screw
37. Overflow tube
38. Seal
39. Plate
40. Needle valve assembly
41. Float pin
42. Drain tube

12

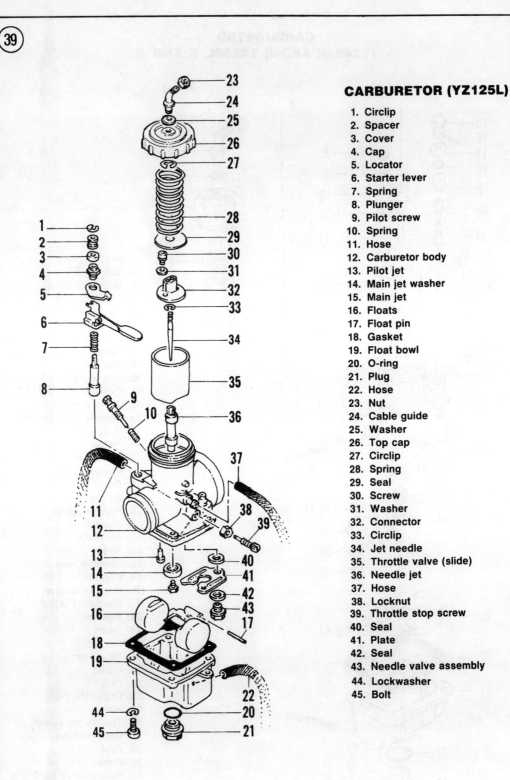

CARBURETOR (YZ125L)

1. Circlip
2. Spacer
3. Cover
4. Cap
5. Locator
6. Starter lever
7. Spring
8. Plunger
9. Pilot screw
10. Spring
11. Hose
12. Carburetor body
13. Pilot jet
14. Main jet washer
15. Main jet
16. Floats
17. Float pin
18. Gasket
19. Float bowl
20. O-ring
21. Plug
22. Hose
23. Nut
24. Cable guide
25. Washer
26. Top cap
27. Circlip
28. Spring
29. Seal
30. Screw
31. Washer
32. Connector
33. Circlip
34. Jet needle
35. Throttle valve (slide)
36. Needle jet
37. Hose
38. Locknut
39. Throttle stop screw
40. Seal
41. Plate
42. Seal
43. Needle valve assembly
44. Lockwasher
45. Bolt

40

CARBURETOR ASSEMBLY (YZ125 K, J AND H)

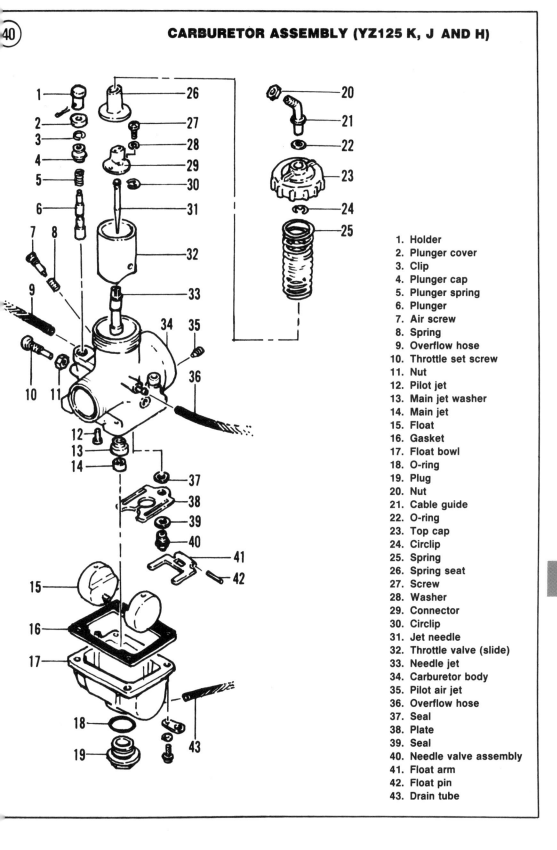

1. Holder
2. Plunger cover
3. Clip
4. Plunger cap
5. Plunger spring
6. Plunger
7. Air screw
8. Spring
9. Overflow hose
10. Throttle set screw
11. Nut
12. Pilot jet
13. Main jet washer
14. Main jet
15. Float
16. Gasket
17. Float bowl
18. O-ring
19. Plug
20. Nut
21. Cable guide
22. O-ring
23. Top cap
24. Circlip
25. Spring
26. Spring seat
27. Screw
28. Washer
29. Connector
30. Circlip
31. Jet needle
32. Throttle valve (slide)
33. Needle jet
34. Carburetor body
35. Pilot air jet
36. Overflow hose
37. Seal
38. Plate
39. Seal
40. Needle valve assembly
41. Float arm
42. Float pin
43. Drain tube

12

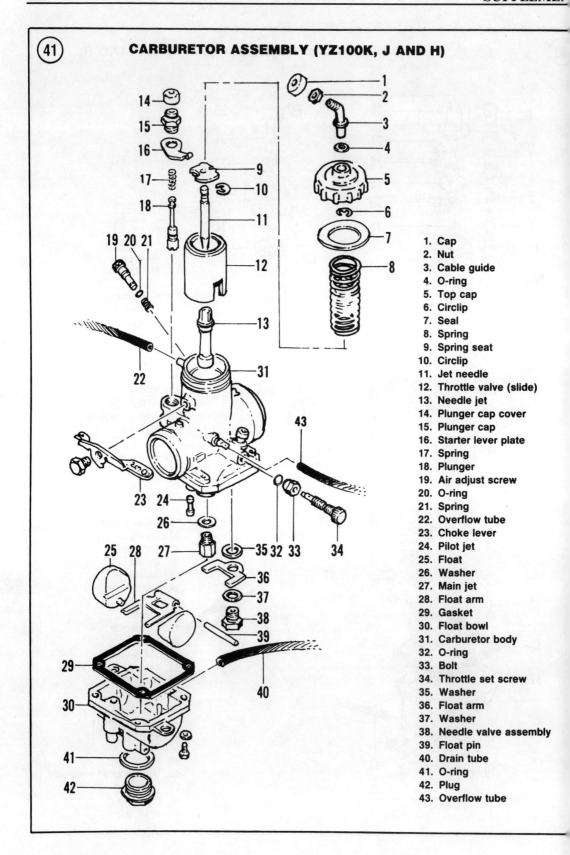

(41) CARBURETOR ASSEMBLY (YZ100K, J AND H)

1. Cap
2. Nut
3. Cable guide
4. O-ring
5. Top cap
6. Circlip
7. Seal
8. Spring
9. Spring seat
10. Circlip
11. Jet needle
12. Throttle valve (slide)
13. Needle jet
14. Plunger cap cover
15. Plunger cap
16. Starter lever plate
17. Spring
18. Plunger
19. Air adjust screw
20. O-ring
21. Spring
22. Overflow tube
23. Choke lever
24. Pilot jet
25. Float
26. Washer
27. Main jet
28. Float arm
29. Gasket
30. Float bowl
31. Carburetor body
32. O-ring
33. Bolt
34. Throttle set screw
35. Washer
36. Float arm
37. Washer
38. Needle valve assembly
39. Float pin
40. Drain tube
41. O-ring
42. Plug
43. Overflow tube

42

CYLINDER/POWER VALVE ASSEMBLY
(YZ250L, K)

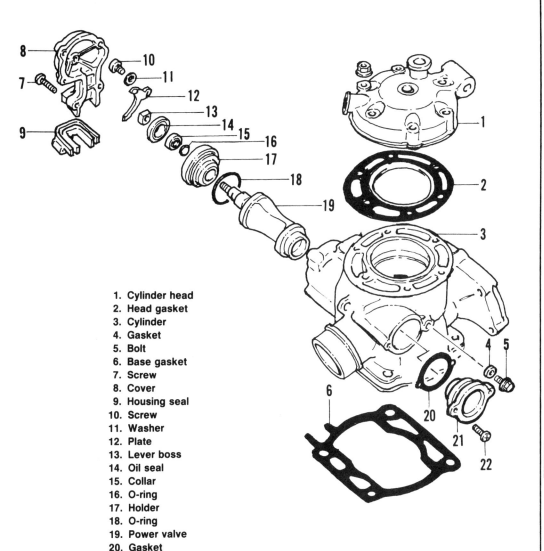

1. Cylinder head
2. Head gasket
3. Cylinder
4. Gasket
5. Bolt
6. Base gasket
7. Screw
8. Cover
9. Housing seal
10. Screw
11. Washer
12. Plate
13. Lever boss
14. Oil seal
15. Collar
16. O-ring
17. Holder
18. O-ring
19. Power valve
20. Gasket
21. Holder
22. Screw

12

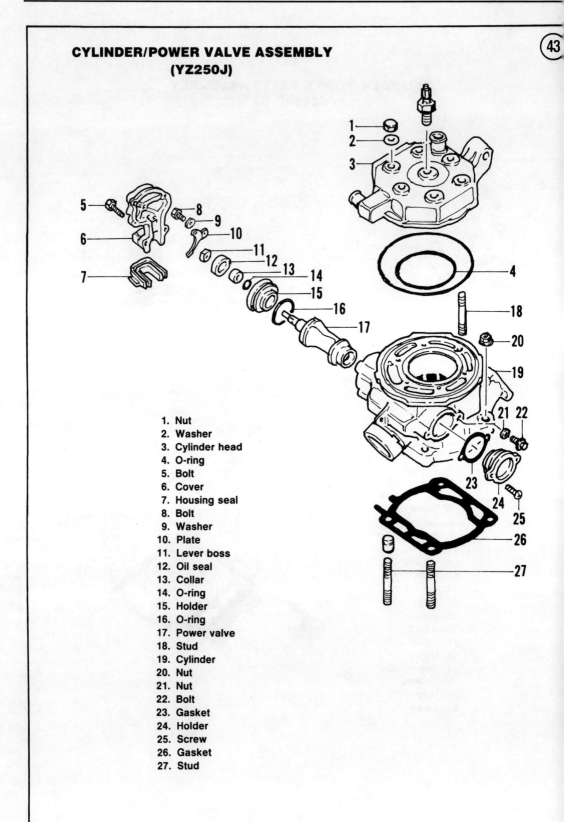

CYLINDER/POWER VALVE ASSEMBLY
(YZ250J)

43

1. Nut
2. Washer
3. Cylinder head
4. O-ring
5. Bolt
6. Cover
7. Housing seal
8. Bolt
9. Washer
10. Plate
11. Lever boss
12. Oil seal
13. Collar
14. O-ring
15. Holder
16. O-ring
17. Power valve
18. Stud
19. Cylinder
20. Nut
21. Nut
22. Bolt
23. Gasket
24. Holder
25. Screw
26. Gasket
27. Stud

44

CYLINDER/POWER VALVE ASSEMBLY
(YZ125L, K)

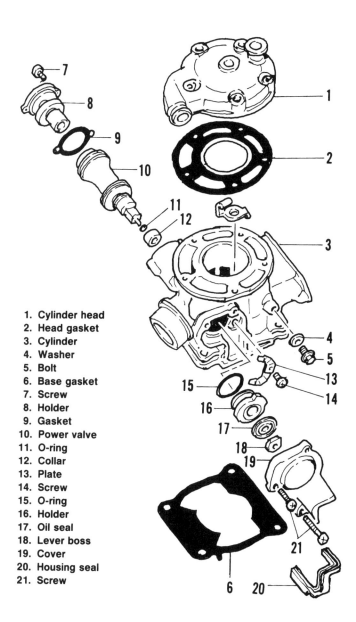

1. Cylinder head
2. Head gasket
3. Cylinder
4. Washer
5. Bolt
6. Base gasket
7. Screw
8. Holder
9. Gasket
10. Power valve
11. O-ring
12. Collar
13. Plate
14. Screw
15. O-ring
16. Holder
17. Oil seal
18. Lever boss
19. Cover
20. Housing seal
21. Screw

12

CYLINDER/POWER VALVE ASSEMBLY (YZ125J)

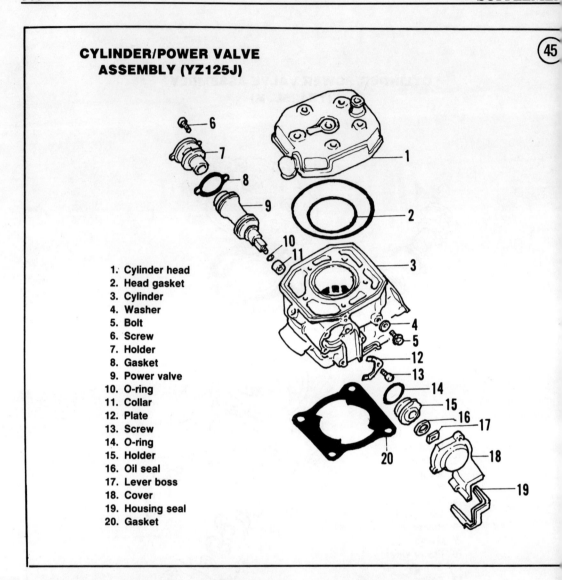

1. Cylinder head
2. Head gasket
3. Cylinder
4. Washer
5. Bolt
6. Screw
7. Holder
8. Gasket
9. Power valve
10. O-ring
11. Collar
12. Plate
13. Screw
14. O-ring
15. Holder
16. Oil seal
17. Lever boss
18. Cover
19. Housing seal
20. Gasket

12. Installation is the reverse of these steps, noting the following.

13. Apply a small amount of molybdenum disulfide grease to the following parts:

  a. Grease the end of the Allen screw used to secure both halves of the power valve unit.

  b. Grease all O-rings and oil seals.

14. Install all new gaskets during reassembly.

15. When aligning the power valve halves, note that alignment pins and holes are used on the mating ends. See **Figure 60**.

NOTE
A flashlight directed up through the exhaust port can be helpful when

*aligning power valve halves. See **Figure 61**.*

16. After installing the power va assembly, turn it by hand so that alignment mark faces up. See **Figure** (YZ250) or **Figure 63** (YZ125). Then ins the lever boss (**Figure 64**) and lever.

17. Lock the power valve lever using a inserted through the lever boss and into cylinder as during disassembly (**Figure 4** Then install the power valve lever nut a tighten to 4 ft.-lb. (5 N•m). After tighteni remove the pin.

18. Check the alignment of the power va lever. The cut in the valve lever should

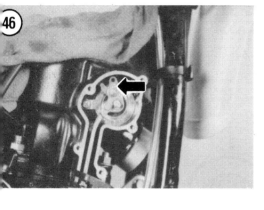

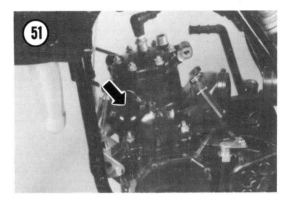

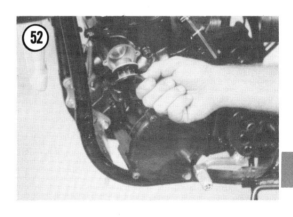

12

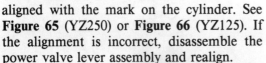

aligned with the mark on the cylinder. See **Figure 65** (YZ250) or **Figure 66** (YZ125). If the alignment is incorrect, disassemble the power valve lever assembly and realign.

19. If the power valve lever is aligned properly with the engine index mark, start the engine without the power valve cover installed. Check the operation of the power valve lever. It should operate smoothly when the engine is revved. If not, there is a problem with the power valve assembly.

CAUTION
Do not rev the engine excessively while performing Step 19.

20. After checking the power valve operation, install all parts previously removed.

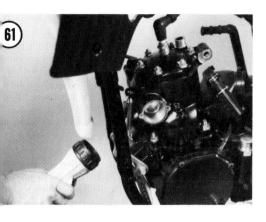

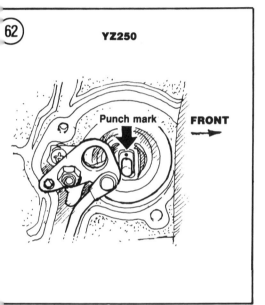

YZ250

Punch mark

FRONT

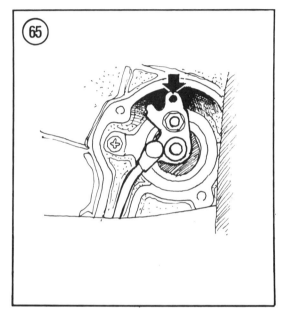

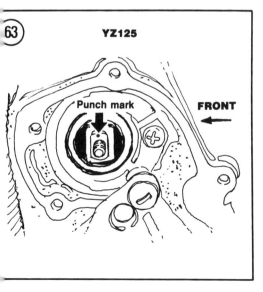

YZ125

Punch mark

FRONT

12

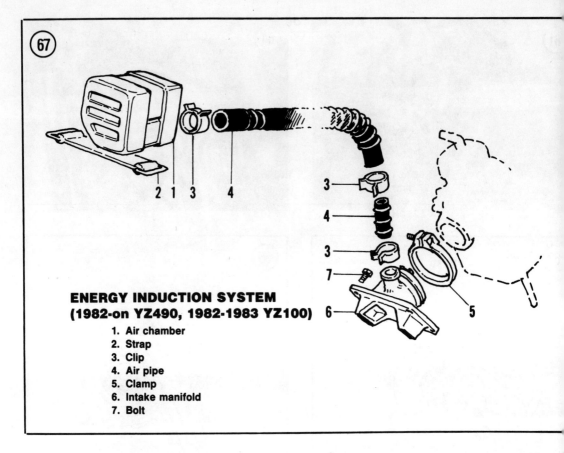

**ENERGY INDUCTION SYSTEM
(1982-on YZ490, 1982-1983 YZ100)**
1. Air chamber
2. Strap
3. Clip
4. Air pipe
5. Clamp
6. Intake manifold
7. Bolt

YAMAHA ENERGY INDUCTION SYSTEM

The Yamaha Energy Induction System (YEIS) is installed on all 1982 and later YZ490 and YZ100 models. The YEIS system increases low- and mid-range power while maintaining maximum engine power by reducing air speed fluctuations through the intake tract. By maintaining a smoother flow of air, carburetor jetting is more precise.

The YEIS system consists of a single air chamber connected to the intake manifold by a hose (**Figure 67**). Because the chamber and hose size determine the operating range of the YEIS system, do not tamper with or alter either. The chamber and hose dimensions on the YZ models are designed to deliver the greatest effect for motocross racing.

Removal/Installation

1. Disconnect the air chamber hose at the intake manifold (**Figure 67**).

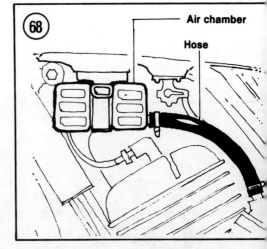

2. Disconnect the YEIS chamber undernea the fuel tank (**Figure 68**) and remove t YEIS chamber and hose.

3. Check the YEIS chamber and hose wear or damage. Replace any parts required.

4. Installation is the reverse of these steps.

Table 17 CARBURETOR SPECIFICATIONS

	YZ465H	YZ490J, K	YZ490L
Model No.	VM38ss	VM38ss	VM40ss
I.D. mark	4V400	23X-00	40T-00
Main jet	390	440	440
Needle jet	Q-2	Q-8	Q-8
Pilot jet	45	50	50
Jet needle	6F16	6F16	7F8
Clip position	3	3	2
Slide cutaway	3.0	3.0	2.5
Float level	1.06 in.	1.06 in.	0.79 in.
	(27 mm)	(27 mm)	(20.1 mm)

	YZ250H	YZ250J	YZ250K
Model No.	VM38ss	VM38ss	VM38ss
I.D. mark	4V300	5X500	24Y-00
Main jet	380	370	260
Needle jet	Q-0	Q-0	P-6
Pilot jet	80	45	50
Jet needle	6F16	6F16	6F45
Clip position	4	2	3
Slide cutaway	3.0	3.0	3.0
Float level	1.06 in.	1.06 in.	1.06 in.
	(27 mm)	(27 mm)	(27 mm)

	YZ250L	YZ125H	YZ125J
Model No.	VM38ss	VM34ss	VM34ss
I.D. mark	39X-00	4V2-10	5X400
Main jet	290	340	260
Needle jet	P-6	P-8	Q-0
Pilot jet	60	80	65
Jet needle	6F45	6F21	6F21
Clip position	3	4	3
Slide cutaway	3.0	2.5	2.5
Float level	1.06 in.	0.92 in.	0.92 in.
	(27 mm)	(23.4)	(23.4 mm)

	YZ125K	YZ125L	YZ100J, K
Model No.	VM34ss	VM36ss	VM30ss
I.D. mark	24X00	39W00	5X300
Main jet	280	360	190
Needle jet	Q-2	P-2	Q-2
Pilot jet	60	50	50
Jet needle	6F21	6F15	6DP10
Clip position	3	2	2
Slide cutaway	2.5	2.0	2.5
Float level	0.92 in.	0.94 in.	0.65 in.
	(23.4 mm)	(24.0 mm)	(16.4 mm)

12

	YZ100H
Model No.	VM30ss
I.D. mark	3R2-00

(continued)

Table 17 CARBURETOR SPECIFICATIONS (continued)

	YZ100H
Main jet	210
Needle jet	Q-2
Pilot jet	40
Jet needle	6DP10
Clip position	2
Slide cutaway	2.5
Float level	0.65 in.
	(16.4 mm)

CHAPTER SEVEN

ELECTRICAL SYSTEMS

New electrical specifications that differ from 1980 and earlier models are in **Table 18**.

MAGNETO OUTER ROTOR

The outer rotor magneto assembly has been changed for YZ490K models. See **Figure 69**. Service procedures remain the same as for YZ465 models. See **Table 15** for magneto torque specifications that have changed.

MAGNETO INNER ROTOR

The inner rotor magneto assembly has bee changed for the following models:
a. YZ250L, K and J.
b. YZ125L, K and J.
c. YZ100K and J.
See **Figure 70**. Service procedures rema the same as for 1981 and earlier models. S **Table 15** for new magneto torq specifications.

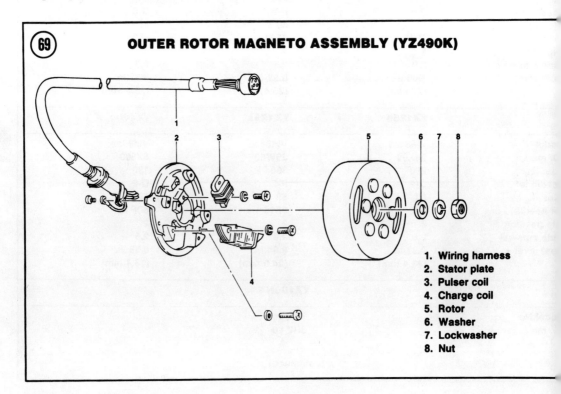

69 **OUTER ROTOR MAGNETO ASSEMBLY (YZ490K)**

1. Wiring harness
2. Stator plate
3. Pulser coil
4. Charge coil
5. Rotor
6. Washer
7. Lockwasher
8. Nut

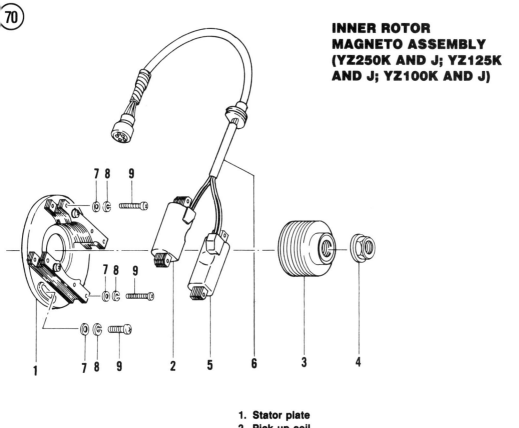

**INNER ROTOR
MAGNETO ASSEMBLY
(YZ250K AND J; YZ125K
AND J; YZ100K AND J)**

70

1. Stator plate
2. Pick up coil
3. Rotor
4. Nut
5. Charge coil
6. Wiring harness
7. Washer
8. Lockwasher
9. Screw

Table 18 ELECTRICAL SPECIFICATIONS

Ignition coil	
Primary resistance	
YZ250L, K, YZ125L, K	0.22 ohms ±10%
Secondary resistance	
YZ250L, K, YZ125L, K	4.4 ohms ±10%

12

CHAPTER EIGHT

FRONT SUSPENSION AND STEERING

New torque specifications are listed in **Table 19** and **Table 20**. New front fork spring free length specifications are in **Table 21**.

STEERING HEAD (YZ250J AND YZ125J AND H)

The steering stem on these models has been redesigned to accommodate the radiator. The steering stem assembly is shown in **Figure 71**.

Removal

1. Remove the front wheel, handlebar an front forks as described in Chapter Eight the main book.
2. Remove the radiator as described in th section of the supplement.
3. Remove the coolant radiator-to-steerir stem joint at the bottom of the steering ster
4. Remove the steering stem flange nut ar O-ring. Then slip the fork crown off t steering stem.

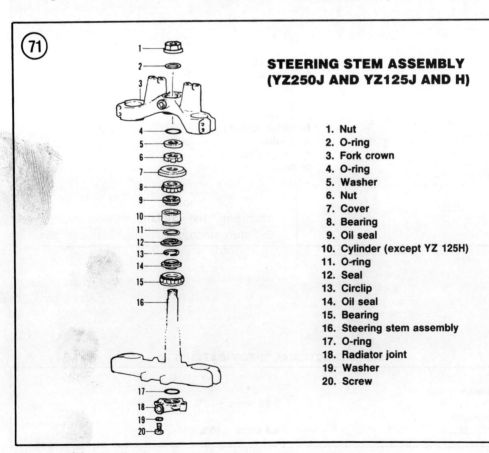

⑦71

STEERING STEM ASSEMBLY (YZ250J AND YZ125J AND H)

1. Nut
2. O-ring
3. Fork crown
4. O-ring
5. Washer
6. Nut
7. Cover
8. Bearing
9. Oil seal
10. Cylinder (except YZ 125H)
11. O-ring
12. Seal
13. Circlip
14. Oil seal
15. Bearing
16. Steering stem assembly
17. O-ring
18. Radiator joint
19. Washer
20. Screw

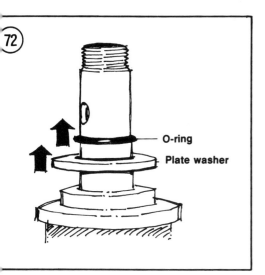

O-ring

Plate washer

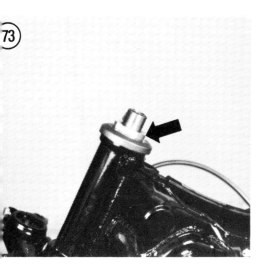

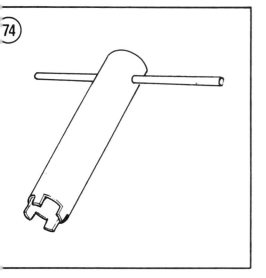

5. Slide the second O-ring off the steering stem and remove the plate washer. See **Figure 72**. Then remove the steering head adjusting nut (**Figure 73**). The steering head nut can be removed by using a large drift and hammer or with an easily improvised tool (**Figure 74**).

6. Remove the upper bearing cap and lower the steering stem assembly down out of the steering head (**Figure 75**).

7. Remove the upper bearing (**Figure 76**) and race (**Figure 77**) from the steering head pipe and the lower bearing from the steering stem.

Inspection

1. Use the *Inspection* procedures in Chapter Eight of the main book plus the following to inspect the steering head assembly.

2. The steering stem and the steering head in the frame are of special design to provide a path for coolant flow. During engine operation, the coolant travels through the radiator, steering stem/head, engine, steering stem/head and back into the radiator. Because the coolant actually travels through the steering stem/head assembly, three special seals are pressed into the steering head to control coolant flow. The top seal prevents coolant from entering the upper bearing area, the middle seal separates the hot and cold coolant as it travels through the system and the bottom seal prevents coolant from entering the lower bearing. Any time the steering stem assembly is removed, these steering head seals should be inspected and replaced if necessary by your Yamaha dealer.

12

3. Examine the steering stem-to-radiator joint and O-ring for damage and replace if required.

4. Inspect the steering crown upper and lower O-ring sealing areas. Replace the steering crown if these areas are damaged or worn in any way; these O-rings prevent coolant leakage as it returns to the radiator.

Bearing and Race Replacement

The headset and steering stem bearing races can be replaced by following the procedures in Chapter Eight of the main book.

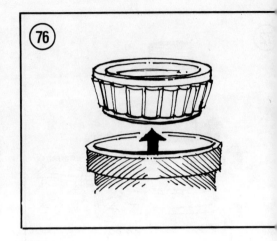

Steering Head Assembly

1. Coat the oil seals and bearings with a heat-resistant grease such as Shell Retinax A before installation.

2. Install the upper and lower bearing oil seals as shown in **Figure 78**.

3. Insert the upper bearing race and bearing into the steering head pipe.

4. With the bottom bearing fitted onto the steering stem and the bottom race fitted into the steering head pipe, insert the steering stem up through the steering head and hold it firmly in place.

5. Install the upper bearing race cover.

6. Install the steering stem adjusting nut (**Figure 73**) and tighten it until is is snug against the upper race, then back it off 1/8 turn.

> *NOTE*
> *The adjusting nut should be just tight enough to remove both horizontal and vertical play (**Figure 79**), yet loose enough so that the assembly will turn to both lock positions under its own weight after an assist.*

7. Install the plate washer and the second steering stem O-ring (**Figure 72**).

> *NOTE*
> *Be sure to install the plate washer as shown in **Figure 80** to ensure that it seats around the O-ring correctly.*

8. Install the upper steering crown. Then install the top O-ring and slide it down into the recess in the steering crown.

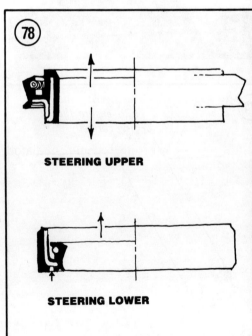

STEERING UPPER

STEERING LOWER

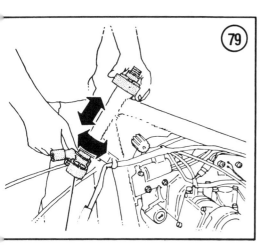

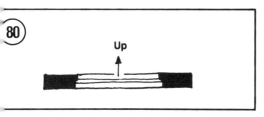

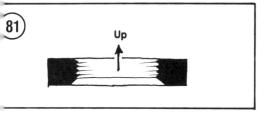

Install the steering nut finger-tight at this ~~~ne.

> *NOTE*
> *Be sure to install the steering nut as shown in **Figure 81** to ensure that it seats around the O-ring correctly.*

~. Push the steering stem-to-radiator ~olant joint up into the lower steering stem ~wn and secure with the attaching bolt.

> *NOTE*
> *Steps 11-13 must be performed in this order to assure proper upper and lower fork crown-to-fork alignment.*

~. Slide both fork tubes into position and ~hten the lower fork bridge bolts to 16 ft.-lb. ~3 N•m).

~. Tighten the steering stem flange nut to 90 ~-lb. (125 N•m).

13. Tighten the upper fork bridge bolts to 16 ft.-lb. (23 N•m).

14. Install the radiator as described in this supplement.

15. Install the handlebar and front wheel.

16. After a few hours of riding the bearings have had a chance to seat; readjust the free play in the steering stem with the steering stem adjusting nut.

STEERING HEAD (MODELS YZ490K AND J; YZ465H; YZ250K; YZ125K; YZ100K AND J)

The steering stem on these models has changed slightly from the type used on 1980 and earlier models. Refer to **Figures 82-84** when servicing the steering head assembly. The service information in Chapter Eight of the main book can be used during steering head service.

RADIATOR

Removal/Installation (YZ250J and YZ125J and H)

1. Drain the cooling system as described in the Chapter Three section of this supplement.

2. Remove the number plate.

3. Remove the screws securing the front fender to the lower steering crown and remove the fender.

4. Disconnect the upper and lower radiator hoses where the hoses attach to the steering crown.

5. Remove the lower radiator attaching bolts and remove the radiator.

6. Examine the radiator cooling surface for damage. Also check along the sides at the lower mounting bushings. If the radiator is damaged in any way it should be replaced.

7. Check the radiator coolant hoses and hose clamps for damage and replace if required.

8. Before installing the radiator, check the coolant hose mountings on the steering head for damage or coolant crust build-up and clean or replace as required.

9. Installation is the reverse of these steps. Keep the following in mind:
   a. Replace all damaged parts before installing the radiator. The radiator is a

12

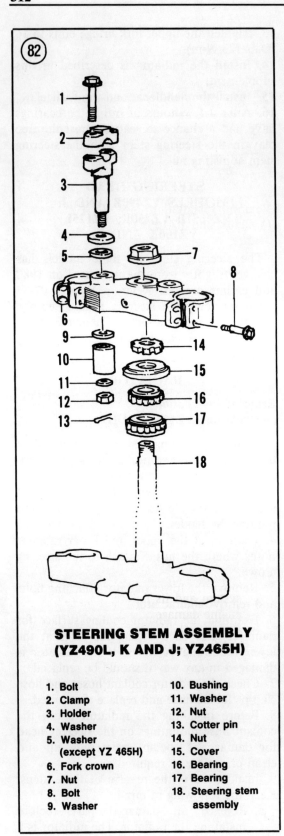

82

**STEERING STEM ASSEMBLY
(YZ490L, K AND J; YZ465H)**

1. Bolt	10. Bushing
2. Clamp	11. Washer
3. Holder	12. Nut
4. Washer	13. Cotter pin
5. Washer	14. Nut
(except YZ 465H)	15. Cover
6. Fork crown	16. Bearing
7. Nut	17. Bearing
8. Bolt	18. Steering stem
9. Washer	assembly

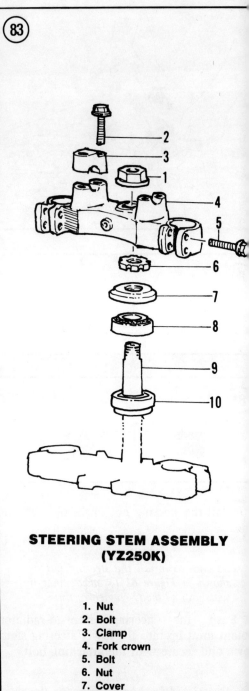

83

**STEERING STEM ASSEMBLY
(YZ250K)**

1. Nut
2. Bolt
3. Clamp
4. Fork crown
5. Bolt
6. Nut
7. Cover
8. Bearing
9. Steering stem assembly
10. Bearing

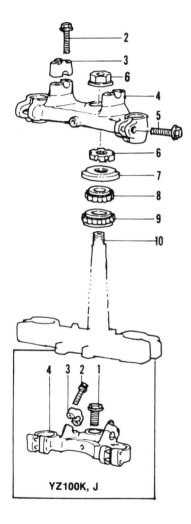

STEERING STEM ASSEMBLY (YZ125L, K; YZ100K AND J)

YZ100K, J

1. Bolt
2. Bolt
3. Clamp
4. Crown
5. Bolt
6. Nut
7. Cover
8. Bearing
9. Bearing
10. Steering stem assembly

critical part in the engine's cooling system and its failure can cause severe engine damage.
b. Ensure that all hose clamps are tightened properly, but not so tight that the clamps tear the hoses.
c. Refill the radiator. Use the correct coolant as specified in the Chapter Three section of this supplement.

Removal/Installation (YZ250K and YZ125K)

1. Drain the cooling system as described in the Chapter Three section of this supplement.
2. Remove the radiator side covers from both sides (**Figure 85**).
3. Remove the air deflectors from both sides (**Figure 86**).
4. Disconnect the hose connecting both radiator housings together (A, **Figure 87**).
5. Disconnect the top (B, **Figure 87**) and bottom (**Figure 88**) hoses at each radiator.
6. Remove the radiator mounting bolts (**Figure 89**) and remove the radiators.
7. Examine the radiator cooling surface for damage. If the radiator is damaged in any way it should be replaced.
8. Check the radiator coolant hoses and hose clamps for damage and replace if required.
9. Installation is the reverse of these steps. Keep the following in mind:
a. Replace all damaged parts before installing the radiator. The radiator is a critical part in the engine's cooling system and its failure can cause severe engine damage.
b. Ensure that all hose clamps are tightened properly, but not so tight that the clamps tear the hoses.
c. Refill the radiator. Use the correct coolant as specified in the Chapter Three section of this supplement.

FRONT FORKS

Disassembly/Assembly (1981-on Except YZ100)

The fork tubes on these models require the use of a hydraulic press for disassembly and a

12

number of special tools for both disassembly and assembly. Because the front forks play an important part in the operation of the motorcycle's handling, refer all front fork disassembly to a qualified Yamaha dealer.

Compression Damping Adjustment (1984)

Compression damping adjustments are provided for all 1984 models. Compression damping adjustments are made by turning the adjuster/fork tube holding bolt at the bottom of the fork tube (**Figure 90**). Adjust as follows.

1. Remove the rubber cap at the bottom of the fork tube.

2. To make compression damping stiffer, turn the adjuster bolt *clockwise* as seen from the front. For softer damping, turn the adjuster *counterclockwise*.

> *NOTE*
> *The standard compression damping adjustment position is 2 1/4 turns out for YZ125 models and 4 turns out for YZ250 and YZ490 models.*

> *WARNING*
> *Do not turn the adjuster more than 8 turns from the seated position. The adjuster bolt also serves as the fork tube holding bolt.*

3. Install the lower fork tube rubber cap to prevent dirt and other debris from obstructing the adjuster bolt threads.

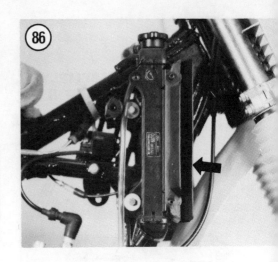

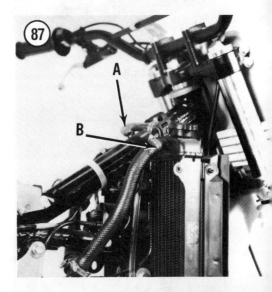

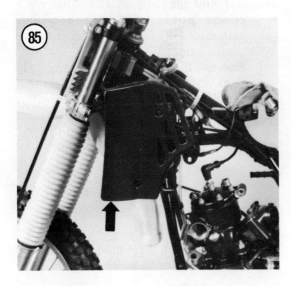

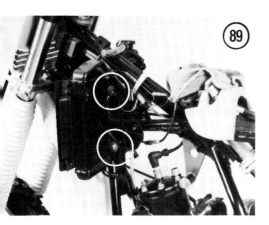

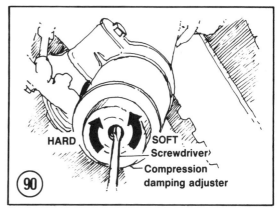

Table 19 FRONT SUSPENSION TORQUE SPECIFICATIONS (YZ490, YZ465 AND YZ250)

Item	ft.-lb.	N•m
Steering stem bolt		
YZ490L	61	85
YZ490K, J; YZ250L, K, J	94	130
YZ465H	94	130
Front axle holder		
YZ250J	14	20
Damper unit		
YZ465H; YZ250H	59	80
YZ250J	40	55
Fork bridge bolts		
YZ250L	17	23
Handlebar holder bolts		
YZ250L	17	23

Table 20 FRONT SUSPENSION TORQUE SPECIFICATIONS (YZ125 AND YZ100)

Item	ft.-lb.	N•m
Steering stem bolt		
YZ125L, K	94	130
YZ125J	85	120
YZ125H	92	125
YZ100K, J, H	39	54
Damper unit		
YZ125J	25	35
Axle holder		
YZ125L, K, J, H	7.2	10
Front axle nut		
YZ100K, J	53	74
YZ100H	36	50
YZ125L	43	60

12

Table 21 FRONT FORK SPRING FREE LENGTH

Model	in.	mm
YZ490L	21.40	543.5
YZ490K	22.0	559
YZ490J	23.07	586
YZ490H	21.7	553
YZ250L	21.4	543.5
YZ250K	22.0	559
YZ250J	23.07	586
YZ250H	21.7	553
YZ125L	22.89	581.5
YZ125K	23.25	590.5
YZ125J, H	25.9	659
YZ100K, J	23.9	607.5
YZ100H	21.32	541.5

CHAPTER NINE

REAR SUSPENSION

New rear suspension specifications are listed in **Table 22** and **Table 23**.

SWING ARM

New swing arm assemblies are used on the following models:

a. YZ490L, K and YZ250L, K—**Figure 91**.
b. YZ490J and YZ250J—**Figure 92**.
c. YZ125L, K—**Figure 93**.
d. YZ125J and YZ100K and J—**Figure 94**.

Refer to the appropriate figure when servicing the swing arm. During swing arm reinstallation, be sure to grease all bearings, oil seal lips, bushings and pivot shafts.

REAR MONOSHOCK (DECARBON MONOCROSS SYSTEM)

Damping Adjustments

Redesigned monoshock units are used the following models:

a. YZ490L; YZ250L—**Figure 95**.
b. YZ125L—**Figure 96**.
c. YZ490K, YZ250K and YZ125K **Figure 97**.
d. YZ490J, YZ250J and YZ125J—**Figu** **98**.
e. YZ100K and J—**Figure 99**.

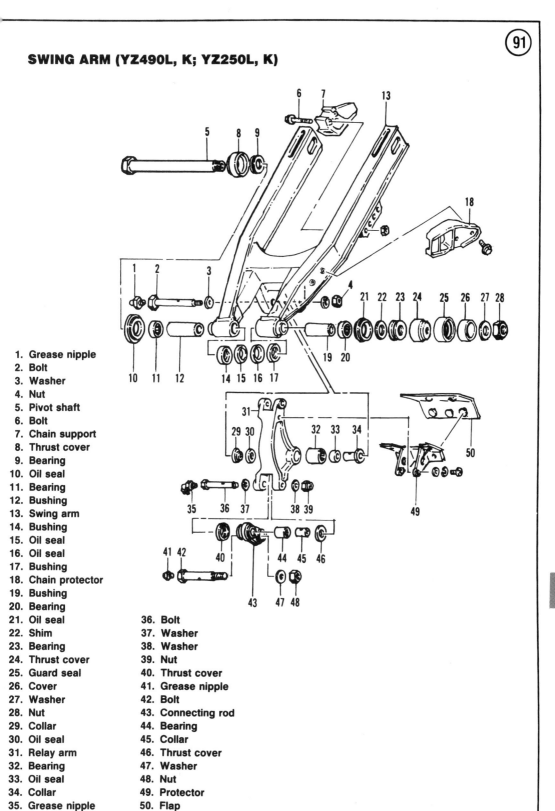

SWING ARM (YZ490L, K; YZ250L, K)

1. Grease nipple
2. Bolt
3. Washer
4. Nut
5. Pivot shaft
6. Bolt
7. Chain support
8. Thrust cover
9. Bearing
10. Oil seal
11. Bearing
12. Bushing
13. Swing arm
14. Bushing
15. Oil seal
16. Oil seal
17. Bushing
18. Chain protector
19. Bushing
20. Bearing
21. Oil seal
22. Shim
23. Bearing
24. Thrust cover
25. Guard seal
26. Cover
27. Washer
28. Nut
29. Collar
30. Oil seal
31. Relay arm
32. Bearing
33. Oil seal
34. Collar
35. Grease nipple

36. Bolt
37. Washer
38. Washer
39. Nut
40. Thrust cover
41. Grease nipple
42. Bolt
43. Connecting rod
44. Bearing
45. Collar
46. Thrust cover
47. Washer
48. Nut
49. Protector
50. Flap

12

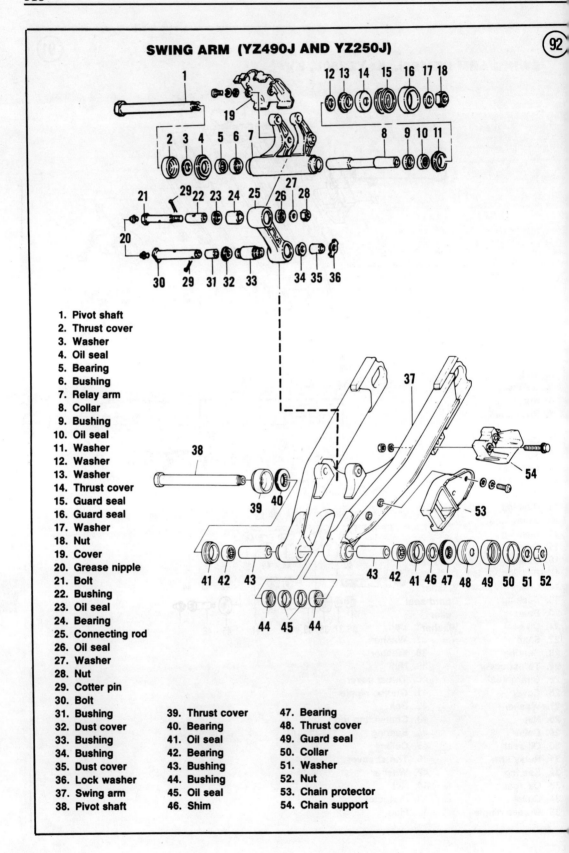

SWING ARM (YZ490J AND YZ250J)

92

1. Pivot shaft
2. Thrust cover
3. Washer
4. Oil seal
5. Bearing
6. Bushing
7. Relay arm
8. Collar
9. Bushing
10. Oil seal
11. Washer
12. Washer
13. Washer
14. Thrust cover
15. Guard seal
16. Guard seal
17. Washer
18. Nut
19. Cover
20. Grease nipple
21. Bolt
22. Bushing
23. Oil seal
24. Bearing
25. Connecting rod
26. Oil seal
27. Washer
28. Nut
29. Cotter pin
30. Bolt
31. Bushing
32. Dust cover
33. Bushing
34. Bushing
35. Dust cover
36. Lock washer
37. Swing arm
38. Pivot shaft

39. Thrust cover
40. Bearing
41. Oil seal
42. Bearing
43. Bushing
44. Bushing
45. Oil seal
46. Shim

47. Bearing
48. Thrust cover
49. Guard seal
50. Collar
51. Washer
52. Nut
53. Chain protector
54. Chain support

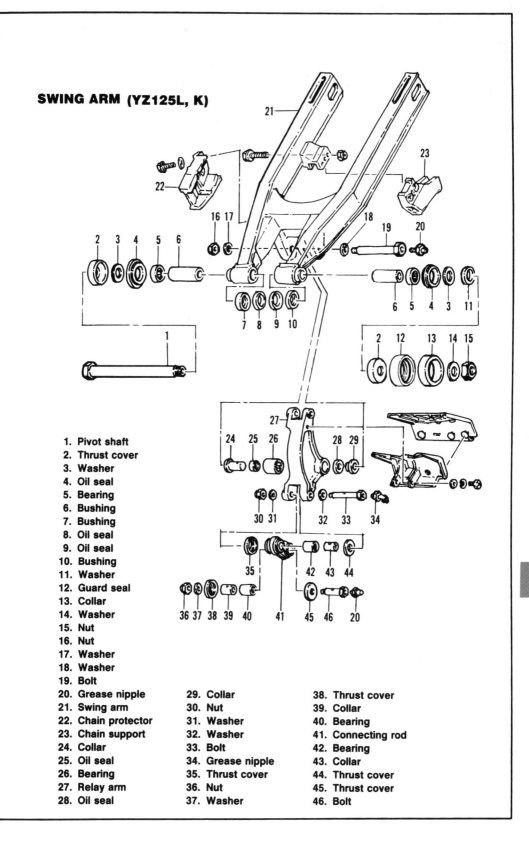

SWING ARM (YZ125L, K)

1. Pivot shaft
2. Thrust cover
3. Washer
4. Oil seal
5. Bearing
6. Bushing
7. Bushing
8. Oil seal
9. Oil seal
10. Bushing
11. Washer
12. Guard seal
13. Collar
14. Washer
15. Nut
16. Nut
17. Washer
18. Washer
19. Bolt
20. Grease nipple
21. Swing arm
22. Chain protector
23. Chain support
24. Collar
25. Oil seal
26. Bearing
27. Relay arm
28. Oil seal
29. Collar
30. Nut
31. Washer
32. Washer
33. Bolt
34. Grease nipple
35. Thrust cover
36. Nut
37. Washer
38. Thrust cover
39. Collar
40. Bearing
41. Connecting rod
42. Bearing
43. Collar
44. Thrust cover
45. Thrust cover
46. Bolt

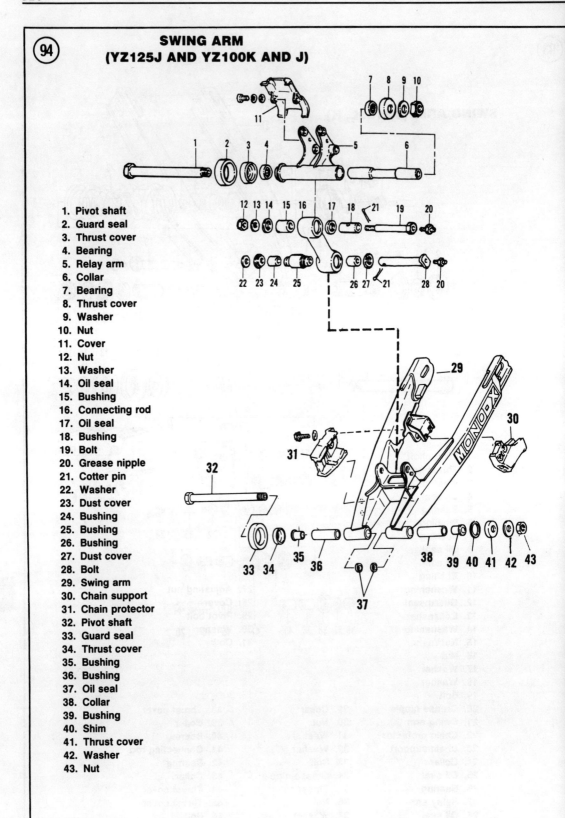

94

SWING ARM
(YZ125J AND YZ100K AND J)

1. Pivot shaft
2. Guard seal
3. Thrust cover
4. Bearing
5. Relay arm
6. Collar
7. Bearing
8. Thrust cover
9. Washer
10. Nut
11. Cover
12. Nut
13. Washer
14. Oil seal
15. Bushing
16. Connecting rod
17. Oil seal
18. Bushing
19. Bolt
20. Grease nipple
21. Cotter pin
22. Washer
23. Dust cover
24. Bushing
25. Bushing
26. Bushing
27. Dust cover
28. Bolt
29. Swing arm
30. Chain support
31. Chain protector
32. Pivot shaft
33. Guard seal
34. Thrust cover
35. Bushing
36. Bushing
37. Oil seal
38. Collar
39. Bushing
40. Shim
41. Thrust cover
42. Washer
43. Nut

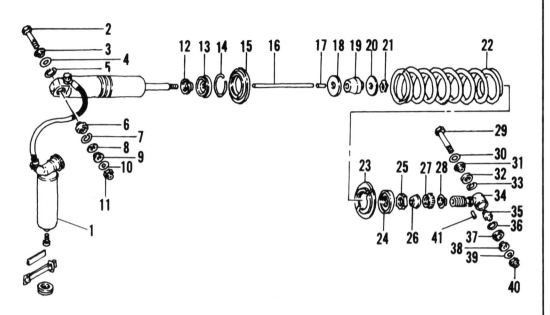

MONOSHOCK ASSEMBLY
(YZ490L; YZ250L)

1. Shock assembly	22. Spring
2. Pivot bolt	23. Spring seat
3. Bushing	24. Seal
4. Washer	25. Locknut
5. Clip	26. Cover
6. Bushing	27. Adjusting nut
7. Clip	28. Cover
8. Washer	29. Pivot bolt
9. Bushing	30. Washer
10. Washer	31. Collar
11. Nut	32. Oil seal
12. Dust seal	33. Circlip
13. Cover	34. Upper bracket
14. Circlip	35. Bearing
15. Spring seat	36. Circlip
16. Pushrod	37. Oil seal
17. Dowel pin	38. Collar
18. Washer	39. Washer
19. Stop	40. Nut
20. Washer	41. Dowel pin
21. Wave washer	

12

MONOSHOCK ASSEMBLY
(YZ125L)

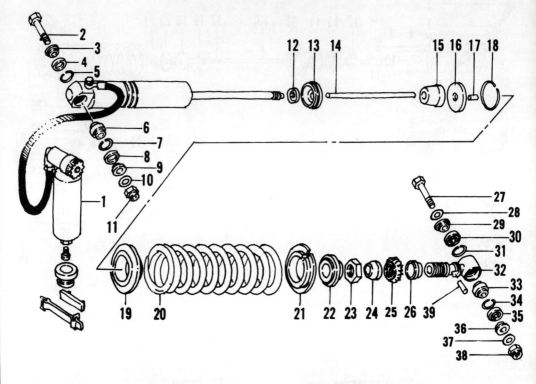

1. Shock assembly	20. Spring
2. Pivot bolt	21. Spring seat
3. Collar	22. Preload adjuster
4. Cover	23. Locknut
5. Circlip	24. Cover
6. Bushing	25. Adjusting nut
7. Circlip	26. Boot
8. Cover	27. Pivot bolt
9. Collar	28. Washer
10. Washer	29. Collar
11. Nut	30. Oil seal
12. Dust seal	31. Circlip
13. Cap	32. Upper bracket
14. Pushrod	33. Collar
15. Stop	34. Circlip
16. Washer	35. Seal
17. Pin	36. Collar
18. Circlip	37. Washer
19. Spring seat	38. Nut
	39. Pin

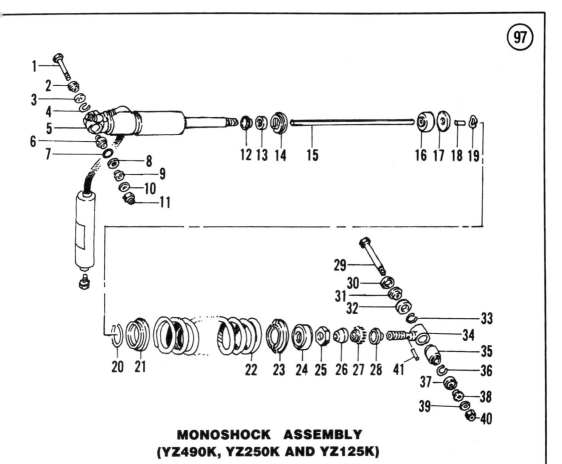

(97)

MONOSHOCK ASSEMBLY
(YZ490K, YZ250K AND YZ125K)

1. Bolt
2. Collar
3. Cover
4. Circlip
5. Monoshock unit
6. Bearing
7. Circlip
8. Cover
9. Collar
10. Washer
11. Nut
12. Dust seal
13. Seal ring housing
  (YZ490 and YZ250K only)
14. Cap
15. Pushrod
16. Stop
17. Support
18. Dowel pin
19. Wave washer
20. Circlip

21. Spring seat
22. Spring
23. Spring seat
24. Seal
25. Nut
26. Cover
27. Adjusting nut
28. Cover
29. Bolt
30. Washer
31. Collar
32. Oil seal
33. Circlip
34. Upper bracket
35. Bearing
36. Circlip
37. Oil seal
38. Collar
39. Washer
40. Nut
41. Dowel pin

12

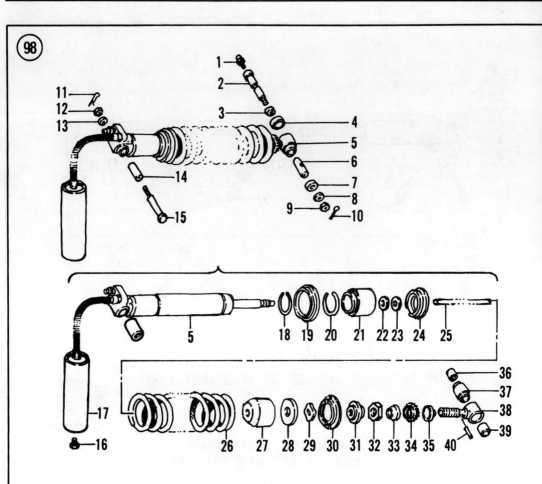

MONOSHOCK ASSEMBLY
(YZ490J; YZ250J AND YZ125J)

1. Grease nipple	21. Spring guide
2. Bolt	22. Dust seal
3. Washer	23. Housing
4. Cover	24. Cap
5. Shock assembly	25. Pushrod
6. Bushing	26. Spring
7. Cover	27. Stop
8. Washer	28. Support
9. Nut	29. Wave washer
10. Cotter pin	30. Spring guide
11. Cotter pin	31. Spring seat
12. Nut	32. Nut
13. Washer	33. Cover
14. Bushing	34. Adjusting nut
15. Bolt	35. Cover
16. Screw	36. Bushing
17. Canister	37. Bushing
18. Circlip	38. Upper bracket assembly
19. Spring seat	39. Bushing
20. Circlip	40. Dowel pin

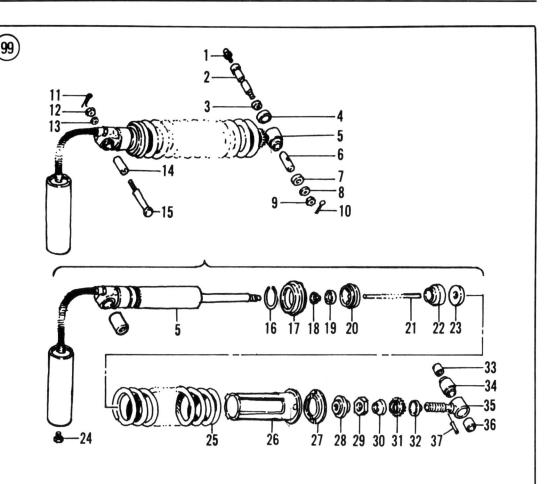

MONOSHOCK ASSEMBLY
(YZ100K AND J)

1. Grease nipple
2. Bolt
3. Washer
4. Cover
5. Shock assembly
6. Bushing
7. Cover
8. Washer
9. Nut
10. Cotter pin
11. Cotter pin
12. Nut
13. Washer
14. Bushing
15. Bolt
16. Circlip
17. Spring seat
18. Dust seal
19. Housing
20. Cap
21. Pushrod
22. Bumper
23. Support
24. Screw
25. Spring
26. Spring guide
27. Spring guide
28. Spring seat
29. Nut
30. Cover
31. Adjusting nut
32. Cover
33. Bushing
34. Bushing
35. Upper bracket assembly
36. Bushing
37. Dowel pin

12

Rebound damping adjustment

Rebound damping adjustments are provided for all 1981 and later models (except for the YZ100H).
1. Remove the seat.
2. Rebound damping adjustments are made by turning the adjusting ring at the shock's rear mount bracket. See **Figure 100**. The adjuster on each model has a specific number of maximum adjustment positions. See **Table 24**. Yamaha recommends changing the rebound damping in increments of 2 click positions; then test ride the bike and make further changes as required. It is not necessary to remove the shock unit to perform this adjustment.
3. To make rebound damping stiffer, turn the adjuster *clockwise* as seen from the rear. For softer damping, turn it *counterclockwise*.

> ### NOTE
> *The standard rebound damping adjustment position is listed in **Table 24**. To set the shock in this position, turn the damping adjuster clockwise until it bottoms, then turn it out the specified number of clicks.*

> ### CAUTION
> *Do not turn the adjuster more than the maximum number of adjustments provided. See **Table 24**.*

Compression damping adjustment (1982-1983)

Compression damping adjustment is provided for all 1982 and 1983 YZ490, YZ250 and YZ125 models.
1. Remove the seat and fuel tank.
2. Compression damping adjustment is made by turning the adjusting ring at the shock's front mount bracket. See **Figure 101**. The adjuster on each model has a maximum number of adjustment positions. See **Table 24**. Yamaha recommends changing the compression damping in increments of 2 click positions; then test ride the bike and make further changes as required. It is not necessary to remove the shock unit to perform this adjustment.

3. To make compression damping stiffe turn the adjuster *clockwise* as seen from th rear. For softer damping, turn *counterclockwise*.

> ### NOTE
> *The standard compression damping adjustment position is listed in **Table 24**. To set the shock in this position, turn the adjuster clockwise until it bottoms, then turn it out the specified number of clicks.*

> ### CAUTION
> *Do not turn the adjuster more than the maximum number of adjustments provided. See **Table 24**.*

Compression damping adjustment (1984)

Compression damping adjustment provided for all 1984 models.
1. Compression damping adjustment is mac by turning the adjusting ring at the shock reservoir mounted on the right-hand side the bike. See **Figure 102**. The adjuster on eac model has a maximum number of adjustmer positions. See **Table 24**. It is not necessary remove the shock unit to perform th adjustment.
2. To make compression damping stiffe turn the adjuster *clockwise* as seen from th front of the adjuster. For softer damping, tu it *counterclockwise*.

> ### NOTE
> *The standard compression adjustment is listed in **Table 24**. To set the shock to this position, turn the adjuster counterclockwise until it bottoms; then turn it in the specified number of turns.*

> ### CAUTION
> *Do not turn the adjuster more than the maximum number of adjustments provided. See **Figure 24**.*

Spring Pre-load Adjustments

Procedures for adjusting the spring pre-lo are the same as for 1980 models; the sprir installed length has changed for some mode Refer to **Table 25**.

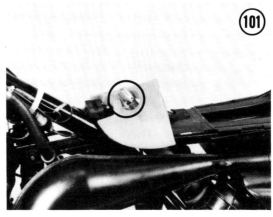

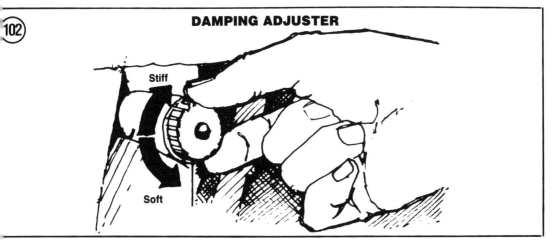

DAMPING ADJUSTER

Stiff

Soft

Table 22 REAR SUSPENSION TORQUE SPECIFICATIONS (YZ490, YZ465 AND YZ250)

Item	ft.-lb.	N•m
Rear axle nut		
YZ490L, K, J; YZ250 all	72	100
YZ465H	72	100
Swing arm pivot nut		
YZ490L, K; YZ250L, K, J	63	85
Relay arm (YZ490L)		
Swing arm	43	60
Rear shock	22	30
Connecting rod	22	30
Connecting rod @ frame	43	60
Relay arm (YZ490K; UZ250L, K)		
Swingarm	43	60
Rear shock	32	45
Connecting rod	32	45
Connecting rod @ frame	43	60
Relay arm (YZ250J)		
Shock to frame	22	30
Shock to L-arm	22	30
L-arm to frame	63	85
L-arm to connecting rod	43	60

12

Table 23 REAR SUSPENSION TORQUE SPECIFICATIONS (YZ125 AND YZ100)

Item	ft.-lb.	N•m
Rear axle nut		
YZ125L, K, J; YZ100K, J, H	63	85
Swing arm pivot nut		
YZ125L, K, J; YZ100K, J	63	85
YZ100H	36	50
Relay arm (YZ125L)		
Swing arm	43	60
Rear shock	22	30
Connecting arm	22	30
Connectirn rod @ frame	43	60
Relay arm (YZ125K)		
Swing arm	43	60
Rear shock	36	50
Connecting rod	32	45
Connecting rod @ frame	43	60
Relay arm (YZ125J; YZ100K, J)		
Frame	63	85
I-arm	43	60
Rear shcok	23	32

Table 24 MONOSHOCK ADJUSTMENT POSITION

	Rebound Standard	Maximum*	Compression Standard	Maximum*
YZ490L	8	21	5	20
YZ490K	7	25	8	20
YZ490J	9	25	6	20
YZ465H	12	24	–	–
YZ250L	8	21	5	20
YZ250K	8	25	7	20
YZ250J	9	25	6	20
YZ250H	12	24	–	–
YZ125L	11	21	5	21
YZ125K	8	25	7	15
YZ125J	10	25	5	20
YZ125H	15	24	–	–
YZ100K	16	25	–	–
YZ100J	16	38	–	–
YZ100H	–	–	–	–

*Never turn the adjuster past the maximum position.

Table 25 MONOSHOCK SPRING LENGTH (INSTALLED)

	Standard in. (mm)	Maximum in. (mm)	Minimum in. (mm)
YZ490L	10.87 (276)	11.14 (283)	9.96 (253)
YZ490K	11.4 (290)	11.6 (295)	10.6 (270)
YZ490J	13.2 (337)	13.7 (350)	12.8 (325)
YZ465H	14.1 (358)	14.2 (360)	13.8 (345)
YZ250L	10.87 (276)	11.14 (283)	9.96 (253)

(continued)

Table 25 MONOSHOCK SPRING LENGTH (INSTALLED)

	Standard in. (mm)	Maximum in. (mm)	Minimum in. (mm)
YZ250K	11.4 (290)	11.6 (295)	10.6 (270)
YZ250J	13.2 (337)	13.7 (350)	12.8 (325)
YZ250H	14.1 (358)	14.2 (360)	13.6 (345)
YZ125L	10.71 (272)	11.06 (281)	10.08 (256)
YZ125K	10.75 (273)	13.7 (350)	12.8 (325)
YZ125J	13.5 (342)	13.7 (350)	12.8 (325)
YZ125H	14.0 (356)	14.2 (360)	13.6 (345)
YZ100K	12.3 (313)	12.5 (318)	11.7 (298)
YZ100J	12.3 (313)	12.5 (318)	11.7 (298)
YZ100H	10.5 (267)	–	–

CHAPTER TEN

BRAKES

Brake specifications that differ from 1980 models are listed in **Table 26**.

Table 26 BRAKE SPECIFICATIONS

Item	in.	mm
Drum ID (new)		
Rear		
YZ490K, J	5.12	130
YZ465H; YZ250H	5.91	150
Shoe spring free length (new)		
Front		
YZ490K; YZ465H; YZ250 all;		
YZ125 all	1.44	36.5
YZ100K, J	Not specified	
YZ100H	1.36	34.5
Rear		
YZ490K; YZ250L, K, J; YZ125 all	1.44	36.5
YZ465H; YZ250H	2.67	68
YZ100K, J	Not specified	
YZ100H	1.44	36.5
Brake shoe OD wear limit	Not specified for these models	

12

INDEX

13

13

YZ100C

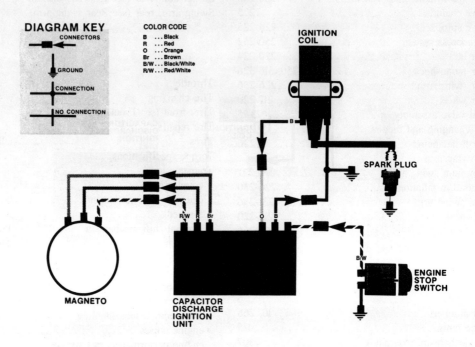

YZ100D, E, F

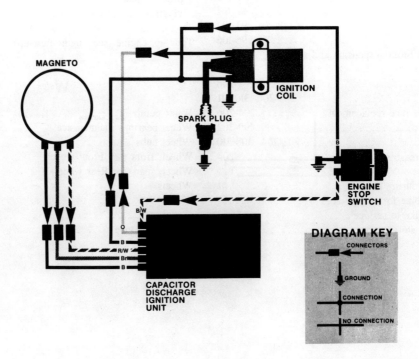

YZ100G, H; YZ125X, C, D, E, F, G, & YZ175C

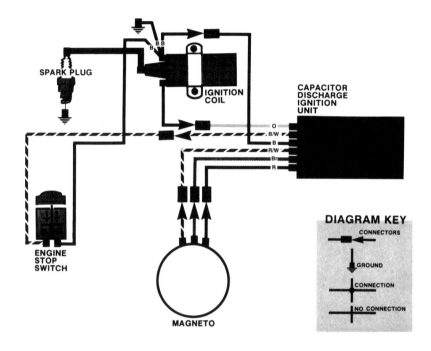

YZ100J, K, & YZ125J, K, L

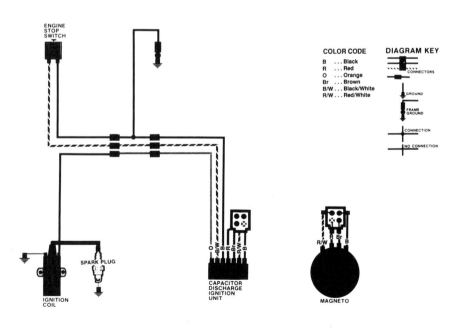

14

YZ125H

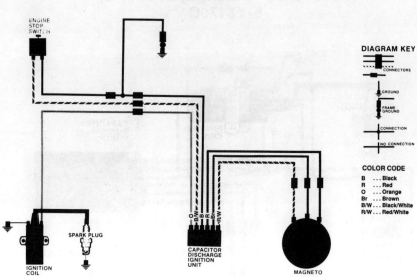

YZ250C, D, E

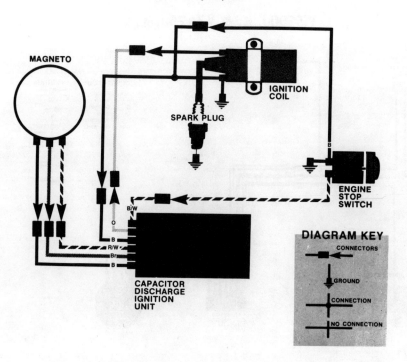

YZ250F, G, H

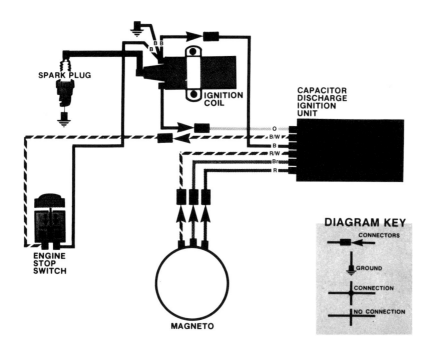

YZ250J, K, L

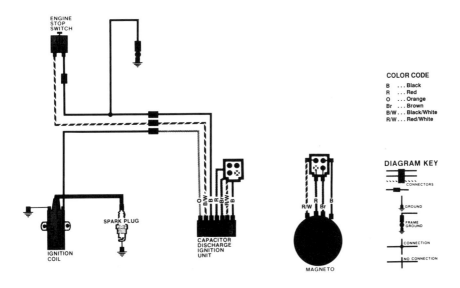

YZ400 (All) & YZ465G, H

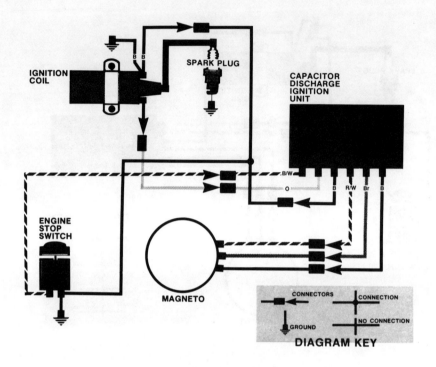

YZ490J, K, L

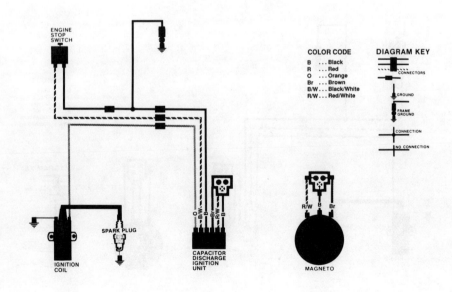

NOTES

NOTES

MAINTENANCE LOG

Date	Miles	Type of Service

BMW

M308	500 & 600 CC Twins, 55-69
M309	F650, 1994-2000
M500-3	BMW K-Series, 85-97
M502-3	BMW R50/5-R100 GSPD, 70-96
M503-2	R850, R1100, R1150 and R1200C, 93-04

HARLEY-DAVIDSON

M419	Sportsters, 59-85
M428	Sportster Evolution, 86-90
M429-4	Sportster Evolution, 91-03
M418	Panheads, 48-65
M420	Shovelheads,66-84
M421-3	FLS/FXS Evolution,84-99
M423	FLS/FXS Twin Cam 88B, 2000-2003
M422-3	FLH/FLT/FXR Evolution, 84-99
M430-2	FLH/FLT Twin Cam 88, 1999-2003
M424-2	FXD Evolution, 91-98
M425-2	FXD Twin Cam, 99-03

HONDA

ATVs

M316	Odyssey FL250, 77-84
M311	ATC, TRX & Fourtrax 70-125, 70-87
M433	Fourtrax 90 ATV, 93-00
M326	ATC185 & 200, 80-86
M347	ATC200X & Fourtrax 200SX, 86-88
M455	ATC250 & Fourtrax 200/ 250, 84-87
M342	ATC250R, 81-84
M348	TRX250R/Fourtrax 250R & ATC250R, 85-89
M456-3	TRX250X 87-92; TRX300EX 93-04
M446-2	TRX250 Recon 97-04
M346-3	TRX300/Fourtrax 300 & TRX300FW/Fourtrax 4x4, 88-00
M200	TRX350 Rancher, 00-03
M459-3	TRX400 Foreman 95-03
M454-2	TRX400EX 99-03
M205	TRX450 Foreman, 98-04
M210	TRX500 Rubicon, 98-04

Singles

M310-13	50-110cc OHC Singles, 65-99
M319	XR50R-XR70R, 97-03
M315	100-350cc OHC, 69-82
M317	Elsinore, 125-250cc, 73-80
M442	CR60-125R Pro-Link, 81-88
M431-2	CR80R, 89-95, CR125R, 89-91
M435	CR80, 96-02
M457-2	CR125R & CR250R, 92-97
M464	CR125R, 1998-2002
M443	CR250R-500R Pro-Link, 81-87
M432-3	CR250R, 88-91 & CR500R, 88-01
M437	CR250R, 97-01
M352	CRF250, CRF250X & CRF450R, 02-05
M312-13	XL/XR75-100, 75-03
M318-4	XL/XR/TLR 125-200, 79-03
M328-4	XL/XR250, 78-00; XL/XR350R 83-85; XR200R, 84-85; XR250L, 91-96
M320-2	XR400R, 96-04
M339-7	XL/XR 500-650, 79-03

Twins

M321	125-200cc, 65-78
M322	250-350cc, 64-74
M323	250-360cc Twins, 74-77
M324-5	Twinstar, Rebel 250 & Nighthawk 250, 78-03
M334	400-450cc, 78-87
M333	450 & 500cc, 65-76
M335	CX & GL500/650 Twins, 78-83
M344	VT500, 83-88
M313	VT700 & 750, 83-87
M314	VT750 Shadow, 98-03
M440	VT1100C Shadow , 85-96
M460-3	VT1100C Series, 95-04

Fours

M332	CB350-550cc, SOHC, 71-78
M345	CB550 & 650, 83-85
M336	CB650,79-82
M341	CB750 SOHC, 69-78
M337	CB750 DOHC, 79-82
M436	CB750 Nighthawk, 91-93 & 95-99
M325	CB900, 1000 & 1100, 80-83
M439	Hurricane 600, 87-90
M441-2	CBR600F2 & F3, 91-98
M445	CBR600F4, 99-03
M434-2	CBR900RR Fireblade, 93-99
M329	500cc V-Fours, 84-86
M438	Honda VFR800, 98-00
M349	700-1000 Interceptor, 83-85
M458-2	VFR700F-750F, 86-97
M327	700-1100cc V-Fours, 82-88
M340	GL1000 & 1100, 75-83
M504	GL1200, 84-87
M508	ST1100/PAN European, 90-02

Sixes

M505	GL1500 Gold Wing, 88-92
M506-2	GL1500 Gold Wing, 93-00
M507	GL1800 Gold Wing, 01-04
M462-2	GL1500C Valkyrie, 97-03

KAWASAKI

ATVs

M465-2	KLF220 & KLF250 Bayou, 88-03
M466-4	KLF300 Bayou, 86-04
M467	KLF400 Bayou, 93-99
M470	KEF300 Lakota, 95-99
M385	KSF250 Mojave, 87-00

Singles

M350-9	Rotary Valve 80-350cc, 66-01
M444-2	KX60, 83-02; KX80 83-90
M448	KX80/85/100, 89-03
M351	KDX200, 83-88
M447-3	KX125 & KX250, 82-91 KX500, 83-04
M472-2	KX125, 92-00
M473-2	KX250, 92-00
M474	KLR650, 87-03

Twins

M355	KZ400, KZ/Z440, EN450 & EN500, 74-95
M360-3	EX500, GPZ500S, Ninja R, 87-02
M356-4	Vulcan 700 & 750, 85-04
M354-2	Vulcan 800 & Vulcan 800 Classic, 95-04
M357-2	Vulcan 1500, 87-99
M471-2	Vulcan Classic 1500, 96-04

Fours

M449	KZ500/550 & ZX550, 79-85
M450	KZ, Z & ZX750, 80-85
M358	KZ650, 77-83
M359-3	900-1000cc Fours, 73-81
M451-3	1000 &1100cc Fours, 81-02
M452-3	ZX500 & 600 Ninja, 85-97
M453-3	Ninja ZX900-1100 84-01
M468	ZX6 Ninja, 90-97
M469	ZX7 Ninja, 91-98
M453-3	900-1100 Ninja, 84-01
M409	Concours, 86-04

POLARIS

ATVs

M496	Polaris ATV, 85-95
M362	Polaris Magnum ATV, 96-98
M363	Scrambler 500, 4X4 97-00
M365-2	Sportsman/Xplorer, 96-03

SUZUKI

ATVs

M381	ALT/LT 125 & 185, 83-87
M475	LT230 & LT250, 85-90
M380-2	LT250R Quad Racer, 85-92
M343	LTF500F Quadrunner, 98-00
M483-2	Suzuki King Quad/ Quad Runner 250, 87-98

Singles

M371	RM50-400 Twin Shock, 75-81
M369	125-400cc 64-81
M379	RM125-500 Single Shock, 81-88
M476	DR250-350, 90-94
M384-2	LS650 Savage, 86-03
M386	RM80-250, 89-95
M400	RM125, 96-00
M401	RM250, 96-02

Twins

M372	GS400-450 Twins, 77-87
M481-4	VS700-800 Intruder, 85-04
M482-2	VS1400 Intruder, 87-01
M484-2	GS500E Twins, 89-02
M361	SV650, 1999-2002

Triple

M368	380-750cc, 72-77

Fours

M373	GS550, 77-86
M364	GS650, 81-83
M370	GS750 Fours, 77-82
M376	GS850-1100 Shaft Drive, 79-84
M378	GS1100 Chain Drive, 80-81
M383-3	Katana 600, 88-96 GSX-R750-1100, 86-87
M331	GSX-R600, 97-00
M478-2	GSX-R750, 88-92 GSX750F Katana, 89-96
M485	GSX-R750, 96-99
M377	GSX-R1000, 01-04
M338	GSF600 Bandit, 95-00
M353	GSF1200 Bandit, 96-03

YAMAHA

ATVs

M499	YFM80 Badger, 85-01
M394	YTM/YFM200 & 225, 83-86
M488-5	Blaster, 88-05
M489-2	Timberwolf, 89-00
M487-5	Warrior, 87-04
M486-5	Banshee, 87-04
M490-3	Moto-4 & Big Bear, 87-04
M493	YFM400FW Kodiak, 93-98
M280-2	Raptor 660R, 01-05

Singles

M492-2	PW50 & PW80, BW80 Big Wheel 80, 81-02
M410	80-175 Piston Port, 68-76
M415	250-400cc Piston Port, 68-76
M412	DT & MX 100-400, 77-83
M414	IT125-490, 76-86
M393	YZ50-80 Monoshock, 78-90
M413	YZ100-490 Monoshock, 76-84
M390	YZ125-250, 85-87 YZ490, 85-90
M391	YZ125-250, 88-93 WR250Z, 91-93
M497-2	YZ125, 94-01
M498	YZ250, 94-98 and WR250Z, 94-98
M406	YZ250F & WR250F, 01-03
M491-2	YZ400F, YZ426F, WR400F WR426F, 98-02
M417	XT125-250, 80-84
M480-3	XT/TT 350, 85-00
M405	XT500 & TT500, 76-81
M416	XT/TT 600, 83-89

Twins

M403	650cc, 70-82
M395-10	XV535-1100 Virago, 81-03
M495-3	V-Star 650, 98-04
M281	V-Star 1100, 99-04

Triple

M404	XS750 & 850, 77-81

Fours

M387	XJ550, XJ600 & FJ600, 81-92
M494	XJ600 Seca II, 92-98
M388	YX600 Radian & FZ600, 86-90
M396	FZR600, 89-93
M392	FZ700-750 & Fazer, 85-87
M411	XS1100 Fours, 78-81
M397	FJ1100 & 1200, 84-93
M375	V-Max, 85-03
M374	Royal Star, 96-03
M461	YZF-R6, 99-04
M398	YZF-R1, 98-03
M399	F21, 01-04

VINTAGE MOTORCYCLES

Clymer® Collection Series

M330	Vintage British Street Bikes BSA, 500–650cc Unit Twins; Norton, 750 & 850cc Commandos; Triumph, 500-750cc Twins
M300	Vintage Dirt Bikes, V. 1 Bultaco 125-370cc Singles; Montesa, 123-360cc Singles; Ossa, 125-250cc Singles
M301	Vintage Dirt Bikes, V. 2 CZ, 125-400cc Singles; Husqvarna 125-450cc Singles; Maico, 250-501cc Singles; Hodaka, 90-125cc Singles
M305	Vintage Japanese Street Bikes Honda, 250 & 305cc Twins Kawasaki, 250-750cc Triples Kawasaki, 900 & 1000cc Four